Josiah Gilbert Holland

Arthur Bonnicastle

An American Novel

Josiah Gilbert Holland

Arthur Bonnicastle
An American Novel

ISBN/EAN: 9783337028985

Printed in Europe, USA, Canada, Australia, Japan

Cover: Foto ©Thomas Meinert / pixelio.de

More available books at **www.hansebooks.com**

ARTHUR BONNICASTLE,

AN

AMERICAN NOVEL.

BY

J. G. HOLLAND,

AUTHOR OF

"THE BAY PATH," "MISS GILBERT'S CAREER," "BITTER-SWEET," "KATHRINA," ETC., ETC.

With twelve full-page Illustrations by MARY A. HALLOCK.

NEW YORK:
SCRIBNER, ARMSTRONG & CO.
1873.

Stereotyped at the
WOMEN'S PRINTING HOUSE,
56, 58 and 60 Park Street,
New York.

CONTENTS.

—:o:—

	PAGE
CHAPTER I. Thank a Blind Horse for Good Luck..........	9
CHAPTER II. I visit an Ogress and a Giant in their Enchanted Castle...	37
CHAPTER III. I go to The Bird's Nest to live, and the Giant persists in his Plans for a Sea Voyage................................	50
CHAPTER IV. In which the Course of True Love is not permitted to run at all...	68
CHAPTER V. The Discipline of The Bird's Nest as illustrated by two startling public Trials......................	77
CHAPTER VI. I become a Member of Mrs. Sanderson's Family and have a wonderful Voyage with Jenks upon the Atlas...........	99
CHAPTER VII. I leave The Bird's Nest and make a great Discovery.	114
CHAPTER VIII. I am introduced to new Characters and enter the Shadow of the great Bedlow Revival.........................	130
CHAPTER IX. I pass through a terrible Tempest into the Sunlight...	151
CHAPTER X. I join a Church that leaves out Mr. Bradford and Millie.	165
CHAPTER XI. The old Portrait is discovered and old Jenks has a real Voyage at Sea...	180
CHAPTER XII. Mrs. Sanderson takes a Companion and I go to College...	195
CHAPTER XIII. The Beginning of College Life.—I meet Peter Mullens, Gordon Livingston, and Temptation.....................	209
CHAPTER XIV. My first Visit to New York, and my first Glass of Wine...	223
CHAPTER XV. I go out to make New-Year's Calls and return in Disgrace...	233

	PAGE
CHAPTER XVI. Peter Mullens acquires a very large Stock of old Clothes	248
CHAPTER XVII. I change my Religious Views to conform with my Moral Practice, and am graduated without Honors	256
CHAPTER XVIII. Henry becomes a Guest at The Mansion by force of Circumstances	272
CHAPTER XIX. Jenks goes far, far away upon the Billow, and never comes back	286
CHAPTER XX. Mr. Bradford tells me a Story which changes the Determinations of my Life	293
CHAPTER XXI. I meet an old Friend who becomes my Rival	309
CHAPTER XXII. Mrs. Sanderson meets her Grandson and I return to my Father's Home	327
CHAPTER XXIII. I take Arthur Bonnicastle upon my own Hands and succeed with him	348
CHAPTER XXIV. In which I learn something about Livingston, Millie Bradford, and Myself	359
CHAPTER XXV. I win a Wife and Home of my own, and The Mansion loses and gains a Mistress	368
CHAPTER XXVI. Which briefly records the Professional Life of Rev. Peter Mullens	384
CHAPTER XXVII. In which I say Good-night to my Friends and the Past, and Good-morrow to my Work and the Future	392

LIST OF ILLUSTRATIONS.

1. WHAT HAVE YOU COME HERE FOR? *Frontispiece.*
2. "ONE THING MORE, PLEASE," I SAID; "I WANT TO TELL YOU THAT I LOVE YOU."
3. "JENKS," SAID THE LADY, "TAKE THIS BOY TO HIS FATHER."
4. THE APPEAL FROM MAN TO WOMAN—FROM JUSTICE TO MERCY.
5. CLAIRE'S HAND LIGHTED THE CANDLE WITH WHICH I LED HIM TO HIS ROOM.
6. STEPPING UP BEHIND HIM, I PUT MY HAND UPON HIS SHOULDER, AND SAID: "WELL, HOW DO YOU LIKE IT?"
7. MRS. BELDEN HELD CLAIRE'S HAND.
8. MR. BRADFORD AND ARTHUR ON THE STEAMER.
9. MRS. BELDEN KNELT AT HENRY'S BED WITH HER ARMS AROUND HIS NECK.
10. THE OLD COOK REGARDED US IN WONDERING SILENCE.
11. THE WATER-LILY'S SECRET.
12. THE REV. PETER MULLENS.

ARTHUR BONNICASTLE.

CHAPTER I.

THANK A BLIND HORSE FOR GOOD LUCK.

LIFE looks beautiful from both extremities. Prospect and retrospect shine alike in a light so divine as to suggest that the first catches some radiance from the gates, not yet closed, by which the soul has entered, and that the last is illuminated from the opening realm into which it is soon to pass.

Now that they are all gone, I wrap myself in dreams of them, and live over the old days with them. Even the feeblest memory, that cannot hold for a moment the events of to-day, keeps a firm grasp upon the things of youth, and rejoices in its treasures. It is a curious process—this of feeling one's way back to childhood, and clothing one's self again with the little frame —the buoyant, healthy, restless bundle of muscles and nerves— and the old relations of careless infancy. The growing port of later years and the ampler vestments are laid aside; and one stands in his slender young manhood. Then backward still the fancy goes, making the frame smaller, and casting aside each year the changing garments that marked the eras of early growth, until, at last, one holds himself upon his own knee— a ruddy-faced, wondering, questioning, uneasy youngster, in his first trousers and roundabout, and dandles and kisses the dear little fellow that he was!

They were all here then—father, mother, brothers and sisters; and the family life was at its fullest. Now they are all gone, and I am alone. All the present relations of my life are those which have originated since. I have wife and children, and troops of friends, yet still I am alone. No one of all the number can go back with me into these reminiscences of my earliest life, or give me sympathy in them.

My father was a plain, ingenious, industrious craftsman, and a modest and thoroughly earnest Christian. I have always supposed that the neighbors held him in contempt or pity for his lack of shrewdness in business, although they knew that he was in all respects their superior in education and culture. He was an omnivorous reader, and was so intelligent in matters of history and poetry that the village doctor, a man of literary tastes, found in him almost his only sympathetic companion. The misfortunes of our family brought them only too frequently together; and my first real thinking was excited by their conversations, to which I was always an eager listener.

My father was an affectionate man. His life seemed bound up in that of my mother, yet he never gave a direct expression to his affection. I knew he could not live without her, yet I never saw him kiss her, or give her one caress. Indeed, I do not remember that he ever kissed me, or my sisters. We all grew up hungry, missing something, and he, poor man, was hungriest of all; but his Puritan training held him through life in slavery to notions of propriety which forbade all impulses to expression. He would have been ashamed to kiss his wife in the presence of his children!

I suppose it is this peculiarity of my father which makes me remember so vividly and so gratefully a little incident of my boyhood. It was an early summer evening; and the yellow moon was at its full. I stood out in the middle of the lawn before the house alone, looking up to the golden-orbed wonder, which—so high were the hills piled around our little valley—seemed very near to me. I felt rather than saw my father approaching me. There was no one looking, and he half knelt and put his arm around me. There was something in the clasp of that strong, warm arm that I have never forgotten. It thrilled me through with the consciousness that I was most tenderly beloved. Then he told me what the moon was, and by the simplest illustrations tried to bring to my mind a comprehension of its magnitude and its relations to the earth. I only remember that I could not grasp the thought at all, and that it all ended in his taking me in his arms and carrying me to my bed.

The seclusion in which we lived among the far New Hampshire hills was like that in which a family of squirrels lives in the forest; and as, at ten years of age, I had never been ten miles from home, the stories that came to my ears of the great world that lay beyond my vision were like stories of fairy-land. Fifty years ago the echoes of the Revolution and the War of 1812 had not died away, and soldiers who had served in both wars were plenty. My imagination had been many times excited by the stories that had been told at my father's fireside; and those awful people, "the British," were to me the embodiment of cruelty and terror. One evening, I remember, my father came in, and remarked that he had just heard the report of a cannon. The phrase was new, and sounded very large and significant to me, and I attributed it at once to the approach of "the British." My father laughed, but I watched the converging roads for the appearance of the red-coats for many days. The incident is of no value except to show how closely between those green hills my life had been bound, and how entirely my world was one of imagination. I was obliged to build the world that held alike my facts and my fancies.

When I was about ten years old, I became conscious that something was passing between my father and my mother of an unusual character. They held long conferences from which their children were excluded. Then a rich man of the neighborhood rode into the yard, and tied his horse, and walked about the farm. From a long tour he returned and entered the stable, where he was joined by my father. Both came into the house together, and went all over it, even down to the cellar, where they held a long conversation. Then they were closeted for an hour in the room which held my father's writing-desk. At last, my mother was called into the room. The children, myself among them, were huddled together in a corner of the large kitchen, filled with wonder at the strange proceedings; and when all came out, the stranger smiling and my father and mother looking very serious, my curiosity was at a painful height; and no sooner had the intruder vanished from the room— pocketing a long paper as he went—than I demanded an explanation.

My sisters were older than I, and to them the explanation was addressed. My father simply said at first: "I have sold the place." Tears sprang into all our eyes, as if a great calamity had befallen us. Were we to be wanderers? Were we to have no home? Where were we to go?

Then my father, who was as simple as a child, undertook the justification of himself to his children. He did not know why he had consented to live in such a place for a year. He told the story of the fallacious promises and hopes that had induced him to buy the farm at first; of his long social deprivations; of his hard and often unsuccessful efforts to make the year's income meet the year's constantly increasing expenses; and then he dwelt particularly on the fact that his duty to his children compelled him to seek a home where they could secure a better education, and have a chance, at least, to make their way in the world. I saw then, just as clearly as I see to-day, that the motives of removal all lay in the last consideration. He saw possibilities in his children which demanded other circumstances and surroundings. He knew that in his secluded home among the mountains they could not have a fair chance at life, and he would not be responsible for holding them to associations that had been simply starvation and torment to him.

The first shock over, I turned to the future with the most charming anticipations. My life was to be led out beyond the hills into an unknown world! I learned the road by which we were to go; and beyond the woods in which it terminated to my vision my imagination pushed through splendid towns, across sweeping rivers, over vast plains and meadows, on and on to the wide sea. There were castles, there were ships, there were chariots and horses, there was a noble mansion swept and garnished, waiting to receive us all, and, more than all, there was a life of great deeds which should make my father proud of his boy, and in which I remember that "the British" were to be very severely handled.

The actual removal hardly justified the picture. There were two overloaded three-horse teams, and a high, old-fashioned wagon, drawn by a single horse, in which were bestowed the family, the family satchels, and the machinery of an eight-day clock—a pet of my father, who had had it all in pieces for repairs every year since I was born. I did not burden the wagon with my presence, but found a seat, when I was not running by the wayside, with the driver of one of the teams. He had attracted me to his company by various sly nods and winks, and by a funny way of talking to his horses. He was an old teamster, and knew not only every inch of the road that led to the distant market-town to which we were going, but every landlord, groom, and bar-keeper on the way. A man of such vast geographical knowledge, and such extensive and interesting acquaintance with men, became to me a most important personage. When he had amused himself long enough with stories told to excite my imagination, he turned to me sharply and said:

"Boy, do you ever tell lies?"

"Yes, sir," I answered, without hesitation.

"You do? Then why didn't you lie when I asked you the question?"

"Because I never lie except to please people," I replied.

"Oh! you are one of the story-tellers, are you?" he said, in a tone of severity.

"Yes, sir."

"Well, then, you ought to be flogged. If I had a story-telling boy I would flog it out of him. Truth, boy—always stand by the truth! It was only this time last year that I was carrying a load of goods down the mountain for a family the same as yours, and there was a little boy who went with me the same as you are going now. I was sure I smelt tobacco. Said I, 'I smell tobacco.' He grew red in the face, and I charged him with having some in his pocket. He declared he had none, and I said, 'We shall see what will come to liars.' I pitied him, for I knew something terrible would happen. A strap broke, and the horses started on a run, and off went the boy. I stopped them as soon as I could, ran back and picked him up insensible, with as handsome a plug of tobacco in his pocket as you ever saw; and the rascal had stolen it from his grandmother! Always speak the truth, my boy, always speak the truth!"

"And did you steal the tobacco from him?" I asked.

"No, lad, I took it and used it, because I knew it would hurt him, and I couldn't bear the thought of exposing him to his grandmother."

"Do you think lying is worse than stealing?" I asked.

"That is something we can't settle. Tobacco is very preserving and cleansing to the teeth, and I am obliged to use it. Do you see that little building we are coming to? That is Snow's store: and now, if you are a boy that has any heart—any *real* heart—and if you have saved up a few pennies, you will go in there and get a stick of candy for yourself and a plug of tobacco for me. That would be the square thing for a boy to do who stands by the truth, and wants to do a good turn to a man that helps him along;" and he looked me in the eye so steadily and persuasively that resistance was impossible, and my poor little purse went back into my pocket painfully empty of that which had seemed like wealth.

We rode along quietly after this until my companion asked me if I knew how tall I was. Of course I did not know anything about it, and wished to learn the reason of the question. He had a little boy of his own at home—a very smart little fellow—who could exactly reach the check-rein of his leading horse. He had been wondering if I could do the same. He should think we were about the same height, and as it would be a tiptoe stretch, the performance would be a matter of spring and skill. At that moment it happened that we came to a watering-trough, which gave me the opportunity to satisfy his curiosity; and he sat smiling appreciatively upon my frantic and at last successful efforts to release the leader's head, and lift it again to its check.

We came to a steep acclivity, and, under the stimulating influence of the teamster's flattery, I carried a stone as large as my head from the bottom to the top, to stay the wheels when the horses paused for breath.

I recall the lazy rascal's practice upon my boyish credulity and vanity more for my interest in my own childishness than for any interest I still have in him; though I cannot think that the jolly old joker was long ago dust, without a sigh. He was a great man to me then, and he stirred me with appeals to my ambition as few have stirred me since. And " standing by the truth," as he so feelingly adjured me to stand, I may confess that his appeals were not the basest to which my life has responded.

The forenoon was long, hot and wearisome, but at its close we emerged upon a beautiful valley, and saw before us a characteristic New England village, with its white houses, large and little, and its two homely wooden spires. I was walking as I came in sight of the village, and I stopped, touched with the poetry of the peaceful scene. Just then the noon-bell pealed forth from one of the little churches—the first church-bell I had ever heard. I did not know what it was, and was obliged to inquire. I have stood under the belfry of Bruges since, and heard, amid the dull jargon of the decaying city, the chimes from its silver-sounding bells with far less of emotion than I experienced that day, as I drank my first draught of the wonderful music. O sweet first time of everything good in life!

Thank heaven that, with an eternity of duration before us,

there is also infinity of resources, with ever-varying supply and ministry, and ever-recurring first times!

My father and the rest of the family had preceded us, and we found them waiting at the village tavern for our arrival. Dinner was ready, and I was quite ready for it, though I was not so much absorbed that I cannot recall to-day the fat old woman with flying cap-strings who waited at the table. Indeed, were I an artist, I could reproduce the pictures on the walls of the low, long dining-room where we ate, so strongly did they impress themselves upon my memory. We made but a short stay, and then in our slow way pressed on. My friend of the team had evidently found something more exhilarating at the tavern than tobacco, and was confidential and affectionate, not only toward me but toward all he met upon the road, of whom he told me long and marvelous histories. But he grew dull and even ill-tempered at last, and I had a quiet cry behind a projecting bedstead, for very weariness and homesickness.

I was too weary when at dusk we arrived at the end of our day's progress to note, or care, for anything. My supper was quickly eaten, and I was at once in the oblivion of sleep. The next day's journey was unlike the first, in that it was crowded with life. The villages grew larger, so as quite to excite my astonishment. I saw, indeed, the horses and the chariots. There were signs of wealth that I had never seen before,—beautifully kept lawns, fine, stately mansions, and gayly-dressed ladies, who humiliated me by regarding me with a sort of stately curiosity; and I realized as I had never done before that there were grades of life far above that to which I had been accustomed, and that my father was comparatively a poor, plain man.

Toward the close of the second afternoon we came in sight of Bradford, which, somewhere within its limits, contained our future home. There were a dozen stately spires, there were tall chimneys waving their plumes of pearly smoke, there were long rows of windows red in the rays of the declining sun, there was a river winding away into the distance between its borders of elm and willow, and there were white-winged craft that glided hither and thither in the far silence.

"What do you think of that, boy?" inquired my friend the teamster.

"Isn't it pretty!" I responded. "Isn't it a grand place to live in?"

"That depends upon whether one lives or starves," he said. "If I were going to starve, I would rather do it where there isn't anything to eat."

"But we are not going to starve," I said. "Father never will let us starve."

"Not if he can help it, boy; but your father is a lamb—a great, innocent lamb."

"What do you mean by calling my father a lamb? He is as good a man as there is in Bradford, any way," I responded, somewhat indignantly.

The man gave a new roll to the enormous quid in his mouth, a solace that had been purchased by my scanty pennies, and said, with a contemptuous smile, "Oh! he's too good. Some time when you think of it, suppose you look and see if he has ever cut his eye-teeth."

"You are making fun of my father, and I don't like it. How should you like to have a man make fun of you to your little boy?"

At this he gave a great laugh, and I knew at once that he had no little boy, and that he had been playing off a fiction upon me throughout the whole journey. It was my first encounter with a false and selfish world. To find in my hero of the three horses and the large acquaintance only a vulgar rascal who could practice upon the credulity of a little boy was one of the keenest disappointments I had ever experienced.

"If I could hurt you, I would strike you," I said in a rage.

"Well, boy," he replied almost affectionately, and quite admiringly, "you will make *your* way, if you have that sort of thing in you. I wouldn't have believed it. Upon my word, I wouldn't have believed it. I take it all back. Your father is a first-rate man for heaven, if he isn't for Bradford; and he's sure to go there when he moves next, and I should like to be the one to move him, but I'm afraid they wouldn't let me in to unload the goods."

There was an awful humor in this strange speech which I fully comprehended, but my reverence for even the name of heaven was so profound that I did not dare to laugh. I simply said: "I don't like to hear you talk so, and I wish you wouldn't."

"Well, then, I won't, my lad. They say the lame and the lazy are always provided for, and I don't know why the lambs are not just as deserving. You'll all get through, I suppose; and a hundred years hence there will be no difference."

"Who provides for the lame and the lazy?" I inquired.

"Well, now you have me tight," said the fellow with a sigh. "Somebody up there, I s'pose;" and he pointed his whip upward with a little toss.

"Don't you know?" I inquired, with ingenuous and undisguised wonder.

"Not a bit of it. I never saw him. I've been lazy all my life, and I was lame once for a year, falling from this very wagon, and a mighty rough time I had of it, too; and so far as I am concerned it has been a business of looking out for number one. Nobody ever let down a silver spoon full of honey to me; and what is more, I don't expect it. If you have that sort of thing in your head, the best way is to keep it. You'll be happier, I reckon, in the long run if you do; but I didn't get it in early, and it is too late now."

"Then your father was a goat, wasn't he?" I said, with a quick impulse.

"Yes," he replied with a loud laugh. "Yes indeed; he was a goat with the biggest and wickedest pair of horns you ever saw. Boy, remember what I tell you. Goodness in this world is a thing of fathers and mothers. I haven't any children, and I shouldn't have any right to them if I had. People who bring children into the world that they are not fit to take care of, and who teach them nothing but drinking and fighting and swearing, ought to be shot. If I had had your start, I snould be all right to-day."

So I had another lesson,—two lessons, indeed,—one in the practical infidelity of the world, and one in social and family influence. They haunted me for many days, and brought to me a deeper and a more intelligent respect for my father and his goodness and wisdom than I had ever entertained.

"I wish I were well down that hill," said my teamster at last, after we had jolted along for half a mile without a word. As he said this he looked uneasily around upon his load, which, with the long transportation, had become loose. He stopped his horses, and gave another turn to the pole with which he had strained the rope that, passing lengthwise and crosswise the load, held it together. Then he started on again. I watched him closely, for I saw real apprehension on his face. His horses were tired, and one of them was blind. The latter fact gave me no apprehension, as the driver had taken much pains to impress upon me the fact that the best horses were always blind. He only regretted that he could not secure them for his whole team, principally on account of the fact that not having any idea how far they had traveled, they never knew when to be tired. The reason seemed sound, and I had accepted it in good faith.

When we reached the brow of the hill that descended into the town, I saw that he had some reason for his apprehension, and I should have alighted and taken to my feet if I had not been as tired as the horses. But I had faith in the driver, and faith in the poor brutes he drove, and so remained on my seat. Midway the hill, the blind horse stepped upon a rolling stone; and all I remember of the scene which immediately followed was a confused and violent struggle. The horse fell prone upon the road, and while he was trying in vain to rise, I was conscious that my companion had leaped off. Then something struck me from behind, and I felt myself propelled wildly and resistlessly through the air, down among the struggling horses, after which I knew no more.

When consciousness came back to me it was night, and I was in a strange house. A person who wakes out of healthy sleep recognizes at once his surroundings, and by a process in which volition has no part reunites the thread of his life with that which was dropped when sleep fell upon him. The unconsciousness which follows concussion is of a different sort, and obliterates for a time the memory of a whole life.

I woke upon a little cot on the floor. Though it was summer, a small fire had been kindled on the hearth, my father was chafing my hands, my brothers and sisters were looking on at a distance with apprehension and distress upon their faces, and the room was piled with furniture in great confusion. The whole journey was gone from my memory; and feeling that I could not lift my head or speak, I could only gasp and shut my eyes and wonder. I knew my father's face, and knew the family faces around me, but I had no idea where we were, or what had happened. Something warm and stinging came to my lips, and I swallowed it with a gulp and a strangle. Then I became conscious of a voice that was strange to me. It was deep and musical and strong, yet there was a restraint and a conscious modulation in its tone, as if it were trying to do that to which it was not well used. Its possessor was evidently talking to my mother, who, I knew, was weeping.

"Ah! madam! Ah! madam! This will never do—never do!" I heard him say. "You are tired. Bless me! You have come eighty miles. It would have killed Mrs. Bradford. All you want is rest. I am not a chicken, and such a ride in such a wagon as yours would have finished me up, I'm sure."

"Ah, my poor boy, Mr. Bradford!" my mother moaned.

"The boy will be all right by to-morrow morning," he replied. "He is opening his eyes now. You can't kill such a little piece of stuff as that. He hasn't a broken bone in his body. Let him have the brandy there, and keep his feet warm. Those little chaps are never good for anything until they have had the daylight knocked out of them half-a-dozen times. I wonder what has became of that rascal, Dennis!"

At this he rose and walked to the window, and peered out into the darkness. I saw that he was a tall, plainly dressed man, with a heavy cane in his hand. One thing was certain: he was a type of man I had never seen before. Perfectly self-possessed, entirely at home, superintending all the affairs of the house, commanding, advising, reassuring, inspiring, he was evidently there to do good. In my speechless helplessness, my own heart went out to him in perfect trust. I had the fullest faith in what he said about myself and my recovery, though at the moment I had no idea what I was to recover from, or, rather, what had been the cause of my prostration.

"There the vagabond comes at last!" said the stranger. He threw open the door, and Dennis, a smiling, good-natured looking Irishman, walked in with a hamper of most appetizing drinks and viands. An empty table was ready to receive them, and hot coffee, milk, bread, and various cold meats were placed one after another upon it.

"Set some chairs, Dennis, and be quick about it," said Mr. Bradford.

The chairs were set, and then Mr. Bradford stooped and offered my mother his arm, in as grand a manner as if he were proffering a courtesy to the Queen of England. She rose and took it, and he led her to the table. My father was very much touched, and I saw him look at the stranger with quivering lips. This was a gentleman—a kind of man he had read about in books, but not the kind of man he had ever been brought much in contact with. This tender and stately attention to my mother was an honor which was very grateful to him. It was a touch of ideal life, too,—above the vulgar, graceless habits of those among whom his life had been cast. Puritan though he was, and plain and undemonstrative in his ways, he saw the beauty of this new manner with a thrill that brought a crimson tint to his hollow cheeks. Both he and my mother tried to express their thanks, but Mr. Bradford declared that he was the lucky man in the whole matter. It was so fortunate that he had happened to be near when the accident occurred; and though the service he had rendered was a very small one, it had been a genuine pleasure to him to render it. Then, seeing that no one touched the food, he turned with a quick instinct to Dennis, and said: "By the way, Dennis, let me see you at the door a moment."

Dennis followed him out, and then my father bowed his head, and thanked the Good Giver for the provision made for his family, for the safety of his boy, and for the prosperous journey, and ended by asking a blessing upon the meal.

When, after a considerable interval, Mr. Bradford and his servant reappeared, it was only on the part of the former to say that Dennis would remain to assist in putting the beds into such shape that the family could have a comfortable night's rest, and to promise to look in late in the morning. He shook hands in a hearty way with my father and mother, said "good-night" to the children, and then came and looked at me. He smiled a kind, good-humored smile, and shaking his long finger at me, said: "Keep quiet, my little man: you'll be all right in the morning." Then he went away, and after the closing of the door I heard his brisk, strong tread away into the darkness.

I have often wondered whether such men as Mr. Bradford realize how strong an impression they make upon the minds of children. He undoubtedly realized that he had to deal with a family of children, beginning with my father and mother—as truly children as any of us; but it is impossible that he could know what an uplift he gave to the life to which he had ministered. The sentiment which he inspired in me was as truly that of worship as any of which I was capable. The grand man, with his stalwart frame, his apparent control of unlimited means, his self-possession, his commanding manner, his kindness and courtesy, lifted him in my imagination almost to the dignity of a God. I wondered if I could ever become such a man as he! I learned in after years that even he had his weaknesses, but I never ceased to entertain for him the most profound respect. Indeed, I had good and special reason for this, beyond what at present appears.

After he departed I watched Dennis. If Mr. Bradford was

my first gentleman, Dennis was my first Irishman. Oh, sweet first time! let me exclaim again. I have never seen an Irish man since who so excited my admiration and interest.

"Me leddy," said Dennis, imitating as well as he could the grand manner of his master, "if ye'll tek an Irish b'y's advice, ye'll contint yoursilf with a shake-down for the night, and set up the frames in the marnin'. I'm thinkin' the Squire will lit me give ye a lift thin, an it's slape ye're wantin' now."

He saw the broad grin coming upon the faces of the children as he proceeded, and joined in their unrestrained giggle when he finished.

"Ah! there's nothing like a fine Irish lad for makin' little gurr'ls happy. It's better nor whisky any day."

My poor father and mother were much distressed, fearing that the proprieties had been trampled on by the laughing children, and apologized to Dennis for their rudeness.

"Och! niver mind 'em. An Irish b'y is a funny bird any way, and they're not used to his chirrup yet."

In the meantime he had lighted half a dozen candles for as many rooms, and was making quick work with the bedding. At length, with the help of my mother, he had arranged beds enough to accommodate the family for the night, and with many professions of good-will, and with much detail of experience concerning moving in his own country, he was about to bid us all "good-night," when he paused at the door and said: "Thank a blind horse for good luck!"

"What do you mean, Dennis?" inquired my father.

"Is it what I mane? ye ask me. Wasn't it a blind horse that fell on the hill, and threw the lad aff jist where the Squire was standin,' and didn't he get him in his arms the furr'st one, and wasn't that the beginnin' of it all? Thank a blind horse for good luck, I till ye. The Squire can no more drap you now than he can drap his blissid ould hearr't, though it's likely I'll have to do the most of it mesilf."

My mother assured Dennis that she was sorry to give him the slightest trouble.

"Never mind me, me leddy. Let an Irish b'y alone for bein' tinder of himsilf. Do I look as if I had too much worr'k and my bafe comin' to me in thin slices?" And he spread out his brawny hands for inspection.

The children giggled, and he went out with a "good-night." Then he reopened the door, and putting only his head in, said, "Remimber what I till ye. A blind horse for good luck;" and, nodding his head a dozen times, he shut the door again and disappeared for the night.

When I woke the next morning, it all came back to me— the long ride, the fearful experience upon the hill, and the observations of the previous evening. We were indebted to the thoughtful courtesy of Mr. Bradford for our breakfast, and, after Dennis had been busy during half the morning in assisting to put the house in order, I saw my gentleman again. The only inconvenience from which I suffered was a sense of being bruised all over; and when he came in I greeted him with such a smile of hearty delight that he took my cheeks in his hands and kissed me. How many thousand times I had longed for such an expression of affection from my father, and longed in vain! It healed me and made me happy. Then I had an opportunity to study him more closely. He was fresh from his toilet, and wore the cleanest linen. His neck was enveloped and his chin propped by the old-fashioned "stock" of those days, his waistcoat was white, and his dark gray coat and trousers had evidently passed under Dennis's brush in the early morning. A heavy gold chain with a massive seal depended from his watch-pocket, and he carried in his hand what seemed to be his constant companion, his heavy cane. At this distance of time I find it difficult to describe his face, because it impressed me as a whole, and not by its separate features. His eyes were dark, pleasant, and piercing—so much I remember; but the rest of his face I cannot describe. I trusted it wholly; but, as I recall the man, I hear more than I see. Impressive as was his presence, his wonderful voice was his finest interpreter to me. I lingered upon his tones and cadences as I have often listened to the voice of a distant waterfall, lifted and lowered by the wind. I can hear it to-day as plainly as I heard it then.

During the visit of that morning he learned the situation of the family, and comprehended with genuine pain the helplessness of my father. That he was interested in my father I could see very plainly. His talk was not in the manner of workingmen, and the conversation was discursive enough to display his intelligence. The gentleman was evidently puzzled. Here was a plain man who had seen no society, who had lived for years among the woods and hills; yet the man of culture could start no subject without meeting an intelligent response.

Mr. Bradford ascertained that my father had but little money, that he had come to Bradford with absolutely no provision but a house to move into, that he had no definite plan of business, and that his desire for a better future for his children was the motive that had induced him to migrate from his mountain home.

After he had made a full confession of his circumstances, with the confiding simplicity of a boy, Mr. Bradford looked at him with a sort of mute wonder, and then rose and walked the room.

"I confess I don't understand it, Mr. Bonnicastle," said he, stopping before him, and bringing down his cane. "You want your children to be educated better than you are, but you are a thousand times better than your circumstances. Men are happiest when they are in harmony with their circumstances. I venture to say that the men you left behind you were contented enough. What is the use of throwing children out of all pleasant relations with their condition? I don't blame you for wanting to have your children educated, but I am sure that educating working people is a mistake. Work is their life; and they worked a great deal better and were a great deal happier when they knew less. Now isn't it so, Mr. Bonnicastle? isn't it so?"

Quite unwittingly Mr. Bradford had touched my father's sensitive point, and as there was something in the gentleman's manner that inspired the conversational faculties of all with whom he came in contact, my father's tongue was loosed, and it did not stop until the gentleman had no more to say.

"Well, if we differ, we'll agree to differ," said he, at last; "but now you want work, and I will speak to some of my friends about you. Bonnicastle—Peter Bonnicastle, I think?"

My father nodded, and said—"a name I inherit from I do not know how many great-grandfathers."

"Your ancestor was not Peter Bonnicastle of Roxbury?"

"That is what they tell me."

"Peter Bonnicastle of Roxbury!"

"Ay, Peter Bonnicastle of Roxbury."

"By Jove, man! Do you know you've got the bluest blood in your veins of any man in Bradford?"

I shall never forget the pleased and proud expression that came into the faces of my father and mother as these words were uttered. What blue blood was, and in what its excellence consisted, I did not know; but it was something to be proud of—that was evident.

"Peter Bonnicastle of Roxbury! Ah yes! Ah yes! I understand it. It's all plain enough now. You are a gentleman without knowing it—a gentleman trying in a blind way to get back to a gentleman's conditions. Well, perhaps you will; I shall not wonder if you do."

It was my first observation of the reverence for blood that I have since found to be nearly universal. The show of contempt for it which many vulgar people make is always an affectation, unless they are very vulgar indeed. My father, who, more than any man I ever knew, respected universal humanity, and ignored class distinctions, was as much delighted and elevated with the recognition of his claims to good family blood as if he had fallen heir to the old family wealth.

"And what is this lad's name?" inquired Mr. Bradford, pointing over his shoulder toward me.

"My name is Arthur Bonnicastle," I replied, taking the words out of my father's mouth.

"And Arthur Bonnicastle has a pair of ears and a tongue," responded Mr. Bradford, turning to me with an amused expression upon his face.

I took the response as a reproof, and blushed painfully.

"Tut, tut, there is no harm done, my lad," said he, rising and coming to a chair near me, and regarding me very kindly. "You know you had neither last night," he added, feeling my hand and forehead to learn if there were any feverish reaction.

I was half sitting, half lying on a lounge near the window, and he changed his seat from the chair to the lounge so that he sat over me, looking down into my face. "Now," said he, regarding me very tenderly, and speaking gently, in a tone that was wholly his own, "we will have a little talk all by ourselves. What have you been thinking about? Your mouth has been screwed up into ever-so-many interrogation points ever since your father and I began to talk."

I laughed at the odd fancy, and told him I should like to ask him a few questions.

"Of course you would. Boys are always full of questions. Ask as many as you please."

"I should like to ask you if you own this town," I began.

"Why?"

"Because," I answered, "you have the same name the town has."

"No, my lad, I own very little of it; but my great-grandfather owned all the land it stands on, and the town was named for him, or rather he named it for himself."

"Was his blood blue?" I inquired.

He smiled and whistled in a comical way, and said he was afraid that it wasn't quite so blue as it might have been.

"Is yours?"

"Well, that's a tough question," he responded. "I fancy the family blood has been growing blue for several generations, and perhaps there's a little indigo in me."

"Do you eat anything in particular?" I inquired.

"No, nothing in particular; it isn't made in that way."

"How is it made?" I inquired.

"That's a tough question, too," he replied.

"Oh! if you can't answer it," I said, "don't trouble yourself; but do you think Jesus Christ had blue blood?"

"Why yes—yes indeed. Wasn't he the son of David—when he got back to him—and wasn't David a King?"

"Oh! that's what you mean by blue blood;—and that's another thing," I said.

"What do you mean by another thing, my boy?" inquired Mr. Bradford.

"I was thinking," I said, "that my father was a carpenter, and so was his; and so his blood was blue and mine too. And there are lots of other things that might have been true."

"Tell me all about them," said my interlocutor. "What have you been thinking about?"

"Oh!" I said, "I've been thinking that if my father had lived when his father lived, and if they had lived in the same country, perhaps they would have worked in the same shop and on the same houses; and then perhaps Jesus Christ and I should have played together with the blocks and shavings. And then, when he grew up and became so wonderful, I should have grown up and perhaps been one of the apostles, and written part of the Bible, and preached and healed the sick, and been a martyr, and gone to heaven, and—and—I don't know how many other things."

"Well, I rather think you would, by Jove," he said, rising to his feet, impulsively.

"One thing more, please," I said, stretching my hands up to him. He sat down again, and put his face close to mine. "I want to tell you that I love you."

His eyes filled with tears; and he whispered: "Thank you, my dear boy: love me always. Thank you."

Then he kissed me again and turned to my father. "I think you are entirely right in coming to Bradford," I heard him say. "I don't think I should like to see this little chap going back to the woods again, even if I could have my own way about it."

One thing more, please, I said, I want to tell you that I love you. (p. 28.)

For some minutes he walked the room backward and forward, sometimes pausing and looking out of the window. My father saw that he was absorbed, and said nothing. At length he stopped suddenly before my father and said: "This is the strangest affair I ever knew. Here you come out of the woods with this large family, without the slightest idea what you are going to do—with no provision for the future whatever. How did you suppose you were going to get along?"

How well I remember the quiet, confident smile with which my father received his strong, blunt words, and the trembling tone in which he replied to them!

"Mr. Bradford," said he, "none of us takes care of himself. I am not a wise man in worldly things, and I am obliged to trust somebody; and I know of no one so wise as He who knows all things, or so kind as He who loves all men. I do the best I can, and I leave the rest to Him. He has never failed me in the great straits of my life, and He never will. I have already thanked Him for sending you to me yesterday; and I believe that by His direction you are to be, as you have already been, a great blessing to me. I shall seek for work, and with such strength as I have I shall do it, and do it well. I shall have troubles and trials, but I know that none will come that I cannot transform, and that I am not expected to transform, into a blessing. If I am not rich in money when the end comes, I shall be rich in something better than money."

Mr. Bradford took my father's hand, and shaking it warmly, responded: "You are already rich in that which is better than money. A faith like yours is wealth inestimable. You are a thousand times richer than I am to-day. I beg your pardon, Mr. Bonnicastle, but this is really quite new to me. I have heard cant and snuffle, and I know the difference. If the Lord doesn't take care of such a man as you are, he doesn't stand by his friends, that's all."

My father's reverence was offended by this familiar way of speaking a name which was ineffably sacred to him, and he made no reply. I could see, too, that he felt that the humility with which he had spoken was not fully appreciated by Mr. Bradford.

Suddenly breaking the thread of the conversation, Mr. Bradford said: "By the way, who is your landlord? I ought to know who owns this little house, but I don't."

"The landlord is not a landlord at all, I believe. The owner is a landlady, though I have never seen her—a Mrs. Sanderson—Ruth Sanderson."

"Oh! I know her well, and ought to have known that this is her property," said Mr. Bradford. "I have nothing against the lady, though she is a little odd in her ways; but I am sorry you have a woman to deal with, for, so far as I have observed, a business woman is a screw by rule, and a woman without a business faculty and with business to do is a screw without rule."

In the midst of the laugh that followed Mr. Bradford's axiomatic statement he turned to the window, and exclaimed: "Well, I declare! here she comes."

I looked quickly and saw a curious turn-out approaching the house. It was an old-fashioned chaise, set low between two high wheels, drawn by a heavy-limbed and heavy-gaited black horse, and driven by a white-haired, thin-faced old man. Beside the driver sat a little old woman; and the first impression given me by the pair was that the vehicle was much too large for them, for it seemed to toss them up and catch them, and to knock them together by its constant motion. The black horse, who had a steady independent trot, that regarded neither stones nor ruts, made directly for our door, stopped when he found the place he wanted, and then gave a preliminary twitch at the reins and reached down his head for a nibble at the grass. The man sat still, looking straight before him, and left the little old woman to alight without assistance; and she did alight in a way which showed that she had little need of it. She was dressed entirely in black, with the exception of the white widow's cap drawn tightly around a little face set far back in a deep bonnet. She had a quick, wiry, nervous way in walking; and coming up the path that led through a little garden lying between the house and the street, she cast furtive glances left and right, as if gathering the condition of her property. Then followed a sharp rap at the door.

The absorbed and embarrassed condition of my father and mother was evident in the fact that neither started to open the door; but Dennis, coming quickly in from an adjoining room where he was busy, opened it, and Mr. Bradford went forward to meet her in the narrow hall. He shook her hand in his own cordial and stately way, and said jocularly: "Well, Madame, you see we have taken possession of your snug little house."

Her lips, which were compressed and thin as if she were suffering pain, parted in a faint smile, and her dark, searching eyes looked up to him in a kind of questioning wonder. There was nothing in her face that attracted me. I remember only that I felt moved to pity her, she seemed so small, and lonely, and careworn. Her hands were the tiniest I had ever seen, and were merely little bundles of bones in the shape of hands.

"Let me present your tenants to you, Mrs. Sanderson, and commend them to your good opinion," said Mr. Bradford.

She stood quietly and bowed to my father and mother, who had risen to greet her. I was young, but quick in my instincts, and I saw at once that she regarded a tenant as an inferior, with whom it would not do to be on terms of social familiarity.

"Do you find the house comfortable?" she inquired, speaking in a quick way and addressing my father.

"Apparently so," he answered; and then he added: "we are hardly settled yet, but I think we shall get along very well in it."

"With your leave I will go over it, and see for myself," she said quietly.

"Oh, certainly!" responded my father. "My wife will go with you."

"If she will; but I want you, too."

They went off together, and I heard them for some minutes talking around in the different parts of the house.

"Any more questions?" inquired Mr. Bradford with a smile, looking over to where I sat on the lounge.

"Yes, sir," I replied. "I have been wondering whether that lady has a crack in the top of her head."

"Well, I shouldn't wonder if she had a very, very small one," he replied; "and now what started that fancy?"

"Because," I continued, "if she is what you call a screw, I was wondering how they turned her."

"Well, my boy, it is so very small indeed," said Mr. Bradford, putting on a quizzical look, "that I'm afraid they can't turn her at all."

When the lady came back she seemed to be ready to go away at once; but Mr. Bradford detained her with the story of the previous night's experiences, including the accident that had happened to me. She listened sharply, and then came over to where I was sitting, and asked me if I were badly hurt. I assured her I was not. Then she took one of my plump hands in her own little grasp, and looked at me in a strange, intense way without saying a word.

Mr. Bradford interrupted her, with an eye to business, by saying: "Mr. Bonnicastle, your new tenant here, is a carpenter; and I venture to say that he is a good one. We must do what we can to introduce him to business."

She turned with a quick motion on her heel, and bent her eyes on my father. "Bonnicastle?" said she, with almost a fierce interrogation.

"Oh! I supposed you knew his name, Mrs. Sanderson," said Mr. Bradford; and then he added, "but I presume your agent did not tell you."

She made no sign to show that she had heard a word that Mr. Bradford had said.

"Peter Bonnicastle," said my father, breaking the silence with the only words he could find.

"Peter Bonnicastle!" she repeated almost mechanically, and continued standing as if dazed.

She stood with her back toward me, and I could only guess at her expression, or the strangely curious interest of the scene, by its reflection in Mr. Bradford's face. He sat uneasily in his chair, and pressed the head of his cane against his chin, as if he were using a mechanical appliance to keep his mouth shut. He knew the woman before him, and was determined to be wise. Subsequently I learned the reason of it all—of his silence at the time, of his reticence for months and even years afterward, and of what sometimes seemed to me and to my father like coolness and neglect.

The silence was oppressive, and my father, remembering the importance which Mr. Bradford had attached to the fact, and moved by a newly awakened pride, said: "I am one of many Peters, they tell me, the first of whom settled in Roxbury."

"Roxbury?" and she took one or two steps toward him. "You are sure?"

"Perfectly sure," responded my father.

She made no explanation, but started for the door, dropping a little bow as she turned away. Mr. Bradford was on his feet in a moment, and, opening the door for her, accompanied her into the street. I watched them from the window. They paused just far enough from the driver of the chaise to be beyond his hearing, and conversed for several minutes. I could not doubt that Mr. Bradford was giving her his impression of us. Then he helped her into the chaise, and the little grayhaired driver, gathering up his reins, and giving a great pull at the head of the black horse, which seemed fastened to a particularly strong tuft of grass, turned up the street and drove off, tossing and jolting in the way he came.

There was a strong, serious, excited expression on Mr. Bradford's face as he came in. "My friend," said he, taking my father's hand, "this is a curious affair. I cannot explain it to you, and the probabilities are that I shall have less to do with and for you than I supposed I might have. Be sure, however, that I shall always be interested in your prosperity; and never hesitate to come to me if you are in serious trouble. And now let me ask you never to mention my name to Mrs. Sanderson, with praise; never tell her if I render you a service. I know the lady, and I think it quite likely that you will hear from her in a few days. In the mean time you will be busy in making your family comfortable in your new home." Then he spoke a cheerful word to my mother, and bade us all a good-morning, only looking kindly at me instead of bestowing upon me the coveted and expected kiss.

When he was gone, my father and mother looked at each other with a significant glance, and I waited to hear what they would say. If I have said little about my mother, it is because she had very little to say for herself. She was a weary, worn woman, who had parted with her vitality in the bearing and rearing of her children and in hard and constant care and work. Life had gone wrong with her. She had a profound respect for practical gifts, and her husband did not possess them. She had long since ceased to hope for anything good in life, and her face had taken on a sad, dejected expression, which it never lost under any circumstances. To my father's abounding hopefulness she always opposed her obstinate hopelessness. This was partly a matter of temperament, as well as a result of disappointment. I learned early that she had very little faith in me, or rather in any natural gifts of mine that in the future might retrieve the fortunes of the family. I had too many of the characteristics of my father.

I see the two now as they sat thinking and talking over the events and acquaintances of the evening and the morning as plainly as I saw them then—my father with his blue eyes all alight, and his cheeks touched with the flush of excitement, and my mother with her distrustful face, depreciating and questioning everything. She liked Mr. Bradford. Mr. Bradford was a gentleman; but what had gentlemen to do with them? It was all very well to talk about family, but what was family good for without money? Mr. Bradford had his own affairs to attend to, and we should see precious little more of him! As for Mrs. Sanderson, she did not like her at all. Poor people would get very little consideration from an old woman whose hand was too good to be given to a stranger who happened to be her tenant.

I have wondered often how my father maintained his courage and faith with such a drag upon them as my mother's morbid sadness imposed, but in truth they were proof against every depressing influence. Out of every suggestion of possible good fortune he built castles that filled his imagination with almost a childish delight. He believed that something good was soon to come out of it all, and he was really bright and warm in the smile of that Providence which had manifested itself to him in these new acquaintances. I pinned my faith to my father's sleeve, and believed as fully and as far as he did. There was a rare sympathy between us. The great sweet boy that he was and the little boy that I was, were one in a charming communion. Oh God! that he should be gone and I here! He has been in heaven long enough to have won his freedom, and I am sure we shall kiss when we meet again!

Before the week closed, the gray-haired old servant of Mrs. Sanderson knocked at the door, and brought a little note. It was from his mistress, and read thus, for I copy from the faded document itself:—

"THE MANSION, BRADFORD.

"MR. PETER BONNICASTLE:—

"I should like to see you here next Monday morning, in regard to some repairs about The Mansion. Come early, and if your little boy Arthur is well enough you may bring him.

"RUTH SANDERSON."

The note was read aloud, and it conveyed to my mind instantaneously a fact which I did not mention, but which filled me with strange excitement and pleasure. I remembered that my name was not once mentioned while Mrs. Sanderson was in the house. She had learned it therefore from Mr. Bradford, while talking at the door. Mr. Bradford liked me, I knew, and he had spoken well of me to her. What would come of it all? So, with the same visionary hopefulness that characterized my father, I plunged into a sea of dreams on which I floated over depths paved with treasure, and under skies bright with promise, until Monday morning dawned. When the early breakfast was finished, and my father with unusual fervor of feeling had commended his family and himself to the keeping and the blessing of heaven, we started forth, he and I, hand in hand, with as cheerful anticipations as if we were going to a feast.

CHAPTER II.

I VISIT AN OGRESS AND A GIANT IN THEIR ENCHANTED CASTLE.

"The Mansion" of Mrs. Sanderson was a long half-mile away from us, situated upon the hill that overlooked the little city. It appeared grand in the distance, and commanded the most charming view of town, meadow and river imaginable. We passed Mr. Bradford's house on the way—a plain, rich, unpretending dwelling—and received from him a hearty good-morning, with kind inquiries for my mother, as he stood in his open doorway, enjoying the fresh morning air. At the window sat a smiling little woman, and, by her side, looking out at me, stood the prettiest little girl I had ever seen. Her raven-black hair was freshly curled, and shone like her raven-black eyes; and both helped to make the simple frock in which she was dressed seem marvelously white. I have pitied my poor little self many times in thinking how far removed from me in condition the petted child seemed that morning, and how unworthy I felt, in my homely clothes, to touch her dainty hand, or even to speak to her. I was fascinated by the vision, but glad to get out of her sight.

On arriving at The Mansion, my father and I walked to the great front-door. There were sleeping lions at the side and there was a rampant lion on the knocker which my father was about to attack when the door swung noiselessly upon its hinges, and we were met upon the threshold by the mistress herself. She looked smaller than ever, shorn of her street costume and her bonnet; and her lips were so thin and her face seemed so full of pain that I wondered whether it were her head or her teeth that ached.

"The repairs that I wish to talk about are at the rear of the house," she said, blocking the way, and with a nod directing my father to that locality. There was no show of courtesy in her words or manner. My father turned away, responding to her bidding, and still maintaining his hold upon my hand.

"Arthur," said she, "come in here."

I looked up questioningly into my father's face, and saw that it was clouded. He relinquished my hand, and said: "Go with the lady."

She took me into a little library, and, pointing me to a chair, said: "Sit there until I come back. Don't stir, or touch anything."

I felt, when she left me, as if there were enough of force in her command to paralyze me for a thousand years. I hardly dared to breathe. Still my young eyes were active, and were quickly engaged in taking an inventory of the apartment, and of such rooms as I could look into through the open doors. I was conscious at once that I was looking upon nothing that was new. Everything was faded and dark and old, except those things that care could keep bright. The large brass andirons in the fireplace, and the silver candlesticks on the mantel-tree were as brilliant as when they were new. So perfect was the order of the apartment—so evidently had every article of furniture and every little ornament been adjusted to its place and its relations—that, after the first ten minutes of my observation, I could have detected any change as quickly as Mrs. Sanderson herself.

Through a considerable passage, with an open door at either end, I saw on the wall of the long dining-room a painted portrait of a lad, older than I and very handsome. I longed to go nearer to it, but the prohibition withheld me. In truth, I forgot all else about me in my curiosity concerning it—forgot even where I was—yet I failed at last to carry away any impression of it that my memory could recall at will.

It may have been half an hour—it may have been an hour—that Mrs. Sanderson was out of the room, engaged with my father. It seemed a long time that I had been left when she returned.

"Have you moved, or touched anything?" she inquired.

"No, ma'am."

"Are you tired?"

"Yes, ma'am."

"What would you like to do?"

"I should like to go nearer to the picture of the beautiful little boy in that room," I answered, pointing to it.

She crossed the room at once and closed the door. Then she came back to me and said with a voice that trembled: "You must not see that picture, and you must never ask me anything about it."

"Then," I said, "I should like to go out where my father is at work."

"Your father is busy. He is at work for me, and I do not wish to have him disturbed," she responded.

"Then I should like a book," I said.

She went to a little case of shelves on the opposite side of the room, and took down one book after another, and looked, not at the contents, but at the fly-leaf of each, where the name of the owner is usually inscribed. At last she found one that apparently suited her, and came and sat down by me, holding it in her lap. She looked at me curiously, and then said: "What do you expect to make of yourself, boy? What do you expect to be?"

"A man," I answered.

"Do you? That is a great deal to expect."

"Is it harder to be a man than it is to be a woman?" I inquired.

"Yes."

"Why?"

"Because it is," she replied almost snappishly.

"A woman isn't so large," I responded, as if that statement might contain a helpful suggestion.

She smiled faintly, and then her face grew stern and sad; and she seemed to look at something far off. At length she turned to me and said : "You are sure you will never be a drunkard?"

"Never," I replied.

"Nor a gambler?"

"I don't know what a gambler is."

"Do you think you could ever become a disobedient, ungrateful wretch, child?" she continued.

I do not know where my responding words or my impulse to utter them came from : probably from some romantic passage that I had read, coupled with the conversations I had recently heard in my home; but I rose upon my feet, and with real feeling, though with abundant mock-heroism in the seeming, I said : "Madame, I am a Bonnicastle !"

She did not smile, as I do, recalling the incident, but she patted me on the head with the first show of affectionate regard. She let her hand rest there while her eyes looked far off again; and I knew she was thinking of things with which I could have no part.

"Do you think you could love me, Arthur?" she said, looking me in the eyes.

"I don't know," I replied, "but I think I could love anybody who loved me."

"That's true, that's true," she said sadly; and then she added : "Would you like to live here with me?"

"I don't think I would," I answered frankly.

"Why?"

"Because it is so still, and everything is so nice, and my father and mother would not be here, and I should have nobody to play with," I replied.

"But you would have a large room, and plenty to eat and good clothes to wear," she said, looking down upon my humble garments.

"Should I have this house when you get through with it?" I inquired.

"Then you would like it without me in it, would you?" she said, with a smile which she could not repress.

"I should think it would be a very good house for a man to live in," I replied, evading her question.

"But you would be alone."

"Oh no!" I said, "I should have a wife and children."

"Humph!" she exclaimed, giving her head a little toss and mine a little rap as she removed her hand, "you will be a man, I guess, fast enough!"

She sat a moment in silence, looking at me, and then she handed me the book she held, and went out of the room again to see my father at his work. It was a book full of rude pictures and uninteresting text, and its attractions had long been exhausted when she returned, flushed and nervous. I learned afterwards that she had had a long argument with my father about the proper way of executing the job she had given him.

My father had presumed upon his knowledge of his craft to suggest that her way of doing the work was not the right way; and she had insisted that the work must be done in her way or not done at all. Those who worked for her were to obey her will. She assumed all knowledge of everything relating to herself and her possessions, and permitted neither argument nor opposition; and when my father convinced her reason that she had erred, she was only fixed thereby in her error. I knew that something had gone wrong, and I longed to see my father, but I did not dare to say anything about it.

How the morning wore away I do not remember. She led me in a dreary ramble through the rooms of the large old house, and we had a good deal of idle talk that led to nothing. She chilled and repressed me. I felt that I was not myself,— that her will overshadowed me. She called nothing out of me that interested her. I remember thinking how different she was from Mr. Bradford, whose presence made me feel that I was in a large place, and stirred me to think and talk.

At noon the dinner-bell rang, and she bade me go with her to the dining-room. I told her my father had brought dinner for me, and I would like to eat with him. I longed to get out of her presence, but she insisted that I must eat with her and there was no escape. As we entered the dining-room, I looked at once for my picture, but it was gone. In its place was a square area of unfaded wall, where it had hung for many years. I knew it had been removed because I wished to see it and was curious in regard to it. The spot where it hung had a fascination for me, and many times my eyes went up to it, as if that which had so strangely vanished might as strangely reappear.

"Keep your eyes at home," said my snappish little hostess, who had placed me, not at her side, but *vis à vis ;* so afterward, when they were not glued to my plate, or were not watching the movements of the old man-servant whom I had previously seen driving his mistress's chaise, they were fixed on her.

I could not but feel that "Jenks," as she called him, disliked me. I was an intruder, and had no right to be at Madame's table. When he handed me anything at the lady's bidding, he bent down toward me, and uttered something between growling and muttering. I had no doubt then that he would have torn me limb from limb if he could. I found afterward that growling and muttering were the habit of his life. In the stable he growled and muttered at the horse. In the garden, he growled and muttered at the weeds. Blacking his mistress's shoes, he growled and muttered, and turned them over and over, as if he were determining whether to begin to eat them at the toe or the heel. If he sharpened the lady's carving-knife, he growled as if he were sharpening his own teeth. I suppose she had become used to it, and did not notice it; but he impressed me at first as a savage monster.

I was conscious during the dinner, to which, notwithstanding all the disturbing and depressing influences, I did full justice, that I was closely observed by my hostess; for she freely undertook to criticise my habits, and to lay down rules for my conduct at the table. After every remark, Jenks growled and muttered a hoarse response.

Toward the close of the meal there was a long silence, and I became very much absorbed in my thoughts and fancies.

My hostess observed that something new had entered my mind—for her apprehensions were very quick—and said abruptly: "Boy, what are you thinking about?"

I blushed and replied that I would rather not tell.

"Tell me at once," she commanded.

I obeyed with great reluctance, but her expectant eye was upon me, and there was no escape.

"I was thinking," I said, "that I was confined in an enchanted castle where a little ogress lived with a gray-headed giant. One day she invited me to dinner, and she spoke very cross to me, and the gray-headed giant growled always when he came near me, as if he wanted to eat me; but I couldn't stir from my seat to get away from him. Then I heard a voice outside of the castle walls that sounded like my father's, only it was a great way off, and it said:

> 'Come, little boy, to me,
> On the back of a bumble-bee.'

Then I tried to get out of my chair, but I couldn't. So I clapped my hands three times, and said: 'Castle, castle, Bonnicastle!' and the little ogress flew out of the window on a broomstick, and I jumped up and seized the carving-knife and slew the gray-headed giant, and pitched him down cellar with the fork. Then the doors flew open, and I went out to see my father, and he took me home in a gold chaise with a black horse as big as an elephant."

I could not tell whether amazement or amusement prevailed in the expression of the face of my little hostess, as I proceeded with the revelation of my fancies. I think her first impression was that I was insane, or that my recent fall had in some way injured my brain, or possibly that fever was coming on, for she said, with real concern in her voice: "Child, are you sure you are quite well?"

"Very well, I thank you, ma'am," I replied, after the formula in which I had been patiently instructed.

Jenks growled and muttered, but as I looked into his face

I was sure I caught the slightest twinkle in his little gray eyes. At any rate, I lost all fear of him from that moment.

"Jenks," said the lady, "take this boy to his father, and tell him I think he had better send him home. If it is necessary, you can go with him."

As I rose from the table, I remembered the directions my mother had given me in the morning, and my tongue being relieved from its spell of silence, I went around to Mrs. Sanderson, and thanked her for her invitation, and formally gave her my hand, to take leave of her. I am sure the lady was surprised not only by the courtesy, but by the manner in which it was rendered; for she detained my hand, and said, in a voice quite low and almost tender in its tone: "You do not think me a real ogress, do you?"

"Oh no!" I replied, "I think you are a good woman, only you are not very much like my mother. You don't seem used to little boys: you never had any, perhaps?"

Jenks overheard me, pausing in his work of clearing the table, and growled.

"Jenks, go out," said Mrs. Sanderson, and he retired to the kitchen, muttering as he went.

As I uttered my question, I looked involuntarily at the vacant spot upon the wall, and although she said nothing as I turned back to her, I saw that her face was full of pain.

"I beg your pardon," I said, in simplicity and earnestness. My quick sense of what was passing in her mind evidently touched her, for she put her arm around me, and drew me close to her side. I had unconsciously uncovered an old fountain of bitterness, and as she held me she said, "Would you like to kiss an old lady?"

I laughed, and said, "Yes, if she would like to kiss a boy."

She strained me to her breast. I knew that my fresh, boyish lips were sweet to hers, and I knew afterwards that they were the first she had pressed for a quarter of a century. It seemed a long time that she permitted her head to rest upon my shoulder, for it quite embarrassed me. She released me at length,

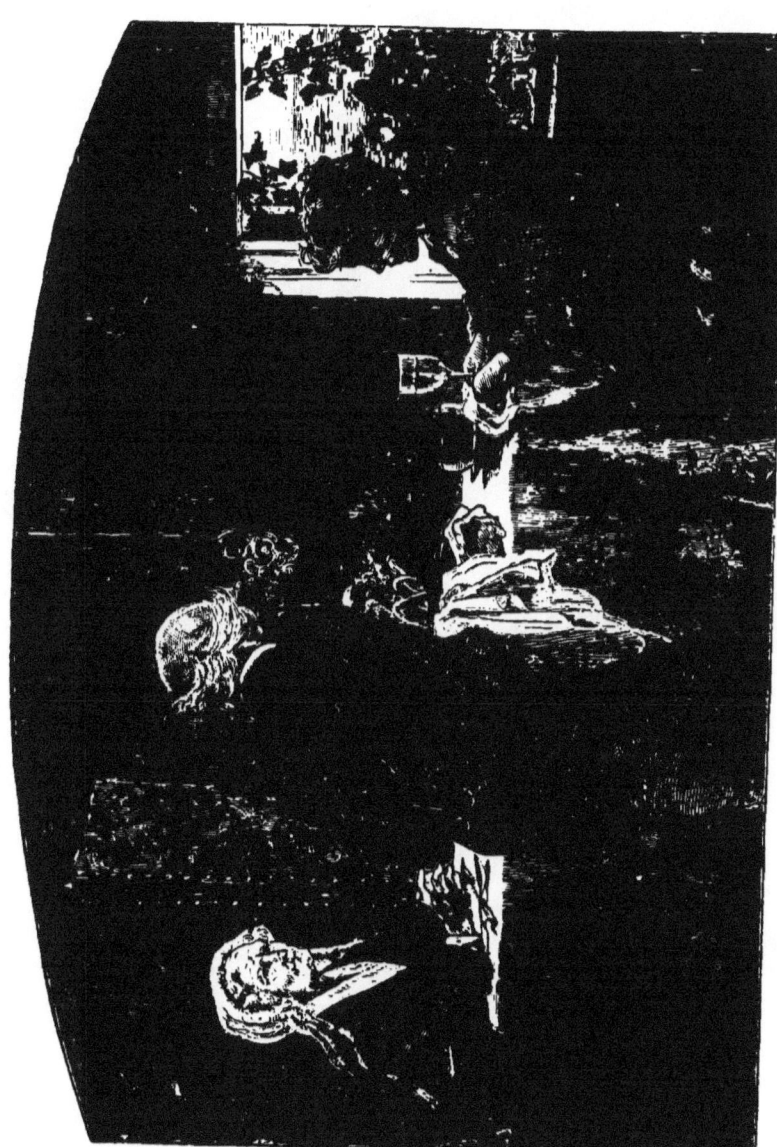

"Jenks," said the lady, "take this boy to his father." (p. 44.)

for Jenks began to fumble at the door, to announce that he was about to enter. Before he opened it, she said quickly: "I shall see you again; I am going to have a talk with your father."

During the closing passages of our interview, my feelings towards Mrs. Sanderson had undergone a most unexpected change. My heart was full of pity for her, and I was conscious that for some reason which I did not know she had a special regard for me. When a strong nature grows tender, it possesses the most fascinating influence in the world. When a powerful will bends to a child, and undertakes to win that which it cannot command, there are very few natures that can withstand it. I do not care to ask how much of art there may have been in Mrs. Sanderson's caresses, but she undoubtedly saw that there was nothing to be made of me without them. Whether she felt little or much, she was determined to win me to her will; and from that moment to this, I have felt her influence upon my life. She had a way of assuming superiority to everybody—of appearing to be wiser than everybody else, of finding everybody's weak point, and exposing it, that made her seem to be one whose word was always to be taken, and whose opinion was always to have precedence. It was in this way, in my subsequent intercourse with her, that she exposed to me the weaknesses of my parents, and undermined my confidence in my friends, and showed me how my loves were misplaced, and almost absorbed me into herself. On the day of my visit to her, she studied me very thoroughly, and learned the secret of managing me. I think she harmed me, and that but for the corrective influences to which I was subsequently exposed, she would well-nigh have ruined me. It is a curse to any child to have his whole personality absorbed by a foreign will,—to take love, law and life from one who renders all with design, in the accomplishment of a purpose. She could not destroy my love for my father and mother, but she made me half ashamed of them. She discovered in some way my admiration of Mr. Bradford, and managed in her own way to modify it. Thus it was with every acquaintance, until, at last, she made herself to me the pivotal point on which the world around her turned.

As I left her, Jenks took me by the hand, and led me out, with the low rumble in his throat and the mangled words between his teeth which were intended to indicate to Mrs. Sanderson that he did not approve of boys at all. As soon, however, as the door was placed between us and the lady, the rumble in his throat was changed to a chuckle. Jenks was not given to words, but he was helplessly and hopelessly under Mrs. Sanderson's thumb, and all his growling and muttering were a pretence. He would not have dared to utter an opinion in her presence, or express a wish. He had comprehended my story of the ogress and the giant, and as it bore rather harder upon the ogress than it did upon the giant, he was in great good humor.

He squeezed my hand and shook me around in what he intended to be an affectionate and approving way, and then gave me a large russet apple, which he drew from a closet in the carriage-house. Not until he had placed several walls between himself and his mistress did he venture to speak.

"Well, you've said it, little fellow, that's a fact."

"Said what?" I inquired.

"You've called the old woman an ogress, he! he! he! and that's just what she is, he! he! he! How did you dare to do such a thing?"

"She made me," I answered. "I did not wish to tell the story."

"That's what she always does," said Jenks. "She always makes people do what they don't want to do. Don't you ever tell her what I say, but the fact is I'm going to leave. She'll wake up some morning and call Jenks, and Jenks won't come! Jenks won't be here! Jenks will be far, far away!"

His last phrase was intended undoubtedly to act upon my boyish imagination, and I asked him with some concern whither he would go.

"I shall plough the sea," said Jenks. "You will find no

Jenks here and no russet apple when you come again. I shall be on the billow. Now mind you don't tell her"—tossing a nod toward the house over his left shoulder—"for that would spoil it all."

I promised him that I would hold the matter a profound secret, although I was conscious that I was not quite loyal to my new friend in keeping from her the intelligence that her servant was about to leave The Mansion for a career upon the ocean.

"Here's your boy," said Jenks, leading me at last to my father. "Mrs. Sanderson thinks you had better send him home, and says I can go with him if he cannot find the way alone."

"I'm very much obliged to Mrs. Sanderson," said my father with a flush on his face, "but I will take care of my boy myself. He will go home when I do."

Jenks chuckled again. He was delighted with anything that crossed the will of his mistress. As he turned away, I said: "Good-by, Mr. Jenks, I hope you won't be very sea-sick."

This was quite too much for the little old man. He had made a small boy believe that he was going away, and that he was going to sea; and he returned to the house so much delighted with himself that he chuckled all the way, and even kicked at a stray chicken that intercepted his progress.

During the remainder of the day I amused myself with watching my father at his work. I was anxious to tell him of all that had happened in the house, but he bade me wait until his work was done. I had been accustomed to watch my father's face, and to detect upon it the expression of all his moods and feelings; and I knew that afternoon that he was passing through a great trial. Once during the afternoon Jenks came out of the house with another apple; and while he kept one eye on the windows he beckoned to me and I went to him. Placing the apple in my hand, he said: "Far, far away, on the billow! Good-by." Not expecting to meet him again, I was much inclined to sadness, but as he did not seem to be very much depressed, I spared my sympathy, and heartily bade him "good luck." So the stupid old servant had had his practice upon the boy, and was happy in the lie that he had passed upon him.

There are boys who seem to be a source of temptation to every man and woman who comes in contact with them. The temptation to impress them, or to excite them to free and characteristic expression, seems quite irresistible. Everybody tries to make them believe something, or to make them say something. I seemed to be one of them. Everybody tried either to make me talk and give expression to my fancies, or to make me believe things that they knew to be false. They practiced upon my credulity, my sympathy, and my imagination for amusement. Even my parents smiled upon my efforts at invention, until I found that they were more interested in my lies than in my truth. The consequence of it all was a disposition to represent every occurrence of my life in false colors. The simplest incident became an interesting adventure; the most common-place act, a heroic achievement. With a conscience so tender that the smallest theft would have made me utterly wretched, I could lie by the hour without compunction. My father and mother had no idea of the injury they were doing me, and whenever they realized, as they sometimes did, that they could not depend upon my word, they were sadly puzzled.

When my father finished his work for the day, and with my hand in his I set out for home, it may readily be imagined that I had a good deal to tell. I not only told of all that I had seen, but I represented as actual all that had been suggested. Such wonderful rooms and dismal passages and marvelous pictures and services of silver and gold and expansive mirrors as I had seen! Such viands as I had tasted—such fruit as I had eaten! And my honest father received all the marvels with hardly a question, and, after him, my mother and the children. I remember few of the particulars, except that the picture of the boy came and went upon the wall of the dining-room as if by magic, and that Mrs. Sanderson wished to have me live with her that I might become her heir. The last statement my father examined with some care. Indeed, I was obliged to tell exactly what was said on the subject, and he learned that, while the lady wished me to live with her, the matter of inheritance had not been suggested by anybody but myself.

CHAPTER III.

I GO TO THE BIRD'S NEST TO LIVE, AND THE GIANT PERSISTS IN HIS PLANS FOR A SEA-VOYAGE.

My father worked for Mrs. Sanderson during the week, but he came home every night with a graver face, and, on the closing evening of the week, it all came out. It was impossible for him to cover from my mother and his family for any length of time anything which gave him either satisfaction or sorrow.

I remember how he walked the room that night, and swung his arms, and in an excitement that was full of indignation and self-pity declared that he could not work for Mrs. Sanderson another week. "I should become an absolute idiot if I were to work for her a month," I heard him say.

And then my mother told him that she never expected anything good from Mrs. Sanderson—that it had turned out very much as she anticipated—though for the life of her she could not imagine what difference it made to my father whether he did his work in one way or another, so long as it pleased Mrs. Sanderson, and he got his money for his labor. I did not at all realize what an effect this talk would have upon my father then, but now I wonder that with his sensitive spirit he did not upbraid my mother, or die. In her mind it was only another instance of my father's incompetency for business, to which incompetency she attributed mainly the rigors of her lot.

Mrs. Sanderson was no better pleased with my father than he was with her. If he had not left her at the end of his first week, she would have managed to dismiss him as soon as she had secured her will concerning myself. On Monday morning I was dispatched to The Mansion with a note from my father which informed Mrs. Sanderson that she was at liberty to suit herself with other service.

Mrs. Sanderson read the note, put her lips very tightly together, and then called Jenks.

"Jenks," said she, "put the horse before the chaise, change your clothes, and drive to the door."

Jenks disappeared to execute her commands, and, in the meantime, Mrs. Sanderson busied herself with preparations. First she brought out sundry pots of jam and jelly, and then two or three remnants of stuffs that could be made into clothing for children, and a basket of apples. When the chaise arrived at the door, she told Jenks to tie his horse and bestow the articles she had provided in the box. When this task was completed she mounted the vehicle, and bade me get in at her side. Then Jenks took his seat, and at Mrs. Sanderson's command drove directly to my father's house.

When we arrived, my father had gone out; and after expressing her regret that she could not see him, she sat down by my mother, and demonstrated her knowledge of human nature by winning her confidence entirely. She even commiserated her on the impracticable character of her husband, and then she left with her the wages of his labor and the gifts she had brought. My mother declared after the little lady went away that she had never been so pleasantly disappointed as she had been in Mrs. Sanderson! She was just, she was generous, she was everything that was sweet and kind and good. All this my father heard when he arrived, and to it all he made no reply. He was too kind to carry anger, and too poor to spurn a freely offered gift, that brought comfort to those whom he loved.

Mrs. Sanderson was a woman of business, and at night she came again. I knew my father dreaded meeting her, as he always dreaded meeting with a strong and unreasonable will. He had a way of avoiding such a will whenever it was possible, and of sacrificing everything unimportant to save a collision with it. There was an insult to his manhood in the mere existence and exercise of such a will, while actual subjection to it was the extreme of torture. But sometimes the exercise of such a will drove him into a corner; and when it did, the shrinking, peaceable man became a lion. He had seen how easily my mother had been conquered, and, although Mrs. Sanderson's gifts were in his house, he determined that whatever might be her business, she should be dealt with frankly and firmly.

I was watching at the window when the little lady alighted at the gate. As she walked up the passage from the street, Jenks exchanged some signals with me. He pointed to the east and then toward the sea, with gestures, which meant that long before the dawning of the morrow's sun Mrs. Sanderson's aged servant would cease to be a resident of Bradford, and would be tossing "on the billow." I did not have much opportunity to carry on this kind of commerce with Jenks, for Mrs. Sanderson's conversation had special reference to myself.

I think my father was a good deal surprised to find the lady agreeable and gracious. She alluded to his note as something which had disappointed her, but, as she presumed to know her own business and to do it in her own way, she supposed that other people knew their own business also, and she was quite willing to accord to them such privileges as she claimed for herself. She was glad there was work enough to be done in Bradford, and she did not doubt that my father would get employment. Indeed, as he was a stranger, she would take the liberty of commending him to her friends as a good workman. It did not follow, she said, that because he could not get along with her he could not get along with others. My father was very silent and permitted her to do the talking. He knew that she had come with some object to accomplish, and he waited for its revelation.

She looked at me, at last, and called me to her side. She put her arm around me, and said, addressing my father: "I suppose Arthur told you what a pleasant day we had together."

"Yes, and I hope he thanked you for your kindness to him," my father answered.

"Oh, yes, he was very polite and wonderfully quiet for a boy," she responded.

My mother volunteered to express the hope that I had not given the lady any trouble.

"I never permit boys to trouble me," was the curt response.

There was something in this that angered my father—something in the tone adopted toward my mother, and something that seemed so cruel in the utterance itself. My father believed in the rights of boys, and when she said this, he remarked with more than his usual incisiveness that he had noticed that those boys who had not been permitted to trouble anybody when they were young, were quite in the habit, when they ceased to be boys, of giving a great deal of trouble. He did not know that he had touched Mrs. Sanderson at a very tender point, but she winced painfully, and then went directly to business.

"Mr. Bonnicastle," said she, "I am living alone, as you know. It is not necessary to tell you much about myself, but I am alone, and with none to care for but myself. Although I am somewhat in years, I come of a long-lived race, and am quite well. I believe it is rational to expect to live for a considerable time yet, and though I have much to occupy my mind it would be pleasant to me to help somebody along. You have a large family, whose fortunes you would be glad to advance, and, although you and I do not agree very well, I hope you will permit me to assist you in accomplishing your wish."

She paused to see how the proposition was received, and was apparently satisfied that fortune had favored her, though my father said nothing.

"I want this boy," she resumed, drawing me more closely to her. "I want to see him growing up and becoming a man under my provisions for his support and education. It is not possible for you to do for him what I can do. It will interest me to watch him from year to year, it will bring a little young blood into my lonely old house occasionally, and in one way and another it will do us all good."

My father looked very serious. He loved me as he loved his life. His great ambition was to give me the education which circumstances had denied to him. Here was the opportunity, brought to his door, yet he hesitated to accept it. After thinking for a moment, he said gravely: "Mrs. Sanderson, God has placed this boy in my hands to train for Himself, and I cannot surrender the control of his life to anybody. Temporarily I can give him into the hands of teachers, conditionally I can place him in your hands, but I cannot place him in any hands beyond my immediate recall. I can never surrender my right to his love and his obedience, or count him an alien from my heart and home. If, understanding my feeling in this matter, you find it in your heart to do for him what I cannot, why, you have the means, and I am sure God will bless you for employing them to this end."

"I may win all the love and all the society from him I can?" said Mrs. Sanderson, interrogatively.

"I do not think it would be a happy or a healthy thing for the child to spend much time in your house, deprived of young society," my father replied. "If you should do for him what you suggest, I trust that the boy and that all of us would make such expressions of our gratitude as would be most agreeable to yourself; but I must choose his teachers, and my home, however humble, must never cease to be regarded by him as his home. I must say this at the risk of appearing ungrateful, Mrs. Sanderson."

The little lady had the great good sense to know when she had met with an answer, and the adroitness to appear satisfied with it. She was one of those rare persons who, seeing a rock in the way, recognize it at once, and, without relinquishing their purpose for an instant, either seek to go around it or to arrive at their purpose from some other direction. She had concluded, for reasons of her own, to make me so far as possible her possession. She had had already a sufficient trial of her power to show her something of what she could do with me, and she calculated with considerable certainty that she could manage my father in some way.

"Very well: he shall not come to me now, and shall never come unless I can make my home pleasant to him," she said. "In the meantime, you will satisfy yourself in regard to a desirable school for him, and we will leave all other questions for time to determine."

Neither my father nor my mother had anything to oppose to this, and my patroness saw at once that her first point was gained. Somehow all had been settled without trouble. Every obstacle had been taken out of the way, and the lady seemed more than satisfied.

"When you are ready to talk decisively about the boy, you will come to my house, and we will conclude matters," she said, as she rose to take her leave.

I noticed that she did not recognize the existence of my little brothers and older sisters, and something subtler than reason told me that she was courteous to my father and mother only so far as was necessary for the accomplishment of her purposes. I was half afraid of her, yet I could not help admiring her. She kissed me at parting, but she made no demonstration of responsive courtesy to my parents, who advanced in a cordial way to show their sense of her kindness.

In the evening, my father called upon Mr. Bradford and made a full exposure of the difficulty he had had with Mrs. Sanderson, and the propositions she had made respecting myself; and as he reported his conversation and conclusions on his return to my mother, I was made acquainted with them. Mr. Bradford had advised that the lady's offer concerning me should be accepted. He had reasons for this which he told my father he did not feel at liberty to give, but there were enough that lay upon the surface to decide the matter. There was nothing humiliating in it, for it was no deed of charity. A great good could be secured for me by granting to the lady what she regarded in her own heart as a favor. She never had been greatly given to deeds of benevolence, and this was the first notable act in her history that looked like one. He advised, however, that my father hold my destiny in his own hands, and keep me as much as possible away from Bradford, never permitting me to be long at a time under Mrs. Sanderson's roof and immediate personal influence. "When the youngster gets older," Mr. Bradford said, " he will manage all this matter for himself, better than we can manage it for him."

Then Mr. Bradford told him about a famous family school in a country village some thirty miles away, which, from the name of the teacher, Mr. Bird, had been named by the pupils "The Bird's Nest." Everybody in the region knew about The Bird's Nest; and multitudinous were the stories told about Mr. and Mrs. Bird; and very dear to all the boys, many of whom had grown to be men, were the house and the pair who presided over it. Mr. Bradford drew a picture of this school which quite fascinated my father, and did much—everything indeed—to reconcile him to the separation which my removal thither would make necessary. I was naturally very deeply interested in all that related to the school, and, graceless as the fact may seem, I should have been ready on the instant to part with all that made my home, in order to taste the new, strange life it would bring me. I had many questions to ask, but quickly arrived at the end of my father's knowledge; and then my imagination ran wildly on until the images of The Bird's Nest and of Mr. and Mrs. Bird and Hillsborough, the village that made a tree for the nest, were as distinctly in my mind as if I had known them all my life.

The interview which Mrs. Sanderson had asked of my father was granted at an early day, and the lady acceded without a word to the proposition to send me to The Bird's Nest. She had heard only good reports of the school, she said, and was apparently delighted with my father's decision. Indeed, I suspect she was quite as anxious to get me away from my father and my home associations as he was to keep me out of The Mansion and away from her. She was left to make her own arrangements for my outfit, and also for my admission to the school, though my father stipulated for the privilege of accompanying me to the new home.

One pleasant morning, some weeks afterward, she sent for me to visit her at The Mansion. She was very sweet and motherly; and when I returned to my home I went clad in a suit of garments that made me the subject of curiosity and envy among my brothers and mates, and with the news that in one week I must be ready to go to Hillsborough. During all that week my father was very tender toward me, as toward some great treasure set apart to absence. He not only did not seek for work, but declined or deferred that which came. It was impossible for me to know then the heart-hunger which he anticipated, but I know it now. I do not doubt that, in his usual way, he wove around me many a romance, and reached forward into all the possibilities of my lot. He was always as visionary as a child, though I do not know that he was more childlike in this respect than in others.

My mother was full of the gloomiest forebodings. She felt as if Hillsborough would prove to be an unhealthy place; she did not doubt that there was something wrong about Mr. and Mrs. Bird, if only we could know what it was; and for her part there was something in the name which the boys had given the school that was fearfully suggestive of hunger. She should always think of me, she said, as a bird with its mouth open, crying for something to eat. More than all, she presumed that Mr. Bird permitted his boys to swim without care, and she would not be surprised to learn that the oldest of them carried guns and pistols and took the little boys with them.

Poor, dear mother! Most fearful and unhappy while living, and most tenderly mourned and revered in memory! why did you persist in seeing darkness where others saw light, and in making every cup bitter with the apprehension of evil? Why were you forever on the watch that no freak of untoward fortune should catch you unaware? Why did you treat the Providence you devoutly tried to trust as if you supposed he meant to trick you, if he found you for a moment off your guard? Oh, the twin charms of hopefulness and trustfulness! What power have they to strengthen weary feet, to sweeten sleep, to make the earth green and the heavens blue, to cheat misfortune of its bitterness and to quench even the poison of death itself!

It was arranged that my father should take me to Hillsborough in Mrs. Sanderson's chaise—the same vehicle in which I had first seen the lady herself. My little trunk was to be attached by straps to the axletree, and so ride beneath us. Taking leave of my home was a serious business, notwithstanding my anticipations of pleasure. My mother said that it was not at all likely we should ever meet again; and I parted with her at last in a passion of tears. The children were weeping too, from sympathy rather than from any special or well-comprehended sorrow, and I heartily wished myself away, and out of sight.

Jenks brought the horse to us, and, after he had assisted my father in fastening the trunk, took me apart from the group that had gathered around the chaise, and said in a confidential way that he made an attempt on the previous night to leave. He had got as far as the window from which he intended to let himself down, but finding it dark and rather cloudy he had concluded to defer his departure until a lighter and clearer night. "A storm, a dark storm, is awful on the ocean, you know," said Jenks, "but I shall go. You will not see me here when you come again. Don't say anything about it, but the old woman is going to be surprised, once in her life. She will call Jenks, and Jenks won't come. He will be far, far away on the billow."

"Good-by," I said; "I hope I'll see you again somewhere, but I don't think you ought to leave Mrs. Sanderson."

"Oh, I shall leave," said Jenks. "The world is large and Mrs. Sanderson is—is—quite small. Let her call Jenks once, and see what it is to have him far, far away. Her time will come." And he shook his head, and pressed his lips together, and ground the gravel under his feet, as if nothing less than an earthquake could shake his determination. The case seemed quite hopeless to me, and I remember that the unpleasant possibility suggested itself that I might be summoned to The Mansion to take Jenks's place.

At the close of our little interview, he drew a long paper box from his pocket, and gave it to me with the injunction not to open it until I had gone half way to Hillsborough. I accordingly placed it in the boot of the chaise, to wait its appointed time.

Jenks rode with us as far as The Mansion, spending the time in instructing my father just where, under the shoulder of the old black horse, he could make a whip the most effective without betraying the marks to Mrs. Sanderson, and, when we drove up to the door, disappeared at once around the corner of the house. I went in to take leave of the lady, and found her in the little library, awaiting me. Before her, on the table, were a Barlow pocket-knife, a boy's playing-ball, a copy of the New Testament, and a Spanish twenty-five cent piece.

"There," she said, "young man, put all those in your pockets, and see that you don't lose them. I want you to write me a letter once a month, and, when you write, begin your letters with 'Dear Aunt.'"

The sudden accession to my boyish wealth almost drove me wild. I had received my first knife and my first silver. I impulsively threw my arms around the neck of my benefactress, and told her I should never, never forget her, and should never do anything that would give her trouble.

"See that you don't!" was the sharp response.

As I bade her good-by, I was gratified by the look of pride which she bestowed on me, but she did not accompany me to the door, or speak a word to my father. So, at last, we were gone, and fairly on the way. I revealed to my father the treasures I had received, and only at a later day was I able to interpret the look of pain that accompanied his congratulations. I was indebted to a stranger, who was trying to win my heart, for possessions which his poverty forbade him to bestow upon me.

Of the delights of that drive over the open country I can

give no idea. We climbed long hills; we rode by the side of cool, dashing streams; we paused under the shadow of wayside trees; we caught sight of a thousand forms of frolic life on the fences, in the forests, and in the depths of crystal pools; we saw men at work in the fields, and I wondered if they did not envy us; we met strange people on the road, who looked at us with curious interest; a black fox dashed across our way, and, giving us a scared look, scampered into the cover and was gone; bobolinks sprang up in the long grass on wings tangled with music, and sailed away and caught on fences to steady themselves; squirrels took long races before us on the road-side rails; and far up through the trees and above the hills white-winged clouds with breasts of downy brown floated against a sky of deepest blue. Never again this side of heaven do I expect to experience such perfect pleasure as I enjoyed that day—a delight in all forms and phases of nature, sharpened by the expectations of new companionships and of a strange new life that would open before I should sleep again.

The half-way stage of our journey was reached before noon, and I was quite as anxious to see the gift which Jenks had placed in my hands at parting as to taste the luncheon which my mother had provided. Accordingly, when my repast was taken from the basket and spread before me, I first opened the paper box. I cannot say that I was not disappointed; but the souvenir was one of which only I could understand the significance, and that fact gave it a rare charm. It consisted of a piece of a wooden shingle labeled in pencil "Atlantick Oshun," in the middle of which was a little ship, standing at an angle of forty-five degrees to the plane of the shingle, with a mast and a sail of wood, and a figure at the bow, also of wood, intended doubtless to represent Jenks himself, looking off upon the boundless waste. The utmost point of explanation to which my father could urge me was the statement that some time something would happen at The Mansion which would explain all. So I carefully put the "Atlantick Oshun" into its box, in which I preserved it for many months, answering all inquiries concerning it with the tantalizing statement that it was "a secret."

Toward the close of the afternoon, we came in sight of Hillsborough, with its two churches, and its cluster of embowered white houses. It was perched, like many New England villages, upon the top of the highest hill in the region, and we entered at last upon the long acclivity that led to it. Halfway up the hill, we saw before us a light, open wagon drawn by two gray horses, and bearing a gentleman and lady who were quietly chatting and laughing together. As we drew near to them, they suddenly stopped, and the gentleman, handing the reins to his companion, rose upon his feet, drew a rifle to his eye and discharged it at some object in the fields. In an instant, a little dog bounced out of the wagon, and, striking rather heavily upon the ground, rolled over and over three or four times, and then, gaining his feet, went for the game. Our own horse had stopped, and, as wild as the little dog, I leaped from the chaise, and started to follow. When I came up with the dog, he was making the most extravagant plunges at a wounded woodchuck, who squatted, chattering and showing his teeth. I seized the nearest weapon in the shape of a cudgel that I could find, dispatched the poor creature, and bore him in triumph to the gentleman, the little dog barking and snapping at the game all the way.

"Well done, my lad! I have seen boys who were afraid of woodchucks. Toss him into the ravine: he is good for nothing," said the man of the rifle.

Then he looked around, and, bowing to my father, told him that as he was fond of shooting he had undertaken to rid the farms around him of the animals that gave their owners so much trouble. "It is hard upon the woodchucks," he added, "but kind to the farmers." This was apparently said to defend himself from the suspicion of being engaged in cruel and wanton sport.

At the sound of his voice, the tired and reeking horse which my father drove whinnied, then started on, and, coming to the back of the other carriage, placed his nose close to the gentleman's shoulder. The lady looked around and smiled, while the man placed his hand caressingly upon the animal's head. "Animals are all very fond of me," said he. "I don't understand it: I suppose they do."

There was something exceedingly winning and hearty in the gentleman's voice, and I did not wonder that all the animals liked him.

"Can you tell me," inquired my father, "where The Bird's Nest is?"

"Oh, yes, I'm going there. Indeed, I'm the old Bird himself."

"Tut! who takes care of the nest?" said the lady with a smile.

"And this is the Mother Bird—Mrs. Bird," said the gentleman.

Mrs. Bird bowed to us both, and, beckoning to me, pointed to her side. It was an invitation to leave my father, and take a seat with her. The little dog, who had been helped into his master's wagon, saw me coming, and mounted into his lap, determined that he would shut that place from the intruder. I accepted the invitation, and, with the lady's arm around me, we started on.

"Now I am going to guess," said Mr. Bird. "I guess your name is Arthur Bonnicastle, that the man behind us is your father, that you are coming to The Bird's Nest to live, that you are intending to be a good boy, and that you are going to be very happy."

"You've guessed right the first time," I responded laughing.

"And I can always guess when a boy has done right and when he has done wrong," said Mr. Bird. "There's a little spot in his eye—ah, yes! you have it!—that tells the whole story," and he looked down pleasantly into my face.

At this moment one of his horses discovered a young calf by the roadside, and, throwing back his ears, gave it chase. I had never seen so funny a performance. The horse, in genuine frolic, dragged his less playful mate and the wagon through the gutter and over rocks for many rods, entirely unrestrained by his driver until the scared object of the chase slipped between two bars at the roadside, and ran wildly off into the field. At this the horse shook his head in a comical way and went quietly back into the road.

"That horse is laughing all over," said Mr. Bird. "He thinks it was an excellent joke. I presume he will think of it, and laugh again when he gets at his oats."

"Do you really think that horses laugh, Mr. Bird?" I inquired.

"Laugh? Bless you, yes," he replied. "All animals laugh when they are pleased. Gyp"—and he turned his eyes upon the little dog in his lap—"are you happy?"

Gyp looked up into his master's face, and wagged his tail.

"Don't you see 'yes' in his eye, and a smile in the wag of his tail?" said Mr. Bird. "If I had asked you the same question you would have answered with your tongue, and smiled with your mouth. That's all the difference. These creatures understand us a great deal better than we understand them. Why, I never drive these horses when I am finely dressed for fear they will be ashamed of their old harness."

Then turning to the little dog again, he said: "Gyp, get down." Gyp immediately jumped down, and curled up at his feet. "Gyp, come up here," said he, and Gyp mounted quickly to his old seat. "Don't you see that this dog understands the English language?" said Mr. Bird; "and don't you see that we are not so bright as a dog, if we cannot learn his? Why, I know the note of every bird, and every insect, and every animal on all these hills, and I know their ways and habits. What is more, they know I understand them, and you will hear how they call me and sing to me at The Bird's Nest."

So I had received my first lesson from my new teacher, and little did he appreciate the impression it had made upon me. It gave me a sympathy with animal life and an interest in its habits which have lasted until this hour. It gave me, too, an insight into him. He had a strong sympathy in the life of a boy, for his own sake. Every new boy was a new study that he entered upon, not from any sense of duty, or from any scheme of policy, but with a hearty interest excited by the boy himself. He was as much interested in the animal play of a boy as he had been in the play of the horse. He watched a group of boys with the same hearty amusement that held him while witnessing the frolic of kittens and lambs. Indeed, he often played with them; and in this sympathy, freely manifested, he held the springs of his wonderful power over them.

We soon arrived at The Bird's Nest, and all the horses were passed into other hands. My little trunk was loosed, and carried to a room I had not seen, and in a straggling way we entered the house.

Before we alighted, I took a hurried outside view of my future home. On the whole, "The Bird's Nest" would have been a good name for it if a man by any other name had presided over it. It had its individual and characteristic beauty, because it had been shaped to a special purpose; but it seemed to have been brought together at different times, and from wide distances. There was a central old house, and a hexagonal addition, and a tower, and a long piazza that tied everything together. It certainly looked grand among the humble houses of the village; though I presume that a professional architect would not have taken the highest pleasure in it. As Mr. Bird stepped out of his wagon upon the piazza, and took off his hat, I had an opportunity to see him and to fix my impressions of his appearance. He was a tall, handsome, strongly-built man, a little past middle life, with a certain fullness of habit that comes of good health and a happy temperament. His eye was blue, his forehead high, and his whole face bright and beaming with good-nature. His companion was a woman above the medium size, with eyes the same color of his own, into whose plainly-parted hair the frost had crept, and upon whose honest face and goodly figure hung that ineffable grace which we try to characterize by the word "motherly."

I heard the shouts of boys at play upon the green, for it was after school hours, and met half-a-dozen little fellows on the piazza, who looked at me with pleasant interest as "the new boy;" and then we entered a parlor with curious angles, and furniture that betrayed thorough occupation and usage. There were thrifty plants and beautiful flowers in the bay-window, for plants and flowers came as readily within the circle of Mr. Bird's sympathies as birds and boys. There was evidently an uncovered stairway near one of the doors, for we heard two or three boys running down the steps with a little more noise than was quite agreeable. Immediately Gyp ran to the door where the noise was manifested, and barked with all his might.

"Gyp is one of my assistants in the school," said Mr. Bird, in explanation, "especially in the matter of preserving order. A boy never runs down-stairs noisily without receiving a scolding from him. He is getting a little old now and sensitive, and I am afraid has not quite consideration enough for the youngsters."

I laughed at the idea of having a dog for a teacher, but with my new notions of Gyp's capacity I was quite ready to believe what Mr. Bird told me about him.

My father found himself very much at home with Mr. and Mrs. Bird, and was evidently delighted with them, and with my prospects under their roof and care. We had supper in the great dining-room with forty hungry but orderly boys, a pleasant evening with music afterward, and an early bed. I was permitted to sleep with my father that night, and he was permitted to take me upon his arm, and pillow my slumbers there, while he prayed for me and secretly poured out his love upon me.

Before we went to sleep my father said a few words to me, but those words were new and made a deep impression.

"My little boy," he said, "you have my life in your hands. If you grow up into a true, good man, I shall be happy, although I may continue poor. I have always worked hard, and I am willing to work even harder than ever, if it is all right with you; but if you disappoint me and turn out badly, you will kill me. I am living now, and expect always to live, in and for my children. I have no ambitious projects for myself. Providence has opened a way for you which I did not anticipate. Do all you can to please the woman who has undertaken to do so much for you, but do not forget your father and mother, and remember always that it is not possible for anybody to love you and care for you as we do. If you have any troubles, come to me with them, and if you are tempted to do wrong pray for help to do right. You will have many struggles and trials—everybody has them—but you can do what you will, and become what you wish to become."

The resolutions that night formed—a thousand times shaken and a thousand times renewed—became the determining and fruitful forces of my life.

The next morning, when the old black horse and chaise were brought to the door, and my father, full of tender pain, took leave of me, and disappeared at last at the foot of the hill, and I felt that I was wholly separated from my home, I cried as if I had been sure that I had left that home forever. The passion wasted itself in Mrs. Bird's motherly arms, and then, with words of cheer and diversions that occupied my mind, she cut me adrift, to find my own soundings in the new social life of the school.

Of the first few days of school-life there is not much to be said. They passed pleasantly enough. The aim of my teachers at first was not to push me into study, but to make me happy, to teach me the ways of my new life, and to give me an opportunity to imbibe the spirit of the school. My apprehensions were out in every direction. I learned by watching others my own deficiencies; and my appetite for study grew by a natural process. I could not be content, at last, until I had become one with the rest in work and in acquirements.

There lies before me now a package of my letters, made sacred by my father's interest in and perusal and preservation of them; and, although I have no intention to burden these pages with their crudenesses and puerilities, I cannot resist the temptation to reproduce the first which I wrote at The Bird's Nest, and sent home. I shall spare to the reader its wretched orthography, and reproduce it entire, in the hope that he will at least enjoy its unconscious humor.

"THE BIRD'S NEST.

"DEAR PRECIOUS FATHER:—

"I have lost my ball. I don't know where in the world it can be. It seemed to get away from me in a curious style. Mr. Bird is very kind, and I like him very much. I am sorry to say I have lost my Barlow knife too. Mr. Bird says a Barlow knife is a very good thing. I don't quite think I have lost the twenty-five cent piece. I have not seen it since yesterday morning, and I think I shall find it. Henry Hulm, who is my chum, and a very smart boy, I can tell you, thinks the money will be found. Mr. Bird says there must be a hole in the top of my pocket. I don't know what to do. I am afraid Aunt Sanderson will be cross about it. Mr. Bird thinks I ought to give my knife to the boy that will find the money, and the money to the boy that will find the knife, but I don't see as I should make much in that way, do you? I love Mrs. Bird very much. Miss Butler is the dearest young lady I ever knew. Mrs. Bird kisses us all when we go to bed, and it seems real good. I have put the testament in the bottom of my trunk, under all the things. I shall keep that if possible. If Mrs. Sanderson finds out that I have lost the things, I wish you would explain it and tell her the testament is safe. Miss Butler has dark eyebrows and wears a belt. Mr. Bird has killed another woodchuck. I wonder if you left the key of my trunk. It seems to be gone. We have real good times, playing ball and taking walks. I have walked out with Miss Butler. I wish mother could see her hair, and I am your son with ever so much love to you and mother and all,

"ARTHUR BONNICASTLE."

CHAPTER IV.

IN WHICH THE COURSE OF TRUE LOVE IS NOT PERMITTED TO RUN AT ALL.

THE first night which I spent in The Bird's Nest, after my father left me, was passed alone, though my room opened into another that was occupied by two boys. On the following day Mr. Bird asked me if I had met with any boy whom I would like for a room-mate; and I told him at once that Henry Hulm was the boy I wanted. He smiled at my selection, and asked for the reason of it; and he smiled more warmly still when I told him I thought he was handsome, and seemed lonely and sad. The lad was at least two years older than I, but among all the boys he had been my first and supreme attraction. He was my opposite in every particular. Quiet, studious, keeping much by himself, and bearing in his dark face and eyes a look of patient self-repression, he enlisted at once my curiosity, my sympathy and my admiration.

Henry was called into our consultation, and Mr. Bird informed him of my choice. The boy smiled gratefully, for he had been shunned by the ruder fellows for the same qualities which had attracted me. As the room I occupied was better than his, his trunk was moved into mine; and while we remained in the school we continued our relations and kept the same apartment. If I had any distinct motive of curiosity in selecting him he never gratified it. He kept his history covered, and very rarely alluded, in any way, to his home or his family.

The one possession which he seemed to prize more highly than any other was an ivory miniature portrait of his mother, which, many a time during our life together, I saw him take from his trunk and press to his lips. I soon learned to respect his reticence on topics which were quite at home on my own lips. I suspect I did talking enough for two boys. Indeed, I threw my whole life open to him, with such embellishments as my imagination suggested. He seemed interested in my talk, and was apparently pleased with me. I brought a new element into his life, and we became constant companions when out of school, as well as when we were in our room.

We were always wakened in the morning by a "whoop" and "halloo" that ran from room to room over the whole establishment. A little bell started it somewhere; and the first boy who heard it gave his call, which was taken up by the rest and borne on from bed to bed until the whole brood was in full cry. Thus the school called itself. It was the voices of merry and wide-awake boys that roused the drowsy ones; and very rarely did a dull and sulky face show itself in the breakfast-room.

This morning call was the key to all the affairs of the day and to the policy of the school. Self-direction and self-government—these were the most important of all the lessons learned at The Bird's Nest. Our school was a little community brought together for common objects—the pursuit of useful learning, the acquisition of courteous manners, and the practice of those duties which relate to good citizenship. The only laws of the school were those which were planted in the conscience, reason, and sense of propriety of the pupils. The ingenuity with which these were developed and appealed to has been, from that day to this, the subject of my unbounded admiration. The boys were made to feel that the school was their own, and that they were responsible for its good order. Mr. Bird was only the biggest and best boy, and the accepted president of the establishment. The responsibility of the boys was not a thing of theory only. It was deeply realized in the conscience and conduct of the school. However careless and refractory a new boy might be, he soon learned that he had a whole school to deal with, and that he was not a match for the public opinion. He might evade the master's or a teacher's will, but he could not evade the eyes or the sentiments of the little fellows around him.

On the first Friday evening of my term, I entered as a charmed and thoroughly happy element into one of the social institutions of the school. On every Friday evening, after the hard labor of the week was over, it was the custom of the school to hold what was called a "reception." Teachers and pupils made the best toilet they could, and spent the evening in the parlors, dancing, and listening to music, and socially receiving the towns-people and such strangers as might happen to be in the village. The piano that furnished the music was the first I had ever heard, and at least half of my first reception-evening was spent by its side, in watching the skillful and handsome fingers that flew over its mysterious keys. I had always been taught that dancing was only indulged in by wicked people; but there were dear Mr. and Mrs. Bird looking on; there was precious Miss Butler without her belt, leading little fellows like myself through the mazes of the figures; there were twenty innocent and happy boys on the floor, their eyes sparkling with excitement; there were fine ladies who had come to see their boys, and village maidens simply clad and as fresh as roses; and I could not make out that there was anything wicked about it.

It was the theory of Mr. Bird that the more the boys could be brought into daily familiar association with good and gracious women the better it would be for them. Accordingly he had no men among his teachers, and as his school was the social center of the village, and all around him were interested in his objects, there were always ladies and young women at the receptions who devoted themselves to the happiness of the boys. Little lads of less than ten summers found no difficulty in securing partners who were old enough to be their mothers and grandmothers; and as I look back upon the patient and hearty efforts of these women, week after week and year after year, to make the boys happy and manly and courteous, it enhances my respect for womanhood, and for the wisdom which laid all its plans to secure these attentions and this influence for us. I never saw a sheepish-looking boy or a sheepish-acting boy who had lived a year at The Bird's Nest. Through the influence of the young women engaged as teachers and of those who came as sympathetic visitors, the boys never failed to become courteous, self-respectful, and fearless in society.

Miss Butler, the principal teacher, who readily understood my admiration of her, undertook early in the evening to get me upon the floor; but it was all too new to me, and I begged to be permitted for one evening to look on and do nothing. She did not urge me; so I played the part of an observer. One of the first incidents of the evening that attracted my attention was the entrance in great haste of a good-natured, rollicking boy, whose name I had learned from the fellows to be Jack Linton. Jack had been fishing and had come home late. His toilet had been hurried, and he came blundering into the room with his laughing face flushed, his neck-tie awry, and his heavy boots on.

Mr. Bird, who saw everything, beckoned Jack to his side. "Jack," said he, "you are a very rugged boy."

"Am I?" And Jack laughed.

"Yes, it is astonishing what an amount of exercise you require," said Mr. Bird.

"Is it?" And Jack laughed again.

"Yes, I see you have your rough boots on for another walk. Suppose you walk around Robin Hood's Barn, and report yourself in a light, clean pair of shoes, as soon as you return."

Jack laughed again, but he made rather sorry work of it; and then he went out. "Robin Hood's Barn" was the name given to a lonely building a mile distant, to which Mr. Bird was in the habit of sending boys whose surplus vitality happened to lead them into boisterousness or mischief. Gyp, who had been an attentive listener to the conversation, and apparently understood every word of it, followed Jack to the door, and, having dismissed him into the pleasant moonlight, gave one or two light yelps and went back into the drawing-room.

Jack was a brisk walker and a lively runner, and before an hour had elapsed was in the drawing-room again, looking as good-natured as if nothing unusual had occurred. I looked at his feet and saw that they were irreproachably incased in light, shining shoes, and that his neck-tie had been readjusted. He came directly to Mr. Bird and said: "I have had a very pleasant walk, Mr. Bird."

"Ah! I'm delighted," responded the master, smiling; and then added:

"Did you meet anybody?"

"Yes, sir; I met a cow."

"What did you say to her?"

"I said 'How do you do, ma'am? How's your calf?'"

"What did she say?" asked Mr. Bird very much amused.

"She said the calf was very well, and would be tough enough for the boys in about two weeks," replied Jack, with a loud laugh.

Mr. Bird enjoyed the sally quite as much as the boys who had gathered round him, and added:

"We all know who will want the largest piece, Jack. Now go to your dancing."

In a minute afterward, Jack was on the floor with a matronly-looking lady to whom he related the events of the evening without the slightest sense of annoyance or disgrace. But that was the last time he ever attended a reception in his rough boots.

The evening was filled with life and gayety and freedom. To my unaccustomed eyes it was a scene of enchantment. I wished my father could see it. I would have given anything and everything I had to give could he have looked in upon it. I was sure there was nothing wrong in such amusement. I could not imagine how a boy could be made worse by such happiness, and I never discovered that he was. Indeed, I can trace a thousand good and refining influences to those evenings. They were the shining goals of every week's race with my youthful competitors; and while they were accounted simply as pleasures by us, they were regarded by the master and the teachers as among the choicest means of education. The manners of the school were shaped by them; and I know that hundreds of boys attribute to them their release from the bondage of bashfulness, under which many a man suffers while in the presence of women during all his life.

I repeat that I have never discovered that a boy was made worse by his experiences and exercises during those precious evenings; and I have often thought how sad a thing it is for a child to learn that he has been deceived or misinformed by his parents with relation to a practice so charged with innocent enjoyment. I enter here no plea for dancing beyond a faithful record of its effect upon the occupants of The Bird's Nest. I suppose the amusement may be liable to abuse: most good things are; and I do not know why this should be an exception. This, however, I am sure it is legitimate to say: that the sin of abuse, be it great or little, is venial compared with that which presents to the conscience as a sin in itself that which is not a sin in itself, and thus charges an innocent amusement with the flavor of guilt, and drives the young, in their exuberant life and love of harmonious play, beyond the pale of Christian sympathy.

As I recall the events of the occasion I find it impossible to analyze the feeling that one figure among the dancers begot in me. Whenever Miss Butler was on the floor I saw only her. Her dark eyes, her heavy shining hair, the inexpressible ease of her motions, her sunny smile,—that combination of graces and manners which makes what we call womanliness,—fascinated me, and inspired me with just as much love as it is possible for a boy to entertain. I am sure no girl of my own age could have felt toward her as I did. I should have been angry with any boy who felt toward her thus, and equally angry with any boy who did not admire her as much, or who should doubt, or undertake to cheapen, her charms. How can I question that it was the dawn within me of the grand passion —an apprehension of personal and spiritual fitness for companionship? Pure as childhood, inspired by personal loveliness, clothing its object with all angelic perfections, this boy-love for a woman has always been to me the subject of pathetic admiration, and has proved that the sweetest realm of love is untainted by any breath of sense.

There was a blind sort of wish within me for possession, even at this early age, and I amused the lady by giving utterance to my feelings. Wearied with the dancing, she took my hand and led me to a retired seat, where we had a delightful chat.

"I think you were born too soon," I said to her, still clinging to her hand, and looking my admiration.

"Oh! if I had been born later," she replied, "I should not be here.. I should be a little girl somewhere."

"I don't think I should love you if you were a little girl," I responded.

"Then perhaps you were not born soon enough," she suggested.

"But if I had been born sooner I shouldn't be here now," I said.

"That's true," said the lady, "and that would be very bad, wouldn't it?"

"Yes, ever so bad," I said. "I wouldn't miss being here with you for a hundred dollars."

The mode in which I had undertaken to measure the pleasure of her society amused Miss Butler very much; and as I felt that the sum had not impressed her sufficiently, I added fifty to it. At this she laughed heartily, and said I was a strange boy, a statement which I received as pleasant flattery.

"Did you ever hear of the princess who was put to sleep for a hundred years and kept young and beautiful through it all?" I inquired.

"Yes."

"Well, I wish Mr. Bird were an enchanter, and would put you to sleep until I get to be a man," I said. .

"But then I couldn't see you for ten years," she replied.

"Oh dear!" I exclaimed, "it seems to be all wrong."

"Well, my boy, there are a great many things in the world that seem to be all wrong. It is wrong for you to talk such nonsense to me, and it is wrong for me to let you do it, and we will not do wrong in this way any more. But I like you, and we will be good friends always."

Thus saying, my love dismissed me, and went back among the boys; but little did she know how sharp a pang she left in my heart. The forbidden subject was never mentioned again, and like other boys under similar circumstances, I survived.

There was one boy besides myself who enacted the part of an observer during that evening. He was a new boy, who had entered the school only a few days before myself. He was from the city, and looked with hearty contempt upon the whole entertainment. He had made no friends during the fortnight which had passed since he became an occupant of The Bird's Nest. His haughty and supercilious ways, his habit of finding fault with the school and everything connected with it, his overbearing treatment of the younger boys, and his idle habits had brought upon him the dislike of all the fellows. His name was Frank Andrews, though for some reason we never called him by his first name. He gave us all to understand that he was a gentleman's son, that he was rich, and, particularly, that he was in the habit of doing what pleased him and nothing else.

He was dressed better than any of the other boys, and carried a watch, the chain of which he took no pains to conceal. During all the evening he stood here and there about the rooms, his arms folded, looking on with his critical eyes and cynical smile. Nobody took notice of him, and he seemed to be rather proud of his isolation. I do not know why he should have spoken to me, for he was my senior, but toward the close of the evening he came up to me and said in his patronizing way:

"Well, little chap, how do you like it?"

"Oh! I think it's beautiful," I replied.

"*Do* you! That's because you're green," said Andrews.

"*Is* it!" I responded, imitating his tone. "Then they're all green—Mr. Bird and all."

"There's where you're right, little chap," said he. "They *are* all green—Mr. Bird and all."

"Miss Butler isn't green," I asserted stoutly.

"Oh! *isn't* she?" exclaimed Andrews, with a degree of sarcasm in his tone that quite exasperated me. "Oh, no! Miss Butler isn't green of course," he continued, as he saw my face reddening. "She's a duck—so she is! so she is! and if you are a good little boy you shall waddle around with her some time, so you shall!"

I was so angry that I am sure I should have struck him if we had been out of doors, regardless of his superior size and age. I turned sharply on my heel, and, retiring to a corner of the room, glared at him savagely, to his very great amusement.

It was at this moment that the bell rang for bed; and receiving, one after another, the kisses of Mr. and Mrs. Bird, and bidding the guests a good-night, some of whom were departing while others remained, we went to our rooms.

CHAPTER V.

THE DISCIPLINE OF THE BIRD'S NEST AS ILLUSTRATED BY TWO STARTLING PUBLIC TRIALS.

SCARCELY less interesting than the exercises of reception-evening were those of the "family meeting," as it was called, which was always held on Sunday. This family meeting was one of the most remarkable of all the institutions of The Bird's Nest. It was probably more influential upon us than even the attendance at church, and our Bible lessons there, which occurred on the same day, for its aim and its result were the application of the Christian rule to our actual, every-day conduct.

I attended the family meeting which was held on my first Sunday at the school with intense interest. I suspect, indeed, that few more interesting and impressive meetings had ever been held in the establishment.

After we were all gathered in the hall, including Mrs. Bird and the teachers, as well as the master, Mr. Bird looked kindly out upon us and said:

"Well, boys, has anything happened during the week that we ought to discuss to-day? Is the school going along all right? Have you any secrets buttoned up in your jackets that you ought to show to me and to the school? Is there anything wrong going on which will do harm to the boys?"

As Mr. Bird spoke, changing the form of his question so as to reach the consciences of his boys from different directions, and get time to read their faces, there was a dead silence. When he paused, every boy felt that his face had been shrewdly read and was still under inspection.

"Yes, there is something wrong: I see it," said Mr. Bird. "I see it in several faces; but Tom Kendrick can tell us just what it is. And he will tell us just what it is, for Tom Kendrick never lies."

All eyes were instantly turned on Tom, a blushing, frank-faced boy of twelve. Close beside him sat Andrews, the new boy, who had so roused my anger on Friday night. His face wore the same supercilious, contemptuous expression that it wore that night. The whole proceeding seemed to impress him as unworthy even the toleration of a gentleman's son, yet I felt sure that he would be in some way implicated in Tom Kendrick's revelations. Indeed, there was, or I thought there was, a look of conscious guilt on his face and the betrayal of excitement in his eye, when Tom rose to respond to Mr. Bird's bidding.

Tom hesitated, evidently very unwilling to begin. He looked blushingly at Mrs. Bird and the teachers, then looked down, and tried to start, but his tongue was dry.

"Well, Tom, we are all ready to hear you," said Mr. Bird.

After a little stammering, Tom pronounced the name of Andrews, and told in simple, straightforward language, how he had been in the habit of relating stories and using words which were grossly immodest; how he had done this repeatedly in his hearing and against his protests, and furthermore, how he had indulged in this language in the presence of smaller boys. Tom also testified that other boys besides himself had warned Andrews that if he did not mend his habit he would be reported at the family meeting.

There was the utmost silence in the room. The dropping of a pin could have been heard in any part of it, for, while the whole school disliked Andrews, his arrogance had impressed them, and they felt that he would be a hard boy to deal with. I watched alternately the accuser and the accused, and I trembled in every nerve to see the passion depicted on the features of the latter. His face became pale at first—deathly pale —then livid and pinched—and then it burned with a hot flame of shame and anger. He sat as if he were expecting the roof to fall, and were bracing himself to resist the shock.

When Tom took his seat Andrews leaned toward him and muttered something in his ear.

"What does he say to you, Tom?" inquired Mr. Bird.

"He says he'll flog me for telling," answered Tom.

"We will attend to that," said Mr. Bird. "But first let us hear from others about this matter. Has any other boy heard this foul language? Henry Hulm, can you tell us anything?"

Henry was another boy who always told the truth; and Henry's testimony was quite as positive as Tom's, though it was given with even more reluctance. Other boys testified in confirmation of the report of Tom and Henry, until, in the opinion of the school, Andrews was shamefully guilty of the matter charged upon him. I was quite ignorant of the real character of the offense, and wondered whether his calling Miss Butler a duck was in the line of his sin, and whether my testimony to the fact was called for. No absurdity, such as this would have been, broke in upon the earnest solemnity of the occasion, however, and the house was silent until Mr. Bird said:

"What have you to say for yourself, Andrews?"

The boy was no whit humbled. Revenge was in his heart and defiance in his eye. He looked Mr. Bird boldly in the face; his lips trembled, but he made no reply.

"Nothing?" Mr. Bird's voice was severe this time, and rang like a trumpet.

Andrews bit his lips, and blurted out: "I think it is mean for one boy to tell on another."

"I don't," responded Mr. Bird; "but I'll tell you what is mean: it is mean for one boy to pollute another—to fill his mind with words and thoughts that make him mean; and I should be sorry to believe that I have any other boy in school who is half as mean as you are. If there is anything to be said about mean boys, you are not the boy to say it."

At first, I confess that I was quite inclined to sympathize with the lad in his view of the dishonor of "telling on" a boy, notwithstanding my old grudge; but my judgment went with the majority at last.

Mr. Bird said that, as there were several new boys in the school, it would be best, perhaps, to talk over this matter of reporting one another's bad conduct to him and to the school.

"When boys first come here," said Mr. Bird, "they invariably have those false notions of honor which lead them to cover up all the wrong-doings of their mates; but they lose them just as soon as they find themselves responsible for the good order of our little community. Now we are all citizens of this little town of Hillsborough, in which we live. We have our own town authorities and our magistrate, and we are all interested in the good order of the village. Suppose a man should come here to live who is in the habit of robbing hen-roosts, or setting barns on fire, or getting drunk and beating his wife and children: is it a matter of honor among those citizens who behave themselves properly to shield him in his crimes, and refrain from speaking of him to the authorities? Why, the thing is absurd. As good citizens—as honorable citizens—we must report this man, for he is a public enemy. He is not only dangerous to us, but he is a disgrace to us. So long as he is permitted to live among us, unreproved and uncorrected, every man in the community familiar with his misdeeds is, to a certain extent, responsible for them. Very well: we have in this house a little republic, and if you can learn to govern yourselves here, and to take care of the enemies of the order and welfare of the school, you will become good citizens, prepared to perform the duties of good citizenship. I really know of nothing more demoralizing to a boy, or more ruinous to a school, than that false sense of honor which leads to the covering up of one another's faults of conduct."

Mr. Bird paused, and, fixing his eye upon Andrews, who had not once taken his eye from him, resumed: "Now here is a lad who has come to us from a good family; and they have sent him here to get him away from bad influences and bad companions. He comes into a community of boys who are trying to lead good lives, and instead of adopting the spirit of the school, and trying to become one with us, he still holds the spirit of the bad companions of his previous life, and goes persistently to work to make all around him as impure and base as himself. Nearly all these boys have mothers and sisters, who would be pained almost to distraction to learn that here, upon these pure hills, they are drinking in social poison with every breath. How am I to guard you from this evil if I do not know of it? How can I protect you from harm if you shield the boy who harms you? There is no mischief of which a boy is capable that will not breed among you like a pestilence if you cover it; and instead of sending you back to your homes at last with healthy bodies and healthy minds and pure spirits, I shall be obliged, with shame and tears, to return you soiled and spotted and diseased. Is it honorable to protect crime? Is it honorable to shield one who dishonors and damages you? Is it honorable to disappoint your parents and to cheat me? Is it honorable to permit these dear little fellows to be spoiled, when the wicked lad who is spoiling them is allowed to go free of arrest and conviction?"

Of course I cannot pretend to reproduce the exact words in which Mr. Bird clothed his little argumentative address. I was too young at the time to do more than apprehend the meaning of it: and the words that I give are mainly remembered from repetitions of the same argument in the years that followed. The argument and the lesson, however, in their substance and practical bearings, I remember perfectly.

Continuing to speak, and releasing Andrews from his regard for a moment, Mr. Bird said: "I want a vote on this question. I desire that you all vote with perfect freedom. If you are not thoroughly convinced that I am right in this matter, I wish you to vote against me. Now all those boys who believe it to be an honorable thing to report the persistently bad conduct of a schoolmate will rise and stand."

Every boy except Andrews rose, and with head erect stood squarely upon his feet. The culprit looked from side to side with a sneer upon his lip, that hardened into the old curl of defiance as he turned his eyes upon Mr. Bird's face again.

"Very well," said Mr. Bird, "now sit down, and remember that you are making rules for the government of yourselves. This question is settled for this term, and there is to be no complaint hereafter about what you boys call "telling on one another." I do not wish you to come to me as tattlers. Indeed, I do not wish you to come to me at all. If any boy does a wrong which I ought to know, you are simply to tell him to report to me what he has done, and if he and I cannot settle the matter together I will call upon you to help us. There will be frictions and vexations among forty boys; I know that, and about these I wish to hear nothing. Settle these matters among yourselves. Be patient and good-natured with each other; but all those things that interfere with the order, purity, and honor of the school—all those things that refuse to be corrected—must be reported. I think we understand one another. The school is never to suffer in order to save the exposure and punishment of a wrong-doer.

"As for this boy, who has offended the school so grossly and shown so defiant a spirit, I propose, with the private assistance of the boys who have testified against him, to make out a literal report of his foul language and forward it to his mother, while at the same time I put him into the stage-coach and send him home."

It was a terrible judgment, and I can never forget the passion depicted upon Andrews' face as he comprehended it. He seemed like one paralyzed.

"Every boy," said Mr. Bird, "who is in favor of this punishment will hold up his right hand."

Two or three hands started to go up among the smaller boys, but as their owners saw that they had no support, they were drawn down again. Four or five of the boys were in tears, and dear Mr. Bird's eyes were full. He gathered at a glance the meaning of the scene, and was much moved. "Well, Tom Kendrick, you were the first to testify against him; what have you to say against this punishment?"

Tom rose with his lips trembling, and every nerve full of

The appeal from man to woman—from justice to mercy.

(p. 83.)

excitement. "Please, sir," said Tom, "I should like to have you give Andrews another chance. I think it's an awful thing to send a boy home without giving him more than one chance."

Tom sat down and blew his nose very loud, as a measure of relief.

I watched Andrews with eager eyes during the closing passages of his trial. When Tom rose on behalf of the whole school to plead for him—that he might have one more chance—the defiant look faded from his face, and he gave a convulsive gulp as if his heart had risen to his throat and he were struggling to keep it down. When Tom sat down, Andrews rose upon his feet and staggered and hesitated for a moment; then, overcome by shame, grief and gratitude, he ran rather than walked to where Mrs. Bird was sitting near her husband, and with a wild burst of hysterical sobbing threw himself upon his knees, and buried his face in the dear motherly lap that had comforted so many boyish troubles before. The appeal from man to woman —from justice to mercy—moved by the sympathy of the boys, was the most profoundly touching incident I had ever witnessed, and I wept almost as heartily as did Andrews himself. In truth, I do not think there was a dry eye in the room.

"Tom," said Mr. Bird, "I think you are right. You have helped me, and helped us all. The lad ought to have another chance, and he shall have one if he desires it. The rest of this matter you can safely leave to Mrs. Bird and myself. Now remember that this is never to be alluded to. If the lad remains and does right, or tries to do right, he is to be received and cherished by you all. No one of us is so perfect that he does not need the charity of his fellows. If Andrews has bad habits, you must help him to overcome them. Be brothers to him in all your future intercourse, as you have been here to-day; and as we have had business enough for one family meeting, you may pass out and leave him with us."

"Gorry!" exclaimed Jack Linton, wiping his eyes and wringing his handkerchief as he left the door, "wasn't that a freshet? Wettest time I ever saw in Hillsborough."

But the boys were not in a jesting mood, and Jack's drolleries were not received with the usual favor. Every thoughtful and sympathetic lad retired with a tableau on his memory never to be forgotten—a benignant man looking tearfully and most affectionately upon him, and a sweet-faced, large-hearted woman pillowing in her lap the head of a kneeling boy, whose destiny for all the untold and unguessed ages was to be decided there and then.

It was more than an hour before we saw anything of Mr. and Mrs. Bird. When they issued from their retirement they were accompanied by a boy who was as great a stranger to himself as he was to the school. Conquered and humbled, looking neither to the right nor the left, he sought his room, and none of us saw his face until the school was called together on Monday morning. His food was borne to his room by Mrs. Bird, who in her own way counseled and comforted him, and prepared him to encounter his new relations with the institution. The good, manly hearts of the boys never manifested their quality more strikingly than when they undertook on Monday to help Andrews into his new life. The obstacles were all taken out of his path—obstacles which his own spirit and life had planted—and without a taunt, or a slight, or a manifestation of revenge in any form, he was received into the brotherhood.

On Monday evening we were somewhat surprised to see him appear, dressed in his best, his hands nicely gloved, making his way across the village green. No one questioned him, and all understood the case as he turned in at the gate which led to the home of the village minister.

When any lad had behaved in an unseemly manner at church, it was Mr. Bird's habit to compel him to dress himself for a call, and visit the pastor with an apology for his conduct. "It is not a punishment, my boy," Mr. Bird used to say, "but it is what one gentleman owes to another. Any boy who so far forgets his manners as to behave improperly in the presence of a clergyman whose ministration he is attending owes him an apology, if he proposes to be considered a gentleman; and he must make it, or he cannot associate with me or my school."

In this case he had made conformity to his rule a test of the genuineness of the boy's penitence, and a trial of his newly-professed loyalty. The trial was a severe one, but the result gratified all the boys as much as it did dear Mr. and Mrs. Bird.

I was very much excited by the exposure of Andrews, and put a good many serious questions to myself in regard to my own conduct. The closing portion of the Sunday evening on which the event occurred was spent by several boys and myself in our rooms. We were so near each other that we could easily converse through the open doors, and I was full of questions.

"What do you think Mr. Bird will do with Andrews?" I inquired of Jack Linton.

"Oh, nothing: he's squelched," said Jack.

"I should think he would punish him," I said, "for I know Mr. Bird was angry."

"Yes," responded Jack, "the old fellow fires up sometimes like everything; but you can't flail a boy when he's got his head in a woman's lap, can you, you little coot?"

"That's the way my mother always flailed me, any way," I said, at which Jack and all the boys gave a great laugh.

"Flailing," said Jack, taking up a moralizing strain, when the laugh was over, "don't pay. The last school I went to before I came here was full of no end of flailing. There gets to be a sort of sameness about it after a while. Confound that old ruler! I used to get it about every day—three or four whacks on a fellow's hand; first it stung and then it was numb; and it always made me mad, or else I didn't care. There isn't quite so much sameness about a raw-hide, for sometimes you catch it on your legs and sometimes on your shoulders, but there gets to be a sort of sameness about that too. But here in this school! My! You never know what's coming. Say, boys, do you remember that day when I was making such a row out in the yard, how Mr. Bird made me take a fish-horn, and blow it at each corner of the church on the green?"

The boys laughed, and Henry Hulm said: "Yes, Jack, but you liked that better than that other punishment when he sent you out into the grove to yell for three-quarters of an hour."

"I'll bet I did," responded Jack. "I got so hoarse that time I couldn't speak the truth for a week, but that's enough better than meditating. If there's anything I hate it's meditating on my misdemeanors and things, kneeling before a tree by the side of the road, like a great heathen luny. I suppose half the people thought I was praying like an old Pharisee. Gorry! If the minister had found me there I believe he'd have kneeled right by the side of a fellow; and wouldn't that have been a pretty show! Did any of you ever hug a tree for an hour?"

None of them ever did. "It's awful tiresome," continued Jack, upon whose punishments Mr. Bird seemed to have exercised all his ingenuities. "It's awful tiresome and it isn't a bit interesting. If it was only a birch-tree a fellow might amuse himself gnawing the bark, but mine was a hemlock with an antheap at the bottom. Oh! I tell you, my stockings wanted tending to when I got through: more ants in 'em than you could count in a week. Got a little exercise out of it, though—fighting one foot with the other. After all it's better than it is when there's so much sameness. It's tough enough when you are at it, but it doesn't make you mad, and it's funny to think of afterwards. I tell you, old Bird—"

"Order! Order! Order!" came from all the boys within hearing.

"Well, what's broke now?" inquired Jack.

"There isn't any Old Bird, in the establishment," said one of them.

"Mr. Bird, then. Confound you, you've put me out. I forget what I was going to say."

Here I took the opportunity to inquire whether any sins of the boys were punishable by "flailing."

"Yes," replied Jack, "big lying and tobacco. Unless a fellow breaks right in two in the middle, as Andrews did to-day, he'd better make his will before he does anything with either of 'em. Old Bird—Mr. Bird, I mean—don't stand the weakest sort of a cigar; and look here, Arthur Bonnicastle" (suddenly turning to me), "you're a little blower, and you'd better hold up. If you don't, you'll find out whether there's any flailing done here."

The conversation went on, but I had lost my interest in it. The possibility of being punished filled me with a vague alarm. It was the first time I had ever been characterized as "a little blower," but my sober and conscientious chum had plainly told me of my fault, and I knew that many statements which I had made during my short stay in the school would not bear examination. I resolved within myself that I would reform, but the next day I forgot my resolution, and the next, and the next, until, as I afterwards learned, my words were good for nothing among the boys as vouchers for the truth. I received my correction in due time, as my narrative will show.

My readers will have seen already that The Bird's Nest was not very much like other schools, though I find it difficult to choose from the great variety of incidents with which my memory is crowded those which will best illustrate its peculiarities. The largest liberty was given to us, and we were simply responsible for the manner in which we used it. We had the freedom of long distances of road and wide spaces of field and forest. Indeed, there was no limit fixed to our wanderings, except the limit of time. There were no feuds between the town-boys and the school. It was not uncommon to see them at our receptions, and everybody in Hillsborough was glad when The Bird's Nest was full.

During the first week of my active study I got very tired, and after the violent exercise of the play-ground I often found myself so much oppressed by the desire for sleep that it was simply impossible for me to hold up my head. It was on one such occasion that my sleepy eyes caught the wide-awake glance of Mr. Bird, and the beckoning motion of his finger. I went to his side, and he lifted me to his knee. Pillowing my head upon his broad breast, I went to sleep; and thus holding me with his strong arm he went on with the duties of the school. Afterwards, when similarly oppressed, or when languid with indisposition, I sought the same resting-place many times, and was never refused. A scene like this was not an uncommon one. It stirred neither surprise nor mirth among the boys. It fitted into the life of the family so naturally that it never occasioned remark.

It must have been three weeks or a month after I entered the school that, on a rainy holiday, as I was walking through one of the halls alone, I was met by two boys who ordered me peremptorily to "halt." Both had staves in their hands, taller than themselves, and one of them addressed me with the words: "Arthur Bonnicastle, you are arrested in the name of The High Society of Inquiry, and ordered to appear before that august tribunal, to answer for your sins and misdemeanors. Right about face!"

The movement had so much the air of mystery and romance that I was about equally pleased and scared. Marching between the two officials, I was led directly to my own room, which I was surprised to find quite full of boys, all of whom were grave and silent. I looked from one to another, puzzled beyond expression, though I am sure I preserved an unruffled manner, and a confident and even smiling face. Indeed, I supposed it to be some sort of a lark, entered upon for passing away the time while confined to the house.

"We have secured the offender," said one of my captors, "and now have the satisfaction of presenting him before this honorable Society."

"The prisoner will stand in the middle of the room, and look at me," said the presiding officer, in a tone of dignified severity.

I was accordingly marched into the middle of the room and left alone, where I stood with folded arms, as became the grand occasion.

"Arthur Bonnicastle," said the officer before mentioned, "you are brought before The High Society of Inquiry on a charge of telling so many lies that no dependence whatever can be placed upon your words. What have you to reply to this charge. Are you guilty or not guilty?"

"I am not guilty. Who says I am?" I exclaimed indignantly.

"Henry Hulm, advance!" said the officer.

Henry rose, and walking by me, took a position near the officer, at the head of the room.

"Henry Hulm, you will look upon the prisoner and tell the Society whether you know him."

"I know him well. He is my chum," replied Henry.

"What is his general character?"

"He is bright and very amiable."

"Do you consider him a boy of truth and veracity?"

"I do not."

"Has he deceived you?" inquired the officer. "If he has, please to state the occasion and circumstances."

"No, your Honor. He has never deceived me. I always know when he lies and when he speaks the truth."

"Have you ever told him of his crimes, and warned him to desist from them?"

"I have," replied Henry, "many times."

"Has he shown any disposition to mend?"

"None at all, your honor."

"What is the character of his falsehood?"

"He tells," replied Henry, "stunning stories about himself. Great things are always happening to him, and he is always performing the most wonderful deeds."

I now began with great shame and confusion to realize that I was to be exposed to ridicule. The tears came into my eyes and dropped from my cheeks, but I would not yield to the impulse either to cry or to attempt to fly.

"Will you give us some specimens of his stories?" said the officer.

"I will," responded Henry, "but I can do it best by asking him questions."

"Very well," said the officer, with a polite bow. "Pursue the course you think best."

"Arthur," said Henry, addressing me directly, "did you ever tell me that, when you and your father were on the way to this school, your horse went so fast that he ran down a black fox in the middle of the road, and cut off his tail with the wheel of the chaise, and that you sent that tail home to one of your sisters to wear in her winter hat?"

"Yes, I did," I responded, with my face flaming and painful with shame.

"And did your said horse really run down said fox in the middle of said road, and cut off said tail; and did you send home said tail to said sister to be worn in said hat?" inquired the judge, with a low, grum voice. "The prisoner will answer so that all can hear."

"No," I replied, and, looking for some justification of my story, I added: "but I did see a black fox—a real black fox, as plain as day!"

"Oh! Oh! Oh!" ran around the room in chorus. "He did see a black fox, a real black fox, as plain as day!"

"The witness will pursue his inquiries," said the officer.

"Arthur," Henry continued, "did you or did you not tell me that when on the way to this school you overtook Mr. and Mrs. Bird in their wagon, that you were invited into the wagon by Mrs. Bird, and that one of Mr. Bird's horses chased a calf on the road, caught it by the ear and tossed it over the fence and broke its leg?"

"I s'pose I did," I said, growing desperate.

"And did said horse really chase said calf, and catch him by said ear, and toss him over said fence, and break said leg?" inquired the officer.

"He didn't catch him by the ear," I replied doggedly, "but he really did chase a calf."

"Oh! Oh! Oh!" chimed in the chorus. "He didn't catch him by the ear, but he really did chase a calf!"

"Witness," said the officer, "you will pursue your inquiries."

"Arthur, did you or did you not tell me," Henry went on, "that you have an old friend who is soon to go to sea, and that he has promised to bring you a male and female monkey, a male and female bird of paradise, a barrel of pineapples, and a Shetland pony?"

"It doesn't seem as if I told you exactly that," I replied.

"Did you or did you not tell him so?" said the officer, severely.

"Perhaps I did," I responded.

"And did said friend, who is soon to go to said sea, really promise to bring you said monkeys, said birds of paradise, said pine-apples, and said pony?"

"No," I replied, "but I really have an old friend who is going to sea, and he'll bring me anything I ask him to."

"Oh! Oh! Oh!" swept round the room again. "He really has an old friend who is going to sea, and he'll bring him anything he asks him to."

"Hulm, proceed with your inquiries," said the officer.

"Did you or did you not," said Henry, turning to me again, "tell me that one day, when dining at your Aunt's, you saw a magic portrait of a boy upon the wall, that came and went, and came and went, like a shadow or a ghost?"

As Henry asked this question he stood between two windows, while the lower portion of his person was hidden by a table behind which he had retired. His face was lighted by a half-smile, and I saw him literally in a frame, as I had first seen the picture to which he alluded. In a moment I became oblivious to everything around me except Henry's face. The portrait was there again before my eyes. Every lineament and even the peculiar pose of the head were recalled to me. I was so much excited that it really seemed as if I were looking again upon the picture I had seen in Mrs. Sanderson's dining-room. Henry was disconcerted, and even distressed by my intent look. He was evidently afraid that the matter had been carried too far, and that I was growing wild with the strange excitement. Endeavoring to recall me to myself, he said in a tone of friendliness:

"Did you or did you not tell me the story about the portrait, Arthur?"

"Yes," I responded, "and it looked just like you. Oh! it did, it did, it did! There—turn your head a little more that way—so! It was a perfect picture of you, Henry. You never could imagine such a likeness."

"You are a little blower, you are," volunteered Jack Linton, from a corner.

"Order! Order! Order!" swept around the room.

"Did said portrait," broke in the voice of the officer, "come and go on said wall, like said shadow or said ghost?"

"It went but it didn't come," I replied, with my eyes still fixed on Henry.

"Oh! Oh! Oh!" resumed the chorus. "It went but it didn't come!"

"Please stand still, Henry! don't stir!" I said. "I want to go nearer to it. She wouldn't let me."

I crept slowly toward him, my arms still folded. He grew pale, and all the room became still. The presiding officer and the members of The High Society of Inquiry were getting scared. "It went but it didn't come," I said. "This one comes but it doesn't go. I should like to kiss it."

I put out my hands towards Henry, and he sank down behind the table as if a ghost were about to touch him. The illusion was broken, and I started as if awakened suddenly from a dream. Looking around upon the boys, and realizing what had been done and what was in progress, I went into a fit of hearty crying, that distressed them quite as much as my previous mood had done. Nods and winks passed from one to another, and Hulm was told that no further testimony was needed. They were evidently in a hurry to conclude the case, and felt themselves cut short in their forms of proceeding. At this moment a strange silence seized the assembly. All eyes were directed toward the door, upon which my back was turned. I wheeled around to find the cause of the interruption. There, in the doorway, towering above us all, and looking questioningly down upon the little assembly, stood Mr. Bird.

"What does this mean?" inquired the master.

I flew to his side and took his hand. The officer who had presided, being the largest boy, explained that they had been trying to break Arthur Bonnicastle of lying, and that they were about to order him to report to the master for confession and correction.

Then Mr. Bird took a chair and patiently heard the whole story.

Without a reproach, further than saying that he thought me much too young for experiments of the kind they had instituted in the case, he explained to them and to me the nature of my misdemeanors.

"The boy has a great deal of imagination," he said, "and a strong love of approbation. Somebody has flattered his power of invention, probably, and, to secure admiration, he has exercised it until he has acquired the habit of exaggeration. I doubt whether the lad has done much that was consciously wrong. It is more a fault of constitution and character than a sin of the will; and now that he sees that he does not win admiration by telling that which is not true, he will become truthful. I am glad if he has learned, even by the severe means which have been used, that if he wishes to be loved and admired he must always tell the exact truth, neither more nor less. If you had come to me, I could have told you all about the lad, and instituted a better mode of dealing with him. He has been through some sudden changes of late that have had the natural tendency to exaggerate his fault. But I venture to say that he is cured. Are n't you, Arthur?" And he stooped and lifted me to his face and looked into my eyes.

"I don't think I shall do it any more," I said.

Bidding the boys disperse, he carried me down stairs into his own room, and charged me with kindly counsel. I went out from the interview humbled and without a revengeful thought in my heart toward the boys who had brought me to my trial.

I saw that they were my friends, and I was determined to prove myself worthy of their friendship.

Jack Linton was waiting for me on the piazza, and wished to explain to me that he hadn't anything against me. "I went in with the rest of 'em because they wanted me to," said Jack, "and because I wanted to see what it would be like; but really, now, I don't object so much to blowing myself. There's a sort of sameness, you know, about always telling the truth that there isn't about blowing, but it's the same thing with hash and bread and butter, and it seems to be necessary."

I told him that I wasn't going to blow any more, and that I had arranged it all with Mr. Bird. He shook hands with me and then stooped down and whispered: "You don't catch me trying any High old Society of Inquiries on a chap of your size again."

As soon as I settled into the routine of my school life the weeks flew away so fast that they soon got beyond my counting. The term was long, but I was happy in my study, happy in my companionships, and happy in the love of Mr. and Mrs. Bird, and in their control and direction. I wrote letters home every week, and received prompt replies from my father. The monthly missives to "My dear Aunt," were regularly written, though I won no replies to them. I learned, however, that Mr. Bird had received communications from her concerning myself. On one occasion she sent her love to me through him, and he delivered the message with an amused look in his eyes that puzzled me.

The summer months passed away, and that great, mysterious change came on which reported the consummation of growth and maturity in the processes and products of the year. The plants that had toiled all summer, evolving flower and fruit, were soothed to sleep. The birds stopped singing lest they should waken them. The locusts by day and the crickets by night crooned their lullaby. A dreamy haze hung around the distant hills, and here and there a woodbine lighted its torch in the darkening dingle, and the maples in mellow fire signalled each other from hill to hill. The year had begun to die. There were chills at night and fevers by day, and stretches of weird silence that impressed me more profoundly than I can possibly reveal. It was as if the angels of the summer had fled at the first frost, and the angels of the autumn had come down, bringing with them a new set of spiritual influences that saddened while they sweetened every soul whose sensibilities were delicate enough to apprehend and receive them.

During those days I felt my first twinges of genuine homesickness. I was conscious that I had grown in body and mind during my brief absence; and I wanted to show myself to the dear ones with whom I had passed my childhood. I imagined the interest with which they would listen to the stories of my life at school; and I had learned enough of the world already to know that there was no love so sweet and strong as that which my home held for me. I had been made glad by my father's accounts of his modest prosperity. Work had been plenty and the pay was sure and sufficient. The family had been reclothed, and new and needed articles of furniture had been purchased.

I wrote to Mrs. Sanderson and asked the privilege of going home to spend my vacation, and through my father's letters I learned that she would send for me. A week or more before the close of the term I received a note addressed to me in a hand-writing gone to wreck through disuse, from old Jenks. If I were to characterize the orthography in which it was clothed, I should say it was eminently strong. I do not suppose it was intended to be blank verse, but it was arranged in disconnected lines, and read thus :

"Bring home your Attlus.
"I stere boldly for the Troppicks.
"Desk and cumpusses in the stable.
"When this you see burn this when this you see.
"The sea rolls away and thare is no old wooman thare.
"Where the spisy breazes blow.
"I shall come for you with the Shaze.
"From an old Tarr

"Theophilus Jenks."

This unique document was not committed to the flames, according to the directions of the writer. It was much too precious for such a destiny, and was carefully laid away between the leaves of my Testament, to be revealed in this later time.

The last evening of the term was devoted to a reception. Many parents of the boys who had come to take their darlings home were present; and sitting in the remotest corner of the dancing-room, shrunken into the smallest space it was possible for him to occupy, was old Jenks, gazing enchanted upon such a scene as had never feasted his little gray eyes before. I had learned to dance, in a boy's rollicking fashion, and during the whole evening tried to show off my accomplishments to my old friend. One after another I led ladies—middle-aged and young—to the floor, and discharged the courtesies of the time with all the confidence of a man of society. Occasionally I went to his side and asked him how he liked it.

"It's great—it's tremenduous," said Jenks. "How do you dare to do it—eh? say!" said he, drawing me down to him by the lappel of my coat: "I've been thinking how I'd like to have the old woman on the floor, and see her tumble down once. I ain't no dancer, you know, but I'd dance a regular break-down over her before I picked her up and set her on her pins again. Wouldn't it be fun to see her get up mad, and limp off into a corner?"

I laughed at Jenks's fancy, and asked him what he thought of the last lady I danced with.

"She's a beauty," said Jenks. "I should like to sail with her—just sit and hold her hand and sail—sail away, and keep sailing and sailing and sailing."

"I'm glad you like her," I said, "for that is my lady-love. That's Miss Butler."

"You don't say!" exclaimed Jenks. "Well, you don't mind what I say, do you?"

"Oh no," I said, "you're too old for her."

"Well, yes, perhaps I am, but isn't she just—isn't she rather—that is, isn't she a bit too old for you?"

"I shall be old enough for her by and by," I replied.

"Well, don't take to heart anything I say," responded Jenks. "I was only talking about sailing, any way. My mind is on the sea a good deal, you know. Now you go on with your dancing, and don't mind me."

The next morning there were all sorts of vehicles at the door. There were calls and farewells and kisses, and promises to write, and hurrahs, and all the incidents and excitements of breaking up. With a dozen kisses warm upon my cheeks, from teachers and friends, I mounted the chaise, and Jenks turned the old horse toward home.

I suppose the world would not be greatly interested in the conversation between the old servant and the boy who that day drove from Hillsborough to Bradford. Jenks had been much moved by the scenes of the previous evening, and his mind, separated somewhat from the sea, out toward whose billowy freedom it had been accustomed to wander, turned upon women.

"I think a woman is a tremenduous being," said Jenks. "When she's right, she's the rightest thing that floats. When she's wrong, she's the biggest nuisance that ploughs the sea, even if she's little and don't draw two feet of water. Perhaps it isn't just the thing to say to a boy like you, but you'll never speak of it, if I should tell you a little something?"

"Oh, never!" I assured him.

"Well, I 'spose I might have been a married man;" and Jenks avoided my eyes by pretending to discover a horse-shoe in the road.

"You don't say so!" I exclaimed in undisguised astonishment, for it had never occurred to me that such a man as Jenks could marry.

"Yes, I waited on a girl once."

"Was she beautiful?" I inquired.

"Well, I should say fair to middling," responded Jenks, pursing his lips as if determined to render a candid judgment. "Fair to middling, barring a few freckles."

"But you didn't leave her for the freckles?" I said.

"No, I didn't leave her for the freckles. She was a good girl, and I waited on her. It don't seem possible now, that I ever ra'aly waited on a girl, but I did."

"And why didn't you marry her?" I inquired warmly.

"It wasn't her fault," said Jenks. "She was a good girl."

"Then why didn't you marry her?" I insisted.

"Well, there was another fellow got to hanging round, and—you know how such things go. I was busy, and—didn't 'tend up very well, I s'pose—and—she got tired waiting for me—or something—and the other fellow married her, but I've never blamed her. She's been sorry enough, I guess."

Jenks gave a sigh of mingled regret and pity, and the subject was dropped.

The lights were shining cheerfully in the windows as we drove into Bradford. When we came in sight of my father's house, Jenks exacted a pledge from me that all the confidences of the day which he had so freely reposed in me should never be divulged. Arriving at the gate, I gave a wild whoop, which brought all the family to the door, and in a moment I was smothered with welcome.

Ah! what an evening was that! What sad, sweet tears drop upon my paper as I recall it, and remember that every eye that sparkled with greeting then has ceased to shine, that every hand that grasped mine is turned to dust, and that all those loving spirits wait somewhere to welcome me home from the school where I have been kept through such a long, eventful term.

CHAPTER VI.

I BECOME A MEMBER OF MRS. SANDERSON'S FAMILY AND HAVE
A WONDERFUL VOYAGE WITH JENKS UPON THE ATLAS.

AT an early hour on the following morning, dressed in my best, I went to pay my respects to Mrs. Sanderson at The Mansion. As I walked along over the ground stiffened with the autumn frost, wondering how "my dear Aunt" would receive me, it seemed as if I had lived half a lifetime since my father led me over the same road, on my first visit to the same lady. I felt older and larger and more independent. As I passed Mr. Bradford's house, I looked at the windows, hoping to see the little girl again, and feeling that in my holiday clothes I could meet her eyes unabashed. But she did not appear, nor did I get a sight of Mr. Bradford.

The autumn was now in its glory, and, as I reached the summit of the hill, I could not resist the temptation to pause and look off upon the meadows and the distant country. I stood under a maple, full of the tender light of lemon-colored leaves, while my feet were buried among their fallen fellows with which the ground was carpeted. The sounds of the town reached my ears mellowed into music by the distance, the smoke from a hundred chimneys rose straight into the sky, the river was a mirror for everything upon it, around it and above it, and all the earth was a garden of gigantic flowers. For that one moment my life was full. With perfect health in my veins, and all my sensibilities excited by the beauty before me, my joy was greater in living than any words can express. Nothing but running, or shouting, or singing, or in some way violently spending the life thus swelled to its flood, could give it fitting utterance ; but, as I was near The Mansion, all these were denied me, and I went on, feeling that passing out of the morning sunlight into a house would be like going into a prison. Before reaching the door I looked at the stable, and saw the old horse with his head out of one window, and Jenks's face occupying another. Jenks and the horse looked at one another and nodded, as much as to say: "That is the little fellow we brought over from Hillsborough yesterday."

That Mrs. Sanderson saw me under the tree, and watched every step of my progress to the house, was evident, for when I mounted the steps, and paused between the sleeping lions, the door swung upon its hinges, and there stood the little old woman in the neatest of morning toilets. She had expected me, and had prepared to receive me.

"And how is Master Bonnicastle this pleasant morning?" she said as I entered.

I was prepared to be led into any manifestation of respect or affection which her greeting might suggest, and this cheery and flattering address moved me to grasp both her hands, and tell her that I was very well and very happy. It did not move me to kiss her, or to expect a kiss from her. I had never been called "Master" Bonnicastle before, and the new title seemed as if it were intended so to elevate me as to place me at a distance.

Retaining one of my hands, she conducted me to a large drawing-room, into which she had admitted the full glow of the morning light, and, seating me, drew a chair near to me for herself, where she could look me squarely in the face. Then she led me into a talk about Mr. and Mrs. Bird, and my life at school. She played the part of a listener well, and flattered me by her little comments, and her almost deferential attention. I do her the justice to believe that she was not altogether playing a part, thoroughly pre-considered, for I think she was really interested and amused. My presence, and my report of what was going on in one little part of the great world which was so far removed from the pursuits of her lonely life, were refreshing influences. Seeing that she was really interested, my tongue ran on without restraint, until I had told all I had to tell.

Many times, when I found myself tempted to exaggerate, I checked my vagrant speech with corrections and qualifications, determined that my old fault should have no further sway.

"Well, my boy," she said at last, in a tone of great kindness, "I find you much improved. Now let us go up-stairs and see what we can discover there."

I followed her up the dark old stairway into a chamber whose windows commanded a view of the morning sun and the town.

"How lovely this is!" I exclaimed.

"You like it, then?" she responded with a gratified look.

"Yes," I said, "I think it is the prettiest room I ever saw."

"Well, Master Bonnicastle, this is your room. This new paper on the walls and all this new furniture I bought for you. Whenever you want a change from your house, which you know is rather small and not exactly the thing for a young gentleman like you, you will find this room ready for you. There are the drawers for your linen, and there is the closet for your other clothes, and here is your mirror, and this is a pin-cushion which I have made for you with my own hands."

She said this, walking from one object named to another, until she had shown me all the appointments of the chamber.

I was speechless and tearful with delight. And this was all mine! And I was a young gentleman, with the prettiest room in the grandest house of Bradford at my command! It was like a dream to me, bred as I had been in the strait simplicity of poverty. Young as I was, I had longed for just this —for something around me in my real life that should correspond with my dreams of life. Already the homely furniture of my father's house, and the life with which it was associated, seemed mean—almost wretched; and I was distressed by my sympathy for those whom I should leave behind in rising to my new estate. By some strange intuition I knew that it would not do to speak to my benefactress of my love for my father. I was full of the thought that my love had been purchased, and fairly paid for. I belonged to Mrs. Sanderson. She who had expended so much money for me, without any reward, had a right to me, and all of my society and time that she desired. If she had asked me to come to her house and make it my only home, I should have promised to do so without reserve, but she did not do this. She was too wise. She did not intend to exact anything from me; but I have no doubt that she took the keenest delight in witnessing the operation and consummation of her plans for gaining an ascendency over my affections, my will, and my life.

Her revelations produced in me a strange disposition to silence which neither she nor I knew how to break. I was troubled with the fear that I had not expressed sufficient gratitude for her kindness, yet I did not know how to say more. At length she said: "I saw you under the maple: what were you thinking about there?"

"I was wondering if the world was not made in the fall," I replied.

"Ah?"

"Yes," I continued, "it seemed to me as if God must have stood under that same maple-tree, when the leaves were changing, and saw that it was all very good."

With something of her old asperity she said she wished my boyish fancies would change as well as the leaves.

"I cannot help having them," I replied, "but if you don't like them I shall never speak of them again."

"Now I tell you what I think," said she, assuming her pleasant tone again. "I think you would like to be left alone for a little while."

"Oh! I should like to be alone here in my own room ever so much!" I responded.

"You can stay here until dinner if you wish," she said, and then she bent down and kissed my forehead, and retired.

I listened as she descended the stairs, and when I felt that she was far enough away, I rose, and carefully locked my door. Then I went to the mirror to see whether I knew myself, and to find what there was in me that could be addressed as "Master," or spoken of as "a young gentleman." Then I ransacked the closet, and climbed to a high shelf in it, with the vague hope that the portrait which had once excited my curiosity was hidden there. Finding nothing I had not previously seen, I went to the window, and sat down to think.

I looked off upon the town, and felt myself lifted immeasurably above it and all its plodding cares and industries. This was mine. It had been won without an effort. It had come to me without a thought or a care. I believed there was not a boy in the whole town who possessed its equal, and I wondered what there was in me that should call forth such munificence from my benefactress. If my good fortune as a boy were so great, what brilliant future awaited my manhood? Then I thought of my father, working humbly and patiently, day after day, for bread for his family, and of the tender love which I knew his heart held for me; and I wondered why God should lay so heavy a burden upon him and so marvelously favor me. Would it not be mean to take this good fortune and sell my love of him and of home for it? Oh! if I could only bring them all here, to share my sweeter lot, I should be content, but I could not even speak of this to the woman who had bestowed it on me.

It all ended in a sweet and hearty fit of crying, in which I sobbed until the light faded out of my eyes, and I went to sleep. I had probably slept two hours when a loud knock awakened me, and, staggering to my feet, and recognizing at last the new objects around me, I went to the door, and found Jenks, in his white apron, who told me that dinner was waiting for me. I gave a hurried glance at the mirror and was startled to find my eyes still red; but I could not wait. As he made way for me to pass down before him, he whispered: "Come to the stable as soon as you can after dinner. The atlas and compasses are ready."

I remembered then that he had borrowed the former of me on the way home, and secreted it under the seat of the chaise.

Mrs. Sanderson was already seated when I entered the dining-room.

"Your eyes are red," she said quickly.

"I have been asleep, I think," I responded.

Jenks mumbled something, and commenced growling. His mistress regarded me closely, but thought best not to push inquiries further.

Conversation did not promise to be lively, especially in the presence of a third party, between whom and myself there existed a guilty secret which threatened to sap the peace of the establishment.

At length I said: "Oh! I did not think to tell you anything about my chum."

"What is his name?" she inquired.

"His name is Henry Hulm," I replied; and then I went on at length to describe his good qualities and to tell what excellent friends we had been. "He is not a bit like me," I said, "he is so steady and quiet."

"Do you know anything about his people?" inquired the lady.

"No, he never says anything about them, and I am afraid he is poor," I replied.

"How does he dress?"

"Not so well as I do, but he is the neatest and carefullest boy in the school."

"Perhaps you would like to invite him here to spend your vacation with you, when you come home again," she suggested.

"May I? Can I?" I eagerly inquired.

"Certainly. If he is a good, respectable boy, and you would like him for a companion here, I should be delighted to have you bring him."

"Oh! I thank you: I am so glad! I'm sure he'll come, and he can sleep in my room with me."

"That will please you very much, will it not?" and the lady smiled with a lively look of gratification.

I look back now with mingled pity of my simple self and admiration of the old lady who thus artfully wove her toils about me. She knew she must not alarm my father, or imprison me, or fail to make me happy in the gilded trap she had set for me. All her work upon me was that of a thorough artist. What she wanted was to sever me and my sympathy from my father and his home, and to make herself and her house the center of my life. She saw that my time would pass slowly if I had no companion; and Henry's coming would be likely to do more than anything to hold me. My pride would certainly move me to bring him to my room, and she would manage the rest.

After dinner, I asked liberty to go to the stable. I was fond of horses and all domestic animals. I made my request in the presence of Jenks, and that whimsical old hypocrite had the hardihood to growl and grumble and mutter as if he regarded the presence of a boy in the stable as a most offensive intrusion upon his special domain. I could not comprehend such duplicity, and looked at him inquiringly.

"Don't mind Jenks," said Madame: "he's a fool."

Jenks went growling out of the room, but, as he passed me, I caught the old cunning look in his little eyes, and followed him. When the door was closed he cut a pigeon-wing, and ended by throwing one foot entirely over my head. Then he whispered: "You go out and stay there until I come. Don't disturb anything." So I went out, thinking him quite the nimblest and queerest old fellow I had ever seen.

I passed half an hour patting the horse's head, calling the chickens around me, and wondering what the plans of Jenks would be. At length he appeared. Walking tiptoe into the stable, he said: "The old woman is down for a nap, and we've got two good hours for a voyage. Now, messmate, let's up sails and be off!"

At this he seized a long rope which depended from one of the great beams above, and pulled away with a "Yo! heave oh!" *sotto voce*, (letting it slide through his hands at every call), as if an immense spread of canvas was to be the result.

"Belay there!" he said at last, in token that his ship was under way, and the voyage begun.

"It's a bit cold, my hearty, and now for a turn on the quarter-deck," he said, as he grasped my hand, and walked with me back and forth across the floor. I was seized with an uncontrollable fit of laughter, but walked with him, nothing loth. "Now we plough the billow," said Jenks. "This is what I call gay."

After giving our blood a jog, and getting into a glow, he began to laugh.

"What are you laughing at?" I inquired.

"She made me promise that I wouldn't tease or trouble you, she did!" and then he laughed again. "Oh yes; Jenks is a fool, he is! Jenks is a tremenduous fool!" Then he suddenly sobered, and suggested that it was time to examine our chart. Dropping my hand, he went to a bin of oats, built like a desk, and opening from the top with a falling lid. To this lid he had attached two legs by hinges of leather, which supported it at a convenient angle. Then he brought forth two three-legged milking-stools and placed them before it, and plunging his hand deep down into the oats drew out my atlas, neatly wrapped in an old newspaper. This he opened before me, and we took our seats.

"Now where are we?" said Jenks.

I opened to the map of the world, and said: "Here is New York, and there is Boston. We can't be very far from either of 'em, but I think we are between 'em."

"Very well, let it be between 'em," said Jenks. "Now what?"

"Where will you go?" I inquired.

"I don't care where I go; let us have a big sail, now that we are in for it," he replied.

"Well, then, let's go to Great Britain," I said.

"Isn't there something that they call the English Channel?" inquired Jenks with a doubtful look.

"Yes, there is," and cruising about among the fine type, I found it.

"Well, I don't like this idea of being out of sight of land.

It's dangerous, and if you can't sleep, there is no place to go to. Let's steer straight for the English Channel—straight as a ramrod."

"But it will take a month," I said; "I have heard people say so a great many times."

"My! A month? Out of sight of land? No old woman and no curry-comb for a month? Hey de diddle! Very well, let it be a month. Hullo! it's all over! Here we are: now where are we on the map?"

"We seem to be pretty near to Paris," I said, "but we don't quite touch it. There must be some little places along here that are not put down. There's London, too: that doesn't seem to be a great way off, but there's a strip of land between it and the water."

"Why, yes, there's Paris," said Jenks, looking out of the stable window, and down upon the town. "Don't you see? It's a fine city. I think I see just where Napoleon Bonaparte lives. But it's a wicked place; let's get away from it. Bear off now;" and so our imaginary bark, to use Jenks's large phrase, "swept up the channel."

Here I suggested that we had better take a map of Great Britain, and we should probably find more places to stop at. I found it easily, with the "English Channel" in large letters.

"Here we are!" I said: "see the towns!"

"My! Ain't they thick!" responded Jenks. "What is that name running lengthwise there right through the water?"

"That's the 'Strait of Dover,'" I replied.

"Well, then, look out! We're running right into it! It's a confounded narrow place, any way. Bear away there; take the middle course. I've heard of them Straits of Dover before. They are dangerous; but we're through, we're through. Now where are we?"

"We are right at the mouth of the Thames," I replied, "and here is a river that leads straight up to London."

"Cruise off! cruise off!" said Jenks. "We're in an enemy's country. Sure enough, there's London;" and he looked out of the window with a fixed gaze, as if the dome of St. Paul's were as plainly in sight as his own nose. After satisfying himself with a survey of the great city, he remarked, interrogatively, "Haven't we had about enough of this? I want to go where the spicy breezes blow. Now that we have got our sea-legs on, let us make for the equator. Bring the ship round; here we go; now what?"

"We have got to cross the Tropic of Cancer, for all that I can see," said I.

"Can't we possibly dodge it?" inquired Jenks with concern.

"I don't see how we can," I replied. "It seems to go clean around."

"What is it, any way?" said he.

"It don't seem to be anything but a sort of dotted line," I answered.

"Oh well, never mind; we'll get along with that," he said encouragingly. "Steer between two dots, and hold your breath. My uncle David had one of them things."

Here Jenks covered his mouth and nose with entire gravity, and held them until the imaginary danger was past. At last, with a red face, he inquired, "Are we over?"

"All over," I replied; "and now where do you want to go?"

"Isn't there something that they call the Channel of Mozambique?" said Jenks.

"Why?" I asked.

"Well, I've always thought it must be a splendid sheet of water! Yes: Channel of Mozambique—splendid sheet of water! Mozambique! Grand name, isn't it?"

"Why, here it is," said I, "away round here. We've got to run down the coast of Africa, and around the Cape of Good Hope, and up into the Indian Ocean. Shall we touch anywhere?"

"No, I reckon it isn't best. The niggers will think we are after 'em, and we may get into trouble. But look here, boy! We've forgot the compasses. How we ever managed to get across the Atlantic without 'em is more than I know. That's one of the carelessest things I ever did. I don't suppose we could do it again in trying a thousand times."

Thereupon he drew from a corner of the oat-bin an old pair of carpenter's compasses, between which and the mariner's compass neither he nor I knew the difference, and said: "Now let us sail by compasses, in the regular way."

"How do you do it?" I inquired.

"There can't be but one way, as I see," he replied. "You put one leg down on the map, where you are, then put the other down where you want to go, and just sail for that leg."

"Well," said I, "here we are, close to the Canary Islands. Put one leg down there, and the other down here at St. Helena."

After considerable questioning and fumbling and adjusting of the compasses, they were held in their place by the ingenious navigator, while we drove for the lonely island. After a considerable period of silence, Jenks broke out with: "Doesn't she cut the water beautiful? It takes the Jane Whittlesey!"

"Oh!" I exclaimed, "I didn't know you had a name for her."

"Yes," said Jenks with a sigh—still holding fast to the compasses, as if our lives depended upon his faithfulness—"Jane Whittlesey has been the name of every vessel I ever owned. You know what I told you about that young woman?"

"Yes," I said; "and was that her name?"

Jenks nodded, and sighed again, still keeping his eye upon the outermost leg of the instrument, and holding it firmly in its place.

"Here we are," he exclaimed at last. "Now let's double over and start again."

So the northern leg came around with a half circle, and went down at the Cape of Good Hope. The Tropic of Capricorn proved less dangerous than the northern corresponding line, and so, at last, sweeping around the cape, we brought that leg of the compasses which we had left behind toward the equator again, and, working up on the map, arrived at our destination.

"Well, here we are in the Channel of Mozambique," I said.

"What's that blue place there on the right hand side of it?" he inquired.

"That's the Island of Madagascar."

"You don't tell me!" he exclaimed. "Well! I never expected to be so near that place. The Island of Madagascar! The Island of Mad-a-gas-car! Let's take a look at it."

Thereupon he rose and took a long look out of the window. "Elephants — mountains — tigers — monkeys — golden sands—cannibals," he exclaimed slowly, as he apprehended *seriatim* the objects he named. Then he elevated his nose, and began to sniff the air, as if some far-off odor had reached him on viewless wings. "Spicy breezes, upon my word!" he exclaimed. "Don't you notice 'em, boy? Smell uncommonly like hay; what do you think?"

We had after this a long and interesting cruise, running into various celebrated ports, and gradually working toward home. I was too busy with the navigation to join Jenks in his views of the countries and islands which we passed on the voyage, but he enjoyed every league of the long and eventful sail. At last the Jane Whittlesey ran straight into Mrs. Sanderson's home inclosures, and Jenks cast anchor by dropping a huge stone through a trap-door in the floor.

"It really seems good to be at home again, and to feel everything standing still, doesn't it?" said he. "I wonder if I can walk straight," he went on, and then proceeded to ascertain by actual experiment. I have laughed a hundred times since at the recollection of the old fellow's efforts to adapt himself to the imaginary billows of the stable-floor.

"I hope I shall get over this before supper-time," said Jenks, "for the old woman will know we have been to sea."

I enjoyed the play quite as well as my companion did, but even then I did not comprehend that it was simply play, with him. I supposed it was a trick of his to learn something of geography, before cutting loose from service and striking out into the great world by way of the ocean. So I said to him: "What do you do this for?"

"What do I do it for? What does anybody go to sea for?" he inquired with astonishment.

"Well, but you don't go to the real sea, you know," I suggested.

"Don't I! That's what the atlas says, any way, and the atlas ought to know," said Jenks. "At any rate it's as good a sea as I want at this time of year, just before winter comes on. If you only think so, it's a great deal better sailing on an atlas than it is sailing on the water. You have only to go a few inches, and you needn't get wet, and you can't drown. You can see everything there is in the world by looking out of the window, and thinking you do; and what's the use spending so much time as people do travelling to the ends of the earth? The only thing that troubles me is that Bradford's Irishman down here has really come across the ocean, and I don't s'pose he cared any more about it than if he'd been a pig. If I could only have had a real sail on the ocean, and got through with it, I don't know but I should be ready to die."

"But you will have, some time, you know," I said encouragingly.

"Do you think so?"

"When you run away you will," I said.

"I don't know," he responded dubiously. "I think perhaps I'd better run away on an atlas a few times first, just to learn the ropes."

Here we were interrupted by the tinkle of a bell, and it was marvelous to see how quickly the atlas disappeared in the oats and the lid was closed over it. Jenks went to the house and I followed him.

Mrs. Sanderson did not inquire how I had spent my time. It was enough for her that I had in no way disturbed her after-dinner nap, and that I came when she wanted me. I told her I had enjoyed the day very much, and that I hoped my father would let me come up soon and occupy my room. Then I went up-stairs and looked the room all over again, and tried to realize the extent and value of my new possession. When I went home, toward night, she loaded me with nice little gifts for my mother and the children, and I lost no time in my haste to tell the family of the good fortune that had befallen me. My mother was greatly delighted with my representations, but my father was sad. I think he was moved to sever my connection with the artful woman at once, and take the risks of the step, but a doubt of his own ability to do for me what it was her intention and power to do withheld him. He consented at last to lose me because he loved me, and on the following day I went out from my home with an uneasy conviction that I had been bought and paid for, and was little better than an expensive piece of property. What she would do with me I could not tell. I had my doubts and my dreams, which I learned to keep to myself; but in the swift years that followed there was never an unkind word spoken to me in my new home, or any unkind treatment experienced which made me regret the step I had taken.

I learned to regard Mrs. Sanderson as the wisest woman living; and I found, as the time rolled by, that I had adopted her judgments upon nearly every person and every subject that called forth her opinion. She assumed superiority to all her neighbors. She sat on a social throne, in her own imagination. There were few who openly acknowledged her sway, but she was imperturbable. Wherever she appeared, men bowed to her with profoundest courtesy, and women were assiduous in their politeness. They may have flouted her when she was out of sight, but they were flattered by her attentions, and were always careful in her presence to yield her the pre-eminence she assumed. No man or woman ever came voluntarily into collision with her will. Keen, quiet, alert, self-possessed, she lived her own independent life, asking no favors, granting few, and holding herself apart from, and above, all around her. The power of this self-assertion, insignificant as she was in physique, was simply gigantic.

To this height she undertook to draw me, severing one by one the sympathies which bound me to my family and my companions, and making me a part of herself. I remember distinctly the processes of the change, and their result. I grew more silent, more self-contained, more careful of my associations. The change in me had its effect in my own home. I came to be regarded there as a sort of superior being; and when I went there for a day the best things were given me to eat, and certain proprieties were observed by the family, as if a rare stranger had come among them. In the early part of my residence at The Mansion, some of the irreverent little democrats of the street called me "Mother Sanderson's Baby," but even this humiliating and maddening taunt died away when it was whispered about that she was educating her heir, and that I should be some day the richest young man in the town.

CHAPTER VII.

I LEAVE THE BIRD'S NEST AND MAKE A GREAT DISCOVERY.

LIFE is remembered rather by epochs than by continuous details. I spent five years at The Bird's Nest, visiting home twice every year, and becoming more and more accustomed to the thought that I had practically ceased to be a member of my own family. My home and all my belongings were at the Mansion; and although I kept a deep, warm spot in my heart for my father, which never grew cold, there seemed to be a difference in kind and quality between me and my brothers and sisters which forbade the old intimacy. The life at home had grown more generous with my father's advancing prosperity, and my sisters, catching the spirit of the prosperous community around them, had done much to beautify and elevate its appointments.

The natural tendency of the treatment I received, both at my father's house and at The Mansion, was for a long time to concentrate my thoughts upon myself, so that when, on my fifteenth birthday, I entered my father's door, and felt peculiarly charmed by my welcome and glad in the happiness which my presence gave, I made a discovery. I found my sister Claire a remarkably pretty young woman. She was two years my senior, and had been so long my profoundest worshipper that I had never dreamed what she might become. She was the sweetest of blondes, with that unerring instinct of dress which enabled her to choose always the right color, and so to drape her slender and graceful figure as to be always attractive. My own advance toward manhood helped me, I suppose, to appreciate her as I had not hitherto done; and before I parted with her, to return to the closing term of Mr. Bird's tuition, I had become proud of her, and ambitious for her future. I found, too, that she had more than kept pace with me in study. It was a great surprise. By what ingenuities she had managed to win her accomplishments, and become the educated lady that she was, I knew not. It was the way of New England girls then as it is now. I had long talks and walks with her, and quite excited the jealousy of Mrs. Sanderson by the amount of time I devoted to her.

In these years Mrs. Sanderson herself had hardly grown appreciably older. Her hair had become a little whiter, but she retained, apparently, all her old vigor, and was the same strong-willed, precise, prompt, opinionated woman she was when I first knew her. Jenks and I had many sails upon the atlas succeeding that which I have described, but something had always interfered to prevent him from taking the final step which would sever his connection with the service of his old mistress forever.

Every time during these five years that I went home to spend my vacation, I invited Henry to accompany me, but his mother invariably refused to permit him to do so. Mrs. Sanderson, in her disappointment, offered to defray all the expenses of the journey, which, in the mean time, had ceased to be made with the old horse and chaise; but there came always from his mother the same refusal. The old lady was piqued at last, and became soured toward him. Indeed, if she could have found a valid excuse for the step, she would have broken off our intimacy. She had intended an honor to an unknown lad in humble circumstances; and to have that honor persistently spurned, without apparent reason, exasperated her. "The lad is a churl, depend upon it, when you get at the bottom of him," was the stereotyped reply to all my attempts to palliate his offence, and vindicate the lovableness of his character.

These years of study and development had wrought great changes in me. Though thoroughly healthy—thanks to the considerate management of my teacher—I grew up tall and slender, and promised to reach the reputed altitude of the old

Bonnicastles. I was a man in stature by the side of my sister Claire, and assumed the dress and carriage of a man. Though Henry was two years older than I, we studied together in everything, and were to leave school together. Our companionship had been fruitful of good to both of us. I stirred him and he steadied me.

There was one aim which we held in common—the aim at personal integrity and thorough soundness of character. This aim had been planted in us both by Christian parents, and it was fostered in every practicable way by Mr. and Mrs. Bird. There was one habit, learned at home, which we never omitted for a night while we were at school—the habit of kneeling at our bedside before retiring to slumber, and offering silently a prayer. Dear Mrs. Bird—that sweet angel of all the little boys—was always with us in our first nights together, when we engaged in our devotions, and sealed our young lips for sleep with a kiss. Bidding us to pray for what we wanted, and to thank our Father for all that we received, with the simple and hearty language we would use if we were addressing our own parents, and adjuring us never, under any circumstances, to omit our offering, she left us at last to ourselves. "Remember," she used to say, "remember that no one can do this for you. The boy who confesses his sins every night has always the fewest sins to confess. The habit of daily confession and prayer is the surest corrective of all that is wrong in your motives and conduct."

In looking back upon this aspect of our life together, I am compelled to believe that both Henry and myself were in the line of Christian experience. Those prayers and those daily efforts at good, conscientious living, were the solid beginnings of a Christian character. I do not permit myself to question that had I gone on in that simple way I should have grown into a Christian man. The germination and development of the seed planted far back in childhood would, I am sure, have been crowned with a divine fruitage. Both of us had been taught that we belonged to the Master—that we had been given to

Him in baptism. Neither of us had been devoted to Him by parents who, having placed His seal upon our foreheads, thenceforth strove to convince us that we were the children of the devil. Expecting to be Christians, trying to live according to the Christian rule of life, never doubting that in good time we should be numbered among Christian disciples, we were already Christian disciples. Why should it be necessary that the aggregate sorrow and remorse for years of selfishness and transgression be crowded into a few hours or days? Why should it be necessary to be lifted out of a great horror of blackness and darkness and tempest, into a supernal light by one grand sweep of passion? Are safe foundations laid in storms and upheavals? Are conviction and character nourished by violent access and reaction of feeling? We give harsh remedies for desperate diseases, and there are such things as desperate diseases. I am sure that Henry and I were not desperately diseased. The whole drift of our aims was toward the realization of a Christian life. The grand influences shaping us from childhood were Christian. Every struggle with that which was base and unworthy within us was inspired by Christian motives. Imperfect in knowledge, infirm in will, volatile in purpose as boys always are and always will be, still we were Christian boys, who had only to grow in order to rise into the purer light and better life of the Christian estate.

I am thus particular in speaking of this, for I was destined to pass through an experience which endangered all that I had won. I shall write of this experience with great care, but with a firm conviction that my unvarnished story has a useful lesson in it, and an earnest wish that it may advance the cause which holds within itself the secret of a world's redemption. I am sure that our religious teachers do not competently estimate the power of religious education on a great multitude of minds, or adequately measure the almost infinite mischief that may be inflicted upon sensitive natures by methods of address and influence only adapted to those who are sluggish in temperament or besotted by vice.

My long stay at The Bird's Nest was a period of uninterrupted growth of mind as well as of body. Mr. Bird was a man who recognized the fact that time is one of the elements that enter into a healthy development of the mind—that mental digestion and assimilation are quite as essential to true growth as the reception of abundant food. Hence his aim was never to crowd a pupil beyond his powers of easy digestion, and never to press to engorgement the receptive faculties. To give the mind ideas to live upon while it acquired the discipline for work, was his steady practice and policy. All the current social and political questions were made as familiar to the boys under his charge as they were to the reading world outside. The issues involved in every political contest were explained to us, and I think we learned more that was of practical use to us in after-life from his tongue than from the text-books which we studied.

Some of the peculiarities of Mr. Bird's administration I have already endeavored to represent, and one of these I must recall at the risk of repetition and tediousness. In the five years which I spent under his roof and care, I do not think one lad left the school with the feeling that he had been unjustly treated in any instance. No bitter revenges were cherished in any heart. If, in his haste or perplexity, the master ever did a boy a wrong, he made instant and abundant reparation, in an acknowledgment to the whole school. He was as tender of the humblest boy's reputation as he was of any man's, or even of his own. When I think of the brutal despotism that reigns in so many schools of this and other countries, and of the indecent way in which thousands of sensitive young natures are tortured by men who, in the sacred office of the teacher, display manners that have ceased to be respectable in a stable, I bless my kind stars —nay, I thank God—for those five years, and the sweet influence that has poured from them in a steady stream through all my life.

The third summer of my school life was "Reunion Summer," and one week of vacation was devoted to the old boys. It was with inexpressible interest that I witnessed the interviews between them and their teacher. Young men from college with downy whiskers and fashionable clothes; young men in business, with the air of business in their manners; young clergymen, doctors, and lawyers came back by scores. They brought a great breeze from the world with them, but all became boys again when they entered the presence of their old master. They kissed him as they were wont to do in the times which had become old times to them. They hung upon his neck; they walked up and down the parlors with their arms around him; they sat in his lap, and told him of their changes, troubles and successes; and all were happy to be at the old nest again.

Ah, what *fêtes* were crowded into that happy week!—what games of ball, what receptions, what excursions, what meetings and speeches, what songs, what delightful interminglings of all the social elements of the village! What did it matter that we small boys felt very small by the side of those young men whose old rooms we were occupying? We enjoyed their presence, and found in it the promise that at some future time we should come back with whiskers upon our cheeks, and the last triumphs of the tailor in our coats!

Henry and I were to leave school in the autumn; and as the time drew near for our departure dear Mr. and Mrs. Bird grew more tender toward us, for we had been there longer than any of the other boys. I think there was not a lad at The Bird's Nest during our last term whom we found there on our entrance five years before. Jolly Jack Linton had become a clerk in a city shop, and was already thrifty and popular. Tom Kendrick was in college, and was to become a Christian minister. Andrews, too, was in college, and was bringing great comfort to his family by a true life that had been begun with so bad a promise. Mr. Bird seemed to take a special pleasure in our society, and, while loosening his claim upon us as pupils, to hold us as associates and friends the more closely. He loved his boys as a father loves his children. In one of our closing interviews, he and Mrs. Bird talked freely of the life they had lived, and its beautiful compensations. They never wearied with their work, but found in the atmosphere of love that enveloped them an inspiration for all their labor and care, and a balm for all their trials and troubles. "If I were to live my life over again," said Mrs. Bird to me one evening, "I should choose just this, and be perfectly content." There are those teachers who have thought and said that "every boy is a born devil," and have taught for years because they were obliged to teach, with a thorough and outspoken detestation of their work. It is sad to think that multitudes of boys have been trained and misunderstood and abused by these men, and to know that thousands of them are still in office, untrusted and unloved by the tender spirits which they have in charge.

My connection with Mrs. Sanderson was a subject to which Mr. Bird very rarely alluded. I was sure there was something about it which he did not like, and in the last private conversation which I held with him it all came out.

"I want to tell you, Arthur," he said, "that I have but one fear for you. You have already been greatly injured by Mrs. Sanderson, and by the peculiar relations which she holds to your life. In some respects you are not as lovable as when you first came here. You have become exclusive in your society, obtrusive in your dress, and fastidious in your notions of many things. You are under the spell of a despotic will, and the moulding power of sentiments entirely foreign to your nature. She has not spoiled you, but she has injured you. You have lost your liberty, and a cunning hand is endeavoring to shape you to a destiny which it has provided for you. Now no wealth can compensate you for such a change. If she make you her heir, as I think she intends to do, she calculates upon your becoming a useless and selfish gentleman after a pattern of her own. Against this transformation you must struggle. To lose your sympathy for your own family and for the great multitude of the poor ; to limit your labor to the nursing of an old and large estate ; to surrender all your plans for an active life of usefulness among men, is to yield yourself to a fate worse than any poverty can inflict. It is to be bought, to be paid for, and to be made a slave of. I can never be reconciled to any such consummation of your life."

This was plain talk, but it was such as he had a right to indulge in; and I knew and felt it to be true. I had arrived at the conviction in my own way before, and I had wished in my heart of hearts that I had had my own fortune to make, like the other boys with whom I had associated. I knew that Henry's winter was to be devoted to teaching, in order to provide himself with a portion of the funds which would be necessary for the further pursuit of his education. He had been kept back by poverty from entering school at first, so that he was no further advanced in study than myself, though the years had given him wider culture and firmer character than I possessed. Still, I felt entirely unable and unwilling to relinquish advantages which brought me immunity from anxiety and care, and the position which those advantages and my prospects gave me. My best ambitions were already sapped. I had become weak and to a sad extent self-indulgent. I had acquired no vices, but my beautiful room at The Mansion had been made still more beautiful with expensive appointments, my wardrobe was much enlarged, and, in short, I was in love with riches and all that riches procured for me.

Mr. Bird's counsel produced a deep impression upon me, and made me more watchful of the changes in my character and the processes by which they were wrought. In truth, I strove against them, in a weak way, as a slave might strive with chains of gold, which charm him and excite his cupidity while they bind him.

Here, perhaps, I ought to mention the fact that there was one subject which Henry would never permit me to talk about, viz., the relations with Mrs. Sanderson upon whose baleful power over me Mr. Bird had animadverted so severely. Why these and my allusions to them were so distasteful to him, I did not know, and could not imagine, unless it were that he did not like to realize the difference between his harder lot and mine. "Please never mention the name of Mrs. Sanderson to me again," he said to me one day, almost ill-naturedly, and quite peremptorily. "I am tired of the old woman, and I should think you would be."

Quite unexpectedly, toward the close of the term, I received a letter from my father, conveying a hearty invitation to Henry to accompany me to Bradford, and become a guest in his house. With the fear of Mrs. Sanderson's displeasure before my eyes, should he accept an invitation from my father which he had once and many times again declined when extended by herself, I was mean enough to consider the purpose of withholding it from him altogether. But I wanted him in Bradford. I wanted to show him to my friends, and so, risking all untoward consequences, I read him the invitation.

Henry's face brightened in an instant, and, without consulting his mother, he said at once: "I shall go."

Very much surprised, and fearful of what would come of it, I blundered out some faint expression of my pleasure at the prospect of his continued society, and the matter was settled.

I cannot recall our parting with Mr. and Mrs. Bird without a blinding suffusion of the eyes. Few words were said. "You know it all, my boy," said Mr. Bird, as he put his arms around me, and pressed me to his side. "I took you into my heart when I first saw you, and you will live there until you prove yourself unworthy of the place."

For several years a lumbering old stage-coach with two horses had run between Hillsborough and Bradford, and to this vehicle Henry and I committed our luggage and ourselves. It was a tedious journey, which terminated at nightfall, and brought us first to my father's house. Ordering my trunks to be carried to The Mansion, I went in to introduce Henry to the family, with the purpose of completing my own journey on foot.

Henry was evidently a surprise to them all. Manly in size, mould and bearing, he bore no resemblance to the person whom they had been accustomed to regard as a lad. There

Claire's hand lighted the candle with which I led him to his room. (p. 123.)

was embarrassment at first, which Henry's quiet and unpretending manners quickly dissipated; and soon the stream of easy conversation was set flowing, and we were all happy together. I quickly saw that my sister Claire had become the real mistress of the household. The evidences of her care were everywhere. My mother was feeble and prone to melancholy; but her young spirit, full of vitality, had asserted its sway, and produced a new atmosphere in the little establishment. Order, taste, and a look of competency and comfort prevailed. Without any particular motive, I watched the interchange of address and impression between Henry and my sister. It was as charming as a play. Two beings brought together from different worlds could not have appeared more interested in each other. Her cheeks were flushed, her blue eyes were luminous, her words were fresh and vivacious, and with a woman's quick instinct she felt that she pleased him. Absorbed in his study of the new nature thus opened to him, Henry so far forgot the remainder of the family as to address all his words to her. If my father asked him a question, he answered it to Claire. If he told a story, or related an incident of our journey homeward, he addressed it to her, as if her ears were the only ones that could hear it, or at least were those which would hear it with the most interest. I cannot say that I had not anticipated something like this. I had wondered, at least, how they would like each other. Claire's hand lighted the candle with which I led him to his room. Claire's hand had arranged the little bouquet which we found upon his table.

"I shall like *all* your father's family very much, I know," said Henry, in our privacy.

I was quick enough to know who constituted the largest portion of the family, in his estimate of the aggregate.

It was with a feeling of positive unhappiness and humiliation that I at last took leave of the delightful and delighted circle, and bent my steps to my statelier lodgings and the society of my cold and questioning Aunt. I knew that there would be no hope of hiding from her the fact that Henry had accompanied me home, and that entire frankness and promptness in announcing it was my best policy; but I dreaded the impression it would make upon her. I found her awaiting my arrival, and met from her a hearty greeting. How I wished that Henry were a hundred miles away!

"I left my old chum at my father's," I said, almost before she had time to ask me a question.

"You did!" she exclaimed, her dark eyes flaming with anger. "How came he there?"

"My father invited him and he came home with me," I replied.

"So he spurns your invitation and mine, and accepts your father's. Will you explain this?"

"Indeed I cannot," I replied. "I have nothing to say, except that I am sorry and ashamed."

"I should think so! I should think so!" she exclaimed, rising and walking up and down the little library. "I should think so, indeed! One thing is proved, at least, and proved to your satisfaction, I hope—that he is not a gentleman. I really must forbid"—here she checked herself, and reconsidered. She saw that I did not follow her with my sympathy, and thought best to adopt other methods for undermining my friendship for him.

"Arthur," she said, at last, seating herself and controlling her rage, "your model friend has insulted both of us. I am an old woman, and he is nothing to me. He has been invited here solely on your account, and, if he is fond of you, he has declined the invitation solely on mine. There is a certain chivalry—a sense of what is due to any woman under these circumstances—that you understand as well as I do, and I shall leave you to accept or reject its dictates. I ask nothing of you that is based in any way on my relations to you. This fellow has grossly, and without any apology or explanation, slighted my courtesies, and crowned his insult by accepting those coming from a humbler source—from one of my own tenants, in fact."

"I have nothing to say," I responded. "I am really not to blame for his conduct, but I should be ashamed to quarrel with anybody because he would not do what I wanted him to do."

"Very well. If that is your conclusion, I must ask you never to mention his name to me again, and if you hold any communication with him, never to tell me of it. You disappoint me, but you are young, and you must be bitten yourself before you will learn to let dogs alone."

I had come out of the business quite as well as I expected to, but it was her way of working. She saw that I loved my companion with a firmness that she could not shake, and that it really was not in me to quarrel with him. She must wait for favoring time and circumstances, and resort to other arts to accomplish her ends—arts of which she was the conscious mistress. She had not forbidden me to see him and hold intercourse with him. She knew, indeed, that I must see him, and that I could not quarrel with him without offending my father, whose guest he was—a contingency to be carefully avoided.

I knew, however, that all practical means would be used to keep me out of his company during his stay in Bradford, and I was not surprised to be met the next morning with a face cleared from all traces of anger and sullenness, and with projects for the occupation of my time.

"I am getting to be an old woman, Arthur," said she, after a cheery breakfast, "and need help in my affairs, which you ought to be capable of giving me now."

I assured her most sincerely that nothing would give me greater pleasure than to make what return I could for the kindness she had shown me.

Accordingly, she brought out her accounts, and as she laid down her books, and package after package of papers, she said: "I am going to let you into some of my secrets. All that you see here, and learn of my affairs, is to be entirely confidential. I shall show you more than my lawyer knows, and more than anybody knows beyond myself."

Then she opened an account book, and in a neat hand made

out a bill for rent to one of her tenants. This was the form she wished me to follow in making out twenty-five or thirty other bills which she pointed out to me. As I did the work with much painstaking, the task gave me employment during the whole of the morning. At its close, we went over it together, and she was warm in her praises of my handwriting and the correctness of my transcript.

After dinner she told me she would like to have me look over some of the papers which she had left on the table. "It is possible," she said, "that you may find something that will interest you. I insist only on two conditions: you are to keep secret everything you learn, and ask me no question about what may most excite your curiosity."

One ponderous bundle of papers I found to be composed entirely of bonds and mortgages. It seemed as if she had her hold upon nearly every desirable piece of property in the town. By giving me a view of this and showing me her rent-roll, she undoubtedly intended to exhibit her wealth, which was certainly very much greater than I had suspected. "All this if you continue to please me," was what the exhibition meant; and, young as I was, I knew what it meant. To hold these pledges of real estate, and to own this rent-roll was to hold power; and with that precious package in my hands there came to me my first ambition for power, and a recognition of that thirst to gratify which so many men had bartered their honor and their souls. In that book and in those papers lay the basis of the old lady's self-assurance. It was to these that men bowed with deferential respect or superfluous fawning. It was to these that fine ladies paid their devoirs; and a vision of the future showed all these demonstrations of homage transferred to me—a young man—with life all before me. The prospect held not only these but a thousand delights—travel in foreign lands, horses and household pets, fine equipage, pictures, brilliant society, and some sweet, unknown angel in the form of a woman, to be loved and petted and draped with costly fabrics and fed upon dainties.

I floated off into a wild, intoxicating dream. All the possibilities of my future came before me. In my imagination I already stood behind that great bulwark against a thousand ills of life which money builds, and felt myself above the petty needs that harass the toiling multitude. I was already a social center and a king. Yet after all, when the first excitement was over, and I realized the condition that lay between me and the realization of my dreams—"all this if you continue to please me"—I knew and felt that I was a slave. I was not my own: I had been purchased. I could not freely follow even the impulses of my own natural affection.

Tiring of the package at last, and of the thoughts and emotions it excited, I turned to others. One after another I took them up and partly examined them, but they were mostly dead documents—old policies of insurance long since expired, old contracts for the erection of buildings that had themselves grown old, mortgages that had been canceled, old abstracts of title, etc., etc. At last I found, at the bottom of the pile, a package yellow with age; and I gasped with astonishment as I read on the back of the first paper: "*James Mansfield to Peter Bonnicastle.*" I drew it quickly from the tape, and saw exposed upon the next paper: "*Julius Wheeler to Peter Bonnicastle.*" Thus the name went on down through the whole package. All the papers were old, and all of them were deeds —some of them conveying thousands of acres of colonial lands. Thus I learned two things that filled me with such delight and pride as I should find it altogether impossible to describe; first, that the fortune which I had been examining, and which I had a tolerable prospect of inheriting, had its foundations laid a century before by one of my own ancestors; and second, that Mrs. Sanderson and I had common blood in our veins. This discovery quite restored my self-respect, because I should arrive at my inheritance by at least a show of right. The property would remain in the family where it belonged, and, so far as I knew, no member of the family would have a better right to it than myself. I presumed that my father was a descendant of this same Peter Bonnicastle, who was doubtless a notable man in his time; and only the accidents of fortune had diverted this large wealth from my own branch of the family.

This discovery brought up to my memory the conversations that had taken place in my home on my first arrival in the town, between Mr. Bradford and my father. Here was where the "blue blood" came from, and Mr. Bradford had known about this all the time. It was his hint to Mrs. Sanderson that had procured for me my good fortune. My first impulse was to thank him for his service, and to tell him that I probably knew as much as he did of my relations to Mrs. Sanderson; but the seal of secrecy was upon my lips. I recalled to mind Mrs. Sanderson's astonishment and strange behavior when she first heard my father's name, and thus all the riddles of that first interview were solved.

Pride of wealth and power had now firmly united itself in my mind with pride of ancestry; and though there were humiliating considerations connected with my relations to Mrs. Sanderson, my self-respect had been wonderfully strengthened, and I found that my heart was going out to the little old lady with a new sentiment—a sentiment of kinship, if not of love. I identified myself with her more perfectly than I had hitherto done. She had placed confidence in me, she had praised my work, and she was a Bonnicastle.

I have often looked back upon the revelations and the history of that day, and wondered whether it was possible that she had foreseen all the processes of mind through which I passed, and intelligently and deliberately contrived to procure them. She must have done so. There was not an instrument wanting for the production of the result she desired, and there was nothing wanting in the result.

The afternoon passed, and I neither went home nor felt a desire to do so. In the evening she invited me to read, and thus I spent a pleasant hour preparatory to an early bed.

"You have been a real comfort to me to-day, Arthur," she said, as I kissed her forehead and bade her good-night.

What more could a lad who loved praise ask than this? I went to sleep entirely happy, and with a new determination to devote myself more heartily to the will and the interests of my benefactress. It ceased to be a great matter that my companion for five years was in my father's home, and I saw little of him. I was employed with writing and with business errands all the time. During Henry's visit in Bradford I was in and out of my father's house, as convenience favored, and always while on an errand that waited. I think Henry appreciated the condition of affairs, and as he and Claire were on charming terms, and my absence gave him more time with her, I presume that he did not miss me. All were glad to see me useful, and happy in my usefulness.

When Henry went away I walked down to bid him farewell. "Now don't cry, my boy," said Henry, "for I am coming back; and don't be excited when I tell you that I have engaged to spend the winter in Bradford. I was wondering where I could find a school to teach, and the school has come to me, examining committee and all."

I was delighted. I looked at Claire with the unguarded impulse of a boy, and it brought the blood into her cheeks painfully. Henry parted with her very quietly—indeed, with studied quietness—but was warm in his thanks to my father and mother for their hospitality, and hearty with the boys, with whom he had become a great favorite.

I saw that Henry was happy, and particularly happy in the thought of returning. As the stage-coach rattled away, he kissed his hand to us all, and shouted "*Au revoir!*" as if his anticipations of pleasure were embraced in those words rather than in the fact that he was homeward-bound.

CHAPTER VIII.

I AM INTRODUCED TO NEW CHARACTERS AND ENTER THE SHADOW OF THE GREAT BEDLOW REVIVAL.

WHILE Henry was a guest at my old home, Mr. Bradford resumed his visits there. That he had had much to do with securing my father's prosperity in his calling, I afterwards learned with gratitude, but he had done it without his humble friend's knowledge, and while studiously keeping aloof from him. I never could imagine any reason for his policy in this matter except the desire to keep out of Mrs. Sanderson's way. He seemed, too, to have a special interest in Henry; and it soon came to my ears that he had secured for him his place as teacher of one of the public schools. Twice during the young man's visit at Bradford, he had called and invited him to an evening walk, on the pretext of showing him some of the more interesting features of the rapidly growing little city.

Henry's plan for study was coincident with my own. We had both calculated to perfect our preparation for college during the winter and following spring, under private tuition; and this work, which would be easy for me, was to be accomplished by him during the hours left from his school duties. I made my own independent arrangements for recitation and direction, as I knew such a course would best please Mrs. Sanderson, and left him to do the same on his return. With an active temperament and the new stimulus which had come to me with a better knowledge of my relations and prospects, I found my mind and my time fully absorbed. When I was not engaged in study, I was actively assisting Mrs. Sanderson in her affairs.

One morning in the early winter, after Henry had returned, and had been for a week or two engaged in his school, I met

Mr. Bradford on the street, and received from him a cordial invitation to take tea and spend the evening at his home. Without telling me what company I should meet, he simply said that there were to be two or three young people beside me, and that he wanted Mrs. Bradford to know me. Up to this time, I had made comparatively few acquaintances in the town, and had entered, in a social way, very few homes. The invitation gave me a great deal of pleasure, for Mr. Bradford stood high in the social scale, so that Mrs. Sanderson could make no plausible objection to my going. I was careful not to speak of the matter to Henry, whom I accidentally met during the day, and particularly careful not to mention it in my father's family, for fear that Claire might feel herself slighted. I was therefore thoroughly surprised when I entered Mrs. Bradford's cheerful drawing-room to find there, engaged in the merriest conversation with the family, both Henry and my sister Claire. Mr. Bradford rose and met me at the door in his own hospitable, hearty way, and, grasping my right hand, put his free arm around me, and led me to Mrs. Bradford and presented me. She was a sweet, pale-faced little woman, with large blue eyes, with which she peered into mine with a charming look of curious inquiry. If she had said: "I have long wanted to know you, and am fully prepared to be pleased with you and to love you," she would only have put into words the meaning which her look conveyed. I had never met with a greeting that more thoroughly delighted me, or placed me more at my ease, or stimulated me more to show what there was of good in me.

"This is my sister, Miss Lester," said she, turning to a prim personage sitting by the fire.

As the lady did not rise, I bowed to her at a distance, and she recognized me with a little nod, as if she would have said: "You are well enough for a boy, but I don't see the propriety of putting myself out for such young people."

The contrast between her greeting and that of Mr. and Mrs. Bradford led me to give her more than a passing look. I concluded at once that she was a maiden of an age more advanced than she should be willing to confess, and a person with ways and tempers of her own. She sat alone, trotting her knees, looking into the fire, and knitting with such emphasis as to give an electric snap to every pass of her glittering needles. She was larger than Mrs. Bradford, and her dark hair and swarthy skin, gathered into a hundred wrinkles around her black eyes, produced a strange contrast between the sisters.

Mrs. Bradford, I soon learned, was one of those women in whom the motherly instinct is so strong that no living thing can come into their presence without exciting their wish to care for it. The first thing she did, therefore, after I had exchanged greetings, was to set a chair for me at the fire, because she knew I must be cold and my feet must be wet. When I assured her that I was neither cold nor wet, and she had accepted the statement with evident incredulity and disappointment, she insisted that I should change my chair for an easier one. I did this to accommodate her, and then she took a fancy that I had a headache and needed a bottle of salts. This I found in my hand before I knew it.

As these attentions were rendered, they were regarded by Mr. Bradford with good-natured toleration, but there issued from the corner where "Aunt Flick" sat—for from some lip I had already caught her home-name—little impatient sniffs, and raps upon the hearth with her trotting heel.

"Jane Bradford," Aunt Flick broke out at last, "I should think you'd be ashamed. You've done nothing but worry that boy since he came into the room. One would think he was a baby, and that it was your business to 'tend him. Just as if he didn't know whether he was cold, or his feet were wet, or his head ached! Just as if he didn't know enough to go to the fire if he wanted to! Millie, get the cat for your mother, and bring in the dog. Something must be nursed, of course."

"Why, Flick, dear!" was all Mrs. Bradford said, but Mr. Bradford looked amused, and there came from a corner of the room that my eyes had not explored the merriest young laugh imaginable. I had no doubt as to its authorship. Seeing that the evening was to be an informal one, I had already begun to wonder where the little girl might be, with whose face I had made a brief acquaintance five years before, and of whom I had caught occasional glimpses in the interval.

Mr. Bradford looked in the direction of the laugh, and exclaiming: "You saucy puss!" started from his chair, and found her seated behind an ottoman, where she had been quietly reading.

"Oh, father! don't, please!" she exclaimed, as he drew her from her retreat. She resisted at first, but when she saw that she was fully discovered, she consented to be led forward and presented to us.

"When a child is still," said Aunt Flick, "I can't see the use of stirring her up, unless it is to send her to bed."

"Why, Flick, dear!" said Mrs. Bradford again; but Mr. Bradford took no notice of the remark, and led the little girl to us. She shook hands with us, and then her mother caught and pulled her into her lap.

"Jane Bradford, why *will* you burden yourself with that heavy child? I should think you would be ill."

Millie's black eyes flashed, but she said nothing, and I had an opportunity to study her wonderful beauty. As I looked at her, I could think of nothing but a gypsy. I could not imagine how it was possible that she should be the daughter of Mr. and Mrs. Bradford. It was as if some unknown, oriental ancestor had reached across the generations and touched her, revealing to her parents the long-lost secrets of their own blood. Her hair hung in raven ringlets, and her dark, healthy skin was as smooth and soft as the petal of a pansy. She had put on a scarlet jacket for comfort, in her distant corner, and the color heightened all her charms. Her face was bright with intelligence, and her full, mobile lips and dimpled chin were charged with the prophecy of a wonderfully beautiful womanhood. I looked at her quite enchanted, and I am sure that she was conscious of my scrutiny, for she disengaged herself gently from her mother's hold, and saying that she wished to finish the chapter she had been reading, went back to her seclusion.

The consciousness of her presence in the room somehow destroyed my interest in the other members of the family, and as I felt no restraint in the warm and free social atmosphere around me, I soon followed her to her corner, and sat down upon the ottoman behind which, upon a hassock, she had ensconced herself.

"What have you come here for?" she inquired wonderingly, looking up into my eyes.

"To see you," I replied.

"Aren't you a young gentleman?"

"No, I am only a big boy."

"Why, that's jolly," said she. "Then you can be my company."

"Certainly," I responded.

"Well, then, what shall we do? I'm sure I don't know how to play with a boy. I never did."

"We can talk," I said. "What a funny woman your Aunt Flick is! Doesn't she bother you?"

She paused, looked down, then looked up into my face, and said decidedly: "I don't like that question."

"I meant nothing ill by it," I responded.

"Yes you did; you meant something ill to Aunt Flick."

"But I thought she bothered you," I said.

"Did I say so?"

"No."

"Well, when I say so, I shall say so to her. Papa and I understand it."

So this was my little girl, with a feeling of family loyalty in her heart, and a family pride that did not choose to discuss with strangers the foibles of kindred and the jars of home life. I was rebuked, though the consciousness of the fact came too slowly to excite pain. It was *her* Aunt Flick; and a stranger had no right to question or criticise. That was what I gathered from her words; and there was so much that charmed me in this fine revelation of character, that I quite lost sight of the fact that I had been snubbed.

"She has a curious name, any way," I said.

At this her face lighted up, and she exclaimed: "Oh! I'll tell you all about that. When I was a little girl, ever so much smaller than I am now, we had a minister in the house. You know mamma takes care of everybody, and when the minister came to town he came here, because nobody else would have him. He stayed here ever so long, and used to say grace at the table and have prayers. Aunt Flick was sick at the time, and he used to pray every morning for our poor afflicted sister, and papa was full of fun with her, just to keep up her courage, I suppose, and called her ''Flicted,' and then he got to calling her 'Flick' for a nickname, and now we all call her Flick."

"But does she like it?"

"Oh, she's used to it, and don't mind."

Millie had closed her book, and sat with it on her lap, her large black eyes looking up into mine in a dreamy way.

"There's one thing I should like to know," said Millie, "and that is, where all the books came from. Were they always here, like the ground, or did somebody make them?"

"Somebody made them," I said.

"I don't believe it," she responded.

"But if nobody made them, how did they come here?"

"They are real things: somebody found them."

"No, I've seen men who wrote books, and women too," I said.

"How did they look?"

"Very much like other people."

"And did they act like other people?"

"Yes."

"Well, that shows that they found them. They are humbugs."

I laughed, and assured her that she was mistaken.

"Well," said she, "if anybody can make books I can; and if I don't get married and keep house I shall."

Very much amused, I asked her which walk of life she would prefer.

"I think I should prefer to be married."

"You are sensible," I said.

"Not to any boy or young man, though," responded the child, with peculiar and suggestive emphasis.

"And why not?"

"They are so silly;" and she gave her curls a disdainful toss. "I shall marry a big man like papa, with gray whiskers—somebody that I can adore, you know."

"Well, then, I think you had better not be married," I replied. "Perhaps, after all, you had better write books."

"If I should ever write a book," said Millie, looking out of the window, as if she were reviewing the long chain of characters and incidents of which it was to be composed, "I should begin at the foundation of the world, and come up through Asia, or Arabia, or Cappadocia . . . and stop under palm-trees . . . and have a lot of camels with bells. . . . I should have a young man with a fez and an old man with a long beard, and a chibouk, and a milk-white steed. . . . I should have a maiden too beautiful for anything, and an Arab chieftain with a military company on horseback, kicking up a great dust in the desert, and coming after her. . . . And then I should have some sort of an escape, and I should hide the maiden in a tower somewhere on the banks of the Danube. . . . And then I'm sure I don't know what I should do with her."

"You would marry her to the young man with the fez, wouldn't you?" I suggested.

"Perhaps—if I didn't conclude to kill him."

"You couldn't be so cruel as that," I said.

"Why, that's the fun of it: you can stab a man right through the heart in a book, and spill every drop of his blood without hurting him a particle."

"Well," I said, "I don't see but you have made a book already."

"Would that really be a book?" she asked, looking eagerly into my face.

"I should think so," I replied.

"Then it's just as I thought it was. I didn't make a bit of it. I saw it. I found it. They're everywhere, and people see them, just like flowers, and pick them up and press them."

It was not until years after this that with my slower masculine intellect and feebler instincts I appreciated the beauty of this revelation and the marvelous insight which it betrayed. These crude tropical fancies she could not entertain with any sense of ownership or authorship. They came of themselves, in gorgeous forms and impressive combinations, and passed before her vision. She talked of what she saw—not of what she made. I was charmed by her vivacity, acuteness, frankness and spirit, and really felt that the older persons at the other end of the drawing-room were talking common-places compared with Millie's utterances. We conversed a long time upon many things; and what impressed me most, perhaps, was that she was living the life of a woman and thinking the thoughts of a woman—incompletely, of course, and unrecognized by her own family!

When we were called to tea, she rose up quickly and whispered in my ear: "I like to talk with you." As she came around the end of the ottoman I offered her my arm, in the manner with which my school habits had familiarized me. She took it without the slightest hesitation, and put on the air of a grand lady.

"Why this is like a book, isn't it?" said she. Then she pressed my arm, and said: "notice Aunt Flick, please."

Aunt Flick had seen us from the start, and stood with elevated nostrils. The sight was one which evidently excited her beyond the power of expression. She could do nothing but sniff as we approached her. I saw a merry twinkle in Mr. Bradford's eyes, and noticed that as he had Claire on his arm, and Henry was leading out Mrs. Bradford, Aunt Flick was left alone. Without a moment's thought, I walked with Millie straight to her, and offered her my other arm.

Aunt Flick was thunder-struck, and at first could only say: "Well! well! well!" with long pauses between. Then she found strength to say: "For all the world like a pair of young monkeys! No, I thank you; when I want a cane I won't choose a corn-stalk. I've walked alone in the world so far, and I think I can do it the rest of the way."

So Aunt Flick followed us out, less vexed than amused, I am sure.

There are two things which, during all my life, have been more suggestive to me of home comforts and home delights than any others, viz.: A blazing fire upon the hearth, and the odor of fresh toast. I found both in Mrs. Bradford's supper-room, for a red-cheeked lass with an old-fashioned toasting-jack in her hand was browning the whitest bread before our eyes, and preparing to bear it hot to our plates. The subtle odor had reached me first in the far corner of the drawing-room, and had grown more stimulating to appetite and the sense of social and home comfort as I approached its source.

The fire upon the hearth is the center and symbol of the family life. When the fire in a house goes out, it is because the life has gone out. Somewhere in every house it burns, and burns, in constant service; and every chimney that sends its incense heavenward speaks of an altar inscribed to Love and Home. And when it ceases to burn, it is because the altar is forsaken. Bread is the symbol of that beautiful ministry of God to human sustenance, which, properly apprehended, transforms the homeliest meal into a sacrament. What wonder, then, that when the bread of life and the fire on the hearth meet, they should interpret and reveal each other in an odor sweeter than violets—an odor so subtle and suggestive that the heart breathes it rather than the sense!

This is all stuff and sentiment, I suppose; but I doubt whether the scent of toast has reached my nostrils since that evening without recalling that scene of charming domestic life and comfort. It seemed as if all the world were in that room —and, indeed, it was all there—all that, for the hour, we could appropriate.

As we took our seats at the table, I found myself by the side of Millie and opposite to Aunt Flick. Then began on the part of the latter personage, a pantomimic lecture to her niece. First she straightened herself in her chair, throwing out her chest and holding in her chin—a performance which Millie imitated. Then she executed the motion of putting some stray hair behind her ear. Millie did the same. Then she tucked an imaginary napkin into her neck. Millie obeyed the direction thus conveyed. Then she examined her knife, and finding that it did not suit her, sent it away and received one that did.

In the mean time, Mrs. Bradford had begun to dispense the hospitalities of the table. She was very cheerful; indeed, she was so happy herself that she overflowed with assiduities that ran far into superfluities. She was afraid the toast was not hot, or that the tea was not sweet enough, or that she had forgotten the sugar altogether, or that everybody was not properly waited upon and supplied. I could see that all this rasped Aunt Flick to desperation. The sniffs, which were light at first, grew more impatient, and after Mrs. Bradford had urged half a dozen things upon me that I did not want, and was obliged to decline, the fiery spinster burst out with :

"Wouldn't you like to read the Declaration of Independence? Wouldn't you like to repeat the Ten Commandments? Wouldn't you like a yard of calico? Do have a spoon to eat your toast with? Just a trifle more salt in your tea, please?"

All this was delivered without the slightest hesitation, and with a rapidity that was fairly bewildering. Poor Millie was overcome by the comical aspect of the matter, and broke out into an irrepressible laugh, which was so hearty that it became contagious, and all of us laughed together except Aunt Flick, who devoted herself to her supper with imperturbable gravity.

"Why, Flick, dear!" was all that Mrs. Bradford could say

to this outburst of scornful criticism upon her well-meant courtesies.

Just as we were recovering from our merriment, there was a loud knock at the street door. The girl with the toasting-jack dropped her implement to answer the unwelcome summons. We all involuntarily listened, and learned from his voice that the intruder was a man. We heard him enter the drawing-room, and then the girl came in and said that Mr. Grimshaw had called upon the family. In the general confusion that followed the announcement, Millie leaned over to me and said: "It's the very man who used to pray for Aunt Flick."

Mr. Bradford, of course, brought him to the tea-table at once, where room was made for him by the side of Aunt Flick, and a plate laid. The first thing he did was to swallow a cup of hot tea almost at a gulp, and to send back the empty vessel to be refilled. Then he spread with butter a whole piece of toast, which disappeared in a wonderfully brief space of time. Until his hunger was appeased he did not seem disposed to talk, replying to such questions as were propounded to him concerning himself and his family in monosyllables.

Rev. Mr. Grimshaw was the minister of a struggling Congregational church in Bradford. He had been hard at work for half a dozen years with indifferent success, waiting for some manifestation of the Master which would show him that his service and sacrifice had been accepted. I had heard him preach at different times during my vacation visits, though Mrs. Sanderson did not attend upon his ministry; and he had always impressed me as a man who was running some sort of a machine. He had a great deal to say about "the plan of salvation" and the doctrines covered by his creed. I cannot aver that he ever interested me. Indeed, I may say that he always confused me. Religion, as it had been presented to my mind, had been a simple thing—so simple that a child might understand it. My Father in Heaven loved me; Jesus Christ had died for me. Loving both, trusting both, and serving both by worship, and by affectionate and helpful good-will toward all around me was religion, as I had learned it; and I never came from hearing one of Mr. Grimshaw's sermons without finding it difficult to get back upon my simple ground of faith. Religion, as he preached it, was such a tremendous and such a mysterious thing in its beginnings; it involved such a complicated structure of belief; it divided God into such opposing forces of justice and mercy; it depended upon such awful processes of feeling; it was so much the product of a profoundly ingenious scheme, that his sermons always puzzled me.

As he sat before me that evening, pale-faced and thin, with his intense, earnest eyes and solemn bearing and self-crucified expression, I could not doubt his purity or his sincerity. There was something in him that awoke my respect and my sympathy.

Our first talk touched only common-places, but as the meal drew toward its close he ingeniously led the conversation into religious channels.

"There is a very tender and solemn state of feeling in the church," said Mr. Grimshaw, "and a great deal of self-examination and prayer. The careless are beginning to be thoughtful, and the backsliders are returning to their first love. I most devoutly trust that we are going to have a season of refreshment. It is a time when all those who have named the name of the Lord should make themselves ready for His coming."

Aunt Flick started from her chair exactly as if she were about to put on her hat and cloak; and I think that was really her impulse; but she sat down again and listened intently.

I could not fail to see that this turn in the conversation was not relished by Mr. Bradford; but Mrs. Bradford and Aunt Flick were interested, and I noticed an excited look upon the faces of both Henry and Claire.

Mrs. Bradford, in her simplicity, made a most natural response to the minister's communication in the words: "You must be exceedingly delighted, Mr. Grimshaw." She said this very sweetly, and with her cheerful smile making her whole countenance light.

"Jane Bradford!" exclaimed Aunt Flick, "I believe you would smile if anybody were to tell you the judgment-day had come."

Mrs. Bradford did not say this time: "Why, Flick, dear!" but she said with great tenderness: "When I remember who is to judge me, and to whom I have committed myself, I think I should."

"Well, I don't know how anybody can make light of such awful things," responded Aunt Flick.

"Of course, I am rejoiced," said Mr. Grimshaw, at last getting his chance to speak, "but my joy is tempered by the great responsibility that rests upon me, and by a sense of the lost condition of the multitudes around me."

"In reality," Mr. Bradford broke in, "you don't feel quite so much like singing as the angels did when the Saviour came to redeem the world. But then, they probably had no such sense of responsibility as you have. Perhaps they didn't appreciate the situation. It has always seemed to me, however, as if that which would set an angel singing—a being who ought to see a little further forward and backward than we can, and a little deeper down and higher up—ought to set men and women singing. I confess that I don't understand the long faces and the superstitious solemnities of what is called a season of refreshment. If the Lord is with his own, they ought to be glad and give him such a greeting as will induce him to remain. I really do not wonder that he flies from many congregations that I have seen, or that he seems to resist their entreaties that he will stay. Half the prayers that I hear sound like abject beseechings for the presence of One who is very far off, and very unwilling to come."

This free expression on the part of Mr. Bradford would have surprised me had I not just learned that the minister had at one time been a member of his family, with whom he had been on familiar terms; yet I knew that he did not profess to be a religious man, and that his view of the matter, whether sound or otherwise, was from the outside. There was a subtle touch of satire in his words, too, that did not altogether please me ; but I did not see what reply could be made to it.

Aunt Flick was evidently somewhat afraid of Mr. Bradford, and simply said: " I hope you will remember that your child is present."

"Yes, I do remember it," said he, "and what I say about it is as much for her ears as for anybody's. And I remember too, that, during all my boyhood, I was made afraid of religion. I wish to save her, if I can, from such a curse. I have read that when the Saviour was upon the earth, he took little children in His arms and blessed them, and went so far as to say that of such was the kingdom of heaven. If He were to come to the earth again, He would be as apt to take my child upon His knee as any man's and bless her, and repeat over her the same words ; and if He manifests His presence among us in any way I do not wish to have her kept away from Him by the impression that there is something awful in the fact that He is here. My God ! if I could believe that the Lord of Heaven and Earth were really in Bradford, with a dispensation of faith and mercy and love in His hands for me and mine, do you think I would groan and look gloomy over it ? Why, I couldn't eat ; I couldn't sleep ; I couldn't refrain from shouting and singing."

Mr. Grimshaw was evidently touched and impressed by Mr. Bradford's exhibition of strong feeling, and said in a calm, judicial way that it was impossible that one outside of the church should comprehend and appreciate the feelings that exercised him and the church generally. The welfare of the unconverted depended so much upon a revival of religion within the church —it brought such tremendous responsibilities and such great duties—that Christian men and women were weighed down with solemnity. The issues of eternal life and death were tremendous issues. Even if the angels sang, Jesus suffered in the garden, and bore the cross on Calvary ; and Christians who are worthy must suffer and bear the cross also.

" Mr. Grimshaw," said Mr. Bradford, still earnest and excited, " I have heard from your own lips that the fact that Christ was to suffer and bear the cross was at least a part of the inspiration of the song which the angels sang. He suffered and bore the cross that men might not suffer. That is one of the essential parts of your creed. He suffered that He might give peace to the world, and bring life and immortality to light. You have taught me that He did not come to torment the world, but to save it. The religion which Christendom holds in theory is a religion of unbounded peace and joy; that which it holds in fact is one of torture and gloom; and I do not hesitate to say that if the Christian world were a peaceful and joyous world, taking all the good things of this life in gratitude and gladness, while holding itself pure from its corruptions, and not only not fearing death, but looking forward with unwavering faith and hope to another and a happier life beyond, the revivals which it struggles for would be perpetual, and the millennium which it prays for would come."

Then Mr. Bradford, who sat near enough to touch me, laid his hand upon my shoulder, and said: "Boy, look at your father, if you wish to know what my ideal of a Christian is,—a man of cheerfulness, trust and hope, under discouragements that would kill me. Such examples save me from utter infidelity and despair, and, thank God, I have one such in my own home."

His eyes filled with tears as he turned them upon his wife, who sat watching him with intense sympathy and affection, while he frankly poured out his heart and thought.

"I suppose," said the minister, "that we should get no nearer together in the discussion of this question than we did when we were more in one another's company, and perhaps it would be well not to pursue it. You undoubtedly see the truth in a single aspect, Mr. Bradford; and you will pardon me for saying that you cannot see it in the aspects which it presents to me. I came in, partly to let you and your family know of our plans, and to beg you to attend our services faithfully. I hope these young people, too, will not fail to put themselves in the way of religious influence. Now is their time. To-morrow or next year it may be too late. Many a poor soul is obliged to take up the lament after every revival: 'The harvest is past, the summer is ended, and my soul is not saved.' Before the spirit takes its flight, all these precious youth ought to be gathered into the kingdom."

I could not doubt the sincerity of this closing utterance, for it was earnest and tearful. In truth, I was deeply moved by it; for while Mr. Bradford carried my judgment and opened before me a beautiful life, I had always entertained great reverence for ministers, and found Mr. Grimshaw's views and feelings most in consonance with those I had been used to hear proclaimed from the pulpit.

The fact that a revival was in progress in some of the churches of the town, had already come to my ears.

I had seen throngs pouring into or coming out of church-doors and lecture-rooms during other days than Sunday; and a vague uneasiness had possessed me for several weeks. A cloud had arisen upon my life. I may even confess that my heart had rebelled in secret against an influence which promised to interfere with the social pleasures and the progress in study which I had anticipated for the winter. The cloud came nearer to me now, and in Mr. Grimshaw's presence quite overshadowed me. Was I moved by sympathy? Was I moved by the spirit of the Almighty? Was superstitious fear at the bottom of it all? Whatever it was, my soul had crossed the line of that circle of passion and experience in whose center a great multitude were groping and crying in the darkness, and striving to get a vision of the Father's face. I realized the fact then and there. I felt that a crisis in my life was approaching.

On Aunt Flick's face there came a look of rigid determination. She was entirely ready to work, and inquired of Mr. Grimshaw what his plans were.

"I have felt," said he, "that the labor and responsibility are too great for me to bear alone, and, after a consultation with our principal men, have concluded to send for Mr. Bedlow, the evangelist, to assist me."

"Mr. Grimshaw," said Mr. Bradford, "I suppose it is none of

my business, but I am sorry you have done this. I have no faith in the man or his methods. Mrs. Bradford and her sister will attend his preaching if they choose : I am not afraid that they will be harmed; but I decidedly refuse to have this child of mine subjected to his processes. Why parents will consent to yield their children to the spiritual manipulation of strangers I cannot conceive."

Mr. Grimshaw smiled sadly, and said : "You assume a grave responsibility, Mr. Bradford."

"*I* assume a grave responsibility?" exclaimed Mr. Bradford: "I had the impression that I relieved you of one. No, leave the child alone. She is safe with her mother; and no such man as Mr. Bedlow shall have the handling of her sensibilities."

We had sat a long time at the tea-table, and as we rose and adjourned to the drawing-room Mr. Grimshaw took sudden leave on the plea that he had devoted the evening to many other calls yet to be made. He was very solemn in his leave-taking, and for some time after he left we sat in silence. Then Mr. Bradford rose and paced the drawing-room back and forth, his countenance full of perplexity and pain. I could see plainly that a storm of utterance was gathering, but whether it would burst in thunder and torrent, or open with strong and healing rain, was doubtful.

At length he paused, and said : "I suppose that as a man old enough to be the father of all these young people I ought to say frankly what I feel in regard to this subject. I do not believe it is right for me to shut my mouth tight upon my convictions. My own measure of faith is small. I wish to God it were larger, and I am encouraged to believe that it is slowly strengthening. I am perfectly aware that I lack peace in the exact proportion that I lack faith; and so does every man, no matter how much he may boast. Faith is the natural and only healthy attitude of the soul. I would go through anything to win it, but such men as Grimshaw and Bedlow cannot help me. They simply distress and disgust me. Their whole conception of Christianity is cramped and mean, and their methods of operation are unwise and unworthy. I know how Mr. Grimshaw feels: he knows that revivals are in progress in the other churches, and sees that his own congregation is attracted to their meetings. He finds it impossible to keep the tide from retiring from his church, and feels the necessity of doing something extraordinary to make it one of the centers and receivers of the new influence. He has been at work faithfully, in his way, for years, and desires to see the harvest which he has been trying to rear gathered in. So he sends for Bedlow. Now I know all about these Bedlow revivals. They come when he comes, and they go when he goes. His mustard-seed sprouts at once, and grows into a great tree, which withers and dies as soon as he ceases to breathe upon it. I never knew an instance in which a church that had been raised out of the mire by his influence did not sink back into a deeper indifference after he had left it, and that by a process which is just as natural as it is inevitable. An artificial excitement is an artificial exhaustion. He breaks up and ruins processes of religious education that otherwise would have gone on to perfection. He has one process for the imbruted, the ignorant, the vicious, the stolid, the sensitive, the delicate, the weak and the strong, the old and the young. I know it is said that the spirit of God is with him, and I hope it is; but one poor man like him does not monopolize the spirit of God, I trust; nor does that spirit refuse to stay where he is not. No, it is Bedlow—it's all Bedlow; and the fact that a revival got up under his influence ceases when he retires, proves that it is all Bedlow, and accounts for the miserable show of permanently good results."

There was great respect for Mr. Bradford in his own household, and there was great respect for him in the hearts of the three young people who listened to him as comparative strangers; and when he stopped, and sank into an arm-chair, looking into the fire, and shading his face with his two hands, no one broke the silence. Aunt Flick had taken to her corner and her knitting, and Mrs. Bradford sat with her hands on her lap, as if waiting for something further.

At length Mr. Bradford looked up with a smile, and regarding the silent group before him, said: "upon my word, we are not having a very merry evening."

"I assure you," responded Henry, "that I have enjoyed every moment of it. I could hear you talk all night."

"So could I," added Claire.

I could not say a word. The eyes of the minister still haunted me: the spell of a new influence was upon me. What Mr. Bradford had said about Mr. Bedlow only increased my desire to hear him, and to come within the reach of his power.

"Well, children," said Mr. Bradford, "for you will let me call you such, I know, I have only one thing more to say to you, and that is to stand by your Christian fathers and mothers, and take their faith just as it is. Not one of you is old enough to decide upon the articles of a creed, but almost any faith is good enough to hold up a Christian character. Don't bother yourselves voluntarily with questions. A living vine grows just as well on a rough trellis of simple branches as on the smoothest piece of ornamental work that can be made. If you ever wish to change the trellis when you get old enough to do it, be careful not to ruin the vine, that is all. I am trying to keep my vine alive around a trellis that is gone to wreck. I believe in God and His Son, and I believe that there is one thing which God delights in more than in all else, and that is Christian character. I hold to the first and strive for the last, though I am looked upon as little better than an infidel by all but one."

A thrill, sympathetically felt by us all, and visible in a blush and eyes suffused, ran through the dear little woman seated at his side, and she looked up into his face with a trustful smile of response.

After this it was difficult to engage in light conversation. We were questioned in regard to our past experiences and future plans. We looked over volumes of pictures and a cabinet of curiosities, and Millie amused us by reading, and at an early hour we rose to go home. Millie went to her corner as soon as we broke up, giving me a look as she passed me. I took the hint and followed her.

"Shall you go to hear Mr. Bedlow?" she inquired.

"I think I shall," I answered.

"I knew you would. I should like to go with you, but you know I can't. Will you tell me what he is like, and all about it?"

"Yes."

I pressed her hand and bade her "good-night."

Mr. Bradford parted with us at the door with pleasant and courteous words, and told Henry that he must regard the house as his home, and assured him that he would always find a welcome there. I had noticed during the evening a peculiarly affectionate familiarity in his tone and bearing toward the young man. I could not but notice that he treated him with more consideration than he treated me. I went away feeling that there were confidences between them, and suffered the suspicion to make me uneasy.

I walked home with Henry and Claire, and we talked over the affairs of the evening together. Both declared their adhesion to Mr. Bradford's views, and I, in my assumed pride of independent opinion, dissented. I proposed to see for myself. I would listen to Mr. Bedlow's preaching. I was not afraid of being harmed, and, indeed, I should not dare to stay away from him.

As I walked to The Mansion, I found my nerves excited in a strange degree. The way was full of shadows. I started at every noise. It was as if the spiritual world were dropped down around me, and I were touched by invisible wings, and moved by mysterious influences. The stars shivered in their high places, the night-wind swept by me as if it were a weird power of evil, and I seemed to be smitten through heart and brain by a nameless fear. As I kneeled in my accustomed way at my bed I lost my confidence. I could not recall my usual words or frame new ones. I lingered on my knees like one crushed and benumbed. What it all meant I could not tell. I only knew that feelings and influences which long had been gathering in me were assuming the predominance, and that I was entering upon a new phase of experience. At last I went to bed, and passed a night crowded with strange dreams and dreary passages of unrefreshing slumber.

CHAPTER IX.

I PASS THROUGH A TERRIBLE TEMPEST INTO THE SUNLIGHT.

I HAD never arrived at any definite comprehension of Mrs. Sanderson's ideas of religion. Whether she was religious in any worthy sense I do not know, even to-day. The respect which she entertained for the clergy was a sentiment which she shared with New Englanders generally. She was rather generous than otherwise in her contributions to their support, yet the most I could make of her views and opinions was that religion and its institutions were favorable to the public order and security, and were, therefore, to be patronized and permanently sustained. I never should have thought of going to her for spiritual counsel, yet I had learned in some way that she thought religion was a good thing for a young man, because it would save him from dissipation and from a great many dangers to which young men are exposed. The whole subject seemed to be regarded by her in an economical or prudential aspect.

I met her on the morning following my visit at the Bradfords, in the breakfast-room. She was cheery and expectant, for she always found me talkative, and was prepared to hear the full story of the previous evening. That I was obliged to tell her that Henry was there with my sister, embarrassed me much, for, beyond the fact that she disliked Henry intensely, there was the further fact—most offensive to her—that Mr. Bradford was socially patronizing the poor, and bringing me, her *protégé*, into association with them. Here was where my chain galled me, and made me realize my slavery. I saw the thrill of anger that shot through her face, and recognized the effort she made to control her words. She did not speak at first, and not until she felt perfectly sure of self-control did she say:

"Mr. Bradford is very unwise. He inflicts a great wrong upon young people without position or expectations, when he undertakes to raise them to his own social level. How he could do such a thing as he did last night is more than I can imagine, unless he wishes either to humiliate you or offend me."

For that one moment how I longed to pour out my love for Henry and Claire, and to speak my sense of justice in the vindication of Mr. Bradford! It was terrible to sit still and hold my tongue while the ties of blood and friendship were contemned, and the motives of my hospitable host were misconstrued so cruelly. Yet I could not open my lips. I dreaded a collision with her as if she had been a serpent, or a furnace of fire, or a hedge of thorns. Ay, I was mean enough to explain that I had no expectation of meeting either Henry or my sister there; and she was adroit enough to reply that she was at least sure of that without my saying so.

Then I talked fully of Mr. Grimshaw's call, and gave such details of the conversation that occurred as I could without making Mr. Bradford too prominent.

"So Mr. Bradford doesn't like Mr. Bedlow," she remarked; "but Mr. Bradford is a trifle whimsical in his likes and dislikes. I'm sure I've always heard Mr. Bedlow well spoken of. He has the credit of having done a great deal of good, and if he is coming here, Arthur, I think you cannot do better than to go and hear him for yourself."

Like a flash of light there passed through my mind the thought that Providence had not only thus opened the way for me, but with an imperative finger had directed me to walk in it. God had made the wrath of woman to praise Him, and the remainder He had restrained. Imagining myself to be thus directed, I should not have dared to avoid Mr. Bedlow's preaching. The whole interview with Mr. Grimshaw, the fact that, contrary to my wont, I had not found myself in sympathy with my old friend, Mr. Bradford, and the strange and unlooked-for result of my conversation with Mrs. Sanderson, shaped themselves into a divine mandate to whose authority my spirit bowed in ready obedience.

Mr. Bedlow made his appearance in Mr. Grimshaw's pulpit on the following Sunday; and a great throng of excited and expectant people, attracted by the notoriety of the preacher, and moved by the influences of the time, were in attendance. The hush of solemnity that pervaded the assembly when these two men entered the desk impressed me deeply. My spirit was thrilled with strange apprehension. My emotional nature was in chaos; and such crystallizations of opinion, thought, and feeling as had taken place in me during a life-long course of religious nurture and education were broken up. Outside of the church, and entirely lacking that dramatic experience of conversion and regeneration which all around me regarded as the only true beginning of a religious life, my whole soul lay open, quick and quivering, to the influences of the hour, and the words which soon fell upon it.

The pastor conducted the opening services, and I had never seen him in such a mood. Inspired by the presence of an immense congregation and by the spirit of the time, he rose entirely out of the mechanisms of his theology and his stereotyped forms of expression, and poured out the burden of his soul in a prayer that melted every heart before him. Deprecating the judgments of the Most High on the coldness and worldliness of the church; beseeching the Spirit of all Grace to come and work its own great miracles upon those who loved the Master, moving them to penitence, self-sacrifice, humility and prayer; entreating that Spirit to plant the arrows of conviction in all unconverted souls, and to bring a great multitude of these into the Kingdom—a multitude so great that they should be like doves flocking to their windows—he prayed like a man inspired. His voice trembled and choked with emotion, and the tears coursed down his cheeks unheeded. It seemed as if he could not pause, or be denied.

Of Mr. Bedlow's sermon that followed I can give no fitting idea. After a severe denunciation of the coldness of the church that grieved and repelled the Spirit of God, he turned to those without the fold—to the unconverted and impenitent. He told us that God was angry with us every day, that every imagination of the thoughts of our hearts was only evil continually, that we were exposed every moment to death and the perdition of ungodly men, and that it was our duty to turn, then and there, from the error of our ways, and to seek and secure the pardon which a pitying Christ extended to us—a pardon which could be had for the taking. Then he painted with wonderful power the joy and peace that follow the consciousness of sin forgiven, and the glories of that heaven which the Saviour had gone to prepare for those who love Him.

I went home blind, staggering, almost benumbed—with the words ringing in my ears that it had been my duty before rising from my seat to give myself to the Saviour, and to go out of the door rejoicing in the possession of a hope which should be as an anchor in all the storms of my life; yet I did not know what the process was. I was sure I did not know. I had not the slightest comprehension of what was required of me, yet the fact did not save me from the impression that I had committed a great sin. I went to my room and tried to pray, and spent half an hour of such helpless and pitiful distress as I cannot describe. Then there arose in me a longing for companionship. I could not unbosom myself to Mrs. Sanderson. Henry's calm spirit and sympathetic counsels were beyond my reach. Mr. Bradford was not in the church, and I could only think of my father, and determine that I would see him. I ate but little dinner, made no conversation with Mrs. Sanderson, and, toward night, left the house and sought my father's home.

I found the house as solemn as death. All the family save Claire had heard Mr. Bedlow, and my mother was profoundly dejected. A cloud rested upon my brothers and sisters. My father apprehended at once the nature of my errand, and, by what seemed to be a mutual impulse and understanding, we passed into an unoccupied room and closed the door. The moment I found myself alone with him I threw my arms around his neck, and bursting into an uncontrollable fit of weeping, exclaimed: "Oh, father! father! what shall I do?"

For years I had not come to him with a trouble. For years I had not reposed in him a single heart-confidence, and for the first time in his life he put both his arms affectionately around me and embraced me. Minutes passed while we stood thus. I could not see his face, for my own was bowed upon his shoulder, but I could feel his heart-beats, and the convulsions of emotion which shook him in every fiber. At last he gently put me off, led me to a seat, and sat down beside me. He took my hand, but he could not speak.

"Oh, father! what shall I do?" I exclaimed again.

"Go to God, my boy, and repeat the same words to him with the same earnestness."

"But he is angry with me," I said, "and you are not. You pity me and love me. I am your child. You cannot help being sorry for me."

"You are his child too, my boy, by relations a thousand times tenderer and more significant than those which make you mine. He loves you and pities you more than I can."

"But I don't know how to give myself to him," I said.

"I have had the impression and the hope," my father responded, "that you had already given yourself to him."

"Oh, not in this way at all," I said.

My father had his own convictions, but he was almost morbidly conscientious in all his dealings with the souls around him. Fearful of meddling with that which the Gracious Spirit had in charge and under influence, and modest in the assertion of views which might possibly weaken the hold of conviction upon me; feeling, too, that he did not know me well enough to direct me, and fearful that he might arrest a process which, perfected, might redeem me, he simply said: "I am not wise; let us pray together, that we may be led aright."

Then he kneeled and prayed for me. Ah! how the blessed words of that prayer have lingered in my memory! Though not immediately fruitful in my experience, they came to me long years after, loaded with the balm of healing. "Oh, Father in Heaven!" he said, "this is our boy,—thy child and mine. Thou lovest and pitiest him more than I can. Help him to go to Thee as he has come to me, and to say in perfect submission, ' Oh, Father, what shall I do ! ' "

I went home at last somewhat calmed, because I had had sympathy, and, for a few moments, had leaned upon another nature and rested. I ate little, and, as soon as the hour arrived, departed to attend the evening service, previously having asked old Jenks to attend the meeting and walk home with me, for I was afraid to return alone.

A strange and gloomy change had come over the sky; and the weather, which had been extremely cold for a week, had grown warm. The snow under my feet was soft and yielding, and already little rivulets were coursing along the ruts worn by the sleighs. The nerves which had been braced by the tonic of the cold, clear air were relaxed, and with the uncertain footing of the streets I went staggering to the church.

In the endeavor now to analyze my feelings I find it impossible to believe that I was convinced that my life had been one of bold and intentional sin. A considerable part of my pain, I know, arose from the fact that I could not realize my own sinfulness as it had been represented to me. I despaired because I could not despair. I was distressed because I could not be sufficiently distressed. There was one sin, however, of which I had a terrified consciousness, viz., that of rejecting the offer of mercy which had been made to me in the morning, and of so rejecting it as to be in danger of forever grieving away the Spirit of God which I believed was at work upon my heart. This was something definite and dreadful, though I felt perfectly ignorant of the exact thing required of me and impotent to perform it. If I could have known the precise nature of the surrender demanded of me, and could have comprehended the effort I was called upon to make, I believe I should have been ready for both; but in truth I had been so mystified by the preacher, so puzzled by his representation of the miracle of conversion, which he made to appear to be dependent on God's sovereign grace entirely, and yet so entirely dependent on me that the whole guilt of remaining unconverted would rest with me; I was so expectant of some mighty, overwhelming influence that would bear me to a point where I could see through the darkness and the discord—an influence which did not come—that I was paralyzed and helpless.

I was early in the church, and saw the solemn groups as they entered and gradually filled the pews. The preachers, too, were early in the desk. Mr. Bedlow sat where he could see me and read my face. I knew that his searching, magnetic eyes were upon me, and in the exalted condition of my sensibilities I felt them. In the great hush that followed the entrance of the crowd and preceded the beginning of the exercises I saw him slowly rise and walk down the pulpit stairs. I had never known anything of his methods, and was entirely unprepared for what followed. Reaching the aisle, he walked directly to where I sat, and raising his finger, pointed it at me and said: "Young man, are you a Christian?"

"I suppose not," I answered.

"Do you ever expect to become one?"

"I do," I replied.

At this he left me, and went to one and another in the congregation, putting his question and making some remark. Sensitive men and women hung their heads, and tried to evade his inquiries by refusing to look at him.

At length he went back to his desk, and said that the church could do no better than to hold for a few minutes a season of prayer, preparatory to the services of the evening; and then he added: "Will some brother pray for a young man who expects to become a Christian, and pray that that expectation may be taken away from him."

Thereupon a young man, full of zeal, kneeled before the congregation and poured out his heart for me, and prayed as he had been asked to pray: that my expectation to become a Christian might be taken away from me. He was, however, considerate and kind enough so far to modify the petition as to beg that I might lose my expectation in the immediate realization of a Christian experience—that my hope to become a Christian might be swallowed up in my hope of a Christian's reward.

This kindness of the young man, however, to whose zeal and good-will I give hearty honor, could not efface the sore sense of wrong I had suffered at the hand of Mr. Bedlow. Why he should have singled me out in the throng for such an awful infliction I did not know, and why he should have asked anybody to pray that all expectation of becoming a Christian should be taken away from me I could not imagine. I felt that I was misunderstood and outraged, at first, and as my anger died away, or was quenched by other emotions, I found that I was still more deeply puzzled than before. Was I not carefully and prayerfully seeking? And was not this expectation the one thing which made my life endurable? Would I not give all the world to find my feet upon the sure foundation? Had I not in my heart of hearts determined to find what there was to be found if I could, or die?

No: Mr. Bedlow, meaning well no doubt, and desiring to lead me nearer to spiritual rest, had thrust me into deeper and wilder darkness; and in that darkness, haunted by forms of torment and terror, I sat through one of the most impressive sermons and exhortations I had ever heard. I went out of the church at last as utterly hopeless and wretched as I could be. There was a God of wrath above me, because there was the guilt of unfulfilled duty gnawing at my conscience. It seemed as if the great tragedy of the universe were being performed in my soul. Sun, moon, stars, the kingdoms and glory of the world—what were all these, either in themselves or to me, compared with the interests of a soul on which rested the burden of a decision for its own heaven or hell?

As I emerged into the open air, I met Jenks at the door, waiting for me, and as I lifted my hot face I felt the cold rain falling upon it. Pitchy darkness, unrelieved save by the dim lights around the town and the blotched and rapidly melting snow, had settled upon the world. I clutched the old servant's arm, and struck off in silence towards home. We had hardly walked the distance of a block before there came a flash of blinding lightning, and we were in the midst of that impressive anomaly, a January thunder-storm. It was strange how harmoniously this storm supplemented the influences of the services at the church, from which I had just retired. To me it was the crowning terror of the night. I had no question that it was directed by the same unseen power which had been struggling with me all day, and that it was expressive of His infinite anger. As we hurried along, unprotected in the pouring rain, flash after flash illuminated the darkness, and peal after peal of thunder hurtled over the city, rolled along the heavens, and echoed among the distant hills. I walked in constant fear of being struck dead, and of passing to the judgment unreconciled and unredeemed. I felt that my soul was dealing directly with the great God, and under the play of his awful enginery of destruction I realized my helplessness. I could only pray to him, with gasps of agony, and in whispers: "Oh, do not crush me! Spare me, and I will do anything! Save my life, and it shall be thine!"

When I arrived at the house I did not dare to go in, for then I should be left alone. Without a word I led Jenks to the stable, and, dripping with the rain, we passed in.

"Oh, Jenks," I said, "I must pray, and you must stay with me. I cannot be left alone."

I knelt upon the stable-floor, and the old man, touched with sympathy, and awed by the passion which possessed me, knelt at my side. Oh, what pledges and promises I gave in that prayer, if God would spare my life! How wildly I asked for pardon, and how earnestly did I beseech the Spirit of all Grace to stay with me, and never to be grieved away, until his work was perfected in me!

The poor old man, with his childish mind, could not understand my abandonment to grief and terror; but while I knelt I felt his trembling arm steal around me, and knew that he was sobbing. His heart was deeply moved by pity, but the case was beyond his comprehension. He could say nothing, but the sympathy was very grateful to me.

And all this time there was another arm around me, whose touch I was too benumbed to feel; there was another heart beside me, tender with sympathy, whose beatings I was too much agitated to apprehend; there was a voice calling to the tempest within me, "Peace! be still!" but I could not hear it. Oh, infinite Father! Oh, loving and pitying Christ! Why could I not have seen thee, as thou didst look down upon and pity thy terror-stricken child? Why could I not have seen thy arms extended toward me, and thy eyes beaming with ineffable love, calling me to thy forgiving embrace? How could I have done thee the dishonor to suppose that the simple old servant kneeling at my side was tenderer and more pitiful than thou?

We both grew chilly at last, and passed quietly into the house. Mrs. Sanderson had retired, but had left a bright fire upon the hearth, at which both of us warmed and dried ourselves. The storm, meantime, had died away, though the lightning still flapped its red wings against the windows, and the dull reverberations of the thunder came to me from the distance. With the relief from what seemed to be the danger of imminent death, I had the strength to mount to my room alone, and, after another prayer which failed to lift my burden, I consigned myself to my bed. The one thought that possessed me as I lay down was that I might never wake if I should go to sleep. My nervous exhaustion was such that when sinking into sleep I started many times from my pillow, tossing the clothes from me, and gasping as if I had been sinking into an abyss. Sleep came at last, however, and I awoke on the morrow, conscious that I had rested, and rejoicing at least in the fact that my day of probation was not yet past. My heart kindled for a moment as I looked from my window into the face of the glorious sun, and the deep blue heaven, but sank within me when I remembered my promises, and felt that the struggle of the previous day was to be renewed.

This struggle I do not propose to dwell upon further in extended detail. If the record of it thus far is as painful to read as it is to write, the reader will have tired of it already. It lasted for weeks, and I never rationally saw my way out of that blindness. There were literally hundreds in the city who professed to have found a great and superlatively joyous peace, but I did not find it, nor did it come to me in any way by which I dreamed it might come.

The vital point with me was to find some influence so powerful that I could not resist it. I felt myself tossing upon a dangerous sea, just outside the harbor, between which and me there stretched an impassable bar. So, wretched and worn with anxious waiting, I looked for the coming in of some mighty wave which would lift my sinking bark over the forbidding obstacle, into the calm waters that mirrored upon their banks the domes and dwellings of the city of the Great King.

Sometimes I tired of Mr. Bedlow, and went to other churches, longing always to hear some sermon or find some influence that would do for me that which I could not do for myself. I visited my father many times, but he could not help me, beyond what he had already done. One of the causes of my perplexity was the fact that Henry attended the prayer-meetings, and publicly participated in the exercises. I heard, too, that, in a quiet way, he was very influential in his school, and that many of his pupils had begun a religious life. Why was he different from myself? Why was it necessary that I should go through this experience of fear and torment, while he escaped it altogether? All our previous experience had been nearly identical. For years we had been subjected to the same influences, had struggled for the same self-mastery, had kneeled at the same bed in daily devotion; yet here he was, busy in Christian service, steadily rejoicing in Christian hope, into which he had grown through processes as natural as those by which the rose-tree rises to the grace of inflorescence. I see it all now, but then it not only perplexed me, but filled me with weak complaining at my harder lot.

During these eventful weeks I often met Millie Bradford on

her way to and from school. I have no doubt that, from her window, she had made herself familiar with my habits of going and coming, and had timed her own so as to fall in with me.

In communities not familiar with the character and history of a New England revival, it would be impossible to conceive of the universality of the influence which they exert during the time of their highest activity. Multitudes of men neglect their business. Meetings are held during every evening of the week, and sometimes during all the days of the week. Children, gathered in their own little chambers, hold prayer-meetings. Religion is the all-absorbing topic, with old and young.

Millie was like the rest of us; and, forbidden to hear Mr. Bedlow preach, she had determined to win her experience at home. It touches me now even to tears to remember how she used to meet me in the street, and ask me how I was getting along, how I liked Mr. Bedlow, and whether he had helped me. She told me that she and her mother were holding little prayer-meetings together, but that Aunt Flick was away pretty much all the time. She was seeking to become a Christian, and at last she told me that she thought she had become one. I was rational enough to see that it was not necessary for an innocent child like her to share my graver experiences. Indeed, I listened eagerly to her expressions of simple faith and trust, and to her recital of the purposes of life to which she had committed herself. One revelation which she made in confidence, but which I am sure was uttered because she wanted me to think well of her father, interested me much. She said her father prayed very much alone, though he did not attend the meetings. The thought of my old friend toiling in secret over the problem which absorbed us all was very impressive.

Thus weeks passed away, and the tide which rose to its flood began to ebb. I could see that the meetings grew less frequent, and that the old habits of business and pleasure were reasserting themselves. Conversions were rarer, and the blazing fervor of action and devotion cooled. As I realized this, and, in realizing it, found that I was just as far from the point at which I had aimed as I was at the beginning, a strange, desperate despair seized me. I could hope for no influences in the future more powerful than those to which I had been subjected. The stimulus to resolution and endeavor was nearly expended. Yet I had many times vowed to the Most High that before that season had passed away I would find Him, and, with him, peace, if He and it were to be found. What was I to do?

At last there came a day of in-gathering. The harvest was to be garnered. A great number of men, women, and youth were to be received into the church. I went early, and took a seat in the gallery, where I could see the throng as they presented themselves in the aisles to make their profession of faith and unite in their covenant. When called upon they took their places, coming forward from all parts of the audience in front of the Communion table. Among them were both Henry and Claire. At sight of them I grew sick. Passage after passage of Scripture that seemed applicable to my condition, crowded into my mind. They came from the North and the South and the East and the West, and sat down in the Kingdom of God, and I, a child of the Kingdom, baptized into the name of the Ineffable, was cast out. The harvest was past, the summer was ended, and my soul was not saved! I witnessed the ceremonies with feelings mingled of despair, bitterness, and desperation. On the faces of these converts, thus coming into the fold, there was impressed the seal of a great and solemn joy. Within my bosom there burned the feeling that I had honestly tried to do my duty, and that my endeavors had been spurned. In a moment, to which I had been led by processes whose end I could not see, my will gave way, and I said, "I will try no longer. This is the end." Every resolution and purpose within me was shivered by the fall.

To what depth of perdition I might be hurled—under what judgment I might be crushed—I could not tell, and hardly cared to imagine. Quite to my amazement, I found myself at perfect peace. What did it mean? Not only was the burden gone, but there thrilled through my soul a quick, strong joy. My spirit was like a broad sea, alive all over with sunlit ripples, with one broad track of glory that stretched across into the unfathomable heaven! I felt the smile of God upon me. I felt the love of God within me. Was I insane? Had satan appeared to me as an angel of light and deceived me? Was this conversion? I was so much in doubt in regard to the real nature of this experience, that when I left the house I spoke to no one of it. Emerging into the open air, I found myself in a new world. I walked the streets as lightly as if wings had been upon my shoulders, lifting me from point to point through all the passage homeward. Ah, how blue the heavens were, and how broad and beautiful the world! What a blessed thing it was to live! How sweet were the faces not only of friends, but even of those whom I did not know! How gladly would I have embraced every one of them! It was as if I had been unclothed of my mortality, and clothed upon with the immortal. I was sure that heaven could hold no joy superior to that.

When passing Mr. Bradford's, I saw Millie at the window. She beckoned to me, and I went to her door. "How is it now?" she said.

"I don't know, Millie," I replied, "but I think it is all right. I never felt before as I do now."

"Oh, I was getting so tired!" said she. "I've been praying for you for days, and days, and days! and hoping and hoping you'd get through."

I could only thank her, and press her little hand; and then I hurried to my home, mounted to my room, shut and locked the door, and sat down to think.

CHAPTER X.

I JOIN A CHURCH THAT LEAVES OUT MR. BRADFORD AND MILLIE.

How shall I write the history of the few weeks that followed my new experience? I had risen, as on wings, from the depths of despair to the heights of hope. I had emerged from a valley of shadows, haunted by ten thousand forms of terror and shapes of anguish, and sat down upon the sunny hills of peace. The world, which had become either mocking or meaningless to me, was illuminated with loving expression in every feature. Far above the deep blue of the winter skies my imagination caught the sheen of winged forms and the far echoes of happy angel-voices. I lifted my face to the sun, and, shutting my eyes, felt the smile of God upon me. Every wind that blew brought its ministry of blessing. Every cloud that swept the sky bore its message of good-will from heaven. I loved life, I loved the world, I loved every living thing I saw, and, more than all, I loved the Great Father who had bestowed upon me such gracious gifts of hope and healing.

Mrs. Sanderson, though she had said little, and had received no confidence from me, had been troubled for many weeks. She had seen in my haggard eyes and weary look the evidences of a great trial and struggle; but without the power to enter into it, or to help me out of it, she had never done more than to ask me if, for my health's sake, it would not be better for me to attend fewer meetings and take more sleep. The weeks that followed were only more satisfactory to her from the conviction that I was happier, for I gave myself with hearty zeal to the work which I felt had been imposed upon me.

My father was happy in my new happiness, never doubting

that it had come to me through the Grace of Heaven. I was assured on every hand that I had passed through that change of regeneration which was the true basis in me, and in many at least, of the new life. Meeting Mr. Bradford, I spoke freely to him of my change, and he told me with a sigh that he was glad I was at peace. He evidently did not say all that he felt, but he said nothing to discourage me.

It soon became known to Mr. Grimshaw and the members of his church that I had become a convert, and I found abundant opportunities at once to exercise such gifts as I possessed to induce others to drink at the fountain from which I had drawn such draughts of peace and pleasure, I prayed in public; I exhorted; I went from one to another of my own age with personal persuasions. Nay, I was alluded to and held up, in public and private, as one of the most notable of the trophies which had been won in the great struggle with the powers of darkness through which the church had passed.

I look back now upon the public life that I lived in those youthful days with wonder. Audiences that I then faced and addressed without embarrassment would now send fever into my lips and tongue, or strike me dumb. I rejoiced then in a prominence from which I should now shrink with a sensitiveness of pain quite insupportable. I was the youthful marvel of the town; and people flocked again to the church where I was to be seen and heard as if a new Bedlow had come down to them from the skies.

This publicity did not please Mrs. Sanderson, but she saw farther, alas! than I did, and knew that such exaltation could not be perpetual. Could I have had a wise counsellor then, it would have saved me years of wandering and years of sorrow. The tendency of this public work was to make me vain, and induce a love of the sound of my own voice. Without experience, flattered by attention, stimulated by the assurance that I was doing a great deal of good, and urged on by my own delight in action, I fairly took the bit in my teeth, and ran such a race as left me at last utterly exhausted. I went from meeting to meeting all over the city. There was hardly a church in which my voice was not heard. Everywhere I was thanked and congratulated. I did not realize then as I do now that I was moved by a thirst for praise, and that motives most human mingled strangely and strongly with the divine in urging me forward. O Heaven! to think that I, a poor child in life and experience, should have labored in Thy name to win a crown to my personal vanity!

I shudder now at the cruelty practiced upon the young nearly everywhere, in bringing them to the front, and exposing them to such temptations as those which then had the power to poison all my motives, to brush away from my spirit the bloom of youthful modesty, and to expose me to a process which was certain to ultimate in spiritual torpor and doubt. I always tremble and sicken when I behold a child or youth delighting in the exercises of a public exhibition; and when I see, inside or outside of church walls, children bred to boldness through the public show of themselves and their accomplishments, and realize what part of their nature is stimulated to predominance by the process, and what graces are extinguished by it, I do not wonder at the lack of reverence in American character, and that exhaustion of sensibility which makes our churches so faint and fitful in feeling.

Having given up all my earlier ideas of religion, and learned to regard them as wholly inadequate and unworthy, I could be in my new work little more than a parrot. I had passed through but a single phase of what I had learned to regard as a genuine religious experience, and my counsels were but the repetitions of what I had heard. If some wise man or woman could have told me of myself—of the proprieties that belong to the position of a neophyte—of the dangers of public labor, and of being publicly petted and exhibited, how well for me would it have been! But I had no such counsellor. On the contrary, I was seized upon at once as a fresh instrumentality for carrying on a work already waning. I am ashamed to think of the immodesty of some of my personal approaches to my elders whom I regarded as needing my ministry, and humiliated by the memory of the considerate forbearance with which I was treated for religion's and my motive's sake.

It was in labors and experiences like these that a few weeks passed away. Another in-gathering of the great spiritual harvest approached. I, among others, was to make a public profession of my faith, and become a member of the church. Mr. Grimshaw put upon me the task of persuading the young of my own age to join me in this solemn self-dedication, and I had great success in my mission.

Among the considerable number whom I had selected as proper subjects of my counsels and persuasions, was my interesting friend Millie Bradford: but I knew she was quite too young to decide so momentous a question, and that her father would not permit her to decide it for herself. To tell the truth, I did not like to meet Mr. Bradford with my proposition, for I anticipated objections, and did not feel qualified to argue with him. I consulted with Mr. Grimshaw in regard to the case, and it was finally decided that we should visit Mr. Bradford together.

Accordingly we called upon him, and spent an evening in conversation, which, although it won no new members to my group, left a deep impression upon my mind and memory.

The conversation was begun by Mr. Grimshaw, who said: "We have called, Mr. Bradford, with the purpose of conferring with you in regard to your daughter Millie. I know but little of her, but I learn through Arthur that she is a sharer in the blessings of our great revival. Have you any objection to her union with our church, provided she shall choose to become a member?"

"Have you no invitation for any one else in the family?" inquired Mr. Bradford, with a smile.

"I was not aware that there were other converts in the family," responded the minister.

"I speak it with great humility, Mr. Grimshaw," said Mr. Bradford, "but I count myself a disciple. I am a learner at the feet of your Master and mine ; and I have been a learner for years. I do not regard myself as having attained, or fully apprehended, but I follow on, and I should like society on the way, as well as any one."

"But your views do not accord with those professed by our church," said Mr. Grimshaw.

"I do not know what business the church may legitimately have with my private opinions. I learn from the New Testament that he who repents and believes on the Lord Jesus Christ shall be saved. A man who does this belongs at least to the invisible church, and I do not recognize the right of a body of men calling themselves a church to shut out from their communion any man or woman who belongs to the church invisible, or any one whom the Master counts among his disciples."

"But we must have some standard of faith and belief," said Mr. Grimshaw.

"I suppose you must," responded Mr. Bradford, "but why should you construct it of non-essential materials? Why should you build a high fence around your church, and insist that every man shall climb every rail, when the first is all that the Master asks him to climb. I recognize repentance and trust as the basis of a Christian character and life, and I regard character as the one grand result at which the Author of Christianity aimed. He desired to make good men out of bad men ; and repentance and trust form the basis of the process. When you go beyond this, with your dogmas and your creeds, you infringe upon the liberty of those whom repentance and trust have made free. Personally, I feel that I am suffering a great wrong, inflicted in ignorance and with good motives no doubt, but still a wrong, in that I am shut out from Christian sympathy and fellowship. I will not profess to believe any more than I do believe. It is simply impossible for me, a rational, honest, mature man, to accept that which you prescribe for me. I am perfectly willing that you should believe what seems to you to be true, touching all these points of doctrine. I only insist that you shall be a Christian in heart and life—an honest disci ple. If you cannot give me the same liberty, under the same conditions, we can never get any nearer together."

"You seem to forget," responded the minister, "that our creed is the product of whole ages of Christian wisdom—that it has been framed by men of wide and profound experience, who have learned by that experience what is essential to the stability and purity of the church."

"And you seem to forget," said Mr. Bradford, "that the making and defense of creeds have rent the seamless garment of the Lord into ten thousand fragments—that they have been the instruments for the destruction of the unity of the church in fact and feeling—that they have not only been the subjects of controversies that have disgraced the church before the world, and embittered the relations of large bodies of Christians, but have instigated the cruelest persecutions and the most outrageous murders and martyrdoms. You are not so bigoted as to deny that there are Christians among all the sects; and you are liberal enough to give to the different sects the liberty of faith which they claim. The world is growing better in this thing, and is not so intolerant as it was. Now, why will you not give me the same liberty, as a man, that you give to churches founded on creeds at variance with yours? You invite the teachers of other sects into your pulpit. You invite their people to your communion table, while you shut me away by conditions that are just as impossible to me as they would be to them."

I could see that Mr. Grimshaw was not only overwhelmed in argument but deeply moved in feeling. He grasped Mr. Bradford's hand, and said: "My dear sir, it would give me one of the greatest pleasures of my life to receive you into our communion, for I believe in your sincerity and in your character, but I could not if I would."

"I know it," responded Mr. Bradford: "your sympathies go beyond your creed, and your most earnest convictions stop short of it. Your hands are tied, and your tongue must be dumb. You and your church will go on in the old way. The young who do not think, and the mature who will not try to think, or do not dare to try, will accept what you prescribe for them. Women, more trustful and religious than men, will constitute the majority of your members. In the mean time, the thinking men—the strong, influential, practical men of society —the men of culture, enterprise, and executive power—will remain outside of the church—shut out by a creed which their reason refuses to accept."

"I am afraid the creed is not altogether to blame for their exclusion," said the minister. "'Not many wise'—you remember the quotation."

"When Christianity was an apostasy from a church to which all the wise and mighty were attached," replied Mr. Bradford, "your quotation was doubtless true as a statement of fact, but we belong to another nation and age. I hold myself a type and representative of a large class, who cannot enter the church without self stultification and a sacrifice of that liberty of thought and opinion which is their birthright. We cannot afford to do without you, and you cannot afford to do without us. It is your business to make a home for us, for we are all passing on to that stage and realm of being where opinions will be of small account, and where character will decide everything."

"We have wandered very far from your daughter, Mr. Bradford, about whom we came to talk," said Mr. Grimshaw.

An expression of pain passed over Mr. Bradford's face. Then he rose, and walking to a door which closed another room, opened it, and called his daughter. Millie entered the room with a question in her eyes, and shaking hands with us, went to her father's side, where she stood with his arm around her during the remainder of the interview.

"Millie," said her father, "Mr. Grimshaw and Arthur have come here to invite you to join the church. Would you like to do so?"

"If you and mamma think I ought to," she replied.

At this moment, Mrs. Bradford, conjecturing, I suppose, the object of our visit, entered the room, and giving us a most friendly greeting, took a seat near her daughter. Mr. Bradford repeated our proposal to her, and Millie's reply to it.

"I should regard it as one of the sweetest satisfactions of my life to have my child with me in church communion," she said, looking down to hide the tears that she felt filling her eyes.

"And I sympathize with you entirely in your feeling," added Mr. Bradford.

"Then," said Mr. Grimshaw, "nothing will stand in the way, provided, upon examination, your daughter gives evidence of an intelligent entrance upon a Christian experience."

"Which means, I suppose," said Mr. Bradford, "that if she will accept your whole creed and scheme on trust, as well as give evidence of having determined upon a Christian life, you will endow her with the privileges of membership."

"We have but one condition for all, as you know," responded the minister.

"I suppose so; and it is my duty to tell you that it is a very cruel thing; for her intelligence reaches no further than the one essential thing which makes her a Christian child, viz., personal loyalty to the Master. Beyond this she knows absolutely nothing, and for her it is enough. To insist that she shall receive a whole body of divinity about which she is utterly ignorant, and which, at present, has no relation to her Christian character and life, is to do that which you have no right to do. When Jesus took little children in his arms and blessed them, and declared that of such was the kingdom of heaven, he did not impose any conditions upon them. It was sufficient for him that they were in his arms, and had trust and confidence enough to nestle and be contented and happy there. You take the responsibility of going beyond him, and of making conditions which cannot be complied with without a surrender of all future liberty of thought and opinion. You have members in your church to-day who committed themselves to opinions when young, or under excitement, that they now hold most loosely, or with questionings that are a constant torture to them. I know it, for they have told me so; and I cannot consent that my child shall be denied the free and unrestrained formation of opinions when her maturer mind becomes able to form them. The reason that has no range but the bounds of a creed, constructed by human hands, will become dwarfed as certainly as the wings of a bird are weakened by the wires of a cage."

Mr. Grimshaw listened attentively to the speaker, and then said : " I fear that your ideas would form a very poor basis for a church. We should be deprived of any principle or power of cohesion, without unity of belief. Such liberty as you desire, or seem to think desirable, would soon degenerate into license. The experience of the church has proved it, and the united wisdom of the church has declared it."

" My ideas of the true basis of the church are very simple," said Mr. Bradford. "I would make it an organization of Christian disciples—of Christian learners ; you would make it a conservatory of those who have arrived at the last conclusions in dogmatic theology. I would make it a society of those who have accepted the Master, and pledged their hearts and lives to him, with everything to learn and the liberty to learn it by such means as they can command ; you would frame it with limits to all progress. You would make it a school where all are professors; I would make it a school where all are learners. In short, you would make a sectarian church, and I would make a Christian church ; and I cannot but believe that there is such a church awaiting us in the future—a church which will receive both me and my daughter, to give me the rest and fellowship I long for, and her the nurture, restraint and support which she will need among the world's great temptations."

I do not know what the minister thought of all this, for he said but little. He had been accustomed to these discussions with Mr. Bradford, and either deemed them unfruitful of good or found it difficult to maintain his position. He felt sure of me, and did not regard it of consequence to talk on my account. As Mr. Bradford closed, he sighed and said :

"Well, Millie, I suppose you will do as your father wishes, and stay away from us."

Millie looked at her father and then at her mother, with a quick, earnest glance of inquiry.

Mrs. Bradford said: "Mr. Bradford and I never differ on anything relating to our child. So far as our creed is concerned I am entirely content with it; but I have no wish to commit my child to it, though I freely instruct her in it."

"Very well," said the minister, "perhaps it will be better to leave her with you for the present."

Then he advanced to Mr. Bradford for a private conference upon some other subject, apparently, and Millie started quickly and walked to the window where I joined her.

"Are n't you sorry?" I inquired.

"No."

"I thought you would be," I said.

"No, it is all right. Father knows. Don't you think he's splendid?"

"I suppose he thinks he is right," I responded.

"Why, I know he's right," she said warmly. "He's always right; and isn't it sweet of him to let me hear him talk about everything?"

Here was the personal loyalty again. Beyond this the girl could not go. She could trust her father and her Master. She could obey both and love both, and it was all of religion that she was capable of. I supposed that the minister must know better than any of us, but I had no doubt of Millie's fitness for the church, and wondered why it was that a baptized child should be shut out of the fold by a creed she was utterly incapable of comprehending. I confess, too, that I sympathized with Mr. Bradford's view of the church as it related to himself, yet I had given my trust to the minister, and it was only my personal loyalty to him that reconciled me to his opposing opinions. Then there flashed upon me the consciousness that I was to profess before God and men a belief in dogmas that I had not even examined, and was entirely without the power of explaining or defending to myself or others. The fact made me tremble, and I dismissed it as soon as possible.

I fear that I should weary my reader by dwelling upon the spiritual experiences that attended the assumption of my vows. Since the memorable day on which I stood among twenty others, and publicly pledged my life to the Redeemer, and gave my unqualified assent to the doctrines of the creed, I have never been able to witness a similar scene without tears. With all the trust natural to youth I received that which was presented to me, and with all the confidence of youth in its own power to fulfill its promises, I entered into the most solemn covenant which man can make. There was no suspicion in me of a possible reaction. There was no anticipation of temptations before which I should tremble or fall. There was no cloud that portended darkness or storm. I regarded myself as entering a fold from which I should go out no more, save under the conduct and ward of a Shepherd who would lead me only through green pastures and beside still waters.

All my friends, including Mrs. Sanderson, were present. Mr. Bradford and his family sat near me, and I saw that he had been deeply moved. He read the future better than I, and saw before my intense and volatile spirit that which I could not see. He knew the history of one human heart, and he interpreted the future of mine by his own. At the close of the services Mrs. Sanderson drove home alone with Jenks; and the Bradfords with Henry and my own family walked home together. As I left my father at his door, with Henry and Claire, I found myself with Millie. We fell behind her father and mother, and after she had looked around to make sure that she was not observed, she unfolded her handkerchief and showed me a crumb of the sacramental bread.

"Where did you get it?" I inquired.

"I prayed that it might drop when it was handed to my mother, and it did," she replied.

"What are you going to do with it?" I inquired.

"I am going to my room when I get home, and have a communion all by myself."

"But do you think it will be right?" I inquired.

"I don't think *He* will care. *He* knows that I love him, and that it is the only chance I have. It is his bread, and came from his table, and Mr. Grimshaw has nothing to do with it."

I was dumb with astonishment, and could offer no remonstrance. Indeed I sympathized with her so much that I could not have deprived her of her anticipated enjoyment.

Then I asked her what she would do for wine.

"I shall kiss my mother's lips," she replied, and then added: "I wonder if she will know that anything is gone, as the Saviour did when the woman touched him?"

I think if I could have retired with Millie to her seclusion, and shared her crumb away from the eyes of a curious world, and the distractions of the public gaze, I should have come out stronger and purer for the feast. I left her at her door, and went slowly home, imagining the little girl at prayer, and tasting the crumb which had fallen from the Master's table. The thought of the reverent kiss which the mother was to receive that night, all unconscious of the draught of spiritual comfort which her child would quaff there, quite overcame me.

And it was this child, with her quick insight and implicit faith, that had been shut out of the fold because she had no opinions! It was her father, too, carefully seeking and prayerfully learning, who had been refused admittance, because he would not surrender his reason and his liberty of thought! Already I began to doubt the infallibility of my Pope. Already there had crept into my mind the suspicion that there was something wrong in a policy which made more of sound opinions than of sound character. Already I felt that there was something about these two persons that was higher in Christian experience than anything I could claim. Already I had become dimly conscious of a spiritual pride in myself, that I did not see in them, and convinced that they were better fitted to adorn a Christian profession than myself.

So the struggle was over, and I was called upon by the rapidly advancing spring to resume the studies which had long been interrupted. As I addressed myself with strong determination to my work, I was conscious of a greatly impaired power of application. The effect of the winter's excitement and absorption had been to dissipate my mental power, and destroy my habits of mental labor. It took me many weeks to get back upon my old track, and I was led through many discouragements. When I had fairly accomplished my purpose and felt that I was making genuine progress, I discovered that it was impossible to keep up the public life I had been leading, and the zeal which had spurred me on in my Christian work. For weeks I faithfully continued my attendance on the meetings of the church, which, by becoming less frequent, had adapted themselves somewhat to my new circumstances, but to my great sorrow I found my zest in their exercises gradually dying away. I prayed often and long that I might not become a back-slider, and that the joy and comfort of the early days might abide with me. It was all in vain. The excitement of sympathetic crowds and the predominance of a single topic in the public mind had passed away, and, unsupported by those stimuli, I was left to stand alone—an uncertain, tottering, self-suspicious youth—with the great work of life all before me.

Gradually the old motives which had actuated me came back and presented themselves; and to my sad surprise they found that in me which responded to them. The wealth which had held before me its glittering promise still possessed its charming power, and suggested its worldly delights. The brilliant college career which I had determined to achieve for honor's and glory's sake came up to me among my suspended purposes, and shone with all its old attractions. The pride of dress and social position was not dead—it had only slept, and waited but a touch and a nod to spring into life again. The temptations which the world held for my sensuous nature found my appetites and passions still unsubdued.

Then there came upon me first the conviction and the consciousness that my life was to be one of warfare, if it was to be a Christian life at all—that I was really back upon my old ground, and that whatever of genuine progress I should make would be through prayerful, rigid, persistent culture. That there was something unspeakably discouraging in this, I need not affirm. It had the power to make the experiences through which I had so recently passed seem altogether hollow and unreal. I had only dreamed of regeneration, after all. The new birth had only been the birth of a purpose, which needed nursing and strengthening and educating like an infant.

Still I would not, could not, admit that I had not made the genuine beginning of a religious life. If I had done this, I should have grown callous or desperate at once.

And now I beg the privilege of saying to those who may be interested in this narrative, that I have not addressed myself to the task of writing down revivals. I am detailing the experiences of a human soul. That revivals are useful in communities where great excitements are necessary to attract the attention of the careless and the vicious, I can well believe. That multitudes begin a religious life through their influence there is no doubt. That they are dangerous passages for the church to pass through would seem also to be well established, as by the laws of the human mind all great excitements and all extraordinary labors are followed by corresponding depressions and exhaustions. I seriously doubt whether Christian growth is greatly forwarded by these exceptional agencies. All true growth in the realm of nature is the result of a steady unfolding from a germ : and the realm of grace is ruled by the same Being who perfects the flower and builds the tree. I can afford to be misconstrued, misunderstood and misrepresented if I can do anything to direct the attention of the church to the fact that there are better methods of progress than those which are attended with such cost and such danger, and that in the Christian nurture of children and the wide opening of the Christian fold to them abides the hope of the church and the world. I shall be ten thousand times repaid for any suspicion of my motives, if I can bring a single pastor, or a single church, to the realization of the fact that true Christian beginnings are not necessarily conformed to any special dramatic experience ; that a pastor can lead his flock better than a stranger whose voice they do not know, and that their creeds are longer and more elaborate than they have any right to make. If the labor expended upon revivals were spread evenly over greater space, and applied with never-flagging persistency to the shaping and the nurture of the plastic and docile minds of the young, I am sure that the Christian kingdom would increase in numbers and advance in power by a progress at once natural, healthy and irresistible. The fiery shower that pours its flood upon the earth in an hour, leaves the ground fresh for the day, but it also leaves it scarred and seamed, the swollen torrents carrying half its wealth into the sea, while the steady rain of days sinks into the earth to nourish the roots of all things, and make the springs perennial.

CHAPTER XI.

THE OLD PORTRAIT IS DISCOVERED AND OLD JENKS HAS A REAL VOYAGE AT SEA.

THE spring passed quickly away, and the fervors of the June sun were upon us. Mrs. Sanderson, whose health had been a marvel of uniformity, became ill, and showed signs of that failure of the vital power which comes at last to all. She was advised by her physician that she needed a change of air, and encouraged to believe that if she should get relief at once she might retain her hold upon life for some years longer. Arrangements were accordingly perfected to send her with a trusty maid to a watering-place a few leagues distant. I have no doubt that she had come to look upon death as not far away from her, and that she had contemplated the possibility of its visitation while absent from home. I could see that her eye was troubled and anxious. Her lawyer was with her for two days before her departure.

On the morning before she left she called me into her little library, and delivering her keys into my keeping, said:

"I have nothing to tell you, Arthur, except that all my affairs are arranged, so that if I should never return you will find everything in order. You know my ways and wishes. Follow out your plans regarding yourself, and my lawyer will tell you of mine. Maintain the position and uphold the honor of this house. It will be yours. I cannot take it with me; I have no one else to leave it to—and yet—"

She was more softened than I had ever seen her, and her sad and helpless look quite overwhelmed me. I had so long expected her munificence that this affected me much less than the change, physical and mental, which had passed over her.

"My dear, precious Aunt," I said, "you are not going to

die. I cannot let you die. I am too young to spare you. You will go away, and get well, and live a long time."

Then I kissed her, and thanked her for her persistent kindness and her splendid gifts, in words that seemed so poor and inadequate that I was quite distressed.

She was deeply moved. Her physical weakness was such that the iron rule of her will over her emotions was broken. I believe she would have been glad to have me take her in my arms, like a child, and comfort her. After sitting awhile in silence, I said: "Please tell me what you were thinking of when you said: 'And yet.'?"

She gave me no direct reply, but said: "Do you remember the portrait of a boy which you saw when you first came to the house?"

"Perfectly," I replied.

"This key," said she, taking the bunch of keys from my hand which I still held, "will open a door in the dining-room which you have never seen opened. You know where it is. After I am gone away, I wish you to open that closet, and take out the portrait, and hang it just where it was before. I wish to have it hang there as long as the house stands. You have learned not to ask any questions. If ever I come back, I shall find it there. If I do not, you will keep it there for my sake."

I promised to obey her will in every particular, and then the carriage drove up to bear her away. Our parting was very quiet, but full of feeling; and I saw her turn and look back affectionately at the old house, as she passed slowly down the hill.

I was thus left alone—with the old servant Jenks—the master of The Mansion. It will be readily imagined that, still retaining my curiosity with regard to the picture, I lost no time in finding it. Sending Jenks away on some unimportant errand, I entered the dining-room, and locked myself in. Under a most fascinating excitement I inserted the key in the lock of the closet. The bolt was moved with difficulty, like one long unused. Throwing open the door, I looked in. First I saw an old trunk, the covering of rawhide, fastened by brass nails which had turned green with rust. I lifted the lid, and found it full of papers. I had already caught a glimpse of the picture, yet by a curious perversity of will I insisted on seeing it last. Next I came upon an old punch-bowl, a reminder of the days when there were men and revelry in the house. It was made of silver, and had the Bonnicastle arms upon its side. How old it was, I could not tell, but it was evidently an heirloom. A rusty musket stood in one corner, of the variety then known as "Queen's Arms." In another corner hung a military coat, trimmed with gold lace. The wreck of an ancient and costly clock stood upon a shelf, the pendulum of which was a swing, with a little child in it. I remember feeling a whimsical pity for the child that had waited for motion so long in the darkness, and so reached up and set him swinging, as he had done so many million times in the years that were dead and gone. I lingered long upon every article, and wondered how many centuries it would take of such seclusion to dissolve them all into dust.

I had no excuse for withholding my eyes from the picture any longer. I lifted it carefully from the nail where it hung, and set it down by the dining-room wall. Then I closed and locked the door. Not until I had carefully cleaned the painting, and dusted the frame, and hung it in its old place, did I venture to look at it with any thought of careful study; and even this observation I determined to take first from the point where I sat when I originally discovered it. I arranged the light to strike it at the right angle, and then opening the passage into the library, went and sat down precisely where I had sat nearly six years before, under the spell of Mrs. Sanderson's command. I had already, while handling it, found the date of the picture, and the name of the painter on the back of the canvas, and knew that the lad whom it represented had become a man considerably past middle life, or, what seemed more probable, remembering Mrs. Sanderson's strange actions in regard to it, a heap of dust and ashes.

With my first long look at the picture, came back the old days; and I was again a little boy, with all my original interest in the beautiful young face. I expected to see a likeness of Henry, but Henry had grown up and changed, and I found it quite impossible to take him back in my imagination to the point where his face answered, in any considerable degree, to the lineaments of this. Still there was a likeness, indefinable, far back in the depths of expression, and hovering around the contour of the face and head, that at first puzzled me, and at last convinced me that, if I could get at the secrets of my friend's life, I should find that he was a Bonnicastle. I had often while at school, in unexpected glimpses of Henry's features, been startled by the resemblance of his face to some of the members of my own family. The moment I studied his features, however, the likeness was gone. It was thus with the picture. Analysis spoiled it as the likeness of my friend, yet it had a subtle power to suggest him, and to convince me that he was a sharer of the family blood.

I cannot say, much as I loved Henry, that I was pleased with my discovery. Nor was I pleased with the reflections which it stirred in me; for I saw through them something of the mercenary meanness of my own character. I was glad that Mrs. Sanderson had never seen him. I was glad that he had declined her invitation, and that she had come to regard him with such dislike that she would not even hear his name mentioned. I knew that if he were an accepted visitor of the house I should be jealous of him, for I was conscious of his superiority to me in many points, and felt that Mrs. Sanderson would find much in him that would please her. His quiet bearing, his steadiness, his personal beauty, his steadfast integrity, would all be appreciated by her; and I was sure she could not fail to detect in him the family likeness.

Angry with myself for indulging such unworthy thoughts, I sprang to my feet, and went nearer to the picture—went where I could see it best. As I approached it, the likeness to Henry gradually faded, and what was Bonnicastle in the distance became something of another name and blood. Another nature mingled strangely with that to which I was consciously kindred. Beneath the soft veil which gentle blood had thrown over the features, there couched something base and brutal. Somewhere in the family history of the person it represented the spaniel had given herself to the wolf. Sheathed within the foot of velvet was hidden a talon of steel. Under those beautiful features lay the capacity of cruelty and crime. It was a wonderful revelation, and it increased rather than lessened the fascination which the picture exerted upon me. Not until an hour had passed away, and I knew that Jenks had returned from his errand, did I silently unlock the doors of the dining-room and go to my chamber for study.

When the dinner-hour arrived, I was served alone. Jenks had set the table without discovering the returned picture, but in one of the pauses of his service he started and turned pale.

"What is the matter, Jenks?" I said.

"Nothing," he replied, "I thought it was burned. It ought to be."

It was the first intimation that I had ever received that he knew anything about the subject of the picture; but I asked him no more questions, first, because I thought it would virtually be a breach of the confidence which its owner had reposed in me, and, second, because I was so sure of Jenks's reticence that I knew I had nothing to gain by asking. He had kept his place because he could hold his tongue. Still, the fact that he could tell me all I wanted to know had the power to heighten my curiosity, and to fill me with a discomfort of which I was ashamed.

A few days of lonely life passed away, in which, for a defense against my loneliness, I devoted myself with unusual diligence to study. The first letter I received from Mrs. Sanderson contained the good news that her strong and elastic constitution had responded favorably to the change of air and place. Indeed, she was doing so well that she had concluded to stay by the sea during the summer, if she should continue to find herself improving in strength. I was very much relieved, for in truth I had no wish to assume the cares of the wealth she would leave me. I was grateful, too, to find that I had a genuine affection for her, and that my solicitude was not altogether selfish.

One warm evening, just before sunset, I took a chair from the hall and placed it upon the landing of the steps that led from the garden to the door, between the sleeping lions, and sat down to enjoy the fresh air of the coming twilight. I had a book in my hand, but I was weary and listless, and sat looking off upon the town. Presently I heard the sound of voices and laughter from the hill below me; and soon there came in sight a little group whose approach made my heart leap with delight. Henry, Claire and Millie were coming to make a call upon their lonely friend.

I greeted them heartily at a distance, and Henry, with his hat in his hand, walking between the two girls, sauntered up to the house, looking it over, as it seemed to me, very carefully. Suddenly, Millie sprang to the side of the road, and plucked a flower which she insisted upon placing in the button-hole of his coat. He bent to her while she fastened it. It was the work of an instant, yet there was in it that which showed me that the girl was fond of him, and that, young as she was, she pleased him. I was in a mood to be jealous. The thoughts I had indulged in while looking at the picture, and the belief that Henry had Claire's heart in full possession, to say nothing of certain plans of my own with regard to Millie, reaching far into the future—plans very vague and shadowy, but covering sweet possibilities—awoke a feeling in my heart towards Henry which I am sure made my courtesies seem strangely constrained.

I invited the group into the house, and Claire and Millie accepted the invitation at once. Henry hesitated, and finally said that he did not care to go in. The evening was so pleasant that he would sit upon the steps until we returned. Remembering his repeated refusals to go home with me from school, and thinking, for a reason which I could not have shaped into words, that I did not wish to have him see the picture in the dining-room, I did not urge him. So the two girls and myself went in, and walked over the house. Millie had been there before with her mother, but it was the first time that Claire's maidenly figure had ever entered the door. The dining-room had already been darkened for the night, and we only looked in and took a hurried glimpse of its shadowy furniture, and left it. Both the girls were curious to see my room, and to that we ascended. The outlook was so pleasant and the chairs were so inviting that, after looking at the pictures and the various tasteful appointments with which the room had been furnished, we all sat down, and in our merry conversation quite forgot Henry, and the fact that he was waiting for us to rejoin him.

Near the close of our pleasant session I was conscious that feet were moving in the room below. Then I heard the sound of opening or closing shutters. My first thought was that Jenks had come in on some errand. Interrupted in this thought by the conversation in progress, the matter was put out of my mind for a moment. Then it returned, and as I reflected that Jenks had no business in that part of the house at that hour, I became uneasy.

"We have quite forgotten Henry," I said; and we all rose to our feet and walked down stairs.

Millie was at the foot in a twinkling, and exclaimed: "Why, he isn't here! He is gone!"

I said not a word, but went straight to the dining-room. Every shutter was open, and there stood Henry before the picture. He appeared to be entirely unconscious of my entrance; so, stepping up behind him, I put my hand upon his shoulder, and said: "Well, how do you like it?"

He started as if I had struck him, trembled, and turned pale.

"The fact is, I got tired with waiting, my boy," he said, "and so came in to explore, you know, ha! ha! ha! Quite an old curiosity-shop, isn't it? Oh! 'How do I like it?' Yes, quite a picture—quite a picture, ha! ha! ha!"

There certainly was no likeness in the picture to the Henry

Stepping up behind him, I put my hand upon his shoulder, and said: "Well, how do you like it."

(p. 186.)

who stood before it then. Haggard, vacant, convulsed with feeling which it was impossible for him to conceal, he stood before it as if fastened to the spot by a relentless spell. I took him by the arm and led him into the open air, with his hollow-sounding voice and his forced, mechanical laugh still ringing in my ears. The girls were alarmed, and asked him if he were ill.

"Not in the least," he replied, with another attempt at a laugh which made me shiver. The quick instinct of his companions recognized the fact that something unpleasant had happened, and so, overcoming the chill which his voice and manner had thrown upon them, they thanked me for showing them the old house, and declared that it was time for them to go home. Bidding me a hearty good-night, they started and went out of the gate. Henry lingered, holding my hand for a moment, and then, finding it impossible to shape the apology he had evidently intended to make, abruptly left me, and joined the girls. They quickly passed out of sight, Claire tossing me a kiss as she disappeared, and I was left alone.

I was, of course, more mystified than ever. I did not think it strange or ill-mannered for Henry to enter the dining-room unattended, for I had invited him in, I had kept him long waiting, and there was no one to be disturbed by his entrance, as he knew; but I was more convinced than ever that there was some strange connection between that picture and his destiny and mine. I was convinced, too, that by some means he had recognized the fact as well as I. I tossed upon my bed until midnight in nervous wakefulness, thinking it over, permitting my imagination to construct a thousand improbable possibilities, and chafing under the pledge that forbade me to ask a question of friend or servant.

It was a week before I saw him again, and then I found him quite self-possessed, though there was a shadow of restraint upon him. No allusion was made to the incident in the dining-room, and it gradually fell back into a memory, among the things that were, to be recalled years afterward in the grand crisis of my personal history.

Not a day passed away in which Jenks did not inquire for the health of "the mistress." He seemed to be lost without her, and to feel even more anxious for her health than I did. "How is she now?" and "When does she say she is coming back?" were always the inquiries, after he had brought me a letter.

One day I said to him: "I thought you did not like my Aunt. You were always wanting to get away from her."

"I don't say that I do like her," said Jenks, with a quizzical expression of countenance, as if he were puzzled to know exactly what his feelings were, "but the fact is she's a good woman to get away from, and that's half the fun of living. When she's here I'm always thinking of leaving her, and that takes up the time and sets me contriving, you know."

"You can't sail quite as much as you used to," I said, laughing.

"No," said he, "I'm getting rather old for the sea, and I don't know but thinking of the salt water so much has given me the rheumatism. I'm as stiff as an old horse. Any way, I can't get away until she comes back, if I want to ever so much. I've nothing to get away from."

"Yes, Jenks," I said, "you and your mistress are both getting old. In a few years you'll both get away, and you will not return. Do you ever think of what will come after?"

"That's so," he responded, "and the thing that bothers me is that I can't get away from the place I go to, whether it's good or bad. How a man is going to kill time without some sort of contriving to get into a better place, I don't know. Do you think there's really such a place as heaven?"

"Of course I do."

"No offense, sir," said Jenks, "but it seems to me sometimes as if it was only a sort of make-believe place, that people dream about just to pass away the time. They go to meeting, and pray and sing, and take the sacrament, and talk about heaven and hell, and then they come home and laugh and carry on and work just the same as ever. It makes a nice way to pass Sunday, and it seems to me just about the same thing as sailing on an Atlas. One day they make believe very hard, and the next it's all over with. Everybody must have his fun, and everybody has his own way of getting it. Now here's this Miss Lester down at Mr. Bradford's. She's got no end of a constitution, and takes it out in work. She goes to all the prayer-meetings, and knits piles of stockings for poor people; but, dear me! she has to do something, or else she couldn't live. So she tramps out in all sorts of weather, and takes solid comfort in getting wet and muddy, and amuses herself thinking she's doing good. It's just so with the stockings. She must knit 'em, any way, and so she plays charity with 'em. I reckon we're all a good deal alike."

"No, Jenks," I said, "there's really and truly such a place as heaven."

"I s'pose there is," he responded, "but I don't see what I can do there. I can't sing."

"And there's another place."

"I s'pose there is—that's what they say, and I don't see what I am going to do there, for I don't like the sort of people that live there. I never had anything to do with 'em here, and I won't have anything to do with 'em anywhere. I've always kept my own counsel and picked my own company, which has been mighty small, and I always expect to."

These last remarks of Jenks were a puzzle to me. I really did not know what to say, at first, but there came back to me the memory of one of our early conversations, and I said: "What if she were to go to one place and you to the other?"

"Well," he replied, his thin lips twitching and quivering, "I shouldn't be any worse off than I am now. She went to one place and I went to another a good while ago; but do you really think people know one another there?"

"I have no doubt of it," I replied.

"Well, I shouldn't care where I was, if I could be with her, and everything was agreeable," said Jenks.

"So you still remember her."

"How do you s'pose I could live if I didn't?"

At this he excitedly unbuttoned the wristband of his left arm, and pulled up his sleeve, and there, pricked patiently into the skin, after the manner of sailors, were the two names in rude letters: "THEOPHILUS JENKS AND JANE WHITTLESEY."

"I did it myself," said Jenks. "Every prick of the needle hurt me, but the more it hurt the happier I was, just to see the two names together where no man could rub 'em out; and I think I could stand 'most anything else for the sake of being with her."

I was much impressed by this revelation of the inner life of the simple old man, and the frankness with which he had given me his confidence. Laboring from day to day, year after year, in a position from which he had no hope of rising, he had his separate life of the affections and the imagination, and in this he held all his satisfactions, and won all his modest mental and spiritual growth. At the close of our conversation I took out my watch, and, seeing that it was time for the mail, I sent him off to obtain it. When he returned, he brought me among other letters one from Mrs. Sanderson. He had placed it upon the top of the package, and, when he had handed it to me, he waited, as had become his custom, to learn the news from his mistress.

When I had opened the letter and read a few lines, I exclaimed: "Oh, Jenks! here's some great news for you." And then I read from the letter:

"My physician sas that I must have a daily drive upon the beach, but I really do not feel as if I should take a moment of comfort without my old horse and carriage and my old driver. If you can manage to get along for two or three weeks with the cook, who is entirely able to take all the service of the house upon her hands, you may send Jenks to me with the horse and carriage. The road is very heavy, however, and it is best for him to put everything on the *Belle of Bradford*, and come with it himself. The *Belle* touches every day at our wharf, and the horse will be ready for service as soon as he lands."

I read this without looking at Jenks's face, but when I finished

I glanced at him, expecting to see him radiant with delight. I was therefore surprised to find him pale and trembling in every fiber of his frame.

"That's just like an old woman," said Jenks. "How does she s'pose a horse is going to sea? What's he to do when the steamer rolls?"

"Oh, horses are very fond of rolling," I said, laughing. "All he will have to do will be to lie down and roll all the way, without straining himself for it."

"And how does she s'pose a carriage is going to keep right side up?"

"Well, you can sit in it and hold it down."

Jenks looked down upon his thin frame and slender legs, and shook his head. "If there's anything that I hate," said he, "it's a steamboat. I think it will scare the old horse to death. They whistle and toot, and blow up and burn up. Now, don't you really think—candid, now—that I'd better drive the old horse down? Don't you think the property'll be safer? She never can get another horse like him. She never'll get a carriage that suits her half as well as that. It don't seem to me as if I could take the responsibility of risking that property. She left it in my hands. 'Take good care of the old horse, Jenks,' was the last words she said to me; and now because she's an old woman, and does'n't know any better, she tells me to put him on a steamboat, where he's just as likely to be banged about and have his ribs broke in, or be burned up or blowed up, as he is to get through alive. It seems to me the old woman is out of her head, and that I ought to do just as she told me to do when she was all right. 'Take good care of the old horse, Jenks,' was the last words she said."

The old man was excited but still pale, and he stood waiting before me with a pitiful, pleading expression upon his wizen features.

I shook my head. "I'm afraid we shall be obliged to risk the property, Jenks," I said. "Mrs. Sanderson is very particular, you know, about having all her orders obeyed to the letter.

She will have no one to blame but herself if the whole establishment goes overboard, and if I were you I wouldn't miss this chance of going to sea at her expense for anything."

Then Jenks resolutely undertook to bring his mind to it. "How long will it take?" he inquired.

"Oh, three hours or so," I replied carelessly.

"Do we go out of sight of land?"

"No, you sail down the river a few miles, then you strike the ocean, and just hug the shore until you get there," I replied.

"Yes; strike the ocean—hug the shore—" he mumbled to himself, looking down and rubbing the bald spot on the top of his head. "Strike the ocean—hug the shore. Three hours—oh! do you know whether they have life-preservers on that steamboat?"

"Stacks of them," I replied. "I've seen them often."

"Wouldn't it be a good plan to slip one on to the horse's neck when they start? He'll think it's a collar, and won't be scared, you know; and if there should happen to be any trouble it would help to keep his nose up."

"Capital plan," I responded.

"What time do we start?"

"At eight o'clock to-morrow morning."

Jenks retired with the look and bearing of a man who had been sentenced to be hanged. He went first to the stable, and made all the necessary arrangements there, and late into the night I heard him moving about his room. I presume he did not once close his eyes in sleep that night. I was exceedingly amused by his nervousness, though I would not have intimated to him that I had any doubt of his courage, for the world. He was astir at an early hour in the morning; and breakfast was upon the table while yet the early birds were singing.

"You will have a lovely day, Jenks," I said, as he handed me my coffee.

As he bent to set the cup beside my plate, there came close to my ear a curious, crepitant rustle. "What have you got about you, Jenks?" I inquired.

He made a sickly attempt to smile, and then pulling open the bosom of his shirt, displayed a collapsed, dry bladder, with a goose-quill in the neck ready for its inflation.

"That's a capital idea, Jenks," I said.

"Do you think so? What do you think of that?" and he showed me the breast pocket of his coat full of corks.

It was impossible for me to restrain my laughter any longer.

"Number one, you know," said Jenks, buttoning up his coat. "Number one, and a stiff upper lip."

"You're a brave old fellow, any way, Jenks, and you're going to have the best time you ever had. I envy you."

I drove down to the boat with him, to make the arrangements for the shipment, and saw him and the establishment safely on board. The bottom of the carriage was loaded with appliances for securing his personal safety in case of an accident, including a billet of wood, which he assured me was to be used for blocking the wheels of the carriage in case of a storm.

I bade him good-by at last, and went on shore, where I waited to see the steamer wheel into the stream. The last view I had of the old man showed that he had relieved himself of hat and boots, and placed himself in light swimming order. In the place of the former he had tied a red bandanna handkerchief around his head, and for the latter he had substituted slippers. He had entirely forgotten me and the existence of such a town as Bradford. Looking dreamily down the river, out towards that mysterious sea, on which his childish imagination had dwelt so long, and of which he stood in such mortal fear, he passed out of sight.

The next evening I heard from him in a characteristic letter. It was dated at "The Glaids," and read thus:—

"The Bell is a noble vessel.
"The horse and carridge is saif.
"She welcomed me from the see.
"It seems to me I am in the moon.
"Once or twise she roaled cerefully.
"But she rited and drove on.

"I count nineteen distant sales.
"If you will be so kind as not to menshun the blader.
"The waves roll in and rore all night.
"The see is a tremenduous thing, and the atlus is nowhare.
"From an old Tarr
"Theophilus Jenks."

A few days afterwards, Henry and I made a flying trip to New Haven, passed our examination for admission to the freshman class, and in the weeks that followed gave ourselves up to recreations which a debilitating summer and debilitating labor had made necessary.

CHAPTER XII.

MRS. SANDERSON TAKES A COMPANION AND I GO TO COLLEGE.

During the closing days of summer, I was surprised to meet in the street, walking alone, the maid who accompanied Mrs. Sanderson to the sea-side. She courtesied quite profoundly to me, after the manner of the time, and paused as though she wished to speak.

"Well, Jane," I said, "how came you here?"

She colored, and her eyes flashed angrily as she replied: "Mrs. Sanderson sent me home."

"If you are willing, I should like to have you tell me all about it," I said.

"It is all of a lady Mrs. Sanderson met at the hotel," she responded,—"a lady with a pretty face and fine manners, who is as poor as I am, I warrant ye. Mighty sly and quiet she was; and your aunt took to her from the first day. They walked together every day till Jenks came, and then they rode together, and she was always doing little things for your aunt, and at last they left me out entirely, so that I had nothing in the world to do but to sit and sew all day on just nothing at all. The lady read to her, too, out of the newspapers and the books, in a very nice way, and made herself agreeable with her pretty manners until it was nothing but Mrs. Belden in the morning, and Mrs. Belden at night, and Mrs. Belden all the time, and I told your aunt that I didn't think I was needed any more, and she took me up mighty short and said she didn't think I was, and that I could go home if I wished to; and I wouldn't stay a moment after that, but just packed up and came home in the next boat."

The disappointed and angry girl rattled off her story as if

she had told it forty times to her forty friends, and learned it all by rote.

"I am sorry, Jane, that you have been disappointed," I responded, "but is my aunt well?"

"Just as well as she ever was in her life."

"But how will she get home without you?" I inquired, quite willing to hear her talk farther.

"She'll manage the same as she does now, faith. You may wager your eyes the lady will come with her. You never saw the like of the thickness there is between 'em."

"Is she old or young?" I inquired.

"Neither the one nor the other," she replied, "though I think she's older than she looks. Oh, she's a sharp one—she's a sharp one! You'll see her. There was a world of quiet talk going on between 'em, when I couldn't hear. They've been at it for more than a month, and it means something. I think she's after the old lady's money."

I laughed, and again telling Jane that I was sorry for her disappointment, and expressing the hope that it would all turn out well, parted with her.

Here was some news that gave me abundant food for reflection and conjecture. Not a breath of all this had come to me on the wings of the frequent missives that had reached me from Mrs. Sanderson's hand; but I had an unshaken faith in her discretion. The assurance that she was well was an assurance that she was quite able to take care of herself. It was natural that the maid should have been irate and jealous, and I did not permit her words to prejudice me against Mrs. Sanderson's new friend. Yet, I was curious, and not quite comfortable, with the thoughts of her, and permitted my mind to frame and dwell upon the possible results of the new connection.

It was a week after this meeting, perhaps, that I received a note from Mrs. Sanderson, announcing the confirmation of her health, stating that she should bring a lady with her on her return to Bradford, and giving directions for the preparation of a room for her accommodation. It would not have been like my aunt to make explanations in a letter, so that I was not disappointed in finding none.

At last I received a letter informing me that the mistress of The Mansion would return to her home on the following day. I was early at the wharf to meet her—so early that the steamer had but just showed her smoking chimneys far down the river. As the boat approached, I detected two female figures upon the hurricane deck which I was not long in concluding to be my aunt and her new friend. Jenks, in his impatience to get quickly on shore, had loosed his horse from the stall, and stood holding him by the bridle, near the carriage, upon the forward deck. He saw me and swung his hat, in token of his gladness that the long trial was over.

The moment the boat touched the wharf I leaped on board, mounted to the deck, and, in an impulse of real gladness and gratitude, embraced my aunt. For a moment her companion was forgotten: then Mrs. Sanderson turned and presented her. I did not wonder that she was agreeable to Mrs. Sanderson, for I am sure that no one could have looked into her face and received her greeting without being pleased with her. She was dressed plainly but with great neatness; and everything in her look and manner revealed the well-bred woman. The whole expression of her personality was one of refinement. She looked at me with a pleased and inquiring gaze which quite charmed me—a gaze that by some subtle influence inspired me to special courtesy toward her. When the carriage had been placed on shore, and had been made ready for the ride homeward, I found myself under the impulse to be as polite to her as to my aunt.

As I looked out among the loungers who always attended the arrival of the *Belle*, as a resort of idle amusement, I caught a glimpse of Henry. Our eyes met for an instant, and I detected a look of eager interest upon his face. My recognition seemed to quench the look at once, and he turned abruptly on his heel and walked away. It was not like him to be among a company of idlers, and I knew that the arrival of Mrs. Sanderson could not have attracted him. It was an incident, however, of no significance save as it was interpreted by subsequent events which wait for record.

Mrs. Sanderson was quite talkative on the way home, in pointing out to her new companion the objects of interest presented by the thriving little city, and when she entered her house seemed like her former self. She was like the captain of a ship who had returned from a short stay on shore, having left the mate in charge. All command and direction returned to her on the instant she placed her foot upon the threshold. She was in excellent spirits, and seemed to look forward upon life more hopefully than she had done for a long time previous. Mrs. Belden was pleased with the house, delighted with her room, and charmed with all the surroundings of the place; and I could see that Mrs. Sanderson was more than satisfied with the impression which her new friend had made upon me. I remember with how much interest I took her from window to window to show her the views which the house commanded, and how much she gratified me by her hearty appreciation of my courtesy and of the home to which circumstances had brought her.

I saw at once that she was a woman to whom I could yield my confidence, and who was wholly capable of understanding me and of giving me counsel. I saw, too, that the old home would become a very different place to me from what it ever had been before, with her gracious womanliness within it. It was love with me at first sight, as it had been with my more critical aunt.

The next morning Mrs. Sanderson called me into her little library and told me the whole story of her new acquaintance. She had been attracted to her by some heartily-rendered courtesy when she found herself among strangers, feeble and alone, and had learned from her that she was without relatives and a home of her own. They had long conversations, and were led, step by step, to a mutual revelation of personal wishes and needs, until it was understood between them that one was in want of a companion in her old age, and the other was in want of a home, for which she was willing to give service and society.

"I have come," said my aunt, "to realize that I am old, and that it is not right for me to stay in the house alone as I have done; and now that you are to be absent for so long a time, I shall need society and help. I am sure that Mrs. Belden is the right woman for me. Although she will be in a certain sense a dependent, she deserves and will occupy the place of a friend. I do not think I can be mistaken in her, and I believe that you will like her as well as I do."

I frankly told my aunt of the pleasant impression the lady had made upon me, and expressed my entire satisfaction with the arrangement; so Mrs. Belden became, in a day, a member of our home, and, by the ready adaptiveness of her nature, fitted into her new place and relations without a jar.

On the same day in which Mrs. Sanderson and I held our conversation, I found myself alone with Mrs. Belden, who led me to talk of myself, my plans, and my associates. I told her the history of my stay at The Bird's Nest, and talked at length of my companion there. She listened to all I had to say with interest, and questioned me particularly about Henry. She thought a young man's intimate companions had much to do with his safety and progress, and was glad to learn that my most intimate friend was all that he ought to be.

"You must never mention him to Mrs. Sanderson," I said, "for he offended her by not accepting her invitation to spend his vacations with me."

"I shall never do it, Arthur," she responded. "You can always rely upon my discretion."

"We are to be chums at college," I said.

"How will you manage it without offending your aunt?" she inquired.

"Oh, she knows that I like him; so we agree not to mention his name. She asks me no questions, and I say nothing. Besides, I think she knows something else and—" I hesitated.

"And what?" inquired Mrs. Belden, smiling.

"I think she knows that he is fond of my sister Claire," I said.

Mrs. Belden gave a visible start, but checking herself, said, coolly enough, "Well, is he?"

"I think so," I answered. "Indeed, I think they are very fond of one another."

Then, at the lady's request, I told her all about my sister—her beauty, her importance in my father's house, and her accomplishments. She listened with great interest, and said that she hoped she should make her acquaintance.

"If you are to be tied to my aunt in the society you meet here you will be pretty sure not to know her," I responded. "My father is Mrs. Sanderson's tenant, and she has very strict notions in regard to poor people, and especially in regard to those who occupy her houses. She has never invited a member of my family into her house, and she never will. She has been very kind to me, but she has her own way about it."

"Yes, I see; but I shall meet your sister in some way, I know, if I remain here," Mrs. Belden replied.

I had never seen Jenks so happy as he appeared the next day after his arrival. He had been elevated immensely by his voyage and adventures, and had been benefited by the change quite as much as his mistress. He went about humming and growling to himself in the old way, seeking opportunities to pour into my amused ears the perils he had encountered and escaped. There had been a terrific "lurch" on one occasion, when everybody staggered; and a suspicious sail once "hove in sight" which turned out to be a schooner loaded with lumber; and there were white caps tossing on a reef which the captain skillfully avoided; and there was a "tremenduous ground swell" during a portion of the homeward passage which he delighted to dwell upon.

But Jenks was in no way content until I had pointed out his passage to him on the map. When he comprehended the humiliating fact that he had sailed only half an inch on the largest map of the region he possessed, and that on the map of the world the river by which he passed to the sea was not large enough to be noticed, he shook his head.

"It's no use," said the old man. "I thought I could do it, but I can't. The world is a big thing. Don't you think, yourself, it would be more convenient if it were smaller? I can't see the use of such an everlasting lot of water. A half an inch! My! think of sailing a foot and a half! I give it up."

"But you really have been far, far away upon the billow," I said encouragingly.

"Yes, that's so—that's so—that *is* so," he responded, nodding his head emphatically: "and I've ploughed the waves, and struck the sea, and hugged the shore, and embarked and prepared for a storm, and seen the white caps, and felt a ground swell, and got through alive, and all that kind of thing. I tell you, that day when we swung into the stream I didn't know whether I was on my head or my heels. I kept saying to myself: 'Theophilus Jenks, is this you? Who's your father and who's your mother and who's your Uncle David? Do you know what you're up to?' I'll bet you can't tell what else I said?"

"No, I'll not try, but you'll tell me," I responded.

"Well, 'twas a curious thing to say, and I don't know but it was wicked to talk out of the Bible, but it came to me and came out of me before I knew it."

"What was it, Jenks? I'm curious to know."

"Says I : 'Great is Diany of the 'Phesians!'"

I laughed heartily, and told Jenks that in my opinion he couldn't have done better.

"That wasn't all," said Jenks. "I said it more than forty times. A fellow must say something when he gets full, and if he doesn't swear, what is he going to do, I should like to know? So always when I found myself running over, I said 'Great is Diany of the 'Phesians,' and that's the way I spilt myself all the way down."

It was a great comfort to me, on the eve of my departure, to feel that the two lives which had been identified with my new home, and had made it what it had been to me, were likely to be spared for some years longer—spared, indeed, until I should return to take up my permanent residence at The Mansion. Mrs. Belden's presence, too, was reassuring. It helped to give a look of permanence to a home which seemed more and more, as the years went by, to be built of very few and frail materials. I learned almost at once to identify her with my future, and to associate her with all my plans for coming life. If my aunt should die, I determined that Mrs. Belden should remain.

There was one fact which gave me surprise and annoyance, viz., that both my father and Mr. Bradford regarded the four years that lay immediately before me as the critical years of my history. Whenever I met them, I found that my future was much upon their minds, and that my experiences of the previous winter were not relied upon by either of them as sufficient guards against the temptations to which I was about to be subjected. They knew that for many reasons, growing out of the softening influence of age and of apprehended helplessness on the part of Mrs. Sanderson, she had become very indulgent towards me, and had ceased to scan with her old closeness my expenditures of money—that, indeed, she had a growing pride in me and fondness for me which prompted her to give me all the money that might be desirable in sustaining me in the position of a rich young gentleman. Even Mr. Bird came all the way from Hillsborough to see his boys, as he called Henry and myself. He, too, was anxious about me, and did not leave me until he had pointed out the mistakes I should be likely to make and exhorted me to prove myself a man, and to remember what he and dear Mrs. Bird expected of me.

These things surprised and annoyed me, because they indicated a solicitude which must have been based upon suspicions of my weakness, yet these three men were all wise. What could it mean? I learned afterwards. They had seen enough of life to know that when a young man meets the world, temptation comes to him, and always seeks and finds the point in his character at which it may enter. They did not know where that point was in me, but they knew it was somewhere, and that my ready sympathy would be my betrayer, unless I should be on my guard.

I spent an evening with Henry in my father's family, and recognized, in the affectionate paternal eye that followed me everywhere, the old love which knew no diminution. I believe there was no great and good deed which my fond father did not deem me capable of performing, and that he had hung the sweetest and highest hopes of his life upon me. He was still working from day to day to feed, shelter and clothe his dependent flock, but he looked for his rewards not to them but to me. The noble life which had been possible to him, under more favorable circumstances, he expected to live in me. For this he had sacrificed my society, and suffered the pain of witnessing the transfer of my affections and interests to another home.

On the day before that fixed for my departure, a note was received at The Mansion inviting us all to spend the evening at Mrs. Bradford's. The good lady in her note of invitation stated that she should be most happy to see Mrs. Sanderson, and though she hardly expected her to break her rule of not leaving her house in the evening, she hoped that her new companion, Mrs. Belden, would bear me company, and so make the acquaintance of her neighbors. My aunt read the note to Mrs. Belden, and said: "Of course I shall not go, and you will act your own pleasure in the matter." Hoping that the occasion would give me an opportunity to present my friend and my sister to Mrs. Belden, I urged her to go with me, and she at last consented to do so.

I had strongly desired to see my friend Millie once more, and was delighted with the opportunity thus offered. The day was one of busy preparation, and Mrs. Belden was dressed and ready to go when I came down from my toilet. As we walked down the hill together toward Mr. Bradford's house, she said: "Arthur, I have been into society so little during the last few years that I feel very uneasy over this affair. Indeed, every nerve in my body is trembling now." I laughed, and told her she was going among people who would make her at home at once —people whom she would soon learn to love and confide in.

I expected to see Henry and Claire, and I was not disappointed. After greeting my hearty host and lovely hostess, and presenting Mrs. Belden, I turned to Henry, who, with a strange pallor upon his face, grasped and fairly ground my hand within his own. He made the most distant of bows to the strange lady at my side, who looked as ghost-like at the instant as himself. The thought instantaneously crossed my mind that he had associated her with Mrs. Sanderson, against whom I knew he entertained the most bitter dislike. He certainly could not have appeared more displeased had he been compelled to a moment's courtesy toward the old lady herself. When Mrs. Belden and Claire met, it was a different matter altogether. There was a mutual and immediate recognition of sympathy between them. Mrs. Belden held Claire's hand, and stood and chatted with her until her self-possession returned. Henry watched the pair with an absorbed and anxious look, as if he expected his beloved was in some way to be poisoned by the breath of her new acquaintance.

At last, in the general mingling of voices in conversation and laughter, both Mrs. Belden and Henry regained their usual manner; and the fusion of the social elements present became complete. As the little reunion was given to Henry and myself, in token of interest in our departure, that departure was the topic of the evening upon every tongue. We talked about it while at our tea, and there were many sportive speculations upon the possible transformations in character and bearing which the next four years would effect in us. As we came out of the tea-room I saw that Mrs. Belden and Claire still clung to each other. After a while Henry joined them, and I could see, as both looked up into his face with amused interest, that he was making rapid amends for the coolness with which he had greeted the stranger. Then Mr. Bradford went and took Claire away, and Mrs. Belden and Henry sat

Mrs. Belden held Claire's hand. (p. 204.)

down by themselves and had a long talk together. All this pleased me, and I did nothing to interfere with their *tête-à-tête;* and all this I saw from the corner to which Millie and I had retired to have our farewell talk.

"What do you expect to make?" said Millie, curiously, continuing the drift of the previous conversation.

"I told Mrs. Sanderson, when I was a little fellow, that I expected to make a man," I answered; "and now please tell me what you expect to make."

"A woman, I suppose," she replied, with a little sigh.

"You speak as if you were sad about it," I responded.

"I am." And she looked off as if reflecting upon the bitter prospect.

"Why?"

"Oh, men and women are so different from children," she said. "One of these years you'll come back with grand airs, and whiskers on your face, and you will find me grown up, with a long dress on; and I'm afraid I shan't like you as well as I do now, and that you will like somebody a great deal better than you do me."

"Perhaps we shall like one another a great deal better than we do now," I said.

"It's only a perhaps," she responded. "No, we shall be new people then. Just think of my father being a little boy once! I presume I shouldn't have liked him half as well as I do you. As likely as any way he was a plague and a pester."

"But we are growing into new people all the time," I said. "Your father was a young man when he was married, and now he is another man, but your mother is just as fond of him as she ever was, isn't she?"

"Why, yes, that's a fact; I guess she is indeed! She just adores him, out and out."

"Well, then, what's to hinder other people from liking one another right along, even if they are changing all the time?"

"Nothing," she replied quickly. "I see it: I understand.

There's something that does'n't change, isn't there? or something that need'n't change: which is it?"

"Whatever it is, Millie," I answered, "we will not let it change. We'll make up our minds about it right here. When I come back to stay, I will be Arthur Bonnicastle and you shall be Millie Bradford, just the same as now, and we'll sit and talk in this corner just as we do now, and there shall be no Mister and Miss between us."

Millie made no immediate response, but looked off again in her wise way, as if searching for something that eluded and puzzled her. I watched her admiringly while she paused. At last a sudden flash came into her eyes, and she turned to me and said: "Oh, Arthur! I've found it! As true as you live, I've found it!"

"Found what, Millie?"

"The thing that does'n't change, or need'n't change," she replied.

"Well, what is it?"

"Why, it's everything. When I used to dress up my little doll and make a grand lady of her, there was the same doll, inside, after all! Don't you see?"

"Yes, I see."

"And you know how they are building a great church right over the little one down on the corner, without moving a single stone of the chapel. The people go to the big church every Sunday, but all the preaching and singing are in the chapel. Don't you see?"

"Yes, I see, Millie," I answered; "but I don't think I should see it without your eyes to help me. I am to build a man and you are to build a woman right over the boy and girl, without touching the boy and girl at all; and so, when we come together again, we can walk right into the little chapel, and find ourselves at home."

"Isn't that lovely!" exclaimed Millie. "I can see things, and you can make things. I couldn't have said that—about our going into the little chapel, you know."

"And I couldn't have said it if you hadn't found the chapel for me," I responded.

"Why, doesn't it seem as if we belonged together, and had been separated in some way?"

At this moment Mr. Bradford rose and came near us to get a book. He smiled pleasantly upon us while we looked up to him, pausing in our conversation. When he had gone back and resumed his seat, Millie said:

"There's a big church over two chapels. He has a young man in him and a boy besides. The boy plays with me and understands me, and the young man is dead in love with mamma, and the old man takes care of us both, and does everything. Isn't it splendid!"

Ah, Millie! I have heard many wise men and wise women talk philosophy, but never one so wise as you; and I have never seen a young man whose growth had choked and destroyed his childhood, or an old man whose youth had died out of him, without thinking of our conversation that night. The dolls are smothered in their clothes, and the little chapels are fated to fall when the grand cathedral walls are finished. The one thing that need not change, the one thing that should not change, the one thing which has the power to preserve the sweetness of all youthful relations up to the change of death, and, doubtless, beyond it, is childhood—the innocent, playful, trusting, loyal, loving, hopeful childhood of the soul, with all its illusions and romances and enjoyment of pure and simple delights.

Millie and I talked of many things that evening, and participated very little in the general conversation which went on at the other end of the drawing-room. I learned from her of the plans already made for sending her away to school, and realized with a degree of pain which I found difficult to explain to myself, that years were to pass before we should meet for such an hour of unrestrained conversation again.

Before I bade the family farewell, Aunt Flick presented to

both Henry and myself a little box containing pins, needles, buttons, thread, and all the appliances for making timely repairs upon our clothing, in the absence of feminine friends. Each box was a perfect treasure-house of convenience, and had cost Aunt Flick the labor of many hours.

"Henry will use this box," said the donor, "but you" (addressing me) "will not."

"I pledge you my honor, Aunt Flick," I responded, "that I will use and lose every pin in the box, and lend all the needles and thread, and leave the cushions where they will be stolen, and make your gift just as universally useful as I can."

This saucy speech set Millie into so hearty a laugh that the whole company laughed in sympathy, and even Aunt Flick's face relaxed as she remarked that she believed every word I had said.

It was delightful to me to see that while I had been engaged with Millie, Mrs. Belden had quietly made her way with the family, and that Henry, who had met her coldly and almost rudely, had become so much interested in her that when the time of parting came he was particularly warm and courteous toward her.

The farewells and kind wishes were all said at last, and with Mrs. Belden upon my arm I turned my steps toward The Mansion. The lady thought the Bradfords were delightful people, that Henry seemed to be a young man of a good deal of intelligence and character, and that my sister Claire was lovely. The opening chapter of her life in Bradford, she said, was the most charming reading that she had found in any book for many years; and if the story should go on as it had begun she should be more than satisfied.

I need not dwell upon my departure further. In the early morning of the next day, Henry and I were on our way, with the sweet memory of tearful eyes in our hearts, and with the consciousness that good wishes and prayers were following us as white birds follow departing ships far out to sea, and with hopes that beckoned us on in every crested wave that leaped before us and in every cloud that flew.

CHAPTER XIII.

THE BEGINNING OF COLLEGE LIFE—I MEET PETER MULLENS, GORDON LIVINGSTON, AND TEMPTATION.

THE story of my college life occupies so large a space in my memory, that in the attempt to write it within practicable limits I find myself obliged to denude it of a thousand interesting details, and to cling in my record to those persons and incidents which were most directly concerned in shaping my character, my course of life, and my destiny.

I entered upon this life panoplied with good resolutions and worthy ambitions. I was determined to honor the expectations of those who had trusted me, and to disappoint the fears of those who had not. Especially was I determined to regain a measure of the religious zeal and spiritual peace and satisfaction which I had lost during the closing months of my stay in Bradford. Henry and I talked the matter all over, and laid our plans together. We agreed to stand by one another in all emergencies—in sickness, in trouble, in danger—and to be faithful critics and Mentors of each other.

Both of us won at once honorable positions in our class, and the good opinion of our teachers, for we were thoroughly in earnest and scrupulously industrious. Though a good deal of society forced itself upon us, we were sufficient for each other, and sought but little to extend the field of companionship.

We went at once into the weekly prayer-meeting held by the religious students, thinking, that whatever other effect it might have upon us, it would so thoroughly declare our position that all that was gross in the way of temptation would shun us. Taking our religious stand early, we felt, too, that we should have a better outlook upon, and a sounder and safer estimate of, all those diversions and dissipations which never fail to come with subtle and specious temptation to large bodies of young men deprived of the influences of home.

The effect that we aimed at was secured. We were classed at once among those to whom we belonged; but, to me, I cannot say that the classification was entirely satisfactory. I did not find the brightest and most desirable companions among those who attended the prayer-meetings. They were shockingly common-place fellows, the most of them—particularly those most forward in engaging in the exercises. There were a few shy-looking, attractive young men, who said but little, took always the back seats, and conveyed to me the impression that they had come in as a matter of duty, to give their countenance to the gatherings, but without a disposition to engage actively in the discussions and prayers. At first their position seemed cowardly to me, but it was only a few weeks before Henry and I belonged to their number. The meetings seemed to be in the possession of a set of young men who were preparing themselves for the Christian ministry, and who looked upon the college prayer-meeting as a sort of gymnasium, where they were to exercise and develop their gifts. Accordingly, we were treated every week to a sort of dress-parade of mediocrity. Two or three long-winded fellows, who seemed to take the greatest delight in public speech, assumed the leadership, and I may frankly say that they possessed no power to do me good. It is possible that the rest of us ought to have frowned upon their presumption, and insisted on a more democratic division of duty and privilege; but, in truth, there was something about them with which we did not wish to come into contact. So we contented ourselves with giving the honor to them, and cherishing the hope that what they did would bring good to somebody.

Henry and I talked about the matter in our walks and times of leisure, and the result was to disgust us with the semi-professional wordiness of the meetings, as well as with the little body of windy talkers who made those meetings so fruitless and unattractive to us. We found ourselves driven in at length upon our own resources, and became content with our daily prayer together. This was our old habit at The Bird's Nest, and to me, for many months, it was a tower of strength.

Toward the close of our first term an incident occurred which set me still more strongly against the set of young men to whom I have made allusion. There was one of them who had been more offensive than all the rest. His name was Peter Mullens. He was an unwholesome-looking fellow, who wore clothes that never seemed as if they were made for him, and whose false shirt-bosom neither fitted him nor appeared clean. There was a rumpled, shabby look about his whole person. His small, cunning eyes were covered by a pair of glasses which I am sure he wore for ornament, while his hair was combed back straight over his head, to show all the forehead he possessed, though it was not at all imposing in its height and breadth. I had made no inquiries into his history, for he was uninteresting to me in the last degree.

One evening, just before bedtime, he knocked at our door and entered. He had never done this before, and as he seemed to be in unusually good spirits, and to come in with an air of good-fellowship and familiarity, both Henry and myself regarded his call with a sort of questioning surprise. After the utterance of a few commonplace remarks about the weather, and the very interesting meetings they were having, he explained that he had called to inquire why it was that we had forsaken the prayer-meetings.

Henry told him at once, and frankly, that it was because he was not interested in them, and because he felt that he could spend his time better.

Still more frankly, and with less discretion, I told him that the meetings seemed to be in the hands of a set of muffs, who knew very little and assumed to know everything.

"The trouble with you fellows," responded Mr. Peter Mullens, "is that you are proud, and will not humble yourselves to learn. If you felt the responsibility of those of us who are fitting for the ministry, you would look upon the matter in a very different way. We have begun our work, and we shall carry it on, whether men will hear or forbear."

"Is it any of your business whether they hear or forbear?" said I, touchily: "because, if it is, Henry and I will sweep the floor and get down on our knees to you."

"It is my business to do my duty, in the face of all the taunts and ridicule which you may heap upon me," replied Mr. Mullens, loftily.

"Excuse me, Mr. Mullens," I said, "but it seems to me that fellows of your sort thrive on taunts and ridicule. Don't you rather like them now?"

Mr. Mullens smiled a sad, pitying smile, and said that no one who did his duty could hope to live a life of gratified pride or of ease.

"Mr. Mullens," said Henry, "I suppose that so far as you know your own motives, those which led you here were good; but lest you should be tempted to repeat your visit, let me say that I relieve you of all responsibility for my future conduct. You have done me all the good that you can possibly do me, except in one way."

"What is that?" inquired Mullens.

"By carefully keeping out of this room, and out of my sight," responded Henry.

"Henry has expressed my feelings exactly," I added; "and now I think there is a fair understanding of the matter, and we can feel ourselves at liberty to change the conversation."

Mullens sat a moment in thought, then he adjusted his spectacles, tucked down his false shirt-bosom, which always looked as if it were blown up and needed pricking, and turning to me, said with an air of cunning triumph: "Bonnicastle, I believe you are one of us."

"What do you mean?" I inquired.

"Why, one of us that have aid, you know—what they call charity students."

"Charity students!" I exclaimed in astonishment.

"Oh, I've found it out. You are luckier than the rest of us, for you have no end of money. I wish you could manage in some way to get the old woman to help me, for I really need more aid than I have. I don't suppose she would feel a gift of fifty dollars any more than she would one of fifty cents. So small a sum as ten dollars would do me a great deal of good, or even five."

"How would you like some old clothes?" inquired Henry, with a quiet but contemptuous smile.

"That is really what I would like to speak about," said Mr. Mullens. "You fellows who have plenty of money throw away your clothes when they are only a little worn; and when you have any to give away, you would oblige me very much by remembering me. I have no new clothes myself. I take the crumbs that fall."

"And that reminds me," resumed Henry, "that perhaps you might like some cold victuals."

"No, I'm provided for, so far as board and lodging are concerned," responded Mr. Mullens, entirely unconscious of the irony of which he was the subject.

Henry turned to me with a hopeless look, as if he had sounded himself in vain to find words which would express his contempt for the booby before him. As for myself, I had been so taken off my guard, so shamed with the thought that he and his confrères regarded me as belonging to their number, so disgusted with the fellow's greed and lack of sensibility, and so angry at his presumption, that I could not trust myself to speak at all. I suspected that if I should begin to express my feelings I should end by kicking him out of the room.

Henry looked at him for a moment, in a sort of dumb wonder, and then said: "Peter Mullens, what do you suppose I think of you?"

There was something in the flash of Henry's eye and in the tone of his voice, as he uttered this question, that brought Mullens to his feet in an impulse to retire.

"Sit down," said Henry.

Mr. Mullens sat down with his hat between his knees, and

mumbled something about having stayed longer than he intended.

"You cannot go yet," Henry continued. "You came in here to lecture us, and to humiliate one of us; and now I propose to tell you what I think of you. There is not the first element of a gentleman in you. You came in here as a bully in the name of religion, you advertise yourself as a sneak by boasting that you have been prying into other people's affairs, and you end by begging old clothes of those who have too much self-respect to kick you for your impudence and your impertinence. Do you suppose that such a puppy as you are can ever prepare for the ministry?"

I think that this was probably the first time Peter Mullens had ever heard the plain truth in regard to himself. He was very much astonished, for his slow apprehension had at last grasped the conclusions that he was heartily despised and that he was in strong hands.

"I—really—really—beg your pardon, gentlemen," said Mr. Mullens, ramming down his rising shirt-bosom, and wiping his hat with his sleeve; "I meant no offense, but really—I—I—must justify myself for asking for aid. I have given myself to the church, gentlemen, and the laborer is worthy of his hire. What more can I do than to give myself? The church wants men. The church must have men; and she owes it to them to see that they are taken care of. If she neglects her duty she must be reminded of it. If I am willing to take up with old clothes she ought not to complain."

Mr. Mullens paused with a vocal inflection that indicated a deeply wounded heart, rammed down his shirt-bosom again, and looked to Henry for a response.

"There is one thing, Mr. Mullens," said Henry, "that the church has no right to ask you to give up; one thing which you have no right to give up; and one thing which, if given up, leaves you as worthless to the church as despicable in yourself, and that is manhood; and I know of nothing that kills manhood quicker than a perfectly willing dependence on others. You are beginning life as a beggar. You justify yourself in beggary, and it takes no prophet to foresee that you will end life as a beggar. Once down where you are willing to sell yourself and take your daily dole at the hand of your purchaser, and you are forever down."

"But what can I do?" inquired Mullens.

"You can do what I do, and what thousands of your betters are doing all the time—work and take care of yourself," replied Henry.

"But the time—just think of the time that would be lost to the cause."

"I am not very old," responded Henry, "but I am old enough to know that the time which independence costs is never wasted. A man who takes fifteen years to prepare himself for life is twice the man, when prepared, that he is who only takes ten; and the best part of his education is that which he gets in the struggle to maintain his own independence. I have an unutterable contempt for this whole charity business, as it is applied to the education of young men. A man who has not pluck and persistence enough to get his own education is not worth educating at all. It is a demoralizing process, and you, Mr. Peter Mullens, in a very small way, are one of its victims."

Henry had been so thoroughly absorbed during these last utterances that he had not once looked at me. I doubt, indeed, whether he was conscious of my presence; but as he closed his sentence he turned to me, and was evidently pained and surprised at the expression upon my face. With a quick instinct he saw how readily I had applied his words to myself, and, once more addressing Mullens, said: "When a childless woman adopts a relative as a member of her family, and makes him her own, and a sharer in her love and fortune, it may be well or ill for him, but it is none of your business, and makes him no fellow of yours. And now, Mr. Mullens, if you wish to go, you are at liberty to do so. If I ever have any old clothes I shall certainly remember you."

"I should really be very much obliged to you," said Mr. Mullens, "and" (turning to me) "if you should happen to be writing to your aunt—"

"For Heaven's sake, Mullens," exclaimed Henry, "go now," and then, overwhelmed with the comical aspect of the matter, we both burst into a laugh that was simply irresistible. Mullens adjusted his spectacles with a dazed look upon his face, brushed back his hair, rammed down his shirt-bosom, buttoned his coat, and very soberly bade us a good-evening.

Under ordinary circumstances we should have found abundant food for merriment between ourselves after the man's departure, but Henry, under the impression that he had unintentionally wounded me, felt that nothing was to be gained by recalling and explaining his words, and I was too sore to risk the danger of further allusion to the subject. By revealing my position and relations to Mullens, Henry had sought, in the kindest way, to place me at my ease, and had done all that he had the power to do to restore my self-complacency. So the moment Mullens left the room some other subject was broached, and in half an hour both of us were in bed, and Henry was sound asleep.

I was glad in my consciousness to be alone, for I had many things to think of. There was one reason for the omission of all comment upon our visitor and our conversation, so far as Henry was concerned, which, with a quick insight, I detected. He had, in his anxiety to comfort me, spoken of me as a relative of Mrs. Sanderson. He had thus revealed to me the possession of knowledge which I had never conveyed to him. It certainly had not reached him from Mrs. Sanderson, nor had he gathered it from Claire, or my father's family; for I had never breathed a word to them of the secret which my aunt had permitted me to discover. He must have learned it from the Bradfords, with whom he had maintained great intimacy. I had long been aware of the fact that he was carrying on a secret life into which I had never been permitted to look. I should not have cared for this had I not been suspicious that I was in some way concerned with it. I knew that he did not like my relations to Mrs. Sanderson, and that he did not wish to speak of them. I had learned to refrain from all mention of her name; but he had talked with somebody about her and about me, and had learned one thing, at least, which my own father did not know.

All this, however, was a small vexation compared with the revelation of the influence which my position would naturally exert upon my character. However deeply it might wound my self-love, I knew that I was under the same influence which made Mr. Peter Mullens so contemptible a person. He was a willing dependent upon strangers, and was not I? This dependence was sapping my own manhood as it had already destroyed his. If Mullens had come to me alone, and claimed fellowship with me,—if Henry had not been near me in his quiet and self-respectful independence to put him down,—I felt that there would have been no part for me to play except that of the coward or the bully. I had no ground on which to stand for self-defense. Mr. Peter Mullens would have been master of the situation. The thought galled me to the quick.

It was in vain that I remembered that I was an irresponsible child when this dependence began. It was in vain that I assured myself that I was no beggar. The fact remained that I had been purchased and paid for, and that, by the subtly demoralizing influence of dependence, I had been so weakened that I shrank from assuming the responsibility of my own life. I clung to the gold that came with the asking. I clung to the delights that only the gold could buy. I shuddered at the thought of taking myself and my fortunes upon my own hands, and I knew by that fact that something manly had sickened or died in me.

I do not know how long I lay revolving these things in my mind. It was certainly far into the night; and when I woke in the morning I found my heart discontented and bitter. I had regarded myself as a gentleman. I had borne myself with a considerable degree of exclusiveness. I had not cared for recognition. Having determined to do my work well, and to seek no man's company as a thing necessary to fix my social status, I had gone on quietly and self-respectfully. Now I was to go out and meet the anger of Peter Mullens and his tribe. I was to be regarded and spoken of by them as a very unworthy member of their own order. My history had been ascertained, and would be reported to all who knew me.

All these reflections and suggestions may seem very foolish and morbid to the reader, but they were distressing to me beyond my power of telling. I was young, sensitive, proud, and self-loving, and though I prayed for help to enable me to face my fellows, and so to manage my life as to escape the harm which my position threatened to inflict upon me, I could not escape the conviction that Peter Mullens and I were, essentially, on the same ground.

Up to this time I had looked for temptations in vain. No temptations to dissipation had presented themselves. I was sure that no enticement to sensuality or gross vice would have power to move me. Steady employment and daily fatigue held in check my animal spirits, and all my life had gone on safely and smoothly. The daily prayer had brought me back from every heart-wandering, had sweetened and elevated all my desires, had strengthened me for my work, and given me something of the old peace. Away from Henry, I had found but little sympathetic Christian society, but I had been entirely at home and satisfied with him. Now I found that it required courage to face the little world around me; and almost unconsciously I began the work of making acquaintances with the better class of students. Although I had held myself apart from others, there were two or three, similarly exclusive, whom I had entertained a private desire to know. One of these was a New Yorker, Mr. Gordon Livingston by name. He had the reputation of belonging to a family of great wealth and splendid connections, and although his standing as a student was not the best, it was regarded as an honor to know him and the little set to which he belonged. I was aware that the morality of the man and his immediate companions was not much believed in, and I knew, too, that the mean envy and jealousy of many students would account for this. At any rate, I was in a mood, after my interview with Mr. Mullens, to regard him very charitably, and to wish that I might be so far recognized by him and received into his set as to advertise to Mullens and his clique my social removal from them. I determined to brace myself around with aristocratic associations. I had the means in my hands for this work. I could dress with the best. I had personal advantages of which I need not boast here, but which I was conscious would commend me to them. I had no intention to cast in my life with them, but I determined to lose no good opportunity to gain their recognition.

One evening, walking alone, outside the limits of the town—for in my morbid mood I had taken to solitary wanderings,—I fell in with Livingston, also alone. We had approached each other from opposite directions, and met at the corners of the road that led to the city, toward which we were returning. We walked side by side, with only the road between us, for a few yards, when, to my surprise, he crossed over, saying as he approached me: "Hullo, Mr. Bonnicastle! What's the use of two good-looking fellows like us walking alone when they can have company?"

As he came up I gave him my hand, and called him by name.

"So you've known me, as I have known you," he said cordially. "It's a little singular that we haven't been thrown together before, for I fancy you belong to our kind of fellows."

I expressed freely the pleasure I felt in meeting him, and told him how glad I should be to make the acquaintance of his friends; and we passed the time occupied in reaching the college in conversation that was very pleasant to me.

Livingston was older than I, and was two classes in advance of me. He was therefore in a position to patronize and pet me —a position which he thoroughly understood and appreciated. In his manner he had that quiet self-assurance and command that only come from life-long familiarity with good society, and the consciousness of unquestioned social position. He had no youth of poverty to look back upon. He had no associations with mean conditions and circumstances. With an attractive face and figure, a hearty manner, a dress at once faultlessly tasteful and unobtrusive, and with all the prestige of wealth and family, there were few young fellows in college whose notice would so greatly flatter a novice as his. The men who spoke against him and affected contempt for him would have accepted attention from him as an honor.

Livingston had undoubtedly heard my story, but he did not sympathize with the views of Mr. Peter Mullens and his friends concerning it. He found me as well dressed as himself, quite as exclusive in my associations, liked my looks and manners, and, with all the respect for money natural to his class, concluded that I belonged to him and his set. In the mood of mind in which I found myself at meeting him, it can readily be imagined that his recognition and his assurance of friendliness and fellowship brought me great relief.

As we entered the town, and took our way across the green, he became more cordial, and pulled my arm within his own. We were walking in this way when we met Mr. Mullens and a knot of his fellows standing near the path. It was already twilight, and they did not recognize us until we were near them. Then they paused, in what seemed to have been an excited conversation, and stared at us with silent impertinence.

Livingston hugged my arm and said coolly and distinctly: "By the way, speaking of mules, have you ever familiarized yourself with the natural history of the ass? I assure you it is very interesting—his length of ear, his food of thistles, his patience under insult, the toughness of his hide—in short—" By this time we were beyond their hearing and he paused.

I gave a scared laugh which the group must also have heard, and said: "Well that was cool, any way."

"You see," said Livingston, "I wanted to have them understand that we had been improving our minds, by devotion to scientific subjects. They were bound to hear what we said and I wanted to leave a good impression."

The cool impudence of the performance took me by surprise, but, on the whole, it pleased me. It was a deed that I never could have done myself, and I was astonished to find that there was something in it that gratified a spirit of resentment of which I had been the unconscious possessor. The utter indifference of the man to their spite was an attainment altogether beyond me, and I could not help admiring it.

Livingston accompanied me to my room, but we parted at the door, although I begged the privilege of taking him in and making him acquainted with my chum. He left me with an invitation to call upon him at my convenience, and I entered my room in a much lighter mood than that which drove me out from it. I did not tell Henry at once of my new acquaintance, for I was not at all sure that he would be pleased with the information. Indeed, I knew he would not be, for he was a fair measurer of personal values, and held Livingston and Mullens in nearly equal dislike. Still I took a strange comfort in the thought that I had entered the topmost clique, and that Mullens, the man who had determined to bring me to his own level, had seen me arm-in-arm with one of the most exclusive and aristocratic fellows in the college.

And now, lest the reader should suppose that Henry had a knowledge of Livingston's immorality of character which justified his dislike of him, I ought to say at once that he was not a bad man, so far as I was able to learn. If he indulged in immoral practices with those of his own age, he never led me into them. I came to be on familiar terms with him and them. I was younger than most of them, and was petted by them. My purse was as free as theirs on all social occasions, and I was never made to feel that I was in any way their inferior.

Henry was a worker who had his own fortune to make, and he proposed to make it. He was conscious that the whole clique of which Livingston was a member held nothing in common with him, and that they considered him to be socially beneath them. He knew they were not actuated by manly aims, and that they had no sympathy with those who were thus actuated. They studied no more than was necessary to avoid disgrace. They intended to have an easy time. They were thoroughly good-natured among themselves, laughed freely about professors and tutors, took a very superficial view of life, and seemed to regard the college as a mill through which it was necessary to pass, or a waiting-place in which it was considered the proper thing to stop until their beards should mature.

The society of these men had no bad effect upon me, or none perceptible to myself for a long time. Braced by them as I was, Mr. Mullens made no headway against me; and I came at last to feel that my position was secure. With the corrective of Henry's society and example, and with the habit of daily devotion unimpaired, I went on for months with a measurable degree of satisfaction to myself. Still I was conscious of a gradually lowering tone of feeling. By listening to the utterance of careless words and worldly sentiments from my new companions, I came to look leniently upon many things and upon many men once abhorrent to me. Unconsciously at the time, I tried to bring my Christianity into a compromise with worldliness, and to sacrifice my scruples of conscience to what seemed to be the demands of social usage. I had found the temptation for which I had sought so long, and which had so long sought without finding me, but alas! I did not recognize it when it **came.**

CHAPTER XIV.

MY FIRST VISIT TO NEW YORK, AND MY FIRST GLASS OF WINE.

RELYING upon my new associations for the preservation of my social position, now that my history had become known in the college, it was necessary for me to be seen occasionally with the set to which I had been admitted and welcomed. This apparent necessity not unfrequently led me to their rooms, in which there were occasional gatherings of the fellows, and in one or two of which a surreptitious bottle of wine was indulged in. Of the wine I steadily refused to be a partaker, and it was never urged upon me but once, when Livingston interposed, and said I should act my own pleasure. This made the attempt to carry on my double life easier, and saved me from being scared away from it. There was no carousing and no drunkenness—nothing to offend, in those modest symposia —and they came at last to wear a very harmless look to me, associated as they were with good fellowship and hospitality.

Walking one day with Livingston, who fancied me and liked to have me with him, he said: "Bonnicastle, you ought to see more of the world. You've been cooped up all your life, and are as innocent as a chicken."

"You wouldn't have me anything but innocent would you?" I said laughing.

"Not a bit of it. I like a clean fellow like you, but you must see something, some time."

"There'll be time enough for that when I get through study," I responded.

"Yes, I suppose so," he said, "but, my boy, I've taken it into my head to introduce you to New York life. I would like to show you my mother and sisters and my five hundred friends. I want to have you see where I live and how I live, and get a taste of my sort of life. Bradford and your aunt are all very well, I dare say, but they are a little old-fashioned, I fancy. Come, now, don't they bore you?"

"No, they don't," I replied heartily. "The best friends I have in the world are in Bradford, and I am more anxious to please and satisfy them than I can tell you. They are very fond of me, and that goes a great way with such a fellow as I am."

"Oh, I understand that," said Livingston, "but I am fond of you too, and, what's more, you must go home with me next Christmas, for I shall leave college when another summer comes, and that will be the last of me, so far as you are concerned. Now you must make that little arrangement with your aunt. You can tell her what a splendid fellow I am, and humbug the old lady in any harmless way you choose; but the thing must be done."

The project, to tell the truth, set my heart bounding with a keen anticipation of delight. Livingston was the first New York friend I had made who seemed to be worth the making. To be received into his family and introduced to the acquaintance of his friends seemed to me to be the best opportunity possible for seeing the city on its better side. I was sure that he would not willingly lead me into wrong-doing. He had always forborne any criticism of my conscientious scruples. So I set myself at work to win Mrs. Sanderson's consent to the visit. She had become increasingly fond of me, and greedy of my presence and society with her increasing age, and I knew it would be an act of self-denial for her to grant my request. However, under my eloquent representations of the desirableness of the visit, on social grounds, she was persuaded, and I had the pleasure of reporting her consent to Livingston.

I pass over the events of the swift months that made up the record of my first year and of the second autumn of my college life, mentioning only the facts that I maintained a respectable position in my class without excellence, and that I visited home twice. Everything went on well in my aunt's family.

She retained the health she had regained; and Mrs. Belden had become, as her helper and companion, everything she had anticipated. She had taken upon herself much of the work I had learned to do, and, so far as I could see, the family life was harmonious and happy.

My vanity was piqued by the reflection that Henry had achieved better progress than I, and was much more generally respected. He had gradually made himself a social center without the effort to do so, and had pushed his way by sterling work and worth. Nothing of this, however, was known in Bradford, and we were received with equal consideration by all our friends.

For months the projected holiday visit to New York had shone before me as a glittering goal; and when at last, on a sparkling December morning, I found myself with Livingston dashing over the blue waters of the Sound toward the great city, my heart bounded with pleasure. Had I been a winged spirit, about to explore a new star, I could not have felt more buoyantly expectant. Livingston was as delighted as myself, for he was sympathetic with me, and anticipated great enjoyment in being the cup-bearer at this new feast of my life.

We passed Hellgate, we slid by the sunny islands, we approached the gray-blue cloud pierced by a hundred shadowy spires under which the city lay. Steamers pushed here and there, forests of masts bristled in the distance, asthmatic little tugs were towing great ships seaward, ferry-boats crowded with men reeled out from their docks and flew in every direction, and a weather-beaten, black ship, crowded with immigrants, cheered us as we rushed by them. As far as the eye could see, down the river and out upon the bay, all was life, large and abounding. My heart swelled within me as I gazed upon the splendid spectacle, and in a moment, my past life and all that was behind me were dwarfed and insignificant.

As we approached the wharf, we saw among the assemblage of hacks and their drivers—drivers who with frantic whips endeavored to attract our attention—a plain, shining carriage, with a coachman and footman in livery on the box. The men saw us, and raised their hats. The footman jumped from his place as we touched the wharf, and, relieved by him of our satchels, we quietly walked through the boisterous crowd, entered the coach, and slowly took our way along the busy streets. To be thus shut in behind the cleanest of cut-glass, to recline upon the most luxurious upholstery, to be taken care of and shielded from all the roughness of that tumultuous out-door world, to be lifted out of the harsh necessities that made that world forbidding, to feel that I was a favored child of fortune, filled me with a strange, selfish delight. It was like entering upon the realization of a great, sweet dream.

Livingston watched my face with much secret pleasure, I do not doubt, but he said little, except to point out to me the more notable edifices on the route. I was in a city of palaces—warehouses that were the homes of mighty commerce and dwellings that spoke of marvelous wealth. Beautiful women, wrapped in costly furs, swept along the pavement, or peered forth from the windows of carriages like our own; shops were in their holiday attire and crowded with every conceivable article of luxury and taste, and the evidences of money, money, money, pressed upon me from every side. My love of beautiful things and of beautiful life—life relieved of all its homely details and necessities—life that came through the thoughtful and skillful ministry of others—life that commanded what it wanted with the waving of a hand or the breathing of a word—life that looked down upon all other life and looked up to none—my love of this life, always in me, and more and more developed by the circumstances which surrounded me, was stimulated and gratified beyond measure.

At length we drew up to a splendid house in a fashionable quarter of the city. The footman opened the door in a twinkling, and we ran up the broad steps to a landing at which an eager mother waited. Smothered with welcoming kisses from her and his sisters, Livingston could not immediately present me, and Mrs. Livingston saved him the trouble by calling my name and taking my hand with a dignified cordiality which charmed me. The daughters, three in number, were shyer, but no less hearty in their greeting than their mother. Two of them were young ladies, and the third was evidently a school-girl who had come home to spend the holidays.

Livingston and I soon mounted to our room, but in the brief moments of our pause in the library and our passage through the hall my eyes had been busy, and had taken in by hurried glances the beautiful appointments of my friend's home. It was as charming as good taste could make it, with unlimited wealth at command. The large mirrors, the exquisite paintings, the luxurious furniture, the rich carvings, the objects of art and *vertu*, gathered from all lands, and grouped with faultless tact and judgment, the carpets into which the foot sank as into a close-cropped lawn, the artistic forms of every article of service and convenience, all combined to make an interior that was essentially a poem. I had never before seen such a house, and when I looked upon its graceful and gracious keepers, and received their gentle courtesies, I went up-stairs with head and heart and sense as truly intoxicated as if I had been mastered by music, or eloquence, or song.

At the dinner-table, for which we made a careful toilet, all these impressions were confirmed or heightened. The ladies were exquisitely dressed, the service was the perfection of quiet and thoughtful ceremony, the cooking was French, the china and glass were objects of artistic study in their forms and decorations, the choicest flowers gathered from a conservatory which opened into the dining-room, breathed a delicate perfume, and all the materials and ministries of the meal were wrapped in an atmosphere of happy leisure. Livingston was evidently a favorite and pet of the family, and as he had come back to his home from another sphere and experience of life, the conversation was surrendered to him. Into this conversation he adroitly drew me, and under the grateful excitements of the hour I talked as I had never talked before. The ladies flattered me by their attention and applause, and nothing occurred to dampen my spirits until, at the dessert, Mrs. Livingston begged the pleasure of drinking a glass of wine with me.

Throughout the dinner I had declined the wine that had been proffered with every course. It was quietly done, with only a motion of the hand to indicate refusal, and I do not think the family had noticed that I had not taken my wine with themselves. Now the case was different. A lady whom I honored, whom I desired to please, who was doing her best to honor and please me—my friend's mother at her own table—offered what she intended to be a special honor. My face flamed with embarrassment, I stammered out some sort of apology, and declined.

"Now, mother, you really must not do anything of that sort," said Livingston, "unless you wish to drive Bonnicastle out of the house. I meant to have told you. It's one of the things I like in him, for it shows that he's clean and plucky."

"But only one little glass, you know—just a sip, to celebrate the fact that we like one another," said Mrs. Livingston, with an encouraging smile.

But I did not drink. Livingston still interposed, and, although the family detected the disturbed condition of my feelings, and did what they could to restore my equanimity, I felt that my little scruple had been a discord in the music of the feast.

Mr. Livingston, the head of the house, had not yet shown himself. His wife regretted his absence, or said she regretted it, but he had some special reason for dining at his club that day; and I may as well say that that red-faced gentleman seemed to have a special reason for dining at his club nearly every day while I remained in New York, although he consented to get boozy at his own table on Christmas.

We had delightful music in the evening, and my eyes were feasted with pictures and statuary and the *bric-à-brac* gathered in long foreign travel; but when I retired for the night I was in no mood for devotion, and I found myself quarreling with the scruple which had prevented me from accepting the special friendly courtesy of my hostess at dinner.

Wine seemed to be the natural attendant upon this high and beautiful life. It was the most delicate and costly language in which hospitality could speak. There were ladies before me, old and young, who took it without a thought of wrong or of harm. Was there any wrong or harm in it? Was my objection to it born of a narrow education, or an austere view of life, or of prejudices that were essentially vulgar? One thing I saw very plainly, viz., that the practice of total abstinence in the society and surroundings which I most courted would make me uncomfortably singular, and, what was most distressing to me, suggest the vulgar rusticity of my associations.

From my childhood wine and strong drink had been represented to me to be the very poison on which vice and immorality lived and thrived. My father had a hatred of them which no words could express. They were the devil's own instruments for the destruction of the souls and lives of men. I was bred to this belief and opinion. Mr. Bradford had warned me against the temptation to drink, in whatever form it might present itself. Mr. Bird was a sworn foe to all that had the power to intoxicate. When I went away from home, it was with a determination, entered into and confirmed upon my knees, that I would neither taste nor handle the seductive draught which had brought ruin to such multitudes of young men.

Yet I lay for hours that first night in my friend's home, while he was quietly sleeping, debating the question whether, in the new and unlooked-for circumstances in which I found myself, I should yield my scruples, and thus bring myself into harmony with the life that had so many charms for me. Then my imagination went forward into the beautiful possibilities of my future life in The Mansion, with the grand old house refitted and refurnished, with its service enlarged and refined, with a graceful young figure occupying Mrs. Sanderson's place, and with all the delights around me that eye and ear could covet, and taste devise and gather.

In fancies like these I found my scruples fading away, and those manly impulses and ambitions which had moved me mightily at first, but which had stirred me less and less with the advancing months, almost extinguished. I was less interested in what I should do to make myself a man, with power and influence upon those around me, than with what I should enjoy. One turn of the kaleidoscope had changed the vision from a mass of plain and soberly tinted crystals to a galaxy of brilliants, which enchained and enchanted me.

I slid at last from fancies into dreams. Beautiful maidens with yellow hair and sweeping robes moved through grand saloons, pausing at harp and piano to flood the air with the rain of heavenly music; stately dames bent to me with flattering words; groups in marble wreathed their snowy arms against a background of flowering greenery; gilded chandeliers blazed through screens of prismatic crystal; fountains sang and splashed and sparkled, yet all the time there was a dread of some lurking presence—some serpent that was about to leap and grasp me in its coils—some gorgon that would show his grinning head behind the forms of beauty that captivated my senses—some impersonated terror that by the shake of its finger or the utterance of a dreadful word would shatter the beautiful world around me into fragments, or scorch it into ashes.

I woke the next morning unrefreshed and unhappy. I woke with that feeling of weariness which comes to every man who tampers with his convictions, and feels that he has lost something that has been a cherished part of himself. This feeling wore away as I heard the roar of carriages through the streets, and realized the novelty of the scenes around me. Livingston was merry, and at the breakfast table, which was crowned with flowers and Christmas gifts, the trials of the previous night were all forgotten.

The Livingstons were Episcopalians—the one Protestant sect which in those days made much of Christmas. We all attended their church, and for the first time in my life I witnessed its beautiful ritual. The music, prepared with great care for the occasion, was more impressive than any I had ever heard. My æsthetic nature was charmed. Everything seemed to harmonize with the order and the appointments of the house I had just left. And there was my stately hostess, with her lovely daughters, kneeling and devoutly responding— she who had offered and they who had drunk without offense to their consciences the wine which I, no better than they, had refused. They could be Christians and drink wine, and why not I? It must be all a matter of education. High life could be devoutly religious life, and religious life was not harmed by wine. My conscience had received its salvo, and oh, pitiful, recreant coward that I was, I was ready to be tempted!

The Christmas dinner brought the temptation. Mr. Livingston was at home, and presided at his table. He had broached a particularly old and choice bottle of wine for the occasion, and would beg the pleasure of drinking with the young men. And the young men drank with him, and both had the dishonor of seeing him stupid and silly before he left the board. I did not look at Mrs. Livingston during the dinner. I had refused to drink with her the day before, and I had fallen from my resolution. The wine I drank did not go down to warm and stimulate the sources of my life, nor did it rise and spread confusion through my brain, but it burned in my conscience as if a torch, dipped in some liquid hell, had been tossed there.

It was a special occasion—this was what I whispered to my conscience—this was the breath that I breathed a hundred times into it to quench the hissing torture. It was a special occasion. What was I, to stand before these lovely Christian women with an assumption of superior virtue, and a rebuke of their habits and indulgences? I did not want the wine; I did not wish to drink again; and thus the fire gradually died away. I was left, however, with the uncomfortable consciousness that I had in no degree raised myself in the estimation of the family. They had witnessed the sacrifice of a scruple and an indication of my weakness. Livingston, I knew, felt sadly about it. It had brought me nothing that I desired or expected.

The days between Christmas and New Year's were packed

with a thousand pleasures. A party was gathered for us in which I was presented to many beautiful girls and their stylish brothers. We visited the theaters, we were invited everywhere, and we often attended as many as two or three assemblies in an evening. The days and nights were a continued round of social pleasures, and we lived in a whirl of excitement. There was no time for thought, and with me, at least, no desire for it.

But the time flew away until we waited only the excitements of New Year's Day to close our vacation, and return to the quiet life we had left under the elms of New Haven. That day was a memorable one to me and demands a chapter for its record.

CHAPTER XV.

I GO OUT TO MAKE NEW YEAR'S CALLS AND RETURN IN DISGRACE.

New Year's morning dawned bright and cold. "A happy New Year to you!" shouted Livingston from his bed. The call woke me from a heavy slumber into delightful anticipations, and the realization of a great joy in living, such as comes only to youth—an exulting, superabounding sense of vitality that care and age never know.

We rose and dressed ourselves with scrupulous pains-taking for calls. On descending to the breakfast-room, we found the young ladies quite as excited as ourselves. They had prepared a little book in which to keep a record of the calls they expected to receive during the day, for, according to the universal custom, they were to keep open house. The carriage was to be at the disposal of my friend and myself, and we were as ambitious concerning the amount of courtesy to be shown as the young ladies were touching the amount to be received. We intended, before bedtime, to present our New Year's greetings to every lady we had met during the week.

Before we left the house, I saw what preparations had been made for the hospitable reception of visitors. Among them stood a row of wine bottles and decanters. The view saddened me. Although I had not tasted wine since "the special occasion," my conscience had not ceased to remind me, though with weakened sting, that I had sacrificed a conscientious scruple and broken a promise. I could in no way rid myself of the sense of having been wounded, stained, impoverished. I had ceased to be what I had been. I had engaged in no debauch, I had developed no appetite, I was not in love with my sin. I could have heartily wished that wine were out of the world. Yet I had consented to have my defenses broken into, and there had been neither time nor practical disposition to repair the breach. Not one prayer had I offered, or dared to offer, during the week. My foolish act had shut out God and extinguished the sense of his loving favor, and I had rushed blindly through my pleasures from day to day, refusing to listen to the upbraidings of that faithful monitor which he had placed within me.

At last, it was declared not too early to begin our visits. Already several young gentlemen had shown themselves at the Livingstons, and my friend and I sallied forth. The coachman, waiting at the door, and thrashing his hands to keep them warm, wished us "a happy New Year" as we appeared.

"The same to you," responded Livingston, "and there'll be another one to-night, if you serve us well to-day."

"Thankee, sir," said the coachman, smiling in anticipation of the promised fee.

The footman took the list of calls to be made that Livingston had prepared, mounted to his seat, the ladies waved their hands to us from the window, and we drove rapidly away.

"Bonnicastle, my boy," said Livingston, throwing his arm around me as we rattled up the avenue, "this is new business to you. Now don't do anything to-day that you will be sorry for. Do you know, I cannot like what has happened? You have not been brought up like the rest of us, and you're all right. Have your own way. It's nobody's business."

I knew, of course, exactly what he meant, but I do not know what devil stirred within me the spirit of resentment. To be cautioned and counseled by one who had never professed or manifested any sense of religious obligation—by one above whose moral plane I had fancied that I stood—made me half angry. I had consciously fallen, and I felt miserably enough about it, when I permitted myself to feel at all, but to be reminded of it by others vexed me to the quick, and rasped my wretched pride.

"Take care of yourself," I responded, sharply, "and don't worry about me. I shall do as I please."

"It's the last time, old boy," said Livingston, biting his lip, which quivered with pain and mortification. "It's the last time. When I kiss a fellow and he spits in my face I never do it again. Make yourself perfectly easy on that score."

Impulsively I grasped his hand and exclaimed: "Oh! don't say that. I beg your pardon. Let's not quarrel: I was a fool and a great deal worse, to answer as I did."

"All right," said he; "but if you get into trouble, don't blame me; that's all."

At this, we drew up to a house to make our first call. It was a grand establishment. The ladies were beautifully dressed, and very cordial, for Livingston was a favorite, and any young man whom he introduced was sure of a welcome. I was flattered and excited by the attention I received, and charmed by the graceful manners of those who rendered it. House after house we visited in the same way, uniformly declining all the hospitalities of the table, on the ground that it was too early to think of eating or drinking.

At last we began to grow hungry for our lunch, and at a bountifully loaded table accepted an invitation to eat. Several young fellows were standing around it, nibbling their sandwiches, and sipping their wine. A glass was poured and handed to me by a young lady with the toilet and manner of a princess. I took it without looking at Livingston, held it for a while, then tasted it, for I was thirsty; then tasted again and again, until my glass was empty. I was as unused to the stimulant as a child; and when I emerged into the open air my face was aflame with its exciting poison. There was a troubled look on Livingston's face, and I could not resist the feeling that he was either angry or alarmed. My first experience was that of depression. This was partly moral, I suppose; but the sharp air soon reduced the feverish sensation about my head and eyes, and then a strange thrill of exhilaration passed through me. It was different from anything I had ever known, and I was conscious, for the first time, of the charm of alcohol.

Then came the longing to taste again. I saw that I was in no way disabled. On the contrary, I knew I had never been so buoyant in spirits, or so brilliant in conversation. My imagination was excited. Everything presented to me its comical aspects, and there were ripples and roars of laughter wherever I went. After repeated glasses, I swallowed at one house a draught of champagne. It was the first I had ever tasted, and the cold, tingling fluid was all that was necessary to make me noisy and hilarious. I rallied Livingston on his long face, assured him that I had never seen a jolly fellow alter so rapidly as he had since morning, begged him to take something that would warm him, and began to sing.

"Now, really you must be quiet in this house," said he, as we drew up to an old-fashioned mansion in the suburbs. "They are quiet people here, and are not used to noisy fellows."

"I'll wake 'em up," said I, "and make 'em jolly."

We entered the door. I was conscious of a singing in my ears, and a sense of confusion. The warm air of the room wrought in a few moments a change in my feelings, but I struggled against it, and tried with pitiful efforts to command myself, and to appear the sober man I was not. There was a little group around us near the windows, and at the other end of the drawing-room—somewhat in shadow, for it was nearly night—there was another. At length a tall man rose from this latter group, and advanced toward the light. Immediately behind him a young girl, almost a woman in stature and bearing, followed. The moment I could distinguish his form and features and those of his companion, I rushed toward them, forgetful for the instant that I had lost my self-control, and embraced them both. Then I undertook to present Mr. Bradford and my friend Millie to Livingston.

It did not seem strange to me to find them in New York. What foolish things I said to Mr. Bradford and what maudlin words to Millie I do not know. Both carried grave faces.

Millie's eyes—for even through all that cloud of stupid insanity, from this far point of distance I see them still—burned first like fire, then filled with tears.

For what passed immediately after this, I am indebted to another memory and not to my own.

After watching me and listening to me for a minute in silence, Millie darted to the side of Livingston, and looking him fiercely in the face, exclaimed: "You are a wicked man. You ought to be ashamed to let him do it. Oh! he was so good and so sweet when he went away from Bradford, and you have spoiled him—you have spoiled him. I'll never forgive you, never!"

"Millie! my daughter!" exclaimed Mr. Bradford.

Millie threw herself upon a sofa, and burying her head in the pillow, burst into hysterical tears.

Livingston turned to Mr. Bradford and said: "I give you my word of honor, sir, that I have not drunk one drop of wine to-day. I have refrained from drinking entirely for his sake, and your daughter's accusation is most unjust."

Mr. Bradford took the young man's hand cordially and said: "I believe you, and you must pardon Millie. She is terribly disappointed, and so am I. She supposed her friend had been tempted by bad companions, and as you were with him, she at once attributed the evil influence to you."

"On the contrary," responded Livingston, "no man has tempted him at all, and no man could tempt him. None but women who prate about their sufferings from drunken husbands and brothers could have moved him from his determination. I am ashamed to tell you who attacked his scruples first. It was one who has reason enough, Heaven knows, to hate wine; but her efforts have been followed by scores of younger women to-day, who have seemed to take delight in leading him into a mad debauch."

Livingston spoke bitterly, and as he closed, Millie sprang from the sofa, and seizing his hand, kissed it, and wet it with her tears.

"Please take him home, and be kind to him," she said. "I am sure he will never do it again."

In the meantime, entirely overcome by the heat of the room, acting upon nerves which had been stimulated beyond the power of endurance, I had sunk helplessly into a chair, where I stared stupidly upon the group, unable to comprehend a word of the conversation.

Mr. Bradford took Livingston aside, and after some words of private conversation, both approached me, and taking me by my arms, led me from the house, and placed me in the carriage. The dusk had already descended, and I do not think that I was observed, save by one or two strangers passing upon the sidewalk. The seal of secrecy was placed upon the lips of the household by the kind offices of Mr. Bradford, and the story, so far as I know, was never told, save as it was afterward told to me, and as I have told it in these pages.

The carriage was driven rapidly homeward. The house of the Livingstons was upon a corner, so that a side entrance was available for getting me to my room without public observation. The strong arms of Livingston and the footman bore me to my chamber, removed my clothing, and placed me in bed, where I sank at once into that heavy drunken slumber from which there is no waking except that of torture.

The morning after New Year's was as bright as that which preceded it, but it had no brightness for me. The heart which had leaped up into gladness as it greeted the New Year's dawn, was a lump of lead. The head that was as clear as the sky itself on the previous morning, was dull and heavy with a strange, throbbing pain. My mouth was dry and hot, and a languor held me in possession from which it seemed impossible to rouse myself. Then all the mad doings of the day which had witnessed my fall came back to me, and it seemed as if the shame of it all would kill me. Livingston brought me some cooling and corrective draught, on the strength of which I rose. The dizzy feeling was not entirely gone, and I reeled in a pitiful way while dressing; but cold water, a cool room, and motion, soon placed me in possession of myself.

"I can't go down to breakfast, Livingston," I said. "I have disgraced you and all the family."

"Oh! women forgive, my boy," said he, with a contemptuous shrug. "Never you mind. If they don't like their own work, let them do it better."

"But I can't face them," I said.

"Face them! Bah! it's they who are to face you. But don't trouble yourself. You'll find them as placid as a summer morning, ignoring everything. They're used to it."

He insisted, and I descended to the breakfast room. Not an allusion was made to the previous day's experiences, except as a round of unalloyed pleasure. The young ladies had received an enormous number of calls, and on the sideboard stood a row of empty decanters. There was no thought of the headaches and heart-burnings with which the city abounded, no thought of suicidal habits begun or confirmed through their agency, no thought of the drunkards they were nursing into husbands. There sat the mother in her matronly dignity, dispensing her fragrant coffee, there were the young ladies chattering over their list, and talking of this one and that one of their callers, and there was I, a confused ruin of hopes and purposes which clustered around a single central point of consciousness and that point hot with shame and remorse.

We were to return on the afternoon boat that day, and I was not sorry. I was quite ready to turn my back on all the splendors that had so charmed me on my arrival, on all the new acquaintances I had made, and on my temptations.

Special efforts were made by Mrs. Livingston and her daughters to reinstate me in my self-respect. They were cordial in their expressions of friendship, begged that I would not forget them, invited me to visit them again and often, and loaded me with all courteous and friendly attentions. Livingston was quiet and cold through it all. He had intended to return me as good as he brought me, and had failed. He was my senior, and had entertained a genuine respect for my conscientious scruples, over which, from the first moment I had known him, he had assumed a sort of guardianship. He was high-spirited, and as I had once repelled his cautioning care, I knew I should hear no more from him.

When we arrived at the boat, I went at once into the cabin, sank into a chair, buried my face in my hands, and gave myself up to my sorrow and shame. I was glad that I should not find Henry in my room on my return. He had been gone a month when I left, for, through the necessities of self-support, he had resumed his school duties in Bradford for the winter. I thought of him in his daily work, and his nightly visits at my father's house; of the long conversations that would pass between him and those whom I loved best about one who had proved himself unworthy of their regard; of the shameful manner in which I had betrayed the confidence of my benefactress, and the disgrace which I had brought upon myself in the eyes of Mr. Bradford and Millie. It then occurred to me for the first time that Mr. Bradford was on a New Year's visit to his daughter, whom he had previously placed in a New York school. How should I ever meet them again? How could they ever forgive me? How could I ever win their respect and confidence again? "O God! O God!" I said, in a whisper of anguish, "how can I ever come to Thee again, when I knew in my inmost heart that I was disobeying and grieving Thee?"

I was conscious at this moment that steps approached me. Then followed a light touch upon my shoulder. I looked up, and saw Mr. Bradford. I had never before seen his countenance so sad, and at the same time so severe.

"Don't reproach me," I said, lifting my hands in deprecation, "don't reproach me: if you do, I shall die."

"Reproach you, my boy?" he said, drawing a chair to my side while his lips quivered with sympathy, "there would be no need of it if I were disposed to do so. Reproach for error between erring mortals is not becoming."

Mr. Bradford and Arthur on the steamer.

(p. 240.)

"Do you suppose you can ever forgive me and trust me again?" I asked.

"I forgive you and trust you now. I give you credit for common-sense. You have proved, in your own experience, the truth of all I have told you, and I do not believe that you need to learn anything further, except that one mistake and misstep like yours need not ruin a life."

"Do you really think," said I, eagerly grasping his arm, "that I can ever be again what I have been?"

"Never again," he replied, sadly shaking his head. "The bloom is gone from the fruit, but if you hate your folly with a hatred which will forever banish it from your life, the fruit is uninjured."

"And are they to know all this in Bradford?" I asked.

"Never from me," he replied.

"You are too kind to me," I said. "You have always been kind."

"I don't know. I have intended to be kind, but if you are ruined through the influence of Mrs. Sanderson's money I shall curse the day on which I suggested the thought that brought you under her patronage."

"Will you accept a pledge from me," I said eagerly, "in regard to the future?"

"No indeed, Arthur. No pledge coming from you to-day, while you are half beside yourself with shame and sorrow, would have the value of a straw. A promise can never redeem a man who loses himself through lack of strength and principle. A man who cannot be controlled by God's Word certainly cannot be controlled by his own. It will take weeks for you to arrive at a point where you can form a resolution that will be of the slightest value, and, when you reach that point, no resolution will be needed. Some influence has changed your views of life and your objects. You have in some way been shaken at your foundations. When these become sound again, you will be restored to yourself, and not until then. You fancied that the religious influences and experiences which we both remember had done much to strengthen you, but in truth they did nothing. They interrupted, and, for the time, ruined the processes of a religious education. You fancied that in a day you had built what it takes a lifetime to build, and you were, owing to the reactions of that great excitement, and to the confusion into which your thoughts and feelings were thrown, weaker to resist temptation than when you returned from The Bird's Nest. I saw it all then, just as plainly as I see it now. I have discounted all this experience of yours—not precisely this, but something like it. I knew you would be tempted, and that into the joints of a harness too loosely knit and fastened some arrow would find its way."

"What am I to do? What can I do?" I said piteously.

"Become a child again," he responded. "Go back to the simple faith and the simple obedience which you learned of your father. Put away your pride and your love of that which enervates and emasculates you, and try with God's help to grow into a true man. I have had so many weaknesses and faults of my own to look after, that I have never had the heart to undertake the instruction of others; but I feel a degree of responsibility for you, and I know it is in you to become a man who will bring joy to your father and pride to me."

"Oh! do believe me, Mr. Bradford, do," I said, "when I tell you that I will try to become the man you desire me to be."

"I believe you," he responded. "I have no doubt that you will try, in a weaker or stronger way and more or less persistently, to restore yourself to your old footing. And now, as you have forced a promise upon me, which I did not wish you to make, you must accept one from me. I have taken you into my heart. I took you into its warmest place when, years ago, on our first acquaintance, you told me that you loved me. And now I promise you that if I see that you cannot be what you ought to be while retaining your present prospects of wealth, I will put you to such a test as will prove whether you have the manhood in you that I have given you the credit for, and whether you are worth saving to yourself and your friends."

His last words wounded me. Nay, they did more—they kindled my anger. Though grievously humiliated, my pride was not dead. I questioned in my heart his right to speak so strongly to me, and to declare his purpose to thrust himself into my life in any contingency, but I covered my feelings, and even thanked him in a feeble way for his frankness. Then I inquired about Henry, and learned in what high respect he was held in Bradford, how much my father and all his acquaintances were delighted in him, and how prosperously his affairs were going on. Even in his self-respectful poverty, I envied him— a poverty through which he had manifested such sterling manhood as to win the hearts of all who came in contact with him.

"I shall miss him more than I can tell you," I said, "when I get back to my lonely room. No one can take his place, and I need him now more than I ever did before."

"It is as well for you to be alone," said Mr. Bradford, "if you are in earnest. There are some things in life that can only be wrought out between a man and his God, and you have just that thing in hand."

Our conversation was long, and touched many topics. Mr. Bradford shook my hand heartily as we parted at the wharf, and Livingston and I were soon in a carriage, whirling towards the town. I entered my silent room with a sick and discouraged feeling, with a sad presentiment of the struggle which its walls would witness during the long winter months before me, and with a terrible sense of the change through which I had passed during the brief week of my absence.

And here, lest my reader be afflicted with useless anticipations of pain, I record the fact that wine never tempted me again. One bite of the viper had sufficed. I had trampled upon my conscience, and even that had changed to a viper beneath my feet, and struck its fangs deep into the recoiling flesh. From that day forward I forswore the indulgence of the cup. While in college it was comparatively easy to do this, for my habit was known, and as no one but Livingston knew of my fall, it was respected. I was rallied by some of the fellows on my sleepy eyes and haggard looks, but none of them imagined the cause, and the storm that had threatened to engulf me blew over, and the waves around me grew calm again,—the waves around me, but not the waves within.

For a whole week after I returned, I was in constant and almost unendurable torture. The fear of discovery took possession of me. What if the men who were passing at the time Mr. Bradford and Livingston lifted me into the carriage had known me? Was Peter Mullens in New York that night, and was he one of them? This question no sooner took possession of my mind, than I fancied, from the looks and whisperings of him and his companions, that the secret was in their possession. I had no peace from these suspicions until I had satisfied myself that he had not left the college during the holidays. Would Mr. Bradford, by some accident, or through forgetfulness of his promise to me, speak of the matter to my father, or Henry, or Mrs. Sanderson? Would Millie write about it to her mother? Would it be carelessly talked about by the ladies who had witnessed my disgrace? Would it be possible for me ever to show myself in Bradford again? Would the church learn of my lapse and bring me under its discipline? Would the religious congregations I had addressed hear of my fall from sobriety, and come to regard me as a hypocrite? So sore was my self-love, so sensitive was my pride, that I am sure I should have lied to cover my shame, had the terrible emergency arisen. It did not rise, and for that I cannot cease to be grateful.

It will readily be seen that, while the fear of discovery was upon me, and while I lived a false life of carelessness and even gayety among my companions, to cover the tumults of dread and suspicion that were going on within me, I did not make much progress in spiritual life. In truth I made none at all. My prayers were only wild beseechings that I might be spared from exposure, and pledges of future obedience should my prayers be answered. So thoroughly did my fears of men possess me, that there was no room for repentance toward God, or such a repentance as would give me the basis of a new departure and a better life. I had already tried to live two lives that should not be discordant with each other; now I tried to live two lives that I knew to be antagonistic. It now became an object to appear to be what I was not. I resumed at intervals my attendance upon the prayer-meetings to make it appear that I still clung to my religious life. Then, while in the society of my companions, I manifested a careless gayety which I did not feel. All the manifestations of my real life took place in the solitude of my room. There, wrestling with my fears, and shut out from my old sources of comfort and strength, I passed my nights. With a thousand luxurious appliances around me, no sense of luxury ever came to me. My heart was a central living coal, and all around it was ashes. I even feared that the coal might die, and that Henry, when he should return, would find his room bereft of all that would give him welcome and cheer.

As the weeks passed away, the fear slowly expired, and alas! nothing that was better came in its place. No sooner did I begin to experience the sense of safety from exposure, and from the temptation which had brought me such grievous harm, than the old love of luxurious life, and the old plans for securing it, came back to me. I felt sure that wine would never tempt me again, and with this confidence I built me a foundation of pride and self-righteousness on which I could stand, and regard myself with a certain degree of complacency.

As for efficient study, that was out of the question. I was in no mood or condition for work. I scrambled through my lessons in a disgraceful way. The better class of students were all surpassing me, and I found myself getting hopelessly into the rear. I had fitful rebellions against this, and showed them and myself what I could do when I earnestly tried: but the power of persistence, which is born of a worthy purpose, held strongly in the soul, was absent, and there could be no true advancement without it.

I blush with shame, even now, to think how I tried to cover my delinquencies from my father and Mrs. Sanderson, by becoming more attentive to them than I had ever been in the matter of writing letters. I knew that there was nothing that carried so much joy to my father as a letter from me. I knew that he read every letter I wrote him, again and again —that he carried it in his pocket at his work—that he took it out at meals, and talked about it. I knew also that Mrs. Sanderson's life was always gladdened by attentions of this sort from me, and that they tended to keep her heart open toward me. In just the degree in which I was conscious that I was unworthy of their affection, did I strive to present to them my most amiable side, and to convince them that I was unchanged.

I lived this hypocritical, unfruitful life during all that winter; and when Henry came to me in the spring, crowned with the fruits of his labor, and fresh from the loves and friendships of his Bradford home, with his studies all in hand, and with such evident growth of manhood that I felt almost afraid of him, he found me an unhappy and almost reckless laggard, with nothing to show for the winter's privileges but a weakened will, dissipated powers, frivolous habits, deadened moral and religious sensibilities, and a life that had degenerated into subterfuge and sham.

My natural love of approbation—the same greed for the good opinion and the praise of others which in my childhood made me a liar—had lost none of its force, and did much to shape my intercourse with all around me. The sense of worthlessness which induced my special efforts to retain the good-will of Mrs. Sanderson, and the admiration and confidence of my father, moved me to a new endeavor to gain the friendship of all my fellow-students. I felt that I could not afford to have enemies. I had lost none of my popularity with the exclusive clique to which I had attached myself, for even Livingston had seen with delight that I was not disposed to repeat the mistake of which he had been so distressed a witness. I grew more courteous and complaisant toward those I had regarded as socially my inferiors, until I knew that I was looked upon by them as a good fellow. I was easy-tempered, ready at repartee, generous and careless, and although I had lost all reputation for industry and scholarship, I possessed just the character and manners which made me welcome to every group. I blush while I write of it, to remember how I curried favor with Mr. Peter Mullens and his set; but to such mean shifts did a mean life force me. To keep the bark of my popularity from foundering, on which I was obliged to trust everything, I tossed overboard from time to time, to meet every rising necessity, my self-respect, until I had but little left.

CHAPTER XVI.

PETER MULLENS ACQUIRES A VERY LARGE STOCK OF OLD CLOTHES.

THOUGH Mr. Peter Mullens had but slender relations to my outer life—hardly enough to warrant the notice I have already taken of him—there was a relation which I recognized in my experience and circumstances that makes it necessary for me to say more of him. He had recognized this relation himself, and it was this that engendered my intense personal dislike of him. I knew that his willing dependence on others had robbed him of any flavor of manhood he might at one time have possessed, and that I, very differently organized, was suffering from the same cause. I watched the effect upon him of this demoralizing influence, with almost a painful curiosity.

Having, as he supposed, given up himself, he felt that he had a right to support. There seemed to him to be no sweetness in bread that could be earned. Everything came amiss to him that came with personal cost. He was always looking for gifts. I will not say that he prayed for them, but I have no doubt that he prayed, and that his temporal wants mingled in his petitions. No gift humiliated him: he lived by gifts. His greed for these was pitiful, and often ludicrous. Indeed, he was the strangest mixture of piety, avarice, and beggarly meanness that I had ever seen.

My second spring in college was verging upon summer. The weather was intensely hot, and all the fellows had put themselves into summer clothing—all but poor Peter Mullens. He had come out of the winter very seedy, and his heavy clothing still clung to him, in the absence of supplies of a lighter character. Although he had a great many pairs of woolen socks and striped mittens, and a dozen or two neckties, which had been sent to him by a number of persons to whom he gave the indefinite designation of "the sisters," there seemed to be no way by which he could transform them into summer clothing. He was really in a distressed condition, and "the sisters" failed to meet the emergency.

At a gathering of the fellows of our clique one night, his affairs were brought up for discussion, and it was determined that we should go through our respective wardrobes and weed out all the garments which we did not intend to wear again, and, on the first dark night, take them to his room. I was to make the first visit, and to be followed in turn by the others.

Accordingly, having made up a huge bundle of garments that would be of use to him, provided he could wear them— and he could wear anything, apparently—I started out one evening, and taking it in my arms, went to his room. This was located in a remote corner of the dormitory, at the bottom of a narrow hall, and as the hall was nearly dark, I deposited my bundle at the door and knocked for admission.

"Come in!" responded Mullens.

I entered, and by good fortune found him alone. He was sitting in the dark, by the single open window of his room, and I could see by the dim light that he was stripped of coat and waistcoat. He did not know me at first, but, rising and striking a light, he exclaimed: "Well, this is kind of you, Bonnicastle. I was just thinking of you."

He then remembered that his glasses had been laid aside. Putting them on, he seemed to regard himself as quite presentable, and made no further attempt to increase his clothing. I looked around the bare room, with its single table, its wretched pair of chairs, its dirty bed, and its lonely occupant, and contrasting it with the cosy apartment I had just left, my heart grew full of pity for him.

"So you were thinking of me, eh?" I said. "That was very kind of you. Pray, what were you thinking? Nothing bad, I hope."

"No, I was thinking about your privileges. I was thinking how you had been favored."

It was strange that it had never occurred to Mullens to think about or to envy those who held money by right, or by the power of earning it. It was only the money that came as a gift that stirred him. There were dozens or hundreds of fellows whose parents were educating them, but these were never the subject of his envious thoughts.

"Let's not talk about my privileges," I said. "How are you getting along yourself?"

"I am really very hard up," he replied. "If the sisters would only send me trousers, and such things, I should be all right, but they don't seem to consider that I want trousers any more than they do, confound them."

The quiet indignation with which this was uttered amused me, and I laughed outright. But Mullens was in sober earnest, and going to his closet he brought forth at least a dozen pairs of thick woolen socks, and as many pairs of striped mittens, and laid them on the table.

"Look at that pile," said Mullens, "and weep."

The comical aspect of the matter had really reached the poor fellow's apprehension, and he laughed heartily with me.

"What are you going to do with them?" I asked.

"I don't know," he replied; "I've thought of an auction. What do you say?"

"Why don't you try to sell them at the shops?" I inquired.

"Let me alone for that. I've been all over the city with 'em," said he. "One fellow said they didn't run even, and I don't think they do, very, that's a fact. Another one said they looked like the fag-end of an old stock; and the last one I went to asked me if I stole them."

"Well, Mullens, the wind is tempered to the shorn lamb," I said, consolingly. "It's June."

"But it don't apply," said Mullens. "I'm not shorn. The trouble is that I've got too much wool."

This was bright for Mullens, and we both laughed again.

After the laugh had passed, I said: "I think I know of eight or ten fellows who will relieve you of your surplus stock, and, as I am one of them, I propose to take a pair of socks and a pair of mittens now."

The manner of the man changed immediately. His face grew animated, and his eyes fairly gleamed through his spectacles. He jumped to his feet as I spoke of purchasing, and exclaimed: "Will you? What will you give? Make us an offer."

"Oh, you must set your own price," I said.

"Well, you see they are very good socks, don't you?" said Mullens. "Now, every stitch in those socks and mittens was knit upon honor. There isn't a mercenary inch of yarn in 'em. Take your pick of the mittens. By the way, I haven't shown you my neck-ties," and, rushing to his closet, he brought forth quite an armful of them.

The humble sufferer had become a lively peddler, bent upon driving the sharpest bargain and selling the most goods possible to a rare customer. Selecting a pair of socks, a pair of mittens, and a neck-tie of a somewhat soberer hue than I had been accustomed to wear, he laid them by themselves, and then, wiping his forehead and his glasses with a little mop of a handkerchief, he put on a mildly judicial face, and said:

"Bonnicastle, my dear friend, I've always taken a great deal of interest in you; and now you have it in your power to do me a world of good. Think, just think, Bonnicastle, of the weary hours that have been spent on these articles of apparel by those of whom the world is not worthy! Think of the benevolence that inspired every stitch. Think of the—of the—thoughts that have run through those devoted minds. Think of those sisters respectively saying to themselves: 'I know not whom I am laboring for—it may be for Mullens or it may be for one more worthy,—but for whomsoever it is, it is for one who will stand up in defense of the truth when I am gone. His feet, bent upon errands of mercy, will be kept comfortable by these stockings. His hands, carrying succor to the fallen and consolation to the afflicted, will be warmed by these mittens. These neck-ties will surround the neck—the—throat—of one who will breathe words of peace and good-will.' My dear Bonnicastle, there is more in these humble articles of apparel than appears to the carnal eye—much more—incalculably more. Try to take it in when we come to the matter of price. Try to take it all in, and then discharge your duty as becomes a man who has been favored."

"Look here, Mullens," said I, "you are working on my feelings, and the articles are getting so expensive that I can't buy them."

"Oh, don't feel that way;" said he, "I only want to have you get some idea what there is in these things. Why, there's love, good-will, self-sacrifice, devotion, and woman's tender heart."

"Pity there couldn't have been some trowsers," said I.

Mullens' lip quivered. He was not sure whether I was joking or not, but he laid his hand appealingly upon my knee, and then settled back in his chair and wiped his forehead and spectacles again. Having made up my mind that Mullens had determined to raise an enormous revenue from his goods, I was somewhat surprised when he said briskly, "Bonnicastle, what do you say to a dollar and a half? That's only fifty cents an article, and the whole stock will bring me only fifteen or twenty dollars at that price."

"I'll take them," said I.

"Good!" exclaimed Mullens, slapping his knee. "Who'll have the next bowl? Walk up, gentlemen!"

Mullens had evidently officiated in an oyster booth at militia musters. In his elated state of feeling, the impulse to run into his old peddler's lingo was irrepressible. I think he felt complimented by the hearty laugh with which I greeted his cry.

"If I'm going into this business," said Mullens, "I really must have some brown paper. Do you suppose, Bonnicastle, that if you should go to one of the shops, and tell them the object,—a shop kept by one of our friends, you know,—one who has the cause at heart—he would give you a package of brown paper? I'd go myself, but I've been around a good deal."

"Wouldn't you rather have me buy some?" I asked.

"Why, no; it doesn't seem to be exactly the thing to pay out money for brown paper," responded Mullens.

"I'm not used to begging," I said.

"Why, it isn't begging, Bonnicastle; it's asking for the cause."

"You really must excuse me, Mullens."

"All right," said he; "here's an old newspaper that will do for your package. Now don't forget to tell all your friends that I am ready for 'em. Tell 'em the cause is a good one—that it really involves the—the welfare of society. And tell 'em the things are dirt cheap. Don't forget that."

Mullens had become as cheerful and lively as a cricket; and while he was doing up my package, I opened the door and brought in my bundle. As I broke the string and unfolded the bountiful contents, he paused in a pleased amazement, and then, leaping forward and embracing me, exclaimed: "Bonnicastle, you're an angel! What do you suppose that pile is worth, now, in hard cash?"

"Oh, I don't know; it's worth a good deal to you," I replied.

"And you really don't feel it at all, do you now? Own up."

"No," I answered, "not at all. You are welcome to the whole pile."

"Yes, Bonnicastle," said he, sliding smoothly back from the peddler into the pious beneficiary, "you've given out of your abundance, and you have the blessed satisfaction of feeling that you have done your duty. I don't receive it for myself, but for the cause. I am a poor, unworthy instrument. Say, Bonnicastle, if you should see some of these things on others, would you mind?"

"Not in the least," I said. "Do you propose to share your good fortune with your friends?"

"Yes," said Mullens, "I shall sell these things to them,

very reasonably indeed. They shall have no cause to complain."

At this moment there was a knock, and Livingston, with a grave face, walked in with his bundle, and opening it, laid it upon the table. Mullens sank into his chair, quite overwhelmed. "Fellows," said he, "this is too much. I can bear one bundle, but under two you must excuse me if I seem to totter."

Another and another followed Livingston into the room, and deposited their burdens, until the table was literally piled. Mullens actually began to snivel.

"It's a lark, fellows," said Mullens, from behind his handkerchief. "It's a lark: I know it. I see it; but oh, fellows! it's a blessed lark—a blessed, blessed lark! Larks may be employed to bring tribute into the storehouse. Larks may be overruled, and used as means. I know you are making fun of me, but the cause goes on. If there isn't room on the table, put them on the floor. They shall all be employed. If I have ever done you injustice in my thoughts, fellows, you must forgive me. This wipes out everything; and as I don't see any boots in your parcels, perhaps you'll be kind enough to remember that I wear tens, with a low instep. Has the last man come? Is the cup full? What do you suppose the whole pile is worth?"

Mullens ran on in this way, muddled by his unexpected good fortune and his greed, with various pious ejaculations which, for very reverence of the words he used, my pen refuses to record.

Then it suddenly occurred to him that he was not making the most of his opportunities. Springing to his feet, and turning peddler in an instant, he said: "Fellows, Bonnicastle has bought a pair of socks, a pair of striped mittens and a necktie from my surplus stock. I've got enough of them to go all around. What do you say to them at fifty cents apiece?"

"We've been rather expecting," said Livingston, with a quiet twinkle in his eye, "that you would make us a present of these."

This was a new thought to Mullens, and it sobered him at once. "Fellows," said he, "you know my heart; but these things are a sacred trust. They have been devoted to a cause, and from that cause I cannot divert them."

"Oh! of course not," said Livingston; "I only wanted to test your faithfulness. You're as sound as a nut."

The conversation ended in a purchase of the "surplus stock," and then, seeing that the boys had not finished their fun, and fearing that it might run into some unpleasant excesses, Livingston and I retired.

The next morning our ears were regaled with an account of the remaining experiences of the evening, but it does not need to be recorded here. It is sufficient to say that before the company left his room, Mullens was arrayed from head to foot with a dress made up from various parcels, and that in that dress he was obliged to mount his table and make a speech. He appeared, however, the next morning, clothed in comfortable garments, which of course were recognized by their former owners, and formed a subject of merriment among them. We never saw them, however, upon any others of his set, and he either chose to cover his good fortune from them by selling his frippery to the Hebrew dealers in such merchandise, or they refused to be his companions in wearing garments that were known in the **college.**

CHAPTER XVII.

I CHANGE MY RELIGIOUS VIEWS TO CONFORM WITH MY MORAL PRACTICE, AND AM GRADUATED WITHOUT HONORS.

From the first hour of my direct violation of my conscience, there began, almost imperceptibly at first, a change of my views of religious doctrine and obligation. It was one of the necessities of my position. Retaining the strict notions of my childhood and younger youth, I should not have enjoyed a moment of peace; and my mind involuntarily went to work to reconcile my opinions to my looser life. It was necessary to bring my convictions and my conscience into harmony with my conduct, else the warfare within me would have been unendurable. The first change related to duty. It seemed to me that God, remembering that I was dust, and that I was peculiarly weak under specific temptations, would be less rigid in his requirements of me than I had formerly supposed. As this conclusion seemed to make him more lovable to me, I permitted it to deceive me wholly. Then there was something which flattered me in being considered less "blue" than the majority of those who made a profession of religion. It was pleasant to be liberal, for liberality carried no condemnation with it of the careless life around me.

But this was not all. It was only the open gate at which I entered a wide field of doubt. All my religious opinions took on an air of unreality. The old, implicit faith which, like an angel with a sword of flame, had stood at the door of my heart, comforting me with its presence, and keeping at a distance all the shapes of unbelief, took its flight, and the dark band gathered closer, with a thousand questions and suggestions. Was there a God? Was the God whom I had learned to worship anything more than a figment of conspiring imaginations? If He were more than this, had he revealed himself in words? Was Jesus Christ a historical character or a myth? Was there any such thing, after all, as personal accountability? Was the daily conduct of so insignificant a person as myself of the slightest moment to a Being who held an infinite universe in charge? Who knew that the soul was immortal, and that its condition here bore any relation to its condition there? Was not half of that which I had looked upon as sin, made sin only by a conscience wrongly educated? Was drinking wine a sin in itself? If not, why had it so wounded me? Other consciences did not condemn an act which had cost me my peace and self-respect. Who knew but that a thousand things which I had considered wrong were only wrong because I so considered them? After all my pains-taking and my prayers, had I been anything better than a slave to a conscience perverted or insufficiently informed?

The path from an open violation of conscience to a condition of religious doubt, is as direct as that which leads to heaven. It was so in my case, and the observation of a long life has shown me that it is so in every case. Just in the proportion that my practice degenerated did my views become modified to accommodate themselves to my life.

I said very little about the changes going on in my mind, except to my faithful companion and friend, Henry. When he returned from Bradford, he, for the first time, became fully aware of the great change that had taken place in me. He was an intense hater of sham and cant, and sympathized with me in my dislike of the type of piety with which we were often thrown in contact. This, I suppose, had blinded him to the fact that I was trying to sustain myself in my criticism of others. I could not hide my growing infidelity from him, however, for it seemed necessary for me to have some one to talk with, and I was conscious of a new disposition to argue and defend myself. Here I was misled again. I fancied that my modification of views came of intellectual convictions, and that I could not be to blame for changes based upon what

I was fond of calling "my God-given reason." I lost sight of the fact that the changes came first, and that the only office to which I put "my God-given reason" was that of satisfying and defending myself. Oh, the wretched sophistries of those wretched days and years!

I do not like to speak so much of prayer as I have been compelled to in these pages, for even this sounds like cant to many ears; but, in truth, I cannot write the story of my life without it. I do not believe there can be such a thing as a truly religious life without prayer. The religious soul must hold converse and communion with the Infinite or its religion can not live. It may be the simple expression of gratitude and desire. It may be the prostration of the soul in worship and adoration. It may be the up-springing of the spirit in strong aspiration; but in some way or form there must be prayer, or religion dies. There must be an open way between the heart of man and the heart of the Infinite—a ladder that reaches from the pillow of stone to the pillars of the Throne, where angels may climb and angels may descend—or the religious life of the soul can have no ministry.

In my changed condition and circumstances, I found myself deprived of this great source of life. First my sin shut me away, and my neglect of known and acknowledged duty. Then my frivolous pursuits and trifling diversions rendered me unfit for the awful presence into which prayer led me. Then, unbelief placed its bar before me. In truth, I found in prayer, whenever I attempted it, only a hollow expression of penitence, from a weak and unwilling heart, toward a being in whose existence I did not more than half believe.

I bowed with Henry at our bed every night, but it was only a mockery. He apprehended it at last, and questioned me about it. One night, after we had risen from our knees, he said: "Arthur, how is it with you? I don't understand how a man who talks as you do can pray with any comfort to himself. You are not at all what you used to be."

"I'll be frank with you, Henry," I answered. "I don't pray

with any comfort to myself, or any profit either. It's all a sham, and I don't intend to do any more of it."

"Oh, Arthur, Arthur, has it come to this!" exclaimed the dear fellow, his eyes filling with tears. "Have you gone so far astray? How can you live? I should think you would die."

"You see!" I said carelessly: "I'm in very good health. The world goes on quite well. There are no earthquakes or hurricanes. The sun rises and sets in the old way, and the wicked prosper like the righteous, the same as they have always done, and get along without any serious bother with their consciences besides. The fact is that my views of everything have changed, and I don't pray as I used to pray, simply because the thing is impossible."

Henry looked at me while I said this, with a stunned, bewildered expression, and then, putting his arms around my neck, bowed his head upon my shoulder and said, half choked with emotion: "I can't bear it; I can't bear it. It must not be so."

Then he put me off, and looked at me. His eyes were dry, and a determined, almost prophetic expression was in them as he said: "It will not be so; it shall not be so."

"How are you going to prevent it?" I inquired, coolly.

"I shall not prevent it, but there is one who will, you may be very sure," he replied. "There is a God, and he hears the prayers of those who love him. You cannot prevent me from praying for you, and I shall do it always. You and I belong to the same church, and I am under a vow to watch over you. Besides, you and I promised to help one another in every emergency, and I shall not forget the promise."

"So I am under a guardian, am I?"

"Yes, you are under a guardian—a very much more powerful guardian than I am," he replied.

"I suppose I shall be taken care of, then," I said.

"Yes, you will be taken care of; if not in the mild way with which you have hitherto been treated, then in a rough way to which you are not used. The prayers and hopes and expectations of such a father as yours are not to be disregarded or go for nothing. By some means, tender or terrible, you are to be brought out of your indifference and saved."

There was something in this talk which brought back to me the covert threat that I had heard from the lips of Mr. Bradford, of which I had not thought much. Were he and Henry leagued together in any plan that would bring me punishment? That was impossible, yet I grew suspicious of both of them. I did not doubt their friendship, yet the thing I feared most was an interference with my prospects of wealth. Was it possible that they, in case I should not meet their wishes, would inform Mrs. Sanderson of my unworthiness of her benefactions, and reduce me to the necessity and shame of taking care of myself? This was the great calamity I dreaded. Here was where my life could only be touched. Here was where I felt painfully sensitive and weak.

A little incident occurred about this time which rendered me still more suspicious. I had been in the habit of receiving letters from Mrs. Sanderson, addressed in the handwriting of Mrs. Belden. Indeed, not a few of my letters from The Mansion were written entirely by that lady, under Mrs. Sanderson's dictation. I had in this way become so familiar with her hand-writing that I could hardly be mistaken in it, wherever I might see it. From the first day of our entering college, Henry had insisted on our having separate boxes at the Post-Office. I had never known the real reason for this, nor had I cared to inquire what it might be. The thought had crossed my mind that he was not willing to have me know how often he received letters from my sister. One morning he was detained by a severe cold from going, in his accustomed way, for his mail, and as I was at the office, I inquired whether there were letters for him. I had no object in this but to do him a brotherly service; but as his letters were handed to me, I looked them over, and was startled to find an address in what looked like Mrs. Belden's hand-writing. I examined it carefully, compared it with several addresses from her hand which I had in my pocket, and became sure that my first suspicions were correct.

Here was food for the imagination of a guilty man. I took the letters to Henry, and handing them to him in a careless way, remarked that, as I was at the office, I thought I would save him the trouble of sending for his mail. He took the package, ran it over in his hand, selected the letter that had attracted my attention, and put it into his pocket unopened. He did not look at me, and I was sure he could not, for I detected a flush of alarm upon his face at the moment I handed the letters to him. I did not pause to see more, or to make any inquiry for Bradford friends, and, turning upon my heel, left the room.

I could not do else than conclude that there was a private understanding of some sort between him and Mrs. Belden. What this was, was a mystery which I taxed my ingenuity to fathom. My mind ran upon it all day. I knew Henry had seen Mrs. Belden at Mr. Bradford's, and even at my father's during the winter, for she had maintained her friendship for Claire. Could there have sprung up a friendly intimacy between her and Henry of which this correspondence was an outgrowth? It did not seem likely. However harmless my surmises might be, I always came back to the conclusion that through Mrs. Belden and Henry an espionage upon my conduct had been established by Mrs. Sanderson, and that all my words and acts had been watched and reported. As soon as this conviction became rooted in my mind, I lost my faith in Henry, and from that hour, for a long time, shut away my confidence from him. He could not but notice this change, and he was deeply wounded by it. Through all the remainder of the time we spent in college together, there was a restraint in our intercourse. I spent as little time with him as possible, though I threw new guards around my conduct, and was careful that he should see and hear nothing to my discredit. I even strove, in a weak way, to regain something of the ground I had lost in study ; but as I was not actuated by a worthy motive, my progress was neither marked nor persistent.

I certainly was not happy. I sighed a thousand times to think of the peace and inspiration I had lost. My better ambitions were gone, my conscience was unsatisfied, my disposition to pray had fled, my Christian hope was extinguished, and my faith was dead. I was despoiled of all that made me truly rich ; and all that I had left were the good-will of those around me, my social position, and the expectation of wealth which, when it should come into my hands, would not only give me the luxurious delights that I craved as the rarest boon of life, but command the respect as well of the rich as of those less favored than myself. I longed to get through with the bondage and the duty of my college life. I do not dare to say that I longed for the death of my benefactress. I will not acknowledge that I had become so base as this, but I could have been reconciled to anything that would irrevocably place in my power the wealth and independence I coveted.

It is useless to linger further over this period of my life. I have traced with sufficient detail the influences which wrought my transformation. They have been painful in the writing, and they must have been equally painful in the reading, to all those who had become interested in my career, welfare and character. My suspicions that Henry was a spy upon my conduct were effaced for the time whenever I went home. Mrs. Sanderson, upon whom the passing years began to lay a heavy finger, showed no abatement of affection for me, and seemed even more impatient than I for the termination of my college life and my permanent restoration to her home and society. Mrs. Belden was as sweet and ladylike and cordial as ever. She talked freely of Henry as one whom she had learned to admire and respect, and thought me most fortunate in having such a companion. There was a vague shadow of disappointment on my father's face, and I saw too, with pain, that time and toil had not left him untouched with change.

My visits in Bradford always made me better. So much was expected of me, so much was I loved and trusted, so sweet and friendly were all my acquaintances, that I never left them to return to my college life without fresh resolutions to industry and improvement. If these resolutions were abandoned, those who know the power of habit and the influence of old and un-renounced companionships will understand the reason why. I had deliberately made my bed, and I was obliged to lie in it. My compliant disposition brought me uniformly under the yoke of the old persuasions to indolence and frivolous pursuits.

Livingston went away when his time came. There was much that was lovable in him. He had a stronger character than I, and he had always been so used to wealth and the expectation of wealth that he was less harmed than I by these influences. Peter Mullens went away, and though I occasionally heard about him, I saw him no more for several years. I became at last the leader of my set, and secured a certain measure of respect from them because I led them into no vicious dissipations. In this I took a degree of pride and satisfaction; but my teachers had long abandoned any hope that I should distinguish myself, and had come to regard me coldly. My religious experiences were things of the past. I continued to show a certain respect for religion, by attending the public services of the church. I did everything for the sake of appearances, and for the purpose of blinding myself and my friends to the deadness and hollowness of a life that had ceased to be controlled by manly and Christian motives.

At last the long-looked-for day of release approached, and although I wished it to come, I wished it were well over and forgotten. I had no honors to receive, and I knew that it was universally expected that Henry would carry away the highest of his class. I do not think I envied him his eminence, for I knew he had nobly earned it, and that in the absence of other advantages it would do him good. I had money and he had scholarship, which, in time, would give him money. In these possessions we should be able to start more evenly in life.

The time passed away, until the day preceding the annual Commencement dawned. In the middle of this day's excitements, as I was sitting in my room, there was a rap at my door. There were a dozen of my fellows with me, and we were in a merry mood. Supposing the caller to be a student, I made a response in some slang phrase, but the door was not opened. I then went to it, threw it wide, and stood face to face with my father. I was not glad to see him, and as my nature was too transparent to permit me to deceive him, and he too sensitive to fail of apprehending the state of my feelings, even if I had endeavored to do so, the embarrassment of the moment may be imagined.

"Well, father!" I said, "this is a surprise!"

The moment I pronounced the word "father," the fellows began to retire, with hurried remarks about engagements, and with promises to call again. It was hardly ten seconds before every man of them was out of my room.

The dear old man had dressed himself in his plain best, and had come to see realized the great hope of his life, and I, miserable ingrate that I was, was ashamed of him. My fellows had fled the room because they knew I was, and because they wished to save me the pain of presenting him to them. As soon as they were gone I strove to reassure him, and to convince him that I was heartily glad to see him. It was easy for him to make apologies for me, and to receive those which I made for myself. He had had such precious faith in me that he did not wish to have it shaken. He had left his work and come to the City of Elms to witness my triumphs. He had intended to give me a glad day. Indeed, he had had dreams of going about to make the acquaintance of the professors, and of being entertained with a view of all the wonders of the college. I knew him so well that I did not doubt that he expected to be taken in hand by his affectionate son on his arrival, and conducted everywhere, sharing his glory. Never in my life had I received so startling a view of the meanness of my own character as on that morning. I could not possibly hide myself from myself;

and my disgust with myself was measureless. Here was a man whom I loved better than I loved, or had ever loved, any other human being—a man worthy of my profoundest respect—the sweetest, simplest, purest, noblest man whom I had ever known, with a love in his heart for me which amounted to idolatry—yet I could have wished him a thousand miles away, rather than have my gay and aristocratic companions find me in association with him, and recognize the relations that existed between us.

What should I do with him? Where could I put him? How could I hide him? The thought of showing him around was torture. Why had he not stayed at home? What could I say to him to explain my failure? How could I break the force of the blow which he must soon receive? I inquired about home and its affairs. I talked of everything but that which he most desired to talk about; and all the time I was contriving ways to cut him adrift, or to cover him up.

I was saved the trouble I anticipated by my good friend Henry, who, when he came, was so heartily delighted to see my father that the whole course of relief was made plain. Henry knew me and my circumstances, and he knew that my father's presence was unwelcome. He at once took it upon himself to say that I had a great many companions, and that they would want me with them. So he should have the pleasure of looking after my father, and of showing him everything he wanted to see. He disregarded all my protests, and good-naturedly told me to go where I was wanted.

The good old man had a pleasant time. He visited the cabinets, he was introduced to the professors when he chanced to meet them, he saw all that was worth seeing. He had a conversation with Henry about me, which saved me the making of apologies that would have been essential falsehoods. I had won no honors, Henry told him, because I had had too much money; but I was popular, was quite the equal of many others, and would receive my degree. I saw them together, going from building to building and walking under the elms and along the streets. That which to my wretched vanity would have been pain was to Henry's self-assured and self-respectful manhood a rare pleasure. I doubt whether he spent a day during his whole college life more delightfully than that which he spent with my father.

At night I had another call. Mr. Bird came in. I went to him in my old way, sat down in his ample lap, and put my arms around his neck.

"Arthur, my boy, I love you," he said. "There is a man in you still, but all that I feared might be the result of your circumstances has happened. Henry has outstripped you, and while we are all glad for him, we are all disappointed in you."

I tried to talk in a gay way about it, but I was troubled and ashamed.

"By the way, I have seen your father to-day," he said.

"And what did he say?" I inquired.

"No matter what he said: he is not happy. You have disappointed him, but he will not upbraid you. He is pained to feel that privileges which seemed to him inestimable should have been so poorly improved, and that the boy from whom he hoped and for whom he has sacrificed so much should have shown himself so careless and unworthy."

"I'm sorry for him," I said.

"Very well, my boy; and now tell me, has the kind of life which has cost him so much pain paid you?"

"No."

"Are you going to change?"

"I don't know: I doubt if I do," I responded.

"Has money been a good thing for you?"

"No; it has been a curse to me."

"Are you willing to relinquish it?"

"No: I'm spoiled for poverty. It's too late."

"Is it? We'll see."

Then the good man, with a stern look upon his face, kissed me as he used to in the old times, and took his leave.

Here was another warning or threat, and it filled me with uneasiness. Long after Henry had fallen asleep that night, I lay revolving it in my mind. I began to feel that I had been cruelly treated. If money had spoiled me, who had been to blame? It was forced upon me, my father consenting. It had wrought out its natural influence upon me. Somebody ought to have foreseen it. I had been wronged, and was now blamed for that which others were responsible for.

Commencement day came, with its crowd of excitements. The church in which the public exercises were held was thronged. Hundreds from the towns and cities around had assembled to witness the bestowal of the honors of study upon their friends and favorites. Our class had, as usual on such occasions, our places together, and as I did not belong to the group of fellows who had appointments for orations, I was with the class. Taking my seat, I looked around upon the multitude. Beautifully dressed ladies crowded the galleries, and I was deeply mortified that I should win neither their smiles nor their flowers. I was, for the time at least, a nonentity. They had eyes for none but those who had won the right to admiration.

At my right I saw a figure which I thought to be that of an acquaintance. His head was turned from me, while he conversed with a strikingly beautiful girl at his side. He looked towards the stage at last, and then I saw that it was Mr. Bradford. Could that young woman be Millie? I had not seen her since I so shamefully encountered her more than two years before. It was Millie. She had ripened into womanhood during this brief interval, and her beauty was conspicuous even among the score of beauties by which she was surrounded.

The orators came and went, receiving their tributes of applause from the audience, and of flowers from their friends; but I had no eyes for any one but Millie. I could regard her without hinderance, for she did not once look at me. I had always carried the thought of her in my heart. The little talks we had had together had been treasured in my memory among its choicest possessions. She had arrived at woman's estate, and I had now no laurels to lay at her feet. This was the one pungent drop of gall in my cup of wormwood, for then and there I acknowledged to myself that in a vague way I had associated her in my imagination with all my future life. When I had dreamed of one who should sit in Mrs. Sanderson's chair, after she had passed away, it was always Millie. I had not loved her with a man's love, but my heart was all open toward her, ready to kindle in her smile or the glance of her marvelous eyes. I knew there was only one whom she had come to see, and rejoiced in the thought that she could be nothing more to him than a friend, yet I grudged the honor which he was that day to win in her eyes.

At last the long list of speakers was exhausted, and Henry came upon the stage to deliver the valedictory. He was received with a storm of cheers, and, perfectly self-possessed, came forward in his splendid young manhood to perform his part. I knew that Mr. Bird was somewhere in the audience, looking on and listening with moistened eyes and swelling heart. I knew that my father, in his lonely sorrow, was thinking of his disappointment in me and my career. I knew that Mr. Bradford and Millie were regarding Henry with a degree of pride and gratification which, for the moment, shut me out of their minds. As his voice rang out over the vast congregation, and cheer after cheer greeted his splendid periods, I bent my head with shame; and tears that had long been strangers to my eyes fell unbidden down my cheeks. I inwardly cursed my indolence, my meanness, and the fortune which had enervated and spoiled me.

As Henry made his bow in retiring, there was a long-continued and universal burst of applause, and a rain of bouquets upon the platform which half-bewildered him. I watched for the Bradfords, and the most beautiful bouquet of all was handed by Millie to her father and tossed by him at Henry's feet. He picked up all the others, then raised this to his lips, and, looking up at the gallery, made a profound bow to the giver and retired. Knowing that with my quicker brain it had been in my power to win that crowning honor, and that it was irrevocably lost to me, the poor diploma that came to me among the others of my class gave me no pleasure.

I knew that the young woman was right. She was true to her womanly instincts, and had no honors to bestow except upon the worker and the hero. The man who had demonstrated his manhood won the honor of her womanhood. Henry was everything; I was nothing. "The girl is right," I said to myself, "and some time she shall know that the stuff she worships is in me."

A young man rarely gets a better vision of himself than that which is reflected from a true woman's eyes, for God himself sits behind them. That which a man was intended to be is that which unperverted womanhood demands that he shall be. I felt at the moment that a new motive had been born in me, and that I was not wholly shorn of power and the possibilities of heroic life.

Before we left New Haven, Mr. Bradford, Mr. Bird, and my father met by appointment. What their business was I did not know, but I had little doubt that it related to me. I was vexed by the thought, but I was too proud to ask any questions. I hoped that the whole Bradford party would find themselves in the same conveyance on the way home; but on the morning following Commencement, my father, Henry, and myself took our seats in the coach, and Mr. Bradford and Millie were left behind. I had not spoken to either of them. I did not like to call upon Millie, and her father had not sought me.

I was not disposed to talk, and all the conversation was carried on by my father and Henry. I saw that the young man had taken a warm place near my father's heart—that they understood and appreciated one another perfectly. Remembering what an idol I had been, and how cruelly I had defaced my own lineaments and proved myself unworthy of the worship, a vision of this new friendship was not calculated to increase my happiness. But I was full of my plans. I would win Millie Bradford's respect or I would die. My imagination constructed all sorts of impossible situations in which I was to play the part of hero, and compel her admiration. I would devote myself to labor; I would acquire a profession; I would achieve renown; I would become an orator; I would win office; I would wrench a bough from the highest laurel, and, dashing it at her feet, say: "There! I have earned your approval and your smile; give them to me!"

The practical power that resides in this kind of vaporing is readily appreciated. I had at last my opportunity to demonstrate my possession of heroism, but it did not come in the form I anticipated and hoped for.

Our welcome home was cordial. My poor mother thought I had grown thin, and was afraid I had studied too much. The unintended sarcasm did not reassure me. Henry and Claire were happy, and I left the beloved group to seek my own lonelier home. There I manifested a delight I did not feel. I tossed my diploma into Mrs. Sanderson's lap, and lightly told her that there was the bit of sheepskin which had cost her so much. Mrs. Belden congratulated me, and the two women were glad to have me at home. I spent the evening with them, and led the conversation, so far as I could, into channels that diverted their minds from uncomfortable inquiries.

Our life soon took on the old habits, and I heartily tried to make myself tributary to the comfort and happiness of the house. Poor old Jenks was crippled with rheumatism, and while he was made to believe that the domestic establishment could not be operated without him, he had in reality become a burden. As the weather grew intensely hot, and Mrs. Sanderson showed signs of weakness, Mrs. Belden took her away to the seaside again, leaving me once more the master of The Mansion.

A little incident occurred on the morning of Mrs. Sanderson's departure which left an uncomfortable impression upon my mind. She went into the dining-room, and closed the door behind her. As the carriage was waiting for her, I unthinkingly opened the door, and found her before the picture. The tears were on her cheeks, and she looked pale and distressed.

I impulsively put my arm around her, bent down and kissed her, and led her away. As I did this, I determined that I would find out the secret of that picture if I could. I was old enough to be trusted with it, and I would have it. I did not doubt that many in the town could tell me all about it, though I knew there were reasons connected with my relations to Mrs. Sanderson which had thus far forbidden them to speak to me about it.

CHAPTER XVIII.

HENRY BECOMES A GUEST AT THE MANSION BY FORCE OF CIRCUMSTANCES.

It was natural that the first business which presented itself to be done after the departure of Mrs. Sanderson, should be the reinstatement of my social relations with the Bradfords, yet how it could be effected without an invitation from them I could not imagine. I knew that they were all at home, and that Henry and Claire had called upon them. Day after day passed, however, and I heard nothing from them. The time began to drag heavily on my idle hands, when, one pleasant evening, Mr. Bradford made his appearance at The Mansion. I had determined upon the course to be pursued whenever I should meet him, and after some common-place conversation, I said to him, with all my old frankness, that I wished to open my heart to him.

"I cannot hide from myself the fact," I said, "that I am in disgrace with you and your family. Please tell me what I can do to atone for a past for which I can make no apology. Do you wish to see me at your house again? Am I to be shut out from your family, and shut up here in a palace which your proscription will make a prison? If I cannot have the respect of those whom I love best, I may as well die."

The tears filled my eyes, and he could have had no doubt as to the genuineness of my emotion, though he made no immediate reply. He looked at me gravely, and hesitated as if he were puzzled as to the best way to treat me.

At length he said: "Well, Arthur, I am glad you have got as far as this—that you have discovered that money cannot buy everything, and that there are things in the world so much more precious than money, that money itself is good for nothing without them. It is well, at least, to have learned so much, but the question with me is: how far will this conviction be permitted to take practical hold of your life? What are your plans? What do you propose to do to redeem yourself?"

"I will do anything," I answered warmly and impulsively.

"That is very indefinite," he responded, "and if you have no plans there is no use in our talking further upon the subject."

"What would you have me do?" I inquired, with a feeling that he was wronging me.

"Nothing—certainly nothing that is not born of a principle. If there is no higher purpose in you than that of regaining the good opinion of your friends and neighbors, you will do nothing. When you wish to become a man for manhood's sake, your purpose of life and work will come, and it will be a worthy one. When your life proceeds from a right principle, you will secure the respect of everybody, though you will care very little about it—certainly much less than you care now. My approval will avail little; you have always had my love and my faith in your ability to redeem yourself. As for my home it is always open to you, and there is no event that would make it brighter for me than to see you making a man's use of your splendid opportunities."

We had further talk, but it was not of a character to reassure me, for I was conscious that I lacked the one thing which he deemed essential to my improvement. Wealth, with its immunities and delights, had debauched me, and though I craved the good opinion of the Bradfords, it was largely because I had associated Millie with my future. It was my selfishness and my natural love of approbation that lay at the bottom of it all; and as soon as I comprehended myself I saw that Mr. Bradford understood me. He had studied me through and through, and had ceased to entertain any hope of improvement except through a change of circumstances.

As I went to the door with him, and looked out into the

night, two dark figures were visible in the middle of the road. They were standing entirely still when the door was opened, for the light from the hall revealed them. They immediately moved on, but the sight of them arrested Mr. Bradford on the step. When they had passed beyond hearing, he turned to me and, in a low voice, said: "Look to all your fastenings tonight. There is a gang of suspicious fellows about town, and already two or three burglaries have been committed. There may be no danger, but it is well to be on your guard."

Though I was naturally nervous and easily excited in my imagination, I was by no means deficient in physical courage, and no child in physical prowess. I was not afraid of anything I could see; but the thought of a night-visitation from ruffians was quite enough to keep me awake, particularly as I could not but be aware that The Mansion held much that was valuable and portable, and that I was practically alone. Mr. Bradford's caution was quite enough to put all my senses on tension and destroy my power to sleep. That there were men about the house in the night I had evidence enough, both while I lay listening, and, on the next morning, when I went into the garden, where they had walked across the flower-beds.

I called at the Bradfords' the next day, meeting no one, however, save Mr. Bradford, and reported what I had heard and seen. He looked grave, and while we were speaking a neighbor entered who reported two burglaries which had occurred on the previous night, one of them at a house beyond The Mansion.

"I shall spend the night in the streets," said Mr. Bradford decidedly.

"Who will guard your own house?" I inquired.

"I shall depend upon Aunt Flick's ears and Dennis's hands," he replied.

Our little city had greatly changed in ten years. The first railroad had been built, manufactures had sprung up, business and population had increased, and the whole social aspect of the place had been revolutionized. It had entirely outgrown its unchanged police machinery and appointments, and now, when there was a call for efficient surveillance, the authorities were sadly inadequate to the occasion. Under Mr. Bradford's lead, a volunteer corps of constables was organized and sworn into office, and a patrol established which promised protection to the persons and property of the citizens.

The following night was undisturbed. No suspicious men were encountered in the street; and the second night passed away in the same peaceable manner. Several of the volunteer constables, supposing that the danger was past, declined to watch longer, though Mr. Bradford and a faithful and spirited few still held on. The burglars were believed by him to be still in the city, under cover, and waiting either for an opportunity to get away, or to add to their depredations. I do not think that Mr. Bradford expected his own house to be attacked, but, from the location of The Mansion, and Mrs. Sanderson's reputation for wealth, I know that he thought it more than likely that I should have a visit from the marauders. During these two nights of watching, I slept hardly more than on the night when I discovered the loiterers before the house. It began to be painful, for I had no solid sleep until after the day had dawned. The suspense wore upon me, and I dreaded the night as much as if I had been condemned to pass it alone in a forest. I had said nothing to Jenks or the cook about the matter, and was all alone in my consciousness of danger, as I was alone in the power to meet it. Under these circumstances, I called upon Henry, and asked as a personal favor that he would come and pass at least one night with me. He seemed but little inclined to favor my request, and probably would not have done so had not a refusal seemed like cowardice. At nine o'clock, however, he made his appearance, and we went immediately to bed.

Fortified by a sense of protection and companionship, I sank at once into a slumber so profound that a dozen men might have ransacked the house without waking me. Though Henry went to sleep, as he afterwards told me, at his usual hour, he slept lightly, for his own fears had been awakened by the circumstances into which I had brought him. We both slept until about one o'clock in the morning, when there came to me in the middle of a dream a crash which was incorporated into my dream as the discharge of a cannon and the rattle of musketry, followed by the groans of the dying. I awoke bewildered, and impulsively threw my hand over to learn whether Henry was at my side. I found the clothes swept from the bed as if they had been thrown off in a sudden waking and flight, and his place empty. I sprang to my feet, conscious at the same time that a struggle was in progress near me, but in the dark. I struck a light, and, all unclad as I was, ran into the hall. As I passed the door, I heard a heavy fall, and caught a confused glimpse of two figures embracing and rolling heavily down the broad stairway. In my haste I almost tumbled over a man lying upon the floor.

"Hold on to him—here's Arthur," the man shouted, and I recognized the voice of old Jenks.

"What are you here for, Jenks?" I shouted.

"I'm hurt," said Jenks, "but don't mind me. Hold on to him! hold on to him!"

Passing Jenks, I rushed down the staircase, and found Henry kneeling upon the prostrate figure of a ruffian, and holding his hands with a grip of iron. My light had already been seen in the street; and I heard shouts without, and a hurried tramping of men. I set my candle down, and was at Henry's side in an instant, asking him what to do.

"Open the door, and call for help," he answered between his teeth. "I am faint and cannot hold on much longer."

I sprang to the door, and while I was pushing back the bolt was startled by a rap upon the outside, and a call which I recognized at once as that of Mr. Bradford. Throwing the door open, he, with two others, leaped in, and comprehended the situation of affairs. Closing it behind him, Mr. Bradford told Henry to let the fellow rise. Henry did not stir. The ruffian lay helplessly rolling up his eyes, while Henry's head dropped upon his prisoner's breast. The brave fellow was badly hurt, and had fainted. Mr. Bradford stooped and lifted his helpless form, as if he had been a child, and bore him up stairs, while his companions pinioned his antagonist, and dragged him out of the door, where his associate stood under guard. The latter had been arrested while running away, on the approach of Mr. Bradford and his posse.

Depositing his burden upon a bed, Mr. Bradford found another candle and came down to light it. Giving hurried directions to his men as to the disposition of the arrested burglars, he told one of them to bring Aunt Flick at once from his house, and another to summon a surgeon. In five minutes the house would have been silent save for the groanings of poor old Jenks, who still lay where he fell, and the screams of the cook, who had, at last, been wakened by the din and commotion.

As soon as Henry began to show signs of recovery from his fainting fit we turned our attention to Jenks, who lay patiently upon the floor, disabled partly by his fall, and partly by his rheumatism. Lifting him carefully, we carried him to his bed, and he was left in my care while Mr. Bradford went back to Henry.

Old Jenks, who had had a genuine encounter with ruffians in the dark, seemed to be compensated for all his hurts and dangers by having a marvelous story to tell and this he told to me in detail. He had been wakened in the night by a noise. It seemed to him that somebody was trying to get into the house. He lay until he felt his bed jarred by some one walking in the room below. Then he heard a little cup rattle on his table— a little cup with a teaspoon in it. Satisfied that there was some one in the house who did not belong in it, he rose, and undertook to make his way to my room for the purpose of giving me the information. He was obliged to reach me through a passage that led from the back part of the house. This he undertook to do in the stealthy and silent fashion of which he was an accomplished master, and had reached the staircase that led from the grand hall, when he encountered the intruder who, taking him at once for an antagonist, knocked him down. The noise of this encounter woke Henry, who sprang from his bed, and, in a fierce grapple with the rascal, threw him and rolled with him to the bottom of the staircase.

I could not learn that the old man had any bones broken, or that he had suffered much except by the shock upon his nervous system and the cruel jar he had received in his rheumatic joints. After a while, having administered a cordial, I left him with the assurance that I should be up for the remainder of the night and that he could sleep in perfect safety. Returning to my room I found Aunt Flick already arrived, and busy with service at Henry's side. The surgeon came soon afterwards, and having made a careful examination, declared that Henry had suffered a bad fracture of the thigh, and that he must on no account be moved from the house.

At this announcement, Mr. Bradford, Henry and I looked at one another with a pained and puzzled expression. We said nothing, but the same thought was running through our minds. Mrs. Sanderson must know of it, and how would she receive and treat it? She had a strong prejudice against Henry, of which we were all aware. Would she blame me for the invitation that had brought him there? would she treat him well, and make him comfortable while there?

"I know what you are thinking of," said Aunt Flick sharply, "and if the old lady makes a fuss about it I shall give her a piece of my mind."

"Let it be small," said Henry, smiling through his pain.

The adjustment of the fracture was a painful and tedious process, which the dear fellow bore with the fortitude that was his characteristic. It was hard for me to think that he had passed through his great danger and was suffering this pain for me, though to tell the truth, I half envied him the good fortune that had demonstrated his prowess and had made him for the time the hero of the town. These unworthy thoughts I thrust from my mind, and determined on thorough devotion to the companion who had risked so much for me, and who had possibly been the means of saving my life.

It seemed, in the occupation and absorption of the occasion, but an hour after my waking, before the day began to dawn; and leaving Aunt Flick with Henry, Mr. Bradford and I retired for consultation.

It was decided at once that Mrs. Sanderson would be offended should we withhold from her, for any reason, the news of what had happened in her house. The question was whether she should be informed of it by letter, or whether Mr. Bradford or I should go to her on the morning boat, and tell her the whole story, insisting that she should remain where she was until Henry could be moved. Mr. Bradford had reasons of his own for believing that it was best that she should get her intelligence from me, and it was decided that while he remained in or near the house, I should be the messenger to my aunt, and ascertain her plans and wishes.

Accordingly, bidding Henry a hasty good-morning, and declining a breakfast for which I had no appetite, I walked down to the steamer, and paced her decks during all her brief passage, in the endeavor to dissipate the excitement of which I had not been conscious until after my departure from the house. I found my aunt and Mrs. Belden enjoying the morning breeze on the shady piazza of their hotel. Mrs. Sanderson rose with excitement as I approached her, while her companion became as pale as death. Both saw something in my face that betokened trouble, and neither seemed able to do more than to utter an exclamation of surprise. Several guests of the house being near us, I offered my arm to Mrs. Sanderson, and said:

"Let us go to your parlor: I have something to tell you."

We went up-stairs, Mrs. Belden following us. When we reached the door, the latter said: "Shall I come in too?"

"Certainly," I responded. "You will learn all I have to tell, and you may as well learn it from me."

We sat down and looked at one another. Then I said: "We have had a burglary."

Both ladies uttered an exclamation of terror.

"What was carried away?" said Mrs. Sanderson sharply.

"The burglars themselves," I answered.

"And nothing lost?"

"Nothing."

"And no one hurt?"

"I cannot say that," I answered. "That is the saddest part of it. Old Jenks was knocked down, and the man who saved the house came out of his struggle with a badly broken limb."

"Who was he? How came he in the house?"

"Henry Hulm; I invited him. I was worn out with three nights of watching."

Mrs. Sanderson sat like one struck dumb, while Mrs. Belden, growing paler, fell in a swoon upon the floor. I lifted her to a sofa, and calling a servant to care for her, after she began to show signs of returning consciousness, took my aunt into her bed-room, closed the door, and told her the whole story in detail. I cannot say that I was surprised by the result. She always had the readiest way of submitting to the inevitable of any person I ever saw. She knew at once that it was best for her to go home, to take charge of her own house, to superintend the recovery of Henry, and to treat him so well that no burden of obligation should rest upon her. She knew at once that any coldness or lack of attention on her part would be condemned by all her neighbors. She knew that she must put out of sight all her prejudice against the young man, and so load him with attentions and benefactions that he could never again look upon her with indifference, or treat her with even constructive discourtesy.

While we sat talking, Mrs. Belden rapped at the door, and entered.

"I am sure we had better go home," she said, tremblingly.

"That is already determined," responded my aunt.

With my assistance, the trunks were packed long before the boat returned, the bills at the hotel were settled, and the ladies were ready for the little journey.

I had never seen Mrs. Belden so thoroughly deposed from her self-possession as she seemed all the way home. Her agitation, which had the air of impatience, increased as we came in sight of Bradford, and when we arrived at the door of The Mansion, and alighted, she could hardly stand, but staggered up the walk like one thoroughly ill. I was equally distressed and perplexed by the impression which the news had made upon her, for she had always been a marvel of equanimity and self-control.

We met the surgeon and Mr. Bradford at the door. They had good news to tell of Henry, who had passed a quiet day; but poor old Jenks had shown signs of feverish reaction, and had been anxiously inquiring when I should return. Aunt Flick was busy in Henry's room. My aunt mounted at once to the young man's chamber with the surgeon and myself.

Aunt Flick paused in her work as we entered, made a distant bow to Mrs. Sanderson, and waited to see what turn affairs would take, while she held in reserve that "piece of her mind" which contingently she had determined to hurl at the little mistress of the establishment.

It was with a feeling of triumph over both Henry and his spirited guardian, that I witnessed Mrs. Sanderson's meeting with my friend. She sat down by his bedside, and took his pale hand in both her own little hands, saying almost tenderly: "I have heard all the story, so that there is nothing to say, except for me to thank you for protecting my house, and to assure you that while you remain here you will be a thousand times welcome, and have every service and attention you need. Give yourself no anxiety about anything, but get well as soon as you can. There are three of us who have nothing in the world to do but to attend you and help you."

A tear stole down Henry's cheek as she said this, and she reached over with her dainty handkerchief, and wiped it away as tenderly as if he had been a child.

I looked at Aunt Flick, and found her face curiously puckered in the attempt to keep back the tears. Then my aunt addressed her, thanking her for her service, and telling her that she could go home and rest, as the family would be quite sufficient for the nursing of the invalid. The woman could not say a word. She was prepared for any emergency but this, and so, bidding Henry good-night, she retired from the room and the house.

When supper was announced, Mrs. Sanderson and I went down stairs. We met Mrs. Belden at the foot, who declared that she was not in a condition to eat anything, and would go up and sit with Henry. We tried to dissuade her, but she was decided, and my aunt and I passed on into the dining-room. Remembering when I arrived there that I had not seen Jenks, I excused myself for a moment, and as silently as possible remounted the stairs. As I passed Henry's door, I impulsively pushed it open. It made no noise, and there, before me, Mrs. Belden knelt at Henry's bed, with her arms around his neck and her cheek lying against his own. I pulled back the door as noiselessly as I had opened it, and half stunned by what I had seen, passed on through the passage that led to the room of the old servant. The poor man looked haggard and wretched, while his eyes shone strangely above cheeks that burned with the flush of fever. I had been so astonished by what I had seen that I could hardly give rational replies to his inquiries.

"I doubt if I weather it, Mr. Arthur; what do you think?" said he, fairly looking me through to get at my opinion.

"I hope you will be all right in a few days," I responded. "Don't give yourself any care. I'll see that you are attended to."

"Thank you. Give us your hand."

I pressed his hand, attended to some trifling service that he required of me, and went down stairs with a sickening misgiving concerning my old friend. He was shattered and worn, and, though I was but little conversant with disease, there was something in his appearance that alarmed me, and made me feel that he had reached his death-bed.

Mrs. Belden knelt at Henry's bed, with her arm around his neck.
(p. 282.)

With the memory of the scene which I had witnessed in Henry's room fresh in my mind, with all its strange suggestions, and with the wild, inquiring look of Jenks still before me, I had little disposition to make conversation. Yet I looked up occasionally at my aunt's face, to give her the privilege of speaking, if she were disposed to talk. She, however, was quite as much absorbed as myself. She did not look sad. There played around her mouth a quiet smile, while her eyes shone with determination and enterprise. Was it possible that she was thinking that she had Henry just where she wanted him? Was she glad that she had in her house and hands another spirit to mould and conquer? Was she delighted that something had come for her to do, and thus to add variety to a life which had become tame with routine? I do not know, but it seemed as if this were the case.

At the close of the meal, I told her of the impression I had received from Jenks's appearance, and begged her to go to his room with me, but she declined. There was one presence into which this brave woman did not wish to pass—the presence of death. Like many another strongly vitalized nature hers revolted at dissolution. She could rise to the opposition of anything that she could meet and master, but the dread power which she knew would in a few short years, at most, unlock the clasp by which she held to life and her possessions filled her with horror. She would do anything for her old servant at a distance, but she could not, and would not, witness the process through which she knew her own frame and spirit must pass in the transition to her final rest.

That night I spent mainly with Jenks, while Mrs. Belden attended Henry. This was according to her own wish; and Mrs. Sanderson was sent to bed at her usual hour. Whenever I was wanted for anything in Henry's room, Mrs. Belden called me; and, as Jenks needed frequent attention, I got very little sleep during the night.

Mrs. Sanderson was alarmed by my haggard looks in the morning, and immediately sent for a professional nurse to attend her servant, and declared that my watching must be stopped.

Tired with staying in-doors, and wishing for a while to separate myself from the scenes that had so absorbed me, and the events that had broken so violently in upon my life, I took a long stroll in the fields and woods. Sitting down at length in the shade, with birds singing above my head and insects humming around me, I passed these events rapidly in review, and there came to me the conviction that Providence had begun to deal with me in earnest. Since the day of my entrance upon my new life at The Mansion, I had met with no trials that I had not consciously brought upon myself. Hardship I had not known. Sickness and death I had not seen. In the deep sorrows of the world, in its struggles and pains and self-denials, I had had no part. Now, change had come, and further change seemed imminent. How should I meet it? What would be its effect upon me? For the present my selfish plans and pleasures must be laid aside, and my life be devoted to others. The strong hand of necessity was upon me, and there sprang up within me, responsive to its touch, a manly determination to do my whole duty.

Then the strange scene I had witnessed in Henry's room came back to me. What relations could exist between this pair, so widely separated by age, that warranted the intimacy I had witnessed? Was this woman who had seemed to me so nearly perfect a base woman? Had she woven her toils about Henry? Was he a hypocrite? Every event of a suspicious nature which had occurred was passed rapidly in review. I remembered his presence at the wharf when she first debarked in the city, his strange appearance when he met her at the Bradfords for the first time, the letter I had carried to him written by her hand, the terrible effect upon her of the news of his struggle and injury, and many other incidents which I have not recorded. There was some sympathy between them which I did not understand, and which filled me with a strange misgiving, both on account of my sister and myself; yet I knew that she and Claire were the closest friends, and I had never received from her anything but the friendliest treatment. Since she had returned, she had clung to his room and his side as if he were her special charge, by duty and by right. One thing I was sure of: she would never have treated me in the way she had treated him.

Then there came to me, with a multitude of thoughts and events connected with my past history, Mrs. Sanderson's singular actions regarding the picture that had formed with me the subject of so many speculations and surmises. Who was the boy? What connection had he with her life and history? Was she tired of me? Was she repentant for some great injustice rendered to one she had loved? Was she sorrowing over some buried hope? Did I stand in the way of the realization of some desire which, in her rapidly declining years, had sprung to life within her?

I do not know why it was, but there came to me the consciousness that events were before me—ready to disclose themselves—shut from me by a thin veil—which would change the current of my life; and the purpose I had already formed of seeking an interview with Mr. Bradford and asking him the questions I had long desired to ask, was confirmed. I would do it at once. I would learn my aunt's history, and know the ground on which I stood. I would pierce the mysteries that had puzzled me and were still gathering around me, and front whatever menace they might bear.

CHAPTER XIX.

JENKS GOES FAR, FAR AWAY UPON THE BILLOW AND NEVER COMES BACK.

On returning to the house I found myself delayed in the execution of my determination by the increasing and alarming sickness of the old servant Jenks, and by his desire that I should be near him. The physician, who was called at once, gave us no hope of his recovery. He was breaking down rapidly, and seemed to be conscious of the fact.

On the following morning, after I had spent the most of the night in his room, he requested the nurse to retire, and calling me to his bedside said he wished to say a few words to me. I administered a cordial, which he swallowed with pain, and after a fit of difficult breathing caused by the effort, he said feebly: "It's no use, Mr. Arthur; I can't hold on, and I don't think I want to. It's a mere matter of staying. I should never work any more, even if I should weather this."

I tried to say some comforting words, but he shook his head feebly, and simply repeated: "It's no use."

"What can I do for you, Jenks?" I said.

"Do you know Jim Taylor's wife?" he inquired.

"I've seen her," I replied.

"She's a hard working woman."

"Yes, with a great many children."

"And Jim don't treat her very well," he muttered.

"So I've heard."

He shook his head slowly, and whispered: "It's too bad; it's too bad."

"Don't worry yourself about Jim Taylor's wife; she's nothing to you," I said.

"Do you think so?—nothing to me? Don't say that; I can't bear it."

"You don't mean to tell me that Jim Taylor's wife is—"

He nodded his head; and I saw that he had not yet finished what he had to say about her.

"Have you any message for her?" I inquired.

"Well, you know, Mr. Arthur, that she's been everything to me, and I'd like to do a little something for her. You don't think she'd take it amiss if I should leave her some money, do you?"

"Oh, no, she's very poor," I said. "I think she would be very grateful for anything you can do to help her along."

His eye lighted, and a feeble smile spread over his wizen features.

"Pull out that little box under the bed," he said. "The key is under my pillow."

I placed the box on the bed, and, after fumbling under his pillow, found the key and opened the humble coffer.

"'There's a hundred clean silver dollars in that bag, that I've been saving up for her for thirty years. I hope they'll do her good. Give them to her, and don't tell Jim. Tell her Jenks never forgot her, and that she's been everything to him. Tell her I was sorry she had trouble, and don't forget to say that I never blamed *her*."

I assured him that I would give her the money and the message faithfully, and he sank back into his pillow with a satisfied look upon his face that I had not seen there since his sickness. The long contemplated act was finished, and the work of his life was done.

After lying awhile with his eyes closed, he opened them and said: "Do you s'pose we shall know one another over yonder?"

"I hope so; I think so," I responded.

"If she comes before Jim, I shall look after her. Do you dare to tell her that?" and he fixed his glazing eyes upon me with a wild, strained look that thrilled me.

"I think it would scare her," I answered. "Perhaps you had better not send her such a message."

"Well, I shall look after her, any way, if I get a chance, and perhaps both of 'em won't go to one place—and—"

What further possibilities ran through the old man's imagination I do not know, for he seemed exhausted, and ceased to speak. I sat for an hour beside his bed, while he sank into a lethargic slumber. At last he woke and stared wildly about him. Then, fixing his eyes on me, he said: "Now's my time! If I'm ever going to get away from this place I must go to-night!"

There was a pathetic and poetic appositeness in these words to the facts of his expiring life that touched me to tears, and I wiped my eyes. Then listening to some strange singing in his ears, he said: "Doesn't it rain? Doesn't it pour? You'll take cold, my boy, and so shall I."

The thought carried him back over the years to the scene in the stable where in agony I knelt, with the elements in tumult above me and his arm around my neck, and prayed.

"Pray again, Arthur. I want to hear you pray."

I could not refuse him, but knelt at once by his bed, and buried my face in the clothes by his side. He tried to lift his hand, but the power to do so was gone. I recognized his wish, and lifted his arm and placed it round my neck. It was several minutes before I could command my voice, and then, choking as on the evening which he had recalled, I tried to commend his departing spirit to the mercy and fatherly care of Him who was so soon to receive it. Having prayed for him it was easier to pray for myself; and I did pray, fervently and long. As I closed, a whispered "Amen" came from his dying lips. "There," he said; "let's go into the house; it's warm there." There was something in these words that started my tears again.

After this his mind wandered, and in his delirium the old passion of his life took full possession of him.

"To-morrow I shall be far, far away on the billow. . . . . ."

The old woman will call Jenks, but Jenks won't be here. Jenks will be gone! . . . . This is the craft: up with her sails: down with the compasses: My! how she slides! Run her straight for the moon! . . . . Doesn't she cut the water beautiful! . . . . The sea rolls and swings, and rolls and swings, and there are the islands! I see 'em! I see 'em! . . . . It's just like a cradle, and I can't keep awake. . . . . Oh, I'm going to sleep! I'm—going—to—sleep. . . . . Tell the old woman I bore her no ill will, but I had to go. . . . . I was obliged to go. . . . . Straight along in the track of the moon."

He said all this brokenly, with his eyes closed; and then he opened them wide, and looked around as if suddenly startled out of sleep. Then life went out of them, and there came on that quick, short breathing, unmistakable in its character, even to a novice, and I rose and called the nurse and Mrs. Belden to witness the closing scene.

So, sailing out upon that unknown sea made bright by a hovering glory, with green islands in view and the soft waves lapping his little vessel, escaping from all his labors and pains, and realizing all his dreams and aspirations, the old man passed away. There was a smile upon his face, left by some sweet emotion. If he was hailed by other barks sailing upon the same sea, if he touched at the islands and plucked their golden fruit, if there opened to his expanding vision broader waters beyond the light of the moon, and bathing the feet of the Eternal City, we could not know. We only knew that his closing thought was a blessed thought, and that it glorified the features which, in a few short days, would turn to dust. It was delightful to think that the harmless, simple, ignorant, dear old boy had passed into the hands of his Father. There I left him without a care—in the hands of One whose justice only is tenderer than His mercy, and whose love only is stronger than His justice.

The superintendence of all the affairs connected with his funeral was devolved upon me; and his burial was like the burial of an old playfellow. I could not have believed that his death would grieve me so. It was the destruction of a part of my home. Now nothing was left but a single frail woman, whose years were almost told; and when her time should be spent, the house would be empty of all but myself, and those whom I might choose to retain or procure.

His remains were followed to the grave by Mrs. Sanderson and myself in the family carriage, and by the Bradfords, with some humble acquaintances. His relatives were all at a distance, if he had any living, or they had left the world before him. The house seemed more lonely after his death than I had ever felt it to be before, and poor Mrs. Sanderson was quite broken down by the event. The presence of death in the house was so sad a remembrancer of previous occurrences of which I had had no knowledge, and was such a suggestion to herself of the brevity of her remaining years, that she was wonderfully softened.

She had, ever since her return, lived apparently in a kind of dream. There was something in Henry's presence and voice that had the power to produce this tender, silent mood, and Jenks's death only deepened and intensified it.

When all was over, and the house had resumed its every-day aspects and employments, I took the little sum that Jenks had saved with such tender care, and bore it to the woman who had so inspired his affection and sweetened his life. I found her a hard-faced, weary old woman, whose life of toil and trouble had wiped out every grace and charm of womanhood that she had ever possessed. She regarded my call with evident curiosity; and when I asked her if she had ever known Jenks, and whether anything had occurred between them in their early life that would make him remember her with particular regard, she smiled a grim, hard smile and said: "Not much."

"What was it? I have good reasons for inquiring."

"Well," said she, "he wanted me to marry him, and I wouldn't. That's about all. You see he was a kind of an innocent, and I s'pose I made fun of him. Perhaps I've had my pay for't."

"Do you know that he has loved you dearly all his life; that he has pricked your name into his arm, and that it was the tenderest and sweetest word that ever passed his lips; that the thought of you comforted him at his work and mingled with all his dreams; that he would have gone through fire and water to serve you; that he saved up money all his life to give you, and that he hopes you will die before your husband, so that he may have the chance to care for you in the other country to which he has gone?"

As I uttered these words slowly, and with much emotion, her dull eyes opened wider and wider, and filled with tears which dropped unregarded from her cheeks. I suppose these were the first words of affection that had been spoken to her for twenty years. Her heart had been utterly starved, and my words were like manna to her taste. She could not speak at first, and then with much difficulty she said: "Are you telling me the truth?"

"I am not telling you half of the truth. He loved you a thousand times more devotedly than I can tell you. He would have worshiped a ribbon that you had worn. He would have kissed the ground on which you stepped. He would have been your slave. He would have done anything, or been anything, that would have given you pleasure, even though he had never won a smile in return."

Then I untied the handkerchief in which I had brought the old man's savings, and poured the heavy silver into her lap. She did not look at it. She only looked into my face with a sad gaze, while the tears filled her eyes anew.

"I don't deserve it: I don't deserve it," she repeated in a hopeless way, "but I thank you. I've got something to think of besides kicks and cuffs and curses. No—they won't hurt me any more."

Her eyes brightened then so that she looked almost beautiful to me. The assurance that one man, even though she had regarded him as a simpleton, had persistently loved her, had passed into her soul, so that she was strengthened for a lifetime. The little hoard and the love that came with it were a mighty re-enforcement against all the trials which a brutal husband and forgetful children had brought upon her.

I left her sitting with her treasure still in her lap, dreaming over the old days, looking forward to those that remained, and thinking of the man who would have asked for no sweeter heaven than to look in and see her thus employed. Afterwards I saw her often. She attended the church which she had long forsaken, with clothes so neat and comfortable that her neighbors wondered where and how she had managed to procure them, and took up the burden of her life again with courage and patience.

She went before Jim.

Whom she found waiting on the other side of that moonlit sea over which my old friend had sailed homeward, I shall know some time; but I cannot turn my eyes from a picture which my fancy sketches, of a sweet old man, grown wise and strong, standing upon a sunny beach, with arms outstretched, to greet an in-going shallop that bears still the name of all the vessels he had ever owned—" the Jane Whittlesey!"

CHAPTER XX.

MR. BRADFORD TELLS ME A STORY WHICH CHANGES THE DETERMINATIONS OF MY LIFE.

I HAVE already alluded to the effect which Henry's presence produced upon Mrs. Sanderson. For a few days after her return, I watched with covert but most intense interest the development of her acquaintance with him. Mrs. Belden had been for so long a time her companion, and was so constantly at Henry's bedside, that my aunt quickly took on the habit of going in to sit for an hour with the lady and her charge. I was frequently in and out, doing what I could for my friend's amusement, and often found both the ladies in attendance. Mrs. Sanderson always sat at the window in an old-fashioned rocking chair, listening to the conversation between Mrs. Belden and Henry. Whenever Henry laughed, or uttered an exclamation, she started and looked over to his bed, as if the sounds were familiar, or as if they had a strange power of suggestion. There was some charm in his voice and look to which she submitted herself more and more as the days went by—a charm so subtle that I doubt whether she understood it or was conscious of its power.

Two or three days passed after I had executed Jenks's will, with relation to his savings, when my old resolution to visit Mr. Bradford recurred. In the meantime, I felt that I had won strength from my troubles and cares, and was better able to bear trial than I had ever been before. I was little needed in the house, now that Jenks was gone, so, one morning after breakfast, I started to execute my purpose. As I was taking my hat in the hall, there came a rap upon the door, and as I stood near it I opened it and encountered Millie Bradford

She met me with a cordiality that spoke her friendship, but with a reserve which declared that the old relations between us had ceased. I know that I blushed painfully, for she had been much in my thoughts, and it seemed, somehow, that she must have been conscious of the fact. I knew, too, that I had disappointed and shamed her.

"My father is busy this morning, Mr. Bonnicastle," she said, "and I have been sent up to inquire after the invalid."

Ah, how her "Mr. Bonnicastle" removed me from her! And how much more lovely she seemed to me than she had ever seemed before! Dressed in a snowy morning wrapper, with a red rose at her throat, and only a parasol to shade her black hair and her luminously tender eyes, and with all the shapely beauty in her figure that the ministry of seventeen gracious years could bestow, she seemed to me almost a goddess.

I invited her in, and called my aunt. Mrs. Belden heard her voice soon afterwards and came down, and we had a pleasant chat. As soon as Mrs. Belden appeared, I noticed that Millie addressed all her inquiries concerning Henry to her, and that there seemed to be a very friendly intimacy between them.

When, at last, the girl rose to go, I passed into the hall with her, and taking my hat, said: "Miss Bradford, I was about to go to your house for a business call upon your father, when you came in. May I have the pleasure of walking home with you?"

"Oh certainly," she replied, though with a shadow of reluctance in her look, "but I fear your walk will be fruitless. My father has gentlemen with him, and perhaps will not be at liberty to see you."

"Still, with your leave I will go. I shall win a walk at least," I responded.

The moment I was alone with her, I found myself laboring under an embarrassment that silenced me. It was easy to talk in the presence of others, but it was "Arthur" and "Millie" no more between us.

She noticed my silence, and uttered some common-place remark about the changes that had taken place in the city.

"Yes," I said, "I see they have the cathedral finished yonder."

"Entirely," she responded, "and the little chapel inside has been torn down."

How much she meant by this, or whether she intended any allusion to the old conversation, every word of which I recollected so vividly, I could not tell, but I gave her the credit of possessing as good a memory as myself, and so concluded that she considered Arthur Bonnicastle, the boy, as a person dead and gone, and Mr. Bonnicastle the young man as one whom she did not know.

As we came in sight of her house, we saw three gentlemen at the door. Two of them soon left, and the third, who was Mr. Bradford, went back into the house.

"I believe those two men are my father and Mr. Bird," I said. "I don't think I can be mistaken."

"You are not mistaken," she responded, looking flushed and troubled.

"What can they want of your father at this time of the morning?" I said.

She made no reply, but quickened her steps, as if she wished to shorten the interview. Whatever their business was, I felt sure that she understood its nature, and almost equally sure that it related to myself. I knew that the three had met at New Haven; and I had no doubt that they had the same business on hand now that they had then. I determined to learn it before I left the house.

As we approached the gate, she suddenly turned to me in her impulsive way, and said:

"Arthur Bonnicastle, are you strong this morning?"

"Yes," I replied, "I can meet anything."

"I am glad; I believe you."

That was all. As we mounted the steps we found Mr. Bradford sitting before the open door, reading, or pretending to read, a newspaper.

"Here's Mr. Bonnicastle, father," Millie said, and passed through the hall and out of sight.

Mr. Bradford rose and gave me his hand. My coming had evidently agitated him, though he endeavored to bear himself calmly.

"I wish to ask you some questions, and to talk with you," I said.

"Let us go where we can be alone," he responded, leading the way into a little library or office which I had never seen before. Throwing open the shutters, and seating himself by the window, at the same time pointing me to a chair opposite to him, he said: "Now for the questions."

"I want you to tell me what person is represented by the picture of a boy in Mrs. Sanderson's dining-room."

"Her own son, and her only child," he replied.

"Is he living or dead?"

"He is dead."

"Will you tell me his history?" I said.

He hesitated a moment, looking out of the window, and then replied slowly: "Yes, I will. It is time you should know it, and everything connected with it. Have you leisure to hear it now?"

"Yes. That is my business here this morning."

"Then I must begin at the beginning," he replied. "I suppose you may have learned before this time that Mrs. Sanderson was a Bonnicastle."

"I know it," I said.

"You have learned, too, that she is a willful woman. In her youth, at least, she was unreasonably so. She was an heiress, and, in her young days, was pretty. For fifty miles around she was regarded as the finest "catch" within the reach of any ambitious young man. Her suitors were numerous, and among them was the one to whom, against the wishes of her parents, she at last gave her hand. He was handsome, bright, gallant, bold and vicious. It was enough for her that her parents opposed his attentions and designs to secure for him her sympathy. It was enough for her that careful friends warned her against him. She turned a deaf ear to them all, and became fixed in her choice by the opposition she encountered. To the sorrow of those who loved her and wished her well, she was married to him. Her parents, living where she lives now, did the best they could to secure her happiness, and opened their home to their new son-in-law, but witnessing his careless treatment of their daughter, and his dissipations, died soon afterwards, of disappointed hopes and ruined peace.

"The death of her parents removed all the restraint which had thitherto influenced him, and he plunged into a course of dissipation and debauchery which made the life of his wife an unceasing torment and sorrow. He gambled, he kept the grossest companions around him, he committed a thousand excesses, and as he had to do with a will as strong as his own, the domestic life of The Mansion was notoriously inharmonious.

"After a few years, a child was born. The baby was a boy, and over this event the father indulged in a debauch from which he never recovered. Paralysis and a softened brain reduced him in a few months to essential idiocy, and when he died the whole town gave a sigh of relief. Self-sufficient in her nature, your aunt was self-contained in her mortification and sorrow. No one ever heard a complaint from her lips, and no one ever dared to mention the name of her husband to her in any terms but those of respect. His debts were paid, and as his time of indulgence had been comparatively short, her large fortune was not seriously impaired.

"Then she gave herself up to the training of her boy. I think she saw in him something of the nature of his father, and set herself to the task of curbing and killing it. No boy in Bradford ever had so rigid a training as Henry Sanderson. She did not permit him to leave her sight. All his early education was received at her hands. Every wish, every impulse, even every aspiration of the child, was subjected to the iron rule of her will. No slave that ever lived was more absorbed, directed and controlled by his master than this unfortunate child was by his mother. Not one taste of liberty did he ever know, until she was compelled to send him away from her to complete his education. The portrait of him which has excited your curiosity for so many years was painted when he was less than twelve years old, though he was not permitted to leave his home until some years later.

"I was young at that time myself, though I was older than Henry—young enough, at least, to sympathize with him, and to wish, with other boys, that we could get him away from her and give him one taste of social freedom and fellowship. When she rode he was with her, looking wistfully and smilingly out upon the boys wherever he saw them playing, and when she walked she held his hand until he was quite as large as herself. Every act of his life was regulated by a rule which consulted neither his wish nor his reason. He had absolutely no training of his own will—no development within his own heart of the principles of right conduct, no exercise of liberty under those wise counsels and restraints which would lead him safely up to the liberty of manhood. He was simply her creature, her tool, her puppet, slavishly obedient to her every wish and word. He was treated as if he were a wild animal, whom she wished to tame—an animal without affection, without reason, without any rights except those which she might give him. She was determined that he should not be like his father.

"I have no doubt that she loved this child with all the strength of her strong nature, for she sacrificed society and a thousand pleasures for the purpose of carrying out her plans concerning him. She would not leave him at home with servants any more than she would give him the liberty of intercourse with other children, and thus she shut herself away from the world, and lived wholly with and for him.

"He was fitted for college in her own house, by the tuition of a learned clergyman of the town, who was glad to eke out a scanty professional maintenance by attending her son, though she was present at every recitation, and never left him for a moment in the tutor's company.

"When the work of preparation was completed, she went through the terrible struggle of parting with her charge, and sending him away from her for the first time. He went from her as dependent and self-distrustful as a child of three—a trembling, bashful, wretched boy, and came back in less than a year just what any wise man would have anticipated—a rough, roystering, ungovernable fellow, who laughed at his mother, turned her orderly home into a pandemonium, flouted her authority, and made her glad before his vacation ended to send him back again, out of her sight. Untrained in self-control and the use of liberty, he went into all excesses, and became the one notorious rowdy of the college. He was rusticated more than once, and would have been expelled but for the strong influence which his mother brought to bear upon the government of the college.

"After his graduation, he was for a time at home; but Bradford was too small to cover up his debaucheries and immoralities. He had all the beauty and boldness of his father, and inherited his dominant animal nature. After a long quarrel with his mother, he made an arrangement with her by which he was allowed a generous annuity, and with this he went away, drifting at last to New Orleans. There he found college classmates who knew of his mother's wealth, and as he had money enough to dress like a gentleman, he was admitted at once into society, and came to be regarded as a desirable match for any one of the many young women he met. He lived a life of gayety, gambled with the fast men into whose society he was thrown, and at last incurred debts which, in desperation, he begged his mother to pay, promising in return immediate and thorough reform. After a long delay his request was granted; and I have no doubt that he honestly undertook the reform he had promised, for at this time he became acquainted with a woman whose influence over him was purifying and ennobling, and well calcuted to inspire and fortify all his good resolutions. She was not rich, but she belonged to a good family, and was well educated.

"Of course he showed her only his amiable side; and the ardent love she inspired in him won her heart, and she married him. At this time he was but twenty-five years old. His mother had been looking forward wearily to the hour when he would see the folly of his course, would complete the sowing of his wild oats, and be glad to return to his home. She had her own ambitious projects concerning a matrimonial alliance for him; and when he married without consulting her, and married one who was poor, her anger was without bounds. Impulsively she sat down and wrote him the cruelest letter that it was in her power to write, telling him that the allowance which she had hitherto sent him would be sent to him no longer, and that her property would be left to others.

"The blow was one from which he never recovered. He was prostrated at once upon a bed of sickness, which, acting upon a system that had been grossly abused, at last carried him to his grave. Once during this sickness his wife wrote to his mother a note of entreaty, so full of tender love for her sick and dying husband, and so appealing in its Christian womanliness, that it might well have moved a heart of stone; but it found no entrance at a door which disappointed pride had closed. The note was never answered, and was undoubtedly tossed into the fire, that the receiver might never be reminded of it.

"The son and husband died, and was buried by alien hands, and his mother never saw his face again."

Here Mr. Bradford paused, as if his story was finished.

"Is this all?" I asked.

"It is, in brief, the history of the boy whose portrait you have inquired about," he replied.

"What became of his widow?" I inquired.

"She returned to her parents, and never wrote a word to Mrs. Sanderson. She had been treated by her in so cruel a manner that she could not. Afterwards she married again, and removed, I have since learned, to one of the Northern States."

I sat in silence for some moments, a terrible question burning in my throat, which I dared not utter. I felt myself trembling in every nerve. I tried to thrust the question from me, but it would not go.

Then Mr. Bradford, who, I doubt not, read my thoughts,

and did not feel ready to answer my question, said: "You see how differently Mrs. Sanderson has treated you. I have no doubt that she reasoned the matter all out, and came to the conclusion that she had acted unwisely. I have no doubt, though she never acknowledged it to any one, that she saw the reason of the failure of the plan of training which she adopted in the case of her son, and determined upon another one for you."

"And that has failed too," I said sadly.

"Yes: I mean no reproach and no unkindness when I frankly say that I think it has. Both plans ignored certain principles in human nature which must be recognized in all sound training. No true man was ever made either by absorbing and repressing his will, or by removing from him all stimulus to manly endeavor."

"Do you think my aunt cares much for these things that happened so long ago?" I inquired.

"Yes, I think that she cares for them more and more as the days go by, and bring her nearer to her grave. She has softened wonderfully within a few years, and I have no doubt that they form the one dark, ever-present shadow upon her life. As she feels the days of helplessness coming, she clings more to companions, and misses the hand that, for sixteen long and laborious years, she tried to teach obedience, and train into helpfulness against the emergency that is almost upon her. She mourns for her child. She bewails in secret her mistakes; and, while she is true to you to-day, I have no doubt that if the son of her youth could come to her in rags and wretchedness, with all his sins upon him, and with the record of his ingratitude unwashed of its stains, she would receive him with open arms, and be almost content to die at once in his embrace."

The tears filled my eyes, and I said: "Poor woman! I wish he could come."

Mr. Bradford's observations and conclusions with regard to her coincided with my own. I had noticed this change coming over her. I had seen her repeatedly standing before the picture. I had witnessed her absorption in revery. Even from the first day of my acquaintance with her I saw the change had been in progress. Her heart had been unfed so long that it had begun to starve. She had clung more and more to me; she had lived more and more in the society of Mrs. Belden; and now that Henry had become an inmate of her house, she evidently delighted to be in his presence. Her strong characteristics often betrayed themselves in her conduct, but they were revealed through a tenderer atmosphere. I pitied her profoundly, and I saw how impossible it was for me, under any circumstances, to fill the place in her heart of one who had been nursed upon it.

We went on talking upon various unimportant matters, both of us fighting away from the question which each of us felt was uppermost in the other's mind. At last, summoning all my resolution and courage, I said: "Was there any child?"

"Yes."

"Is that child living?"

"Yes; I think so—yes."

I knew that at this reply to my question the blood wholly forsook my face. My head swam wildly, and I reeled heavily upon my feet, and came close to the window for air. Mr. Bradford sprang up, and drew my chair close to where I stood, and bade me be seated. I felt like a man drifting resistlessly toward a precipice. The rocks and breakers had been around me for days, and I had heard indistinctly and afar the roar of tumbling waters; but now the sound stunned my ears, and I knew that my hurrying bark would soon shoot into the air, and pitch with me into the abyss.

"Does Mrs. Sanderson know of this child?"

"I do not think she does. There has been no one to tell her. She communicates with no one, and neither child nor mother would ever make an approach to her in any assertion of their relations to her, even if it were to save them from starving. But the man undoubtedly lives to-day to whom Mrs.

Sanderson's wealth will belong by every moral and natural right, when she shall have passed away."

The truth had come at last, and although I had anticipated it, it was a plunge into warring waters that impelled, and held, and whelmed, and tossed me like some poor weed they had torn from sunny banks far away and above. Would they play with me for an hour, and then carry me with other refuse out to the sea, or would they leave me upon the shore, to take root again in humbler soil and less dangerous surroundings? I did not know. For the moment I hardly cared.

Nothing was said for a long time. I looked with compressed lips and dry eyes out of the window, but I knew that Mr. Bradford's eyes were upon me. I could not but conclude that it was the intention of my friends that Mrs. Sanderson should be informed that her grandson was living, else Mr. Bradford would not have told me. I knew that Mrs. Sanderson had arrived at that point in life when such information would come to her like a voice from heaven. I knew that the fortune I had anticipated was gone; that my whole scheme of life was a shattered dream; that I was to be subjected to the task of taking up and bearing unassisted the burden of my destiny; that everybody must know my humiliation, and that in my altered lot and social position I could not aspire to the hand of the one girl of all the world whose love I coveted.

The whole dainty fabric of my life, which my imagination had reared, was carried away as with the sweep of a whirlwind, and the fragments filled the air as far as I could see.

When reaction came, it was at first weak and pitiful. It made me angry and petulant. To think that my own father and my old teacher should have been plotting for months with my best friend to bring me into this strait, and that all should not only have consented to this catastrophe, but have sought it, and laid their plans for it, made me angry.

"Mr. Bradford," I said, suddenly and fiercely, rising to my feet, "I have been abused. You led me into a trap, and now my own father and Mr. Bird join with you to spring it upon me.

You have wheedled them into it; you have determined to ruin me, and all my hopes and prospects for life, because I do not choose to model my life on your stingy little pattern. Who knows anything about this fellow whom you propose to put in my place? A pretty story to be trumped up at this late day, and palmed off upon an old woman made weak by remorse, anxious to right herself before she goes to her grave! I will fight this thing to the death for her and for myself. I will not be imposed upon; nor will I permit her to be imposed upon. Thank you for nothing. You have treated me brutally, and I take your grand ways for just what they are worth."

I whirled upon my feet, and, without bidding him good morning, attempted to leave the room. His hand was on my shoulder in an instant, and I turned upon him savagely, and yelled: "Well, what more do you want? Isn't it enough that you ruin me? Have you any new torture?"

He lifted his free hand to my other shoulder, and looked me calmly and with a sad smile in the face.

"I forgive it all, Arthur," he said, "even before you repent of it. The devil has been speaking to me, and not Arthur Bonnicastle. I expected just this, and now that it is come, let us forget it. This is not the mood in which a wise man encounters the world, and it is not the mood of a man at all, but of a child."

At this, I burst into tears, and he drew me to his breast, where I wept with painful convulsions. Then he led me back to my seat.

"When you have had time to think it all over," he said calmly and kindly, "you will find before you the most beautiful opportunity to begin a true career that man ever had. It would be cruel to deprive you of it. Your aunt will never know of this heir by your father's lips, or Mr. Bird's, or my own. Neither the heir nor his mother will ever report themselves to her. Everything is to be done by you, of your own free will. You have it in your power to make three persons superlatively happy, and, at the same time, to make a man of yourself. If you cannot appropriate such an opportunity as this, then your manhood is more thoroughly debased, or lost, than I supposed."

I saw how kindly and strongly they had prepared it all for me, and how all had been adjusted to a practical appeal to my manhood, to my sense of justice, and to my gratitude.

"I must have time," I said at last; "but where is this man?"

"In his grandmother's house, with a broken leg, suffered in the service of his friendship for you; and his mother is nursing him!"

"Grandmother's house? . . . Henry Hulm? . . . Mrs. Belden?"

I was so stunned by the information that I uttered the words in gasps, with long pauses between.

"Yes, the Providence that has cared for you and me has brought them there, and fastened them in the home where they belong. There has been no conspiracy, no intrigue, no scheme. It has all been a happening, but a happening after a plan that your father learned long before I did to recognize as divine."

"Do they know where they are?"

I asked the question blindly, because it seemed so strange that they should know anything about it.

"Certainly," Mr. Bradford said, "and Henry has always known his relations to Mrs. Sanderson, from the first day on which you told him of your own. When you first went to her, I knew just where both mother and son were, and was in communication with them; but I knew quite as well then that any attempt to reconcile Mrs. Sanderson to the thought of adopting them would have been futile. Things have changed with her and with you."

"Why are they here under false names? Why have they kept up this deception, and carried on this strange masquerade?" I asked.

"Henry very naturally took his step-father's name, because he was but a child at his mother's second marriage; and Mrs. Belden Hulm chose to be known by a part of her name only, for the purpose of hiding her personality from Mrs. Sanderson, whom she first met entirely by accident."

"Do they know that you have intended to make this disclosure?" I inquired.

"No, they know nothing of it. It was once proposed to them, but they declared that if such a thing were done they would fly the city. Under Mr. Bird's and your father's advice I have taken the matter into my own hands, and now I leave it entirely in yours. This is the end of my responsibility, and here yours begins."

"Will you be kind enough to send a messenger to Mrs. Sanderson, to tell her that I shall be absent during the day?" I said. "I cannot go home now."

"Yes."

I shook his hand, and went out into the sunlight, with a crushed, bruised feeling, as if I had passed through a great catastrophe. My first impulse was to go directly to my father, but the impulse was hardly born before I said aloud, as if moved by some sudden inspiration: "No; this thing shall be settled between God and myself." The utterance of the words seemed to give me new strength. I avoided the street that led by my father's door, and walked directly through the town. I met sun-browned men at work, earning their daily bread. On every side I heard the din of industry. There were shouts and calls, and snatches of song, and rolling of wheels, and laughter of boys. There was no sympathy for me there, and no touch of comfort or healing.

Then I sought the solitude of the woods, and the silence of nature. Far away from every sight and sound of man I sat down, but even there went on the ceaseless industries of life. The bees were plundering the flowers with not a thought of me or of play. A humming bird probed a honeysuckle at my side, and darted away like a sunbeam. A foraging squirrel picked up his dinner almost at my feet, and ran up a tree, where he sat to eat it and scold me for my idleness. A spring of water, twinkling in the light, gushed from under a rock, and went singing down the valley on its mission of service. Back and forth a robin flew, carrying food to her young. The air was loaded with the breath of flowers and the scent of balsams, beauty appealed to my eyes wherever I turned them, and the summer breezes fanned my feverish cheeks. Industry and ministry—these were the words of the world, and God had uttered them.

I looked up through the trees into the deep blue Heaven, and thought of the Being of whom that sky was but an emanation, with its life-giving sun and its wilderness of unseen stars wheeling in infinite cycles of silence, and there came unbidden to my lips those words—a thousand times divine—"My father worketh hitherto, and I work." I realized that to live outside of work was to live outside of the universal plan, that there could be no true godliness without work, and that manliness was simply godliness made human.

I thought I knew from the first what I should do in the end; but I felt the necessity of being led to my act by deliberation. I need not tell how many aspirations went up from my heart that day. I threw my soul wide open to every heavenly influence, and returned at night strong.

On the way, I thought over all that had occurred in my intercourse with Henry, and wondered why I had not apprehended the facts which now seemed so plain to me. I thought of his reticence, his reluctance to enter the door of his friend and companion, his likeness to his father's portrait, his intimacy with Mrs. Belden, of a thousand incidents that pointed to this one conclusion, and could never have led to anything else. It is more than likely that the reader of this history anticipated all that I have recorded, but to me it was a staggering surprise that would have been incredible, save for the conspiring testimony of every event and fact in our intercourse and history.

I entered the house with a new glow upon my face, and a new light in my eyes. Mrs. Sanderson noticed my altered look, and said she was glad I had spent the day away.

In the evening, I went out upon the broad acres that lay

about me, looked up at the grand old house and the splendid elms that stood around, and said : " I can do it, and I will."

Then I went to bed, and with that sweet and strong determination locked in my breast, I slept, brooded over and wrapt around by a peace that held every nerve and muscle of my body and every faculty of my soul in downy bonds until morning.

CHAPTER XXI.

I MEET AN OLD FRIEND WHO BECOMES MY RIVAL.

When I woke, on the following morning, it was with a start and a pang. It was like the shrinking shiver one feels in passing from a room full of warmth and the perfume of flowers and the appliances of comfort into one that is bare and chill; or, it was like rising from a bed, sweet with invitations to dreams and languid luxury, to an icy bath and a frosty toilet. The pang, however, did not last long. With the consciousness that I was relinquishing the hopes and plans of a life, there was mingled a sense of power over other lives that was very stimulating and pleasant. It was a great thing to be able to crown my benefactress with the highest earthly blessing she could wish for. It was a great thing to be able to make my faithful friend and fellow rich, and to restore to him his rights. It was a great thing to have the power to solve the problems of three lives by making them one.

Mr. Bradford and his advisers were exceedingly wise in leaving everything to me, and placing all the responsibility upon me. The appeal to my sense of justice—to my manliness—was simply irresistible. If Henry had been other than what he was—if he had been a young man inheriting the nature of his father—I should doubtless have had difficulty enough with him, but they would have stood by me. He would have made my place hot with hate and persecution, and they would have supported me and turned against him; but they knew that he was not only the natural heir to all that had been promised to me, but that he would use it all worthily, in carrying out the purposes of a manhood worthily won.

It was strange how my purposes with regard to the inmates

of The Mansion glorified them all in my sight. Mrs. Sanderson shone like a saint in the breakfast-room that morning. Mrs. Belden was as fresh and beautiful as a maiden. I sat with Henry for an hour, and talked, not lightly, but cheerfully. The greatness of my sacrifice, prospective though it was, had already enlarged me, and I loved my friend as I had never loved him before. My heart reached forward into the future, and took hold of the new relations which my sacrifice would establish between us; and I drank of his new love, even before it had welled from his heart.

Thus all that morning I bore about my secret; and, so long as I remained in the presence of those whom I had the power and the purpose to make happy, I was content and strong; but when, at length, I went out into the street, and met the courteous bows and warm greetings that came to me from every side as the heir of Mrs. Sanderson, and appreciated the difference between that position and the one to which I should fall as soon as my duty should be done to my benefactress and my friend, I groaned with pain, and, lifting my eyes, exclaimed: "God help me! God help me!"

Without a very definite purpose in my walk, I bent my steps toward my father's house, and on my way was obliged to pass the house of Mr. Bradford. The moment I came in sight of it, I recognized the figure of Millie at work among her flowers in the garden. I saw a quick motion of her head, as she caught the sound of my steps approaching upon the opposite side of the way, and then she rose without looking at me and walked into the house. I had already begun to cross the street toward her; but I returned and passed the house with many bitter thoughts.

It had come to this! As the heir of a large property, I was one whose acquaintance was worth the keeping. As a penniless young man, with his fortune to make, I was quite another person. I wondered if Millie Bradford, the young woman, flattered herself with the supposition that Millie Bradford, the little girl, was still in existence!

The helpless position in which I found myself with relation to this girl worried me and discouraged me. Loyal to her father in every thought and affection, I knew she would not and could not approve my course, unless I followed out his conviction concerning my duty. Yet, if I should do this, what had I to offer her but poverty and a social position beneath her own? I could never make her my wife without her father's approval, and when I had secured that, by the sacrifice of all my expectations, what had I left to offer but a partnership in a struggle against odds for the means and ministries of the kind of life to which she had been bred? To surrender all that I had expected would be my own, and Millie Bradford too, was more than I had bargained for, in my negotiation with myself.

I had not yet learned that a duty undone is always in the way—that it stands so near and high before the feet that it becomes a stumbling-block over which thousands are constantly plunging into disaster. Since those days, in which I was taking my first lessons in life, I have learned that to do one's next duty is to take a step towards all that is worth possessing—that it is the one step which may always be taken without regard to consequences, and that there is no successful life which is not made up of steps thus consecutively taken.

I reached home, not expecting to find my father there, but I was informed by my mother, with many sighs and with the expression of many confidential fears, that he was breaking down and had taken to his bed. Something, she said, had been preying on his mind which she was unable to induce him to reveal. She was glad I had come, and hoped I would ascertain what the trouble was. She had been looking forward to something of this kind for years, and had frequently warned my father of it. Mr. Bird had been there, and had accompanied my father to Mr. Bradford's, whence he had returned with a terrible headache. She always had believed there was something wrong about Mr. Bird, and she always should believe thus. As for Mr. Bradford, she had nothing to say about him; but she had noticed that men with strange notions about religion were not to be trusted.

I listened to the long and doleful story, conscious all the time that my father's illness was one into which he had been thrown by his sympathy for me. He had been trying to do his duty by me, and it had made him ill. In a moment, Millie Bradford went out of my mind, and I only delayed going into his room long enough to prepare myself to comfort him. I presume that he had heard my voice, for, when I entered the dear old man's chamber, his face was turned to the wall, and he was feigning unconsciousness of my presence in the house.

"Well, father, what's the matter?" I said cheerfully.

"Is that you?" he responded feebly, without turning his head.

"Yes."

"How are you?"

"I was never better in my life," I responded.

"Have you seen Mr. Bradford?"

"Yes."

"And had a talk with him?"

"Yes."

"Has he told you?"

"Yes."

"Are you going to do it?"

"Yes."

I was laughing,—I could not help it,—when I was sobered at once by seeing that he was convulsed with emotion. The bed shook with his passion, and he could not say a word, but lay with his face covered by his hands. I did not know what to say, and concluded to say nothing, and to let his feeling take its natural course. For many long minutes he lay silently trying to recover the mastery of himself. At last he seized the wet handkerchief with which he had been trying to assuage the pain and fever of his head, and threw it into a corner of the room, and then turned toward me, laughing and crying together, and stretched his arms toward me. I bowed to his embrace, and so the long years of the past were blotted out in our mutual tears, and we were boys once more.

I brought him his clothes, and he put them on. Then I turned the key in the door, and, sitting down side by side upon the bed, we talked the matter all over. I confessed to him my idleness, my meanness, my shameless sacrifice of golden opportunities, my weakness and my hesitations, and promised that when the right time should come I would do what I could to give Henry and his mother the home that belonged to them, and to bestow upon my benefactress the boon which she would prize a thousand times more than all the money she had ever expended upon me.

"And you are not going to be unhappy and blame me?" he said.

"Never."

"And are you coming home?"

"Yes, to look after and serve you all, so long as you may live."

We looked in one another's faces, and the same thought thrilled us. We knelt at the bed, and my father poured out his gratitude for the answer that had come with such sweet and beautiful fulfillment to his prayers. There was but little of petition in his utterances, for his heart was too full of thankfulness to give a place to his own wants or to mine. When he rose, there was the peace of heaven on his features, and the light of a new life in his faded blue eyes.

"Does my mother know of this," I inquired.

"No," he replied; "and this is the one great trouble that lies before me now."

"Let me break it to her, then, while you go out of the house," I said.

In the state of mind in which my father found himself at the close of our interview, it would have been cruel to subject him to the questions and cavils and forebodings of my mother. So, taking his way out of the house by a side door, he left me at liberty to seek her, and to reconcile her to the new determinations of my life.

I do not suppose it would be interesting to recount the long and painful conversation I had with her. She had foreseen that something of this kind would occur. She had never believed that that great fortune would come to me, but she had never dreamed that I should be the one to give it up. She was disappointed in Henry, and, as for Mrs. Belden, she had always regarded her as a schemer. She presumed, too, that as soon as Henry found himself the possessor of a fortune he would forsake Claire—a step which she was sure would kill her. It all came of mingling with people who have money. Mr. Bradford was very officious, and she was glad that I had found out Mr. Bird at last. Her life had been a life of trial, and she had not been deceived into supposing that it would be anything else.

During all the time I had been in the house, Claire and the boys had been out. My task with my mother was interrupted at last by the sound of Claire's voice at the door. She was trolling in her own happy way the refrain of a familiar song. I had only time to impress upon my mother the necessity of keeping all knowledge of the new phase of my affairs from her and the rest of the family, and to secure her promise in accordance with it, before Claire entered the room. I knew it would be best that my sister should learn everything from the lips of Henry. She would have been distressed beyond measure at the change in my prospects as well as the change in her own. I knew she had learned to look forward upon life as a struggle with poverty, by the side of a brave man, equipped for victory. She had dreamed of helping him, solacing him, blessing him with faith and love, and rising with him to the eminence which she felt sure he had the power to achieve. No wildest dream of her young imagination had ever enthroned her in The Mansion, or made her more than a welcome visitor there after its present mistress should have passed away.

I exchanged a few pleasant words with her, assuring her that I had cured my father by a few talismanic touches, and sent him out to get some fresh air, and was trying my cure upon my mother when she interrupted me. Then we talked about Henry, and his rapid progress toward recovery. I knew that she did not expect or wish to see him, because the visit that such a step would render necessary would be regarded as the advertisement of an engagement which had not yet been openly confessed. But she was glad to hear all about him, and I gratified her by the rehearsal of all the details that I could remember. I could not help thinking, as I talked with her, that I had in hand still another destiny. It was astonishing how fruitful a good determination was, when it took the path of Providence and of natural law. I had already four for one, and felt that I could not foresee how many more would be added to the gain already made.

When, at last, I bade my mother and Claire a "good morning," the only question left upon my mind concerned the time and manner of the announcement to Mrs. Sanderson of the relations of Mrs. Belden and Henry to her. Henry, I knew, was still too weak to be subjected to strong excitement without danger, and this fact made it absolutely necessary to defer the proposed revelation and the changes that were sure to follow.

I went out upon the street with a buoyant feeling, and with that sense of strength that one always feels when his will is consciously in harmony with the Supreme will, and his determinations proceed from his better nature. But my trials had not all been seen and surmounted.

Making a detour among the busier streets, that my passage to The Mansion might be longer and more varied, I saw, walking before me, an elegant young man, in the jauntiest of morning costumes. I could not see his face, but I knew at once that he was a stranger in the city, and was impressed with the conviction that I was familiar with his gait and figure. If I had seen him where I had previously known him, his identity would have been detected at once; but he was the young man furthest from my thoughts, and the one old companion whom I had learned to count out of my life. I quickened my steps, and, as I approached him, some sudden and characteristic movement of his head revealed my old college friend Livingston.

"Well, well, well! Man in the Moon! When did you drop, and where did you strike?" I shouted, running up behind him.

He wheeled and grasped both my hands in his cordial way, pouring out his greetings and compliments so freely that passengers involuntarily stopped upon the walk to witness the meeting.

"I was wondering where you were, and was about to inquire," he said.

"Were you? How long have you been in town?"

"Two or three days," he replied.

"You must have been very desirous to find me," I responded. "I have a good mind to leave you, and send you my address. Permit me to bid you good-morning. This meeting in the street is very irregular."

"None of your nonsense, my boy," said he. "I came here on business, and pleasure comes after that, you know."

"Oho! Business! We are becoming useful are we? Can I assist you? I assure you I have nothing else to do."

"Bonnicastle," said he, "you are hungry. You evidently want something to stop your mouth. Let's go into the hotel and get a lunch."

Saying this, he grasped my arm, and we walked together back to his hotel, and were soon seated at a table in his parlor, doing the duty of two hearty young men to a chop and a salad.

We talked of old times, then of his employments since he left me at college two years before, and then I told him of myself, of the encounter at The Mansion which had resulted in Henry's confinement there with a broken limb, and of the way in which I had been passing my time.

"What are you going to do next?" he inquired.

"That's a secret," I said, with a blush, all the frolic going out of me in a moment.

"I know what you are going to do."

"What?"

"You are going to Europe and the East with me. We are

to be gone two years, and to see everything. We'll sing Yankee Doodle on the Pyramids, have a fish-fry on the shores of Galilee, light our cigars at Vesuvius, call on the Pope, see all the pictures, and dance with all the pretty girls from Vienna and Paris to St. Petersburg, and call it study. On very rainy days, we'll write dutiful letters to our friends, conveying assurances of our high consideration, and asking for remittances."

Little did the merry fellow imagine, as he rattled off his programme, what a temptation he was placing before me. It presented the most agreeable path out of my difficulty. I believed Mrs. Sanderson would deny me nothing, even should I renounce all my expectations, and surrender my home to him to whom it naturally belonged. The act of surrender would place her under such obligations to me that any request that might come with it would, I supposed, be sure to be granted. Then it would let me down easily, and save me the necessity of facing my townsmen under my new circumstances. It would furnish me with a knowledge of the world which would be useful to me in the future task of providing for myself. It would complete my education, and give me the finest possible start in life. Livingston's connections would carry me into the best society, and bring me advantages such as I could not secure by means within my own command.

"Are you in earnest?" I inquired, hesitatingly.

"I never was more so in my life."

"You tempt me."

"Well, you know just how much my rattle means," said he, sobered by the tone of my inquiry. "You know I take care of myself, and others too—when they let me. We can have a good time and one that will do us good."

While I felt pretty sure that I should not go with him, unless Mrs. Sanderson should voluntarily offer me the means for the journey, and my friends should urge me to accept them, I told him I would think of it.

"That's right," he said, "and you'll conclude to go."

"When?"

"Next month."

Was this Providence too? Was my road out of my difficulty to be strewn with flowers? How could I tell? Unexpectedly, at the exact moment when it would meet with a greedy welcome, came this proposition. To accept it would be to take me away from every unpleasant association, and all the apprehended trials attending the execution of my great purpose, and give me pleasure that I coveted and culture that I needed. To reject it was to adopt a career of hardship at once, to take up my life beneath my father's humble roof, to expose myself to the triumphant sneers of the coarse men who had envied me, and to forsake forever those associations which had become so precious to me. I could do justice to Henry and my benefactress, and secure this great pleasure to myself also. Had Providence directed all this?

Many things have been accepted first and last, among men, as providential, under the mistaken supposition that the devil does not understand the value of times and opportunities. Evil has its providences as well as Good; and a tempted man is often too much befogged to distinguish the one from the other. Interpreting providences by wishes is the favorite trick of fools.

After a long and discursive talk on the subject of foreign travel generally, and of the project before us particularly, I was bold enough to ask Livingston what business it could be that had brought him to Bradford. He fought shy of the question and seemed to be embarrassed by it. Licensed by the familiarly friendly terms of our previous intercourse, I good-naturedly pressed my question. He gave all kinds of evasive and unsatisfactory replies; and then I pushed the matter further by asking him what friends he had in the place, and endeavoring to ascertain what new acquaintances he had made. I could not learn that he knew anybody in Bradford but Henry and myself, and I became satisfied at last that he had not been frank with me. It is true that he was not accountable to me, and that I had no right to pry into his affairs; but he had volunteered to say that his errand was a business errand; and I felt that in a place where I was at home, and he was not, I could serve him if he would permit me to do so.

As soon as he could divert me from my purpose, he put me the question whether I had remained heart and fancy free; "for you know," he said, "that it will never do for rovers to leave pining maidens behind them."

I assured him (with those mental reservations with which uncommitted lovers so ingeniously sophisticate the truth) that there was not a woman in the world, with the exception of certain female relatives, who had any claim upon my affection.

"By the way," said Livingston with sudden interest, as if the thought had struck him for the first time, "what has become of that little Bradford girl, whom we met on that memorable New Year's at the Spencers'; you remember that old house in the suburbs? or were you too foggy for that?"

If Livingston had realized how painful such an allusion would be to me, he would not have made it; but his standard of morality, so far as it related to excesses in drink, was so different from mine, that it was impossible for him to appreciate the shame which my fall had caused me, and the shrinking sorrow with which I still looked back upon it.

I told him frankly that I remembered the meeting imperfectly, and that I heartily wished I had no memory of it whatever. "I made an ass of myself," I said, "and worse; and I doubt whether it has ever been forgotten, or ever will be."

There was a quiet lighting of his eye as he heard this; and then he went on to say that her New York friends told very extravagant stories about her beauty and attractiveness, and that he should really like to fall in with her again. Then he went on to moralize, after the wise manner of young men, on the heartlessness of city life, and particularly of city girls, and said that he had often told his mother that no hot-house rose should ever adorn his button-hole, provided he could pluck a satisfactory wayside daisy.

A jealous lover has no rival in the instantaneous construction of a hypothesis. I saw at once the whole trick. Tiring of his New York life, having nothing whatever to do, remembering the beautiful face and hearty manner of Millie Bradford, and moved by some recent conversations about her with her friends, he had started off from home with the determination to meet her in some way. Endeavoring first to assure himself that I had no claim upon her, he undoubtedly intended to engage my services to bring about a renewal of his acquaintance with her.

I had met my rival; for I could not but feel that if he had been impressed by her when she was little more than a child, her charms of womanhood—her beautiful person, and her bright, pure nature—would impress him still more. It was a bitter draught for me to drink, without the privilege of making a wry face or uttering a protest. He was maturer than I, and possessed of every personal attraction. He carried with him, and had behind him, the highest social consideration and influence. He was rich, he was not base, he was the best of his set, he was the master of himself and of all the arts of society; he was one of those young men whose way with women is easy. What was I by the side of a man like him? The only occasion on which Millie Bradford had ever seen him was one associated with my disgrace. She could never meet him again without recalling my fall, and his own honorable freedom from all responsibility for it. The necessity of getting him out of the country by a period of foreign travel seemed laid upon me. To have him within an easy distance, after I had voluntarily forsaken my fortune, and before I had had an opportunity to prove my power to achieve a fortune for myself, was to live a life of constant misery, with the chances of having the one grand prize of existence torn from my hands and borne hopelessly beyond my reach.

"Oh, it's a daisy business, is it?" I said, with a pale face and such carelessness of tone as I could assume. "There are lots of them round here. They're a bit dusty, perhaps, in dry weather, but are fresh after a shower. You would never be contented with one: what do you say to a dozen?"

Livingston laughed, and laughed in such a way that I knew he had no business in Bradford. But why had he kept away from me? Why had he been three days in the town without apprising me of his presence?

He held up his hand and looked at it with a curious smile. "Bonnicastle," said he, "do you see anything peculiar on the back of that hand?"

"Nothing," I replied, "except that it seems to be clean."

"Does it seem to you that there is one spot on it that is cleaner than all the rest?" he inquired.

I confessed that I was unable to detect any such locality.

"Well, my boy, there is a spot there which I could define to you, if I should try, that I have kept clean for two years, and which has a life and sacredness of its own. It once had a sensation—the sweetest and most thrilling that you can imagine. It was pressed by a pair of innocent lips, and wet by as sweet a dew-drop as ever nestled in the heart of a rose. You never thought me romantic, but that little touch and baptism have set that hand apart—for the present, any way."

"If you wish to give me to understand that Milly Bradford ever kissed your hand and dropped a tear upon it, you have brought your chaff to the wrong market," I said, the anger rising in my heart and the color mounting to my face.

"Don't be hasty, old fellow," said he, reaching over and patting me on my shoulder. "I've said nothing about Millie Bradford. I've lived among roses and daisies all my life."

Whether Livingston saw that I had a little personal feeling about the matter, or felt that he had been foolishly confidential, or were afraid that I should push him to an explanation, which would compel him to reveal the circumstances under which Millie had begged his forgiveness with a kiss, for charging him with my intoxication—a fact of which I was too stupid at the time to be conscious—I do not know; but he assured me that he had been talking nonsense, and that I was to lay up and remember nothing that he had said.

We had already pushed back from the table, and he had

rung for a waiter to have it cleared. In response to the bell, a man came with his tray in one hand and a card in the other. Handing the latter to Livingston, the young man took it with a strange, embarrassed flush on his face. Turning it over, and looking at it the second time, he exclaimed: "I wonder how he knew me to be here. It's your friend Mr. Bradford." Then turning to the waiter, he added: "Take these dishes away and ask him up."

I rose at once to go; and he did not detain me, or suggest a future meeting. I shook his hand and bade him "good-morning," but was arrested at the door by finding Mr. Bradford waiting outside. Seeing Livingston within, he came forward, and, while he took my arm and led me back, said: "I am somewhat in haste this morning, and so have followed my card at once. I am not going to separate two fellows like you; so, Arthur, sit down."

I did not believe my presence welcome to Livingston during this interview; but as I was curious to witness it, and had a sufficient apology for doing so, I sat down, and remained.

"I have just taken from the office," Mr. Bradford went on, "a letter from my friends the Spencers, who tell me that you are to be here for a few days; and as the letter has evidently been detained on the way, I have called at once to apologize for not having called before."

Livingston was profuse in his protestations that it was not of the slightest consequence, and that while he should have been glad to meet Mr. Bradford, he had passed his time quite pleasantly. I saw at once what had occupied him during those three days, in which he had not announced his presence to me. He had been awaiting the arrival of this letter. He had chosen to be introduced in this way, rather than bear the letter himself. It was a cunningly-contrived, but a very transparent, proceeding.

Livingston was invited to the Bradfords to dine the next day, of course, and quite of course, as I was present when the invitation was given, I was invited to meet him. This was satisfactory to me, though I doubt whether Livingston was pleased with the arrangement, for he had evidently intended to see Millie Bradford before he announced himself to me.

Inviting my friend to call at The Mansion during the afternoon and make my aunt's acquaintance, and renew his acquaintance with Henry, I took my leave of him and passed out with Mr. Bradford. I was not a little surprised to learn how pleasantly the latter remembered my college acquaintance, and how high an estimate he placed upon him. If Livingston could have heard his hearty words of praise, he would have learned how smoothly the way was paved to the accomplishment of his hopes and his possible purposes. In my jealousy, every word he uttered was full of discouragement, for I was sure that I knew the motive which had drawn Livingston to the town, while Mr. Bradford was as innocent as a child of any suspicions of such a motive.

As we came near his house, I said: "You are in haste this morning, but I wish to see you soon—before to-morrow, if you can spare me the time."

"Come in to-night, then," he responded.

At night, accordingly, I went, and he received me alone, as he did on the previous day. I told him of my interview with my father and mother, and of the determination at which I had arrived with relation to Mrs. Sanderson and Henry. He listened to me with warm approval, which was evident, though he said but little; but when I told him of Livingston's proposition to travel, and my wishes in regard to it, he dropped his head as if he were disappointed. I urged the matter, and frankly gave him the reasons for my desire to absent myself for a while after the change in my circumstances.

He made me no immediate reply, but rose and walked the room, as if perplexed and uncertain concerning the response which he ought to make to the project. At length he paused before me, and said: "Arthur, you are young, and I am afraid that I expect too much of you. I see very plainly, however, that if you go away for a protracted absence, to live still longer on Mrs. Sanderson's benefactions, you will return more disqualified than you are at this moment to take up an independent life. I do not approve of your plan, but I will not lift a finger to thwart it. After you have surrendered your place in Mrs. Sanderson's family, you will be in a better position to judge whether your plan be either desirable or practicable."

Then he laid his hand upon my shoulder, in an affectionate way, and added: "I confess I should be sorry to lose sight of you for the next two years. Your father needs you, and will need you more and more. Besides, the next two years are to confirm you more than you can see in the style of character and manhood which you are to carry through life. I am very anxious that these two years should be made the most of."

The interview was a brief one, and I left the presence and house of my friend under the impression that he not only did not approve my plan, but that he thought it very doubtful whether I should have the opportunity to realize it. He said but little, yet I saw that his faith in Mrs. Sanderson's generosity, where her own selfish ends were not involved, was not very hearty.

On the following day I met Livingston at Mr. Bradford's table. The family were all at home, and Millie, most becomingly dressed, never had seemed so beautiful to me. Livingston was evidently very much impressed by her charms, and showed by the attention he bestowed upon her his desire to appear at his best in her presence. I was distressed by my own youth, and the easy superiority which he manifested in all his manners and conversation.

It was strange, too, to see how the girl's quick nature had shot beyond mine into maturity, and how, in her womanliness, she matched my friend better than myself. I was full of embarrassment and jealousy. The words that were addressed to me by the other members of the family were half unheard and but clumsily replied to, absorbed as I was in watching Livingston and Millie, and seeing how happily they carried on their conversation. I was enraged with myself—I who had always been quick and careless—for I knew that I did not appear well, and felt that the girl, whose senior I was by several years, regarded me as a youth in whom the flavor and power of maturity were lacking. Livingston was a man, she was a woman, and I was a boy. I saw it all and felt it all, with pangs that none may know save those who have experienced them.

The evening did not pass away, however, without giving me an opportunity for a quiet talk with Millie. There was one woman whose sharp vision did not fail to detect the real state of affairs. Aunt Flick was on the alert. She had watched the play from the first, with eyes that comprehended the situation, and in her own perverse way she was my friend. She managed to call Livingston away from Millie, and then I took a seat at her side. I tried to lead her into conversation on the subject most interesting to me, but she declined to say a word, though I knew that she was aware of all that was occurring in relation to my life.

The moments were precious, and I said impulsively, out of the burden of my heart, "Miss Bradford, I am passing through a great trial."

"I know it," she replied, looking away from me.

"Are you sorry?"

"No,"—still looking away.

"Are you my friend?"

"That depends."

"I get very little sympathy," I responded bitterly. "No one but my dear old father seems to understand how hard this is, and how hard all have helped to make it for me. The revolution of one's life is not a pleasant process. A dozen words, spoken to me by the right lips, would make many things easy and anything possible."

She turned to me in a startled way, as if I had given her sudden pain, and she had been moved to ask me why I had done it. I was thrilled by the look, and thoroughly ashamed of the words that had inspired it. What right had I to come to her with my troubles? What right had I to seek for her sympathy?

Was it manly for me to seek help from her to be a man? If she had not pitied me and seen further than I did, she would have spurned me.

This conversation was nothing but a brief episode in the evening's experiences, but it made a healthy impression upon me.

Livingston and I left the Bradfords together, and, as we were to take opposite directions to our lodgings, we parted at the door. Not a word was said about Millie; and all that he said about the Bradfords was in the guarded words: "These friends of yours seem to be very nice people." I knew that he would be there again, as soon as it would be practicable, and that he would be there without me. I was quite reconciled to this, for I saw that he monopolized attention, and that I could be nothing but a boy by his side, when he chose that I should be.

He remained in the town for a week, calling upon the Bradford family nearly every day, and on one occasion taking a drive with them in the family carriage. In the meantime Henry made rapid strides toward recovery, and the dreaded hour approached when it would be necessary for me to take the step which would abruptly change the current of my life.

When I parted with Livingston, he still entertained the project of travel, and said that he should return in a fortnight to ascertain my conclusions.

CHAPTER XXII.

MRS. SANDERSON MEETS HER GRANDSON AND I RETURN TO MY FATHER'S HOME.

LIVINGSTON had been gone three or four days when, one morning, Henry's surgical attendant came down stairs from his regular visit to the young man, and announced that his patient was sitting in a chair by the window, and that he would soon be able to take a little passive exercise in the open air. Having given me directions with regard to getting him back to his bed, when he should become tired with sitting, he went away. The sudden realization that Henry was so near the point of perfect recovery sent the blood to my heart with a dull throb that made me tremble. I knew that he would endeavor to get away as soon as possible, and that he would go whenever his mother should consider it safe for him to be separated from her.

"Are you well to day?" I said, lifting my eyes to my aunt.

"Perfectly well."

"Are you willing to have a long talk with me this morning?" I inquired.

She looked at me with a quick, sharp glance, and seeing that I was agitated, replied with the question: "Is it a matter of great importance?"

"Yes, of the greatest importance."

"H'm! You're not in love, I hope?"

"No," I responded, coloring in spite of the terrible depression that had come upon me, "though I probably should not tell of it if I were."

"I'm sure I don't see why you shouldn't," she answered quickly.

"No," I said, "it has nothing to do with that. I wish it had, but it doesn't look as if anything of that kind would ever come to me."

"Psh! You're a boy. Don't worry yourself before your time."

We were seated in the little library where she first received me. I rose from my chair, went to the door that opened into the hall, and locked it. The door into the dining-room stood ajar, and I threw it wide open. Then I went back to my chair and sat down. She watched these movements in silent astonishment, and her eyes fairly burned with excited curiosity when I concluded them.

Looking into the dining-room upon the picture that still hung where I had replaced it, I said: "Aunt, you must forgive me; but I have learned all about that picture, and I know the whole history of the person whom it represents."

"Who has been base enough to tell you?" she almost screamed.

"A person who wishes no harm either to you or me," I replied.

She had risen to her feet at the first announcement, but she sank back into her chair again, and covered her face with her hands. Suddenly steeling herself against the feelings that were overwhelming her, she dropped her hands, and said, with a voice equally charged with fright and defiance: "So, this is the important business, is it! You have listened to the voice of a slanderer, who has represented me to be little better than a fiend; and I am to be lectured, am I? You, to whom I have given my bread and my fortune—you, to whom I have given my love—are turning against me, are you? You have consented to sit still and hear me maligned and condemned, have you? Do you wish to forsake me? Have I done anything to deserve such treatment at your hands? Does my presence defile you? Do I go about meddling with other people's business? Have I meddled with anything that was not my own? I would like to know who has been poisoning your mind against me. Has there been anything in my treatment of you that would lead you to think me possessed of the devil?"

She poured out these words in a torrent so impetuous and continuous that I could not even attempt to interrupt her; and it was better that she should spend the first gush of her passion without hinderance. It was to me a terrible revelation of the condition of her mind, and of the agitations to which it was familiar. This was doubtless the first utterance to which those agitations had ever forced her.

I paused for a minute to collect my thoughts, while she buried her face in her hands again. Then I said: "Mrs. Sanderson, I have noticed, since my return from college particularly, that you have been in trouble. I have seen you many times before that picture, and known that it was associated in your mind with distressing thoughts. It has troubled me, because it has given me the impression that I am in some way, directly or indirectly, connected with it. I have sought for the explanation and found it. No one has prejudiced my mind against you, as I will prove to you by such a sacrifice as few men have been called upon to make. You have been very kind to me, and I do not now see how it is possible for me ever to cease to be grateful to you. You have been my most generous and indulgent benefactress, and it is partly because I am grateful, and desire to prove my gratitude, that I have sought this interview."

She looked up to me with a dazed, distressed expression upon her sharpened features, as if waiting for me to go on.

"There was once a little boy," I said, "who grew up in this old house, under his mother's care; and then he went away, and went wrong. His mother was distracted with his ingratitude and his excesses, and finally cut him adrift, with the means of continuing his dissipations. After a time he married one of God's own angels."

"You know nothing about it," she interrupted, spitefully. "You know nothing about her. She was a poor girl without any position, who managed to weave her net about him and inveigle him into marriage. I cursed her then, and I curse her still."

"Don't, aunt," I said. "I am sure you have done some things in your life that you are sorry for, and I know you will be sorry for this."

"Don't lecture me, boy."

"I don't lecture you. I don't presume to do anything of the kind, but I know I speak the truth."

"Well, then, what about the angel?"

"She did her best to make him what his mother had failed to make him."

"And the angel failed," she said contemptuously. "Certainly a woman may be excused for not accomplishing what a superior being failed to accomplish."

"Yes, the angel failed, mainly because his mother would not help her."

"I tell you again that you know nothing about it. I am a fool for listening to another word."

It was a strange thing to me, as I sat before this agitated woman, quarreling with her own history, and helplessly angry with me and with the unknown man who had given me my information, to find myself growing cool and strong with every burst of her passion. I had found and pierced the joints of her closely-knit harness. I was in the center of the rankling secret of her life, and she was self-contained no longer. I was in power, and she was fretfully conscious that she was not.

"Yes, the angel failed, because his mother would not help her. I presume the mother intended to drive that angel to forsake him, and compel him to return to herself. If she did not have so good a motive as this, she intended to drive him to the grave into which he was soon gathered."

"Oh, Arthur! Arthur! Arthur! Don't say it! don't say it!"

The anger was gone, and the old remorse which had been eating at her heart for years resumed its sway. She writhed in her chair. She wrung her hands. She rose and paced the room, in a painful, tottering way, which distressed me, and made me fear that I had been harsh, or had chosen the wrong plan for approaching her and executing my purpose.

"Yes, aunt, the woman was an angel. If she had not been, she would have become a torment to you. Did she ever write to you? Did she ever ask a favor of you? Do you suppose that she would ever receive from you a farthing of the wealth that her husband would rightly have inherited, unless first you had poured out your heart to her in a prayer for forgiveness? Has she acted like a mercenary woman? No, aunt, it is you who know nothing about her."

"She was nothing to me," Mrs. Sanderson said. "She never could have been anything to me."

"That you don't know."

"Well, what else have you to say?"

"She is living to-day, and, in a self-respectful way, is earning her own livelihood."

"I tell you again she is nothing to me," my aunt responded. "She is doing to-day what I presume she did before her marriage. I know of no reason why she should not earn her living. She probably knows me well enough to know that I will do nothing for her, and can be nothing to her. If you have taken it into your head to try to bring me to recognize her and give her money, I can tell you that you have undertaken a very foolish and fruitless enterprise. If this is all you have to say to me, we may as well stop our conversation at once. It is a boy's business, and if you know what is for your own good you will never allude to her again."

She rose impatiently as if determined to close the interview, but I did not stir; so, seeing me determined, she sat down again.

"Mrs. Sanderson," I said, "is your heart satisfied with me? Have you not, especially in these last years and months, longed for some one of your own blood on whom to bestow your affections? I grant that you have treated me like a son. I grant that I not only have nothing to complain of, but that I have a thousand things to be grateful for. You have tried to love me. You have determined with all your power of will to make me everything to yourself; but, after all, are you satisfied?

Though one of your kindred, my blood does not come near enough to yours to make me yours. Have you not longed to do something before you die to wipe out the memories that haunt you?"

She watched me with sad, wide-open eyes, as I firmly and tenderly said all this, and then, as if she could conceive of but one conclusion, her anger rose again, and she exclaimed: "Don't talk to me any more about this woman! I tell you I will have nothing to do with her."

"I am saying nothing about this woman, aunt," I responded. "I am going to talk about some one besides this woman, for she had a child, of whom your son was the father."

"What?"

Half exclamation, half interrogation, the word pierced my ears like a scream.

"Mrs. Sanderson, you are the grandmother of as noble a man as breathes."

She cried; she laughed; she exclaimed: "Oh, Arthur! Oh God!" She covered her face; she threw her handkerchief upon the floor; she tore open her dress to relieve her throbbing heart, and yielded herself to such a tumult of conflicting passions as I had never witnessed before—such as I hope I may never be called upon to witness again. I sat frightened and dumb. I feared she would die—that she could not survive such agitations.

"Ha! ha! ha! I have a grandson! I have a grandson! Oh, Arthur! Oh, God! Is it so? Is it so? You lie! You know you lie! You are deceiving me. Is it so, Arthur? Say it again. It can't be so. I should have known it. Somebody has lied to you. Oh, how could you, how could you deceive an old woman, with one foot in the grave—an old woman who has loved you, and done all she could for you? How could you, Arthur?"

Thus she poured out her emotions and doubts and deprecations, unmindful of all my attempts to interrupt her, and I saw at once that it was the only mode by which she could ever be come composed enough to hear the rest of my story. The storm could only resolve itself into calm through the processes of storm. When she had exhausted herself she sank back in her chair. Then, as if moved by an impulse to put me under the strongest motive to truthfulness, she rose and came to me. With a movement so sudden that I was entirely unprepared for it, she threw herself upon my lap, and clasping her arms around my neck, placed her lips close to my ear, and said in a voice surcharged with tender pleading: "Don't deceive me, dear! Don't be cruel to me! I have never used you ill. Tell me all about it, just as it is. I am an old woman. I have only a little while to live."

"I have told you everything just as it is," I responded.

"And I have a grandchild?"

"One that you may love and be proud of."

"And can I ever see him?"

"Yes."

"Do you know him?"

"Yes."

"Do you suppose he will come to live with me, if I ask him?"

"I don't know."

"Does he hate me?"

"I don't think he hates anybody."

"Is he with his mother?"

"Yes."

"Is he fond of her?"

"So fond of her," I answered, "that he will accept no invitation from you that does not include her."

"I take it all back, Arthur," she said. "He is right. He is a Bonnicastle. When can I see him?"

"Soon, I think."

"And I have really a grandson—a good grandson? how long have you known it?"

"Only a few days."

"Perhaps I shall not live forty-eight hours. I must see him at once."

"You shall see him soon."

Then she patted my cheek and kissed me, and played with my hair like a child. She called me her good boy, her noble boy. Then, struck suddenly with the thought of the changes that were progressing in her own mind and affections, and the changes that were imminent in her relations to me, she rose and went back to her chair. When I looked her in the face again, I was astonished at the change which a single moment of reflection had wrought upon her. Her anger was gone, her remorse had vanished, her self-possession had come back to her, enveloping her as with an armor of steel, and she was once more the Mrs. Sanderson of old. How was she to get rid of me? What arrangement could she make to get me out of the house, loosen my hold upon my expectations, and instal the rightful heir of her wealth in her home? She turned to her new life and her new schemes with the eager determination of a woman of business.

"What has led you to this announcement, Arthur?" she inquired.

"A wish to do justice to all the parties to whom it relates," I replied.

"You have done right," she said, "and of course you have counted the cost. If my grandson comes here, you will not expect to stay. Have you made any plans? Have you any reward to ask for your sacrifice? I trust that in making up your mind upon this point, you will remember what I have done for you. You will find my expenses on your account in a book which I will give you."

The cool cruelty of the woman, at this supreme moment of her life, angered and disgusted me. I bit my lips to keep back the hot words that pressed for utterance. Then, with all the calmness I could command, I said: "Do you suppose that I have come to you to-day to sell your grandson to you for money? Do you suppose that your dollars weigh a pin with me? Can't you realize that I am voluntarily relinquishing the hopes and expectations of a lifetime? Can't you see that I am going from a life of independence to one of labor and struggle?"

"Don't be angry, Arthur," she responded coolly. "I have given you your education, and taken care of you for years. I have done it under the impression that I had no heir. You tell me that I have one, and now I must part with you. You foresaw this, and I supposed that you had made your plans for it. The simple question is, how much do you want in consideration of your disappointment? How are we to separate, so that you shall feel satisfied that I have done you justice?"

"I have no stipulations to make," I answered; "I understand that you have done much for me, and that I have done very little for you, indeed; that I have very poorly improved the privileges you have bestowed upon me. I understand that you do not consider yourself under the slightest obligation to me, and that so soon as you may get your grandson into your possession, through my means, you will drop me and be glad to be rid of me forever."

"You speak bitterly, Arthur. I shall always be interested in your welfare, and shall do what I can to serve you; but when we separate we must be quits. You know my mode of doing business. I exact my rights and pay my dues."

"I have no bargains to make with you, Mrs. Sanderson," I said. "We are quits now. I confess that I have had a dream of travel. I have hoped to go away after this change in my life, and to forget it among new scenes, and prepare myself to take up and bear a burden for which my life here has done much to unfit me. I have dreamed of getting away from Bradford for a time, until the excitement that will attend these changes shall have blown over. I confess that I shrink from meeting the questions and sneers that await me; but we are quits now."

"Have you any idea what the expenses of a foreign tour will be?" she inquired in a cool, calculating tone.

"Mrs. Sanderson, you have just come into the possession of the most precious knowledge the world holds for you, and through it you expect to receive the great boon of your life. All this comes through me. Neither your daughter-in-law nor your grandson would ever have made themselves known to you, and now, when I have sacrificed the expectations of a life to them and to you, you talk about the price of a foreign trip for me, as if you were bargaining for a horse. No, madam; I wash my hands of the whole business, and it is better for us both to talk no more about this matter. We are quits to-day. I shall feel better by and by, but you have disappointed me and made me very unhappy."

Even while I talked, I could see her face harden from moment to moment. Her heart had gone out toward her heir with a selfish affection, which slowly, quietly, and surely shut out every other human being. She grudged me every dollar of her fortune on his behalf. The moment she ceased to regard me as her heir, I stood in the same relation to her that any other poor young man in Bradford occupied. Her wealth was for her grandson. She would pay to him, on his father's account, every dollar she held. She would lavish upon him every affection, and every service possible. She would offer herself and her possessions to atone for wrongs for which her conscience had upbraided her more and more, as her life had approached its close. She longed for this consummation, and looked to it for peace.

Thus I reached the moment of transition, and in disappointment and bitterness—feeling that my sacrifice was not appreciated, and that my benefactress had lost all affection for and interest in me—I took up the burden of my own life, determined that on no consideration would I receive, beyond the clothes I wore, one dollar more of the fortune on which I had lived.

"When can I see my grandson?"

"When you choose."

"To day?"

"Yes."

"Bring him to me."

"I must go to my room first," I said.

I mounted to my chamber, and threw myself into my accustomed chair by the window. I had passed into a new world. The charming things about me, which I had counted my own, were another's. The old house and the broad, beautiful acres which stretched around it were alienated forever. I realized that every dollar that had been bestowed upon me, and every privilege, service, and attention I had received, had come from a supremely selfish heart, through motives that sought only to fill an empty life, and to associate with an honored ancestral name the wealth which could not be taken out of the world with its possessor. A mercenary value had been placed upon every sentiment of gratitude and respect and love which my benefactress had inspired in me. I had been used as a thing of convenience, and being a thing of convenience no longer, I was dropped as a burden. I was humiliated, shamed, angered by the way in which I had been treated, but I was cured. The gifts that I had received looked hateful to me. The position I had occupied—the position in which I had not only grown to be content, but in which I had nursed and developed a degree of aristocratic pride—seemed most unmanly. I had been used, played with, petted, fed with daily indulgences and great promises, and then cast away, there being no further use for me.

"Never again!" I said to myself—"never again! I would not take another dollar from this estate and its owner to keep myself from starving."

The dream of travel was shattered. My new life and relations were squarely before me. Where and what I should be in a week I did not know. What old friends would fall away from me, what new friends I should make, how I should earn the bread which had thus far been supplied, was all uncertain.

I believed, however, that I had done my duty; and out of all my shame and disappointment and disgust and apprehension, there rose within me a sentiment of self-respect and a feeling of strength. And when I thought of all the circumstances that had conspired to bring me to this point, I could not doubt that Providence—the great will that embraces all wills—the supreme plan that subordinates and weaves into serviceable relations all plans—the golden fabric that unrolls from day to day, with the steady revolutions of the stars, and rolls up again, studded thick with the designs of men—had ordered everything, and ordered it aright. It was best for me that I had gone through with my indulgences and my discipline. It was best for me that I had passed through the peculiar experiences of my life. It was best for Mrs. Sanderson that she had been tormented, and that, at last, she was passing into the hands that were strong and steady—hands that would lead her aright—hands into which she was ready to throw herself, with self-abandoning love and trust. It was best that Henry had struggled and learned the worth of money, and acquired sympathy and respect for the poor. It was best that the feet of all the persons concerned in this great change of relations should be brought together at last, by a series of coincidences that seemed well-nigh miraculous.

One thing struck me as being very singular, viz.: that Mrs. Sanderson was so easily satisfied that she had a grandson, and that I not only knew him, but that he was close at hand. It only showed how eagerly ready she was to believe it, and to believe that I had prepared everything to satisfy her desire. In another frame of mind—if another frame of mind had been possible—she would have questioned me—doubted me—put me to the proof of my statements; but she was ready to accept anything on my simple assurance. After sitting quietly for an hour, I rose with a long sigh. I had still the duty of presenting Henry Sanderson—for that was his real name—to his grandmother. My heart throbbed wildly every time the thought of this meeting came to me. I had said nothing to Henry, for I knew that it would distress him beyond measure, —nay, that, disabled as he was, he would contrive some way to get out of the house and out of the town. Nothing but a sense of freedom from detection and discovery had ever reconciled him and his mother to an hour's residence in The Mansion. Hidden away in this New England town, toward which they had drifted from the far South, partly on the current of circumstances, and partly by the force of a desire to see and know the early home and associations of the husband and father, they did not doubt that they could cover their identity so perfectly that it would not be suspected. Henry had studiously kept away from the house. His mother had met Mrs. Sanderson entirely by accident, and had taken a sweet and self-amusing revenge by compelling her to love and trust her. They had confided their secret to but one man, and he had had their permission to confide it to his family. Through all these long years, the two families had been intimate friends, and Mr. Bradford had endeavored in every possible way to obtain their consent to the course he had pursued, but in vain. After the death of Mrs. Sanderson, he would doubtless have informed me of Henry's natural claims to the estate, relying upon my sense of justice and my love for him for its division between us; but he saw that my prospects were ruining me, and so had taken the matter into his own hands, simply confiding the facts of the case to my father and Mr. Bird, and acting with their advice and consent.

I drew out my trunk, and carefully packed my clothing. Not an article in the room that was not necessary to me did I take from its place. It would be Henry's room, and all the choice ornaments and appointments that I had had the happy pains to gather, were left to please his eye and remind him of me. The occupation, while it pained me, gave me strength and calmness. When the work was done, I locked my trunk, put the key in my pocket, and was about to leave the room when there came to me the sense of a smile from the skies. A cloud had been over the sun, and as it passed a flood of sunlight filled the room, growing stronger and stronger until my eyes were almost blinded by the sweet effulgence. I was not superstitious, but it seemed as if God had given me His benediction.

I turned the key in my door, and bowed at my bed. "Dear

Father," I said, " at last nothing stands between Thee and me. That which I have loved better than Thee is gone, and now I beg Thee to help me and lead me in Thine own way to Thyself. I shrink from the world, but Thou hast made it. I shrink from toil and struggle, but Thou hast ordained them. Help me to be a man after Thine own heart. Give me wisdom, guidance, and assistance. Help me to lay aside my selfishness, my love of luxury and ease, and to go down heartily into the work of the world, and to build my life upon sure foundations."

Then there rose in me a flood of pity and charity for one who had so long been my benefactress; and I prayed for her— that in her new relations she might be blessed with content and satisfaction, and that her last days might be filled with something better than she had known. I forgave her for her quick and complete renunciation of myself, and the cruel wounds she had inflicted upon my pride, and felt the old good-will of childhood welling in my heart. I enveloped her with my charity. I crowned her with the grace of pardon.

When I went down stairs I found her awaiting me in the room where I had left her. She sat holding a paper in her hand. She had dressed herself in her best, as if she were about to receive a prince. There was a bright spot of red on either thin and wrinkled cheek, and her eyes shone like fire.

"You are sure you have made no mistake, Arthur?" she said, with a voice quite unnatural in its quavering sharpness.

"Quite sure," I answered.

"This," said she, holding up her paper, " is my will. There is no will of mine beside this in existence. I have no time to ask my lawyer here to-day to make another. Life is uncertain, and there must be no mistake. I wish you to go with me to the kitchen."

She rose and I followed her out. I could not imagine what she would do, but she went straight to the old-fashioned fireplace, where the dinner was cooking, and holding the paper in her hands, opened it, and asked me to read the beginning of it and the signatures. I did so, and then she laid it upon the

The old cook regarded us in wondering silence. (p. 341.)

coals. The quick flame shot up, and we both looked on in silence, until nothing was left of it but white ashes, which a breath would scatter. The elements had swallowed all my claim to her large estate. The old cook regarded us in wondering silence, with her hands upon her hips, and watched us as we turned away from the fire, and left her alone in her domain.

When we returned to the library, Mrs. Sanderson said: "The burning of that will is equivalent to writing another in favor of my grandson; so, if I make no other, you will know the reason."

She pressed her hand upon her heart in a distressed way, and added; "I am as nearly ready as I ever can be to see—"

"Henry Sanderson," I said.

"Is that his name? Is that his real name?" she asked, eagerly.

"It is."

"And it will all go to Henry Sanderson!"

The intense, triumphant satisfaction with which she said this was almost enough, of itself, to repay me for the sacrifice I had made.

"Mrs. Sanderson," I said, "I have put into my trunk the clothes I need, and when I go away I will send for them. I have left everything else."

"For Henry—my Henry Sanderson!"

"Yes, for your Henry; and now I must go up and see my Henry, and Mrs. Belden; for after I have presented your grandson to you I shall go away."

I mounted the stairs with a throbbing heart, and a face that told the tale of a terrible excitement and trouble. Both Henry and his mother started as I came into the room, and simultaneously uttered the words, "What is it, Arthur?"

"Nothing, except that my aunt and I have had a talk, and I am going away."

A quick, involuntary glance passed between the pair, but both waited to hear my announcement.

"I am glad you are here," I said. "You can stay as long

as you wish, but I am going away. I shall see you again, but never as an inmate of this house. I want to thank you for all your kindness and love, and to assure you that I shall always remember you. Mrs. Belden, you never kissed me: kiss me now."

The dear woman looked scared, but obeyed my wish. I sat down on Henry's bed and laid my head beside his. "Good-by, old boy; good-by! Thank you for all your faithfulness to me and for your example. I hope some time to be half as good as you are."

My eyes were flooded with tears, and both Mrs. Belden and Henry were weeping in sympathy.

"What is it, Arthur? what is it? Tell us. Perhaps we can help you."

"Whatever it is, it is all right," I answered. "Some time you will know, and you will find that I am not to blame."

Then I shook their hands, went abruptly out of the room, and ran down stairs to Mrs. Sanderson. She saw that I was strangely agitated, and rose feebly as I entered.

"I wish you to go up stairs with me before I leave," I said. "Will you be kind enough to go with me now?"

There was no dawning suspicion in her heart of what I had prepared for her. She had expected me to go out and bring in a stately stranger for whose reception she had prepared her toilet. She had wondered how he would look, and by what terms she should address him.

I gave her my arm and we slowly walked up the stairs together, while my heart was beating so heavily that I could hear it, blow upon blow, in my ears. I knocked at Henry's door and entered. The moment Henry and his mother saw us together, and caught the agitated look that both of us wore, they anticipated the announcement that was imminent, and grew pale as ghosts.

"Mrs. Sanderson," I said, without offering her a seat, "this is Mrs. Belden Hulm, your daughter-in-law, and this (turning to Henry) is your grandson, Henry Sanderson. May God bless you all!"

I dropped her arm and rushed to the door. A hurried glance behind me showed that she was staggering and falling. Turning swiftly back, I caught her, while Mrs. Hulm supported her upon the other side, and together we led her to Henry's bed. Then she dropped upon her knees and Henry threw his arms around her neck, and said softly: "Grandmother!"

"My boy, my boy!" was all she could say, and it was enough.

Then I left them. I heard Henry say: "Don't go," but I did not heed him. Running down stairs, with limbs so weak with excitement that I could hardly stand, I seized my hat in the hall, and went out of doors, and hurriedly took my way toward my father's house. I did not even cast a glance at the Bradford residence, so absorbed was I in the events in which I had been an actor. The vision of the three persons clustered at Henry's bed, the thought of the powerful emotions that were surging in them all, the explanations that were pouring from Henry's lips, the prayers for forgiveness that my old benefactress was uttering, and the dreams of the new life of The Mansion which I had inaugurated blotted out the sense of my own sacrifice, and made me oblivious to all around me. Men spoke to me on the street, and I remembered afterwards that I did not answer them. I walked in a dream, and was at my father's door before I was aware. I felt that I was not ready to go in, so I turned away and continued my walk. Up the long streets I went, wrapped in my dream. Down through the busy life along the wharves I wandered, and looked out upon the water. The sailors were singing, children were playing, apple-women were chaffing, but nothing could divert me. My heart was in the room I had left. The scene was burnt indelibly upon my memory, and no new impression could take its place.

Slowly I turned toward home again. I had mastered myself sufficiently to be able to think of my future, and of the necessities and proprieties of my new position. When I reached my father's house, I found Mrs. Sanderson's man-servant—old Jenks's successor—waiting at the gate with a message from Henry, desiring my immediate return to The Mansion, and requesting that I bring with me my sister Claire. This latter request was one that brought me to myself. I had now the responsibility of leading another through a great and unanticipated excitement. Dismissing the servant, with a promise to obey his new master's wish, I went into the house, and found myself so much in self-possession that I told Claire with calmness of the message, and refrained from all allusion to what had occurred. Claire dressed herself quickly, and I could see as she presented herself for the walk that she was full of wonder. Nothing was said as we passed out. There was a strange silence in the family. The message meant a great deal, and all so thoroughly trusted Henry that no questions were asked.

When we were away from the house, I said: "Claire, you must be a woman to-day. Strange things have happened. Brace yourself for anything that may come."

"What can you mean? Has anything happened to—to him?"

"Yes, much,—much to him, and much to me; and something very strange and unexpected will happen to you."

She stopped short in the street, and grasping my two hands nervously, exclaimed: "Tell me what it is."

"My dear," I said, "my life at Mrs. Sanderson's has ceased. I am no more her heir, for Henry is discovered to be her own grandson."

"You deceive me; you can't mean it."

"It is just as I tell you."

She burst into a fit of weeping so passionate and uncontrollable that in a low voice I said, "You must command yourself. You are observed."

We resumed our walk, but it was a long time before she could speak. At length she said, "I am so sorry for you, and so sorry for myself. I do not want it so. It changes all my plans. I never can be to him what I could be if he were poor; and you are to work. Did he know he was her grandson?"

"Yes, he has always known it."

"And he never told me a word about it. How could he treat me so like a child?"

She was half angry with the thought that he had shut from her the most important secret of his life. As to the fortune which was opened to her, it did not present to her a single charm. The thought of it oppressed and distressed her. It made her life so large that she could not comprehend it. She had had no natural growth up to it and into it.

When we reached The Mansion she was calm; and it seemed, as we stood at the door and I looked inquiringly into her face, as if her beauty had taken on a maturer charm while we had walked. I led her directly to Henry's room, and there, in the presence of Mrs. Sanderson, who sat holding Henry's hand as if she were determined that her newly-found treasure should not escape her, and in the presence of Henry's mother, neither of whom she either addressed or regarded, she stooped and received her lover's kiss. I saw simply this, and with tears in my eyes went out and closed the door softly behind me. What occurred during that interview I never knew. It was an interview so tenderly sacred that neither Henry nor Claire ever alluded to it afterwards. I went down stairs, and awaited its conclusion. At the end of half an hour, I heard voices whispering above, then the footsteps of Mrs. Sanderson going to her chamber, and then the rustle of dresses upon the stairs. I went out into the hall, and met Mrs. Hulm and Claire with their arms around each other. Their eyes were wet, but they were luminous with a new happiness, and I knew that all had been settled, and settled aright.

"Henry wishes to see you," said his mother.

I cannot tell how much I dreaded this interview. I knew of course that it would come, sooner or later, and I dreaded it as much on Henry's account as on my own.

I sat down by his bed, and gave to his eager grasp both

my hands. He looked at me with tears rolling down his cheeks, with lips compressed and with the perspiration standing unbrushed from his forehead, but without the power to speak a word. I pulled out my handkerchief, and wiped his forehead and his cheeks.

"Are you happy, Henry?" I said.

"Yes, thank God and you," he answered, with choking emotion.

"So am I."

"Are you? Are you? Oh Arthur! What can I ever do to show you my gratitude? How can I look on and see you toiling to win the bread you have voluntarily given to me?"

"You have had your hard time, and I my easy one. Now we are to change places, that's all, and it is right. You have learned the value of money, and you will spend this which has come to you as it ought to be spent."

"But it is not the money; it is the home of my father—the home of my ancestors. It is a home for my mother. It is rest from uncertain wandering. I cannot tell you what it is. It is something so precious that money cannot represent it. It is something so precious that I would willingly work harder all my life for having found it. And now, my dear fellow, what can I do for you?"

"Nothing—only love me."

"But I must do more. Your home must be here. You must share it with me."

"No, Henry, the word is spoken. You have come to your own, and I shall go to mine. My lot shall be my father's lot, until I can make it better. We shall be friends forever. The surrender I have made shall do me more good than it has done you. You did not absolutely need it, and I did. You could do without it and I could not. And now, let's not talk about it any more."

We embraced and kissed as if we had been lovers, and I left him, to walk back with Claire. That night the story was all told in our little home. My trunk was brought and carried to my bare and cramped chamber; and when the accustomed early hour for retirement came I knelt with the other children and worshipped as of old. My father was happy, my mother was reconciled to the change, for Claire had been recognized at The Mansion, and I went to bed and rested through a dreamless sleep until the morning light summoned me to new changes and new duties.

CHAPTER XXIII.

I TAKE ARTHUR BONNICASTLE UPON MY OWN HANDS AND SUCCEED WITH HIM.

In a small town like Bradford, the birds have a way of collecting and carrying news, quite unknown in more considerable cities; and, apparently, a large flock of them had been around The Mansion during the events narrated in the preceding chapter; for, on the following day, the community was alive with rumors concerning them. A daily paper had just been established, whose enterprising editor deemed it his special duty and privilege to bruit such personal and social intelligence as he could gain by button-holing his victims on the street, or by listening to the voluntary tattle of busy-bodies. My good angel, Mr. Bradford, apprehending an unpleasant notoriety for me, and for the occurrences associated with my name, came to me at once and heard my story. Then he visited the editor, and so represented the case to him that, on the second morning after taking up my home with my father, I had the amusement of reading a whole column devoted to it. The paper was very wet and very dirty; and I presume that that column was read with more interest, by all the citizens of Bradford, than anything of national import which it might have contained. I will reproduce only its opening and closing paragraphs :

ROMANCE IN HIGH LIFE.—Our little city was thrown into intense excitement yesterday, by rumors of a most romantic and extraordinary character, concerning occurrences at

A CERTAIN MANSION,

which occupies an elevated position, locally, socially, and historically. It appears that a certain estimable young man, whose heroic feat cost him so dearly in a recent struggle with

A MIDNIGHT ASSASSIN,

is the natural heir to the vast wealth which he so gallantly rescued from spoliation, and that

A CERTAIN ESTIMABLE LADY,

well known to our citizens as the companion of a certain other lady, also well known, is his mother. Nothing more startling than the developments in this case has occurred in the eventful history of our city.

A MYSTERY

has always hung around these persons, and we are not among those who are surprised at the solution. But the most remarkable part of the story is that which relates to the young man who has been reared with the expectation of becoming the owner of this magnificent estate. Upon learning the relations of the young man previously alluded to, to his benefactress, he at once, in loyalty to his friend and his own personal honor, renounced forever his expectations, surrendered his position to the heir so strangely discovered, and took up his abode in his father's humble home. This act, than which none nobler was ever performed, was, we are assured by as good authority as there is in *Bradford*, wholly voluntary.

WE GIVE THAT YOUNG MAN OUR HAT—

Miller & Sons' best—and assure him that, in whatever position he may choose to take in this community, he will have such support as our humble editorial pen may give him. We feel that no less than this is due to his nobility of character.

After half a dozen paragraphs in this strain, the article closed as follows :—

It is rumored that the newly-found heir has formed

A TENDER ALLIANCE

with a beautiful young lady—a blonde—who is not a stranger in the family of our blue-eyed hero—an alliance which will enable her to

SHARE HIS BONNY CASTLE,

and unite the fortunes of the two families in indissoluble bonds. Long may they wave!

Far be it from us, enthroned upon the editorial tripod, and wielding the scepter of the press, to invade the sanctities of private life, and we therefore withhold all names. It was due to the parties concerned and to the public, however, to state the facts, and put an end to gossip and conjecture among those who have no better business than that of tampering with the secrets of the hearthstone and the heart.

During the day, I broke through the reluctance which I naturally felt to encounter the public gaze, after this exposure of my affairs, and went out upon the street. Of course, I found myself the object of universal curiosity and the subject of universal remark. Never in my life had I been treated with more deference. Something high in position had been won back to the sphere of common life; and common life was profoundly interested. My editorial friend had so represented the case as to win for me something better than sympathy; and a good-natured reticence under all inquiries, on my own part, seemed to enhance the respect of the people for me. But I had something more important on hand than seeking food for my vanity. I had myself on hand and my future; and the gossip of the community was, for the first time in my life, a matter of indifference.

It occurred to me during the day that an academy, which a number of enterprising people had built two or three years before, had been abandoned and closed, with the conclusion of the spring term, for lack of support, and that it would be possible for me to secure it for the field of my future enterprise. I called at once upon those who held the building in charge, and, before I slept, closed a bargain, very advantageous to myself, which placed it at my disposal for a term of three years. The next day I visited my friend the editor, whom I found with bare arms, well smeared with ink, at work at his printer's case, setting up the lucubrations of the previous night. He was evidently flattered by my call, and expressed the hope that what he had written with reference to myself was satisfactory. Assuring him that I had no fault to find with him, I exposed my project, which not only met with his hearty approval, but the promise of his unstinted support. From his office I went directly to the chambers of the principal lawyer of the city, and entered my name as a student of law. I took no advice, I sought no aid, but spoke freely of my plans to all around me. I realized almost at once how all life and circumstance bend to the man who walks his own determined way, toward an object definitely apprehended. People were surprised by my promptness and energy, and indeed I was surprised by myself. My dreams of luxury and ease were gone, and the fascinations of enterprise and action took strong possession of me. I was busy with my preparations for school and with study all day, and at night, every moment stolen from sleep was filled with planning and projecting. My father was delighted, and almost lived and moved and had his being in me. To him I told everything; and the full measure of his old faith in me was recovered.

When the autumn term of the academy opened, of which I was principal, and my sister Claire the leading assistant, every seat was full. Many of the pupils had come from the towns around, though the principal attendance was from the city, and I entered at once upon a life of the most fatiguing labor and the most grateful prosperity. My purse was filled at the outset with the advanced installment upon the term-bills, so that both Claire and myself had a delightful struggle with my father in our attempt to compel him to receive payment for our board and lodgings. Our little dwelling was full of new life. Even my mother was shaken from her refuge of faithlessness, and compelled to smile. Since those days I have had many pleasant experiences; but I doubt whether I have ever spent three years of purer happiness than those which I passed with Claire beneath the roof of that old academy—old, now, for though put to strange uses, the building is standing still.

There was one experience connected with this part of my history of which it is a pain to speak, because it relates to the most subtle and sacred passage of my inner life; but having led the reader thus far, I should be disloyal to my Christian confession were I to close my lips upon it and refuse its revelation.

From the hour when I first openly joined a band of Christian disciples, I had been conscious of a mighty arm around me. Within the circuit of that restraining power I had exercised an almost unrestricted liberty. I had violated my conscience in times and ways without number, yet, when tempted to reckless wandering, I had touched the obstacle and recoiled. In whatever direction I might go, I always reached a point where I became conscious of its living pulsations and its unrelaxing embrace. Unseen, impalpable, it was as impenetrable as adamant and as strong as God. The moment I assumed responsibility over other lives, and gave my own life in counsel and labor for the good of those around me, the arm came closer, and conveyed to me the impression of comfort and health and safety. I thanked God for the restraint which that voluntary act of mine had imposed upon me.

But this was not all. My life had come into the line of the divine plan for my own Christian development. I had been a recipient all my life; now I had become an active power. I had all my life been appropriating the food that came to me, and amusing myself with the playthings of fancy and imagination; now I had begun to act and expend in earnest work for worthy objects. The spiritual attitude effected by this change was one which brought me face to face with all that was unworthy in me and my past life, and I felt myself under the operations of a mighty regenerating power, which I had no disposition to resist. I could not tell whence it came or whither it went. If it was born of myself, it was a psychological experience which I could neither analyze nor measure. It was upon me for days and weeks. It was within me like leaven in the lump, permeating, enlivening, lifting me. It was like an eye-stone in the eye, searching for dust in every place and plication, and removing it, until the orb was painless and the vision pure. There was no outcry, no horror of great darkness, no disposition to publish, but a subtle, silent, sweet revolution. As it went on within me, I grew stronger day by day, and my life and work were flooded with the light of a great and fine significance. Sensibility softened and endurance hardened under it.

Spirit of God! Infinite Mother! Thou didst not thunder on Sinai amidst smoke and tempest; but in the burning bush thou didst appear in a flame that warmed without withering, and illuminated without consuming. Thou didst not hang upon the cross on Calvary, but thou didst stir the hearts of the bereaved disciples as they walked in the way with their risen Lord. All gentle ministries to the spiritual life of men emanate from Thee. Thou brooding, all-pervading presence, holding a weeping world in thy maternal embrace, with counsel and tender chastening and holy inspirations, was it thy arms that had been around me all these years, and came closer and closer, until I felt myself folded to a heart that flooded me with love? I only know that streams rise no higher than their fountain, and that the fountain of spiritual life in me had sunk and ceased to flow long before this time. Could anything but a long, strong rain from the skies have filled it? All the things we see are types of things we do not see—visible expressions of the things and thoughts of God. All the phenomena of nature—the persistent radiance of the sun and moon—the coming, going, and unloading, and the grace and glory of the clouds—the changes of the seasons and of the all-enveloping atmosphere, are revelations to our senses and our souls of those operations and influences which act upon our spiritual natures. I find no miracle in this; only nature speaking without material interpreters—only the God of nature shunning the coarser passages of the senses, and finding his way direct to the Spirit by means and ministries and channels of his own.

Was this conversion? It was not an intellectual matter at all. I had changed no opinions, for the unworthy opinions I had acquired had fallen from me, one by one, as my practice had conformed more and more to the Christian standard. Indeed, they were not my opinions at all, for they had been assumed in consequence of the necessity of somewhat bringing my spiritual and intellectual natures into harmony. My deepest intellectual convictions remained precisely what they had always been. No, it was a spiritual quickening. It had been winter with me, and I had been covered with snow and locked with ice. Did I melt the bonds which held me, by warmth self-generated? Does the rose do this or the violet? There was a sun in some heaven I could not see that shone upon me. There was a wind from some far latitude that breathed upon me. To be quickened is to be touched by a vital finger. To be quickened is to receive a fructifying flood from the great source of life.

The change was something better than had happened to me under Mr. Bedlow's preaching, long years before; but neither change was conversion. Far back in childhood, at my mother's knee, at my father's side, and in my own secret chamber, those changes were wrought which had directed my life toward a Christian consummation. My little rivulet was flowing toward the sea, increasing as it went, when it was disturbed by the first awful experiences of my life; and its turbid waters were never, until this latter time, wholly clarified. My little plant, tender but upright, was just rising out of its nursing shadows into the light when the great tempest swept over it. If my later experience was conversion, then conversion may come to a man every year of his life. It was simply the revivification and reinforcement of the powers and processes of spiritual life. It was ministry, direct and immediate, to development and growth; and with me it was complete restoration to the track of my Christian boyhood, and a thrusting out of my life of all the ideas, policies and results of that terrible winter which I can never recall without self-pity and humiliation.

The difference in the respective effects of the two great crises of my spiritual history upon my power to work illustrated better than anything else, perhaps, the difference in their nature. The first was a dissipation of power. I could not work while it lasted, and it was a long time before I could gather and hold in hand my mental forces. The second was an accession of strength and the power of concentration. I am sure that I never worked harder or better than I did during the time that my late change was in progress. It was an uplifting, enlightening and strengthening inspiration. One was a poison, the other was a cure; one disturbed, the other harmonized; one was surcharged with fear, the other brimmed with hope; one exhausted, the other nourished and edified me; one left my spirit halting and ready to stumble, the other left it armed and plumed.

After my days at the academy, came my evening readings of the elementary books of the profession which I had chosen. There were no holidays for me; and during those three years I am sure I accomplished more professional study than nine-tenths of the young men whose every day was at their disposal. I was in high health and in thorough earnest. My physical powers had never been overtasked, and I found myself in the possession of vital resources which enabled me to accomplish an enormous amount of labor. I have no doubt that there were those around me who felt a measure of pity for me, but I had no occasion to thank them for it. I had never before felt so happy, and I learned then, what the world is slow to learn, that there can be no true happiness that is not the result of the action of harmonious powers steadily bent upon pursuits that seek a worthy end. Comfort of a certain sort there may be, pleasure of a certain quality there may be, in ease and in the gratification of that which is sensuous and sensual in human nature; but happiness is never a lazy man's dower nor a sensualist's privilege. That is reserved for the worker, and can never be grasped and held save by true manhood and womanhood. It was a great lesson to learn, and it was learned for a lifetime; for, in this eventide of life, with the power to the rest, I find no joy like that which comes to me at the table on which, day after day, I write the present record.

During the autumn and winter which followed the assumption of my new duties, I was often at The Mansion, and a witness of the happiness of its inmates. Mrs. Sanderson was living in a new atmosphere. Every thought and feeling seemed to be centered upon her lately discovered treasure. She listened to his every word, watched his every motion, and seemed to feel that all her time was lost that was not spent in his presence. The strong, indomitable, self-asserting will which she had exercised during all her life was laid at his feet. With her fortune she gave herself. She was weary with the long strain and relinquished it. She trusted him, leaned upon him, lived upon him. She was in the second childhood of her life, and it was better to her than her womanhood. He became in her imagination the son whom long years before she had lost. His look recalled her boy, his voice was the repetition of the old music, and she found realized in him all the dreams she had indulged in concerning him who so sadly dissipated them in his own self-ruin.

The object of all this trust and tenderness was as happy as she. It always touched me deeply to witness the gentleness of his manner toward her. He anticipated all her wants, deferred to her slightest wish, shaped all his life to serve her own. The sense of kindred blood was strongly dominant within him, and his grandmother was held among the most sacred treasures of his heart. Whether he ever had the influence to lead her to higher sources of joy and comfort than himself, I never knew, but I know that in the old mansion that for so many years had been the home of revelry or of isolated selfishness, an altar was reared from which the incense of Christian hearts rose with the rising sun of morning and the rising stars of night.

Henry passed many days with me at the academy. In truth, my school was his loitering place, though his loitering was of a very useful fashion. I found him so full of the results of experience in the calling in which I was engaged that I won from him a thousand valuable suggestions; and such was his love for the calling that he rarely left me without hearing a recitation, which he had the power to make so vitally interesting to my pupils that he never entered the study-hall without awakening a smile of welcome from the whole school. Sometimes he went with Claire to her class-rooms; and, as many of her pupils had previously been his own, he found himself at home everywhere. There was no foolish pride in his heart that protested against her employment. He saw that she was not only useful but happy, and knew that she was learning quite as much that would be useful to her as those who engaged her efforts. Her office deepened and broadened her womanhood; and I could see that Henry was every day more pleased and satisfied with her. If she was ill for a day, he took her place, and watched for and filled every opportunity to lighten her burdens.

Mr. Bradford was, perhaps, my happiest friend. He had had so much responsibility in directing and changing the currents of my life, that it was with unbounded satisfaction that he witnessed my happiness, my industry and my modest prosperity. Many an hour did he sit upon my platform with me, with his two hands resting upon his cane, his fine, honest face all aglow with gratified interest, listening to the school in its regular exercises; and once he came in with Mr. Bird who had traveled all the way from Hillsborough to see me. And then my school witnessed such a scene as it had never witnessed before. I rushed to my dear old friend, threw my arms around him and kissed him. The silver had begun to show itself in his beard and on his temples, and he looked weary. I gave him a chair, and then with tears in my eyes I stood out upon the platform before my boys and girls, and told them who he was, and what he had been to me. I pictured to them the life of The Bird's Nest, and assured them that if they had found anything to approve in me, as a teacher and a friend, it was planted and shaped in that little garden on the hill. I told them further that if any of them should ever come to regard me with the affection I felt for him, I should feel myself abundantly repaid for all the labor I had bestowed upon them—nay, for the labor of a life. I was roused to an eloquence and touched to a tenderness which were at least new to them, and their eyes were wet. When I concluded, poor Mr. Bird sat with his head in his hands, unable to say a word.

As we went out from the school that night, arm in arm, he said: "It was a good medicine, Arthur—heroic, but good."

"It was," I answered, "and I can never thank you and Mr. Bradford enough for it."

First I took him to my home, and we had a merry tea-drinking, at which my mother yielded up all her prejudices against him. I showed him my little room, so like in its dimensions and appointments to the one I occupied at The Bird's Nest, and then I took him to The Mansion for a call upon Henry. After this we went to Mr. Bradford's, where we passed the evening, and where he spent the night.

CHAPTER XXIV.

IN WHICH I LEARN SOMETHING ABOUT LIVINGSTON, MILLIE BRADFORD AND MYSELF.

SINCE the old days of my boyhood, when Millie Bradford and I had been intimate, confidential friends, she had never received me with the cordiality that she exhibited on that evening. I suppose she had listened to the account which her father gave of my meeting with my old teacher, and of the words which that meeting had inspired me to utter. I have no doubt that my later history had pleased her, and done much to awaken her old regard for me. Whatever the reasons may have been, her grasp was hearty, her greeting cordial, and her face was bright with welcome. I need not say that all this thrilled me with pleasure, for I had inwardly determined to earn her respect, and to take no steps for greater intimacy until I had done so, even if it should lead me to abandon all hope of being more to her than I had been.

It was easy that evening to win her to our old corner in the drawing-room. Mrs. Bradford and Aunt Flick were ready listeners to the conversation in progress between Mr. Bradford and Mr. Bird, and we found ourselves at liberty to pursue our own ways, without interruption or observation.

She questioned me with great interest about my school, and as that was a subject which aroused all my enthusiasm, I talked freely, and amused her with incidents of my daily work. She could not but have seen that I was the victim of no vain regrets concerning my loss of position and prospects, and that all my energies and all my heart were in my new life. I saw that she was gratified; and I was surprised to find that she was profoundly interested in my success.

"By the way," I said, after having dwelt too long upon a topic that concerned myself mainly, "I wonder what has become of Livingston? He was going to Europe, but I have not heard a word from him since I parted with him months ago. Do you know anything of him?"

"Have n't heard from him?" she said, with a kind of incredulous gasp.

"Not a word."

"Have n't you seen him?"

"Why, I have n't been out of the town."

"No, but you have seen him here?"

"Not once."

"You are sure?"

"Perfectly sure," I responded, with a smile at her obstinate unbelief.

"I don't understand it," she said, looking away from me.

"Has he been here?" I inquired.

"Twice."

I saw that she was not only puzzled, but deeply moved; and I was conscious of a flush of mingled anger and indignation sweeping over my own tell-tale face.

"Did he call on Henry when he was here?" I inquired.

"He did, on both occasions. Did not Henry tell you?"

"He did not."

"That is strange, too," she remarked.

"Miss Bradford," I responded, "it is not strange at all. I comprehend the whole matter. Henry knew Livingston better than I did, and, doubting whether he would care to continue his acquaintance with me after the change in my circumstances, had not mentioned his calls to me. He knew that if I had met him, I should speak of it; and as I did not speak of it, he concluded that I had not met him, and so covered from me by his silence the presence of my old friend in the city. Livingston did not call upon me because, having nothing further in common with me, he chose to ignore me altogether, and to count all that had appeared like friendship between us for nothing. I was no longer an heir to wealth. I was a worker for my own bread, with my position to make by efforts whose issue was uncertain. I could be his companion no further; I could be received at his father's home no more. Every attention or courtesy he might render me could be rendered no more except as a matter of patronage. I can at least give him the credit for having honesty and delicacy enough to shun me when he could meet me no more on even terms."

"Even terms!" exclaimed the girl, with a scorn in her manner and voice which verged closely upon rage. "Is that a style of manhood that one may apologize for?"

"Well," I answered, "considering the fact that I was attracted to him at first by the very motives which control him now, I ought to be tolerant and charitable."

"Yes, if that is true," she responded; "but the matter is incredible and incomprehensible."

"It begins to seem so now, to me," I replied, "but it did not then. Our clique in college were all fools together, and fancied that, because we had some worldly advantages not shared by others, we were raised by them above the common level. We took pride in circumstances that were entirely independent of our manhood—circumstances that were gathered around us by other hands. I am heartily ashamed of my old weakness, and despise myself for it; but I can appreciate the strength of the bonds that bind Livingston, and I forgive him with all my heart."

"I do not," she responded. "The slight he has put upon you, and his new friendship for Henry, disgust me more than I can tell you. His conduct is mercenary and unmanly, and offends me from the crown of my head to the sole of my foot."

In the firm, strong passion of this true girl I saw my old self, and realized the wretched slough from which I had been lifted. I could not feel as she did, however, toward Livingston. After the first flush of anger had subsided, I saw that, without some radical change in him, he could not do otherwise than he had done. Though manly in many of his characteristics, his scheme of life was rotten at its foundation, in that it ignored manliness. His standard of respectability was not natural, it was conventional; and so long as he entertained no plan of life that was based in manliness and manly work, his associations would be controlled by the conventional standard to which he and those around him bowed in constant loyalty.

After her frank expression of indignation, she seemed inclined to drop the subject, and only a few more words were uttered upon either side concerning it. I saw that she was troubled, that she was angry, and that, during the moments devoted to the conversation, she had arrived at some determination whose nature and moment I could not guess. Sometimes she looked at me: sometimes she looked away from me; and then her lips were pressed together with a strange spasm of firmness, as if some new resolution of her life were passing step by step to its final issue.

I did guess afterward, and guessed aright. Livingston had fascinated her, while she had so wholly gained his affection and respect, and so won his admiration, that he was laying siege to her heart by all the arts and appliances of which he was so accustomed and accomplished a master. He was the first man who had ever approached her as a lover. She had but just escaped from the seclusion of her school-life, and this world of love, of which she had only dreamed, had been opened to her by the hands of a prince. He was handsome, accomplished in the arts of society, vivacious and brilliant; and while he had made comparatively little progress in winning her heart, he had carried her fancy captive and excited her admiration, and only needed more abundant opportunity to win her wholly to himself.

The revelation of the real character of the man, and of his graceless dealing with me—the hollow-heartedness of his friendship, and the transfer of his regard and courtesy from me to Henry—offended all that was womanly within her. From the moment when she comprehended his position—its meanness, its injustice and unmanliness—she determined that he should be forever shut out of her heart. She knew that her judgment and conscience could never approve either his conduct or him—that this one act could never be justified or apologized for. The determination cost her a struggle which called into action all the forces of her nature. I have been a thousand times thankful that I did not know what was passing in her mind, for I was thus saved from all temptation to attempt to turn her heart against him, and turn it toward myself.

She wrote him a letter, as I subsequently learned, which was intended to save him the mortification of visiting her again; but he came again, armed with his old self-possession, determined to win the prize upon which he had set his heart; and then he went away, visiting neither Henry nor myself. Afterward he went to Europe, and severed forever all his relations to the lives of his Bradford acquaintances.

When Millie and I closed our conversation about Livingston, I found her prepossessed and silent; and, as if by mutual impulse and consent, we rose from our seats, and returned to the other end of the drawing-room, where the remainder of the family were gathered. There we found a conversation in progress which I had no doubt had been suggested by my own personality and position; and as it was very fruitfully suggestive to me, and became a source of great encouragement to me, I am sure my readers will be interested in it. We came within hearing of the conversation, just as Mr. Bird was saying:—

"I never saw a man with anything of the real Shakspeare in him—using him as our typical man—who could not be any sort of a man that he chose to be. A genuinely practical man—a man who can adapt himself to any sort of life—is invariably a man of imagination. These young men who have the name of being eminently practical—especially among women, who usually consider all practical gifts to be those which relate to making money and providing for a family—are the least practical, in a wide sense, of anybody. They usually have a strong bent toward a certain industrial or commercial pursuit, and if they follow that bent, persistently, they succeed; but if by any chance they are diverted from it, they fail irrevocably.

Now the man of imagination is he who apprehends and comprehends the circumstances, proprieties and opportunities of every life in which his lot may be cast, and adapts himself to and employs them all. I have a fine chance to notice this in my boys; and whenever I find one who has an imagination, I see ten chances to make a man of him where one exists in those less generously furnished."

"Yet our geniuses," responded Mr. Bradford, "have not been noted for their skill in practical affairs, or for their power to take care of themselves."

"No," said Mr. Bird, "because our geniuses, or what by courtesy we call such, are one-sided men, who have a single faculty developed in exceptionally large proportion. They are practical men only in a single direction, like the man who has a special gift for money-making, or affairs; and the latter is just as truly a genius as the former, and both are necessarily narrow men, and limited in their range of effort. This is not at all the kind of man I mean; I allude to one who has fairly symmetrical powers, with the faculty of imagination among them. Without this latter, a man can never rise above the capacity of a kind of human machine, working regularly or irregularly. A man who cannot see the poetical side of his work, can never achieve the highest excellence in it. The ideal must always be apprehended before one can rise to that which is in the highest possible sense practical. I have known boys who were the despair of their humdrum fathers and mothers, because, forsooth, they had the faculty of writing verses in their youth. They were regarded by these parents with a kind of blind pride, but with no expectation for them except poverty, unsteady purposes and dependence. I have seen these same parents, many times, depending in their old age upon their verse-writing boys for comfort or luxury, while their practical brothers were tugging for their daily bread, unable to help anybody but themselves and their families."

Mr. Bradford saw that I was intensely interested in this talk of Mr. Bird, and said, with the hope of turning it more thoroughly to my own practical advantage : " Well, what have you to say to our young man here ? He was so full of imagination when a lad that we could hardly trust his eyes or his conscience."

He said this with a laugh, but Mr. Bird turned toward me with his old affectionate look, and replied : " I have never seen the day since I first had him at my side, when I did not believe that he had the making of a hundred different men in him. He was always a good student when he chose to be. He would have made, after a time, an ideal man of leisure. He is a good teacher to-day. He has chosen to be a lawyer, and it rests entirely with him to determine whether he will be an eminent one. If he had chosen to be a preacher, or an author, or a merchant, he would meet no insurmountable difficulty in rising above mediocrity, in either profession. The faculty of imagination, added to symmetrical intellectual powers, makes it possible for him to be anything that he chooses to become. By this faculty he will be able to see all the possibilities of any profession, and all the possibilities of his powers with relation to it."

"As frankness of speech seems to be in order," said Mr. Bradford, "suppose you tell us whether you do not think that he spends money rather too easily, and that he may find future trouble in that direction."

Mr. Bird at once became my partisan. "What opportunity has the boy had for learning the value of money ? When he has learned what a dollar costs, by the actual experiment of labor, he will be corrected. Thus far he has known the value of a dollar only from one side of it. He knows what it will buy, but he does not know what it costs. Some of the best financiers I ever met were once boys who placed little or no value upon money. No man can measure the value of a dollar justly who cannot place by its side the expenditure of time and labor which it costs. Arthur is learning all about it."

"Thank you," I responded, "I feel quite encouraged about myself."

"Now, then, what do you think of Henry, in his new circumstances?" inquired Mr. Bradford.

"Henry," replied Mr. Bird, "never had the faculty to learn the value of a dollar, except through the difficulty of getting it. The real superiority of Arthur over Henry in this matter is in his faculty, not only to measure the value of a dollar by its cost, but to measure it by its power. To know how to win money and at the same time to know how to use it when won, is the prerogative of the highest style of practical financial wisdom. Now that money costs Henry nothing, he will cease to value it; and with his tastes I think the care of his fortune will be very irksome to him. Indeed, it would not be strange if, in five years, that care should be transferred to the very hands that surrendered the fortune to him. So our practical boy is quite likely, in my judgment, to become a mere baby in business, while our boy whose imagination seemed likely to run away with him, will nurse him and his fortune together."

"Why, that will be delightful," I responded. "I shall be certain to send the first business-card I get printed to Henry, and solicit his patronage."

There was much more said at the time about Henry's future as well as my own, but the conversation I have rehearsed was all that was of vital importance to me, and I will not burden the reader with more. I cannot convey to any one an idea of the interest which I took in this talk of my old teacher. It somehow had the power to place me in possession of myself. It recognized, in the presence of those who loved but did not wholly trust me, powers and qualities which, in a half-blind way, I saw within myself. It strengthened my self-respect and my faith in my future.

Ah! if the old and the wise could know how the wisdom won by their experience is taken into the heart of every earnest young man, and how grateful to such a young man recognition is, at the hand of the old and the wise, would they be stingy with their hoard and reluctant with their hand? I do not believe they would. They forget their youth, when they drop peas instead of pearls, and are silly rather than sage.

When I left the house to return to my home, I was charged with thoughts which kept me awake far into the night. The only man from whom I had anything to fear as a rival was in disgrace. My power to win a practical man's place in the world had been recognized in Millie Bradford's presence, by one whose opinion was very highly prized. I had achieved the power of looking at myself and my possibilities through the eyes of a wisdom-winning experience. I was inspired, encouraged and strengthened, and my life had never seemed more full of meaning and interest than it did then.

Early the next morning I went for Mr. Bird, accompanied him to the stage-office, and bade him good-by, grateful for such a friend, and determined to realize all that he had wished and hoped for me.

CHAPTER XXV.

I WIN A WIFE AND HOME OF MY OWN, AND THE MANSION LOSES AND GAINS A MISTRESS.

In those early days, professional study was carried on very generally without the aid of professional schools; and during my three years at the academy, accomplished with sufficient pecuniary success, I read all the elementary books of the profession I had chosen, and, at the close, was admitted to the bar, after an examination which placed me at once at the head of the little clique of young men who had fitted themselves for the same pursuit. Henry, meantime, had realized a wish, long secretly cherished, to study divinity, and, under a license from the ministerial association of the county, had preached many times in the vacant pulpits of the city and the surrounding country. Mrs. Sanderson always went to hear him when the distance did not forbid her; and I suppose that the city did not hold two young men of more unwearied industry than ourselves.

My acquaintance with Millie Bradlord ripened into confidential friendship, and, so far as I was concerned, into something warmer and deeper, yet nothing of love was ever alluded to between us. I saw that she did not encourage the advances of other young men which were made upon every side, and I was quite content to let matters rest as they were, until my prospects for life were more definite and reliable than they were then. We read the same books, and talked about them. We engaged in the same efforts to arouse the spirit of literary culture and improvement in the neighborhood. In the meantime her womanhood ripened day by day, and year by year, until she became the one bright star of my life. I learned to look at my own character and all my actions through her womanly eyes. I added her conscience to my own. I added her sense of that which was proper and becoming and tasteful to my own. Through her sensibilities I learned to see things finely, and by persuasions which never shaped themselves to words, I yielded myself to her, to be led to fine consummations of life and character. She was a being ineffably sacred to me. She was never associated in my mind with a coarse thought. She lifted me into a realm entirely above the atmosphere of sensuality, from which I never descended for a moment; and I thank God that I have never lost that respect for woman which she taught me.

I have seen, since those days, so charged with pure and precious memories, many women of unworthy aims, and low and frivolous tastes, yet I have never seen anything that bore the form of woman that did not appeal to my tender consideration. I have never seen a woman so low that her cry of distress or appeal for protection did not stir me like a trumpet, or so base that I did not wish to cover her shame from ribald eyes, and restore her to that better self which, by the grace of her nature, can never be wholly destroyed.

Soon after the term had closed which severed the connection of Claire and myself with the academy, I was made half wild with delight by an invitation, extended to Henry and Claire, as well as to Millie and myself, to visit Hillsborough, and join the Bird's Nest in their biennial encampment. I knew every rod of ground around the beautiful mountain-lake upon whose shores the white tents of the school were to be planted, for, though six miles away from my early school, I had visited it many times during holidays, and had sailed and angled and swam upon its waters. For many years it had been Mr. Bird's habit, at stated intervals, to take his whole school to this lovely spot during the fervors of the brief New England summer and to yield a fortnight to play. The boys looked forward to this event, through the long months of their study, with the most

16*

charming anticipations, and none of them could have been more delighted with the prospect than Henry and myself. We were now the old boys going back, to be looked at and talked about by the younger boys. We were to renew our boyhood and our old associations before undertaking the professional work of our lives.

As both Mr. Bradford and my father trusted Mr. and Mrs. Bird, it was not difficult to obtain their consent that Millie and Claire should accompany us; and when the morning of our departure arrived, we were delighted to find that we should be the only occupants of the old stage-coach which was to bear us to our destination. The day was as beautiful as that on which my father and I first made the journey over the same route. The objects along the way were all familiar to Henry and myself, but it seemed as if we had lived a whole lifetime since we had seen them. We gave ourselves up to merriment. The spirit of play was upon us all; and the old impassive stage-driver must have thought us half insane. The drive was long, but it might have been twice as long without wearying us.

I was going back to the fountain from which I had drunk so much that had come as a pure force into my life. Even the privilege to play, without a thought of work, or a shadow of care and duty, I had learned from the teachings of Mr. Bird. I had been taught by him to believe—what many others had endeavoured to make me doubt—that God looked with delight upon his weary children at play,—that the careless lambs that gambolled in their pasture, and the careless birds singing and flying in the air, were not more innocent in their sports than men, women and children, when, after work faithfully done, they yielded to the recreative impulse, and with perfect freedom gave themselves to play. I believed this then, and I believe it still; and I account that religion poor and pitiful which ascribes to the Good Father of us all less delight in the free and careless sports of his children than we take in the frolic of our own.

The whole school was out to see the new-comers when we

arrived, and we were received literally with open arms by the master and mistress of the establishment. Already the tents and cooking utensils had gone forward. A few of the older boys were just starting on foot for the scene of the fortnight's play, to sleep in neighboring barns, so as to be on the ground early to assist in raising the tents. They could have slept in beds, but beds were at a discount among lads whose present ambition was to sleep upon the ground. The whole building was noisy with the notes of preparation. Food was preparing in incredible quantities, and special preparations were in progress for making Millie and Claire comfortable; for it was supposed that "roughing it" was something foreign to their taste and experience.

On the following morning, I was roused from my dreams by the same outcry of the boys to which I had responded, or in which I had joined, for a period of five happy years. I was obliged to rub my eyes before I could realize that more than seven years lay between me and that golden period. When at last I remembered how, under that roof, breathed the woman dearer to me than all the rest of the world, and that for two precious weeks she would be my companion, amid the most enchanting scenes of nature, and under circumstances so fresh and strange as to touch all her sensibilities, I felt almost guilty that I could not bring to Mr. and Mrs. Bird an undivided heart, and that The Bird's Nest, and the lake, and the camp-fires, and the free life of the wilderness would be comparatively meaningless to me without her.

Our breakfast was a hurried one. The boys could hardly wait to eat anything, and started off by pairs and squads to make the distance on foot. A huge lumber-wagon, loaded with supplies, was the first carriage dispatched. Then those who would need to ride took their seats in such vehicles as the school and village afforded, and the straggling procession moved on its way. Henry and I spurned the thought of being carried, and took our way on foot. We had not gone half the distance, however, when Millie and Claire insisted on joining us. So our little party bade the rest good-by, and we were left to take our own time for the journey.

We were the last to arrive at the encampment, and the sun was already hot in the sky. Poor Claire was quite exhausted, but Millie grew stronger with every step. The flush of health and happiness upon her face drew forth a compliment from Mr. Bird which deepened her color, and made her more charming than ever. The life was as new to her as if she had exchanged planets; and she gave herself up to it, and all the pleasant labor which the provision for so many rendered necessary, with a ready and hearty helpfulness that delighted every one. She could not move without attracting a crowd of boys. She walked and talked with them; she sang to them and read to them; and during the first two or three days of camp-life, I began to fear that I should have very little of her society.

The days were not long enough for our pleasures. Bathing, boating, ball-playing and eating through the day, and singing and story-telling during the evening, constituted the round of waking delights, and the nights, cool and sweet, were long with refreshing and dreamless slumber.

There is no kinder mother than the earth, when we trustfully lay our heads upon her bosom. She holds balm and blessing for the rich and the poor, for the hardy and the dainty alike, which the bed of luxury never knows. Pure air to breathe, pure water to drink and a pillow of stone—ah! how easy it is for the invisible ministers of health and happiness to build ladders between such conditions and heaven!

Far back over the dim years that have come between, I see those camp-fires glowing still, through evenings full of music and laughter. I see the groups of merry boys dancing around them. I hear their calls for Echo to the woods, and then, in the pauses, the plash of oars, as some group of late sailors comes slowly in, stirring the lake into ripples that seem phosphorescent in the firelight. I watch those fires crumbling away, and dying at last into cloudy darkness, or into the milder moonlight which then asserts its undivided sway, and floods lake and forest and mountain, and all the night-sweet atmosphere with its steady radiance. I see the tent in which my sister and my love are sleeping, and invoke for them the guardian care of God and all good angels. I go at last to my own tent, and lie down to a sleep of blessed, blank unconsciousness, from which I am roused by the cry of healthy lungs that find no weariness in play, and by the tramping of feet around me that spring to the tasks and sports of the day with unflagging appetite and interest.

Did Mr. and Mrs. Bird know how much pleasure they were giving to the young life around them? Did they know that they were enabling us all to lay up memories more precious than gold? Did they know they were developing a love of nature and of healthful and simple pleasures that should be a constant guard around those young feet, when they should find themselves among the slippery places of life and the seductive influences of artificial society. Did they know that making the acquaintance of the birds and flowers and open sky and expanding water and rough life was better than the culture and restraint of drawing-rooms? Did they know that these boys, deprived of this knowledge and these influences, would go through life lacking something inexpressibly valuable? Surely they did, or they would not have sacrificed labour and care and comfort to achieve these objects and results. A thousand blessings on you, my wise, patient, self-sacrificing friends! It is no wonder that all who have lived under your ceaseless and self-devoted ministry love you!

The moon was new when we went into camp, and as it grew larger the weather grew finer, until, as the fortnight waned, it came to its glorious full, on a night whose events made it forever memorable to me.

I do not know why it is that a boy, or a collection of boys, is so keen in the discovery of tender relations between young men and young women, but I think that, from the first, the school understood exactly the relations of Henry to Claire and of Millie to myself. There was a lively family interest in us all, and the young rogues seemed to understand that matters were all settled between the former pair, and that they had not reached a permanent adjustment between the latter. Henry and Claire could always be with each other without interruption. They could go down to the shore at any time of the day or evening, enter a boat, and row out upon the lake, and find nothing to interfere with their privacy; but Millie and I could never approach a boat without finding half a dozen little fellows at our side, begging to be taken out with us upon the water. There was always mischief in their eyes, and an evident wish to make the course of true love rough to us. There was something so amusing in all this, to me, that I never could get angry with them, but Millie was sometimes disturbed by their good-natured persecutions.

On one of the later evenings, however, Millie and I took advantage of their momentary absorption in some favorite game, and quietly walked to the shore, unnoticed by any of them. She took her seat in the boat, and, shoving it from the sand, I sprang in after her, and we were afloat and free upon the moonlit water. For some minutes I did not touch the oars, but let the boat drift out with the impulse I had given it, while we watched the outlines of the white tents against the sky, and the groups which the camp-fires made fantastic.

It was the first time, since our residence at the camp, that I had been alone with her under circumstances which placed us beyond hearing and interruption. I had been longing and laboring for this opportunity, and had determined to bring matters between us to a crisis. I had faithfully tried to do those things and to adopt those plans and purposes of life which would command her respect and confidence. I had been so thoroughly sincere, that I had the consciousness of deserving her esteem, even though her heart might not have been drawn toward me with any tenderer regard. I had been in no haste to declare my passion, but the few days I had spent with her in camp had so ripened and intensified it, that I saw I could not carry it longer, uncertain of its issue, without present torment or prospective danger. It seemed, sometimes to my great horror, as if my life hung entirely upon hers—as if existence would be a curse without her companionship.

After a while spent in silence and a strange embarrassment, I took the oars, and as quietly as possible rowed out into the middle of the lake. The deep blue sky and the bright moon were above us, and the pure water below ; and all the sounds that came to us from the shore were softened into music.

At last I broke the spell that had held my voice with what I intended for a common-place, and said : " It seems a comfort to get away from the boys for a little while, doesn't it ! "

" Does it ? " she responded. " You know you have the advantage of me ; I haven't that pleasure yet."

" Oh ! thank you," I said. " I didn't know that you still regarded me as a boy."

" You were to remain a boy, you know. Didn't you promise ? Have you forgotten ? "

" Have I fulfilled my promise ? "

" Yes, after a weary time."

" And you recognize the boy again, do you ? "

" I think so."

" Are you pleased ? "

" I have no fault to find, at least."

" And you are the same girl I used to know ? " I said.

" Yes."

" Does the fact forbid us to talk as men and women talk ? "

" We are here to play," she replied, " and I suppose we may play that we are man and woman."

" Very well," I said, " suppose we play that we are man and woman, and that I am very fond of you and you are very fond of me."

" It seems very difficult to play this, especially when one of us is so very much in earnest."

" Which one ? "

" The one who wishes to play."

" Ah ! Millie," I said, " you really must not bandy words

with me. Indeed, I am too much in earnest to play. I have a secret to tell you, and this is my first good opportunity to tell it, and you must hear it."

"A secret? do you think so? I doubt it."

"Do you read me so easily?"

She reached out her hand upon the water to grasp a dark little object, past which we were slowly drifting, and broke off from its long, lithe stem a water-lily, and tossed it to my feet. "There's a secret in that little cone," she said, "but I know what it is as well as if the morning sun had unfolded it."

"Do you mean to say that my secret has opened under the spell of your eyes every day like the water-lily to the sun?"

"Yes, if you insist on putting it in that very poetical way."

"Are you fond of water-lilies?"

"Very: fonder of them than of any other flower I know."

"Well," I responded, "I'm a man, or a boy—just which you choose—and don't pretend to be a water-lily, though I wish my roots were as safely anchored and my life as purely surrounded and protected. I believe that maidenhood monopolizes all the lilies for its various impersonations, but for the present purpose, I should really like to ask you if you are willing to take the water-lily for the one flower of your life, with all its secrets which you claim to understand so fully."

"Charmingly done," she said—"for a boy."

"You taunt me."

"No, Arthur," she responded, "but you really are hurrying things so. Just think of trying to settle everything in five minutes, and think, too, of the inconvenience of this little boat. You cannot get upon your knees without upsetting us, and then you know I might be compelled to adopt a water-lily."

"Particularly if the lily should save your life."

"Yes."

"Suppose we go ashore."

"Not for the world."

"Ah! Millie, I think I know your secret," I said.

The Water-Lily's Secret.

"It isn't hard to discover."

"Well, then let's not talk in riddles any more. I love you more than life, Millie! may I continue to love you?"

She paused, and I saw tears upon her face, glittering in the moonlight.

"Yes," she said, "always."

"Thank you! thank God!" I said with a hearty impulse. "Life is all bright to me now, and all full of promise. I wish I could come to you and close this business in the good old orthodox fashion."

She laughed at my vexation, and counseled patience.

There is something very provoking about the coolness of a woman under circumstances like those in which I found myself. For many days I had permitted myself to be wrought into an exalted state of feeling. Indeed, I had been mustering strength for this interview during all the time I had lived in the camp. I was prepared to make a thousand protestations of everlasting devotion. I was ready to cast at her feet my hopes, my life, my all; yet she had anticipated everything, and managed to hold the conversation in her own hands. Then she apparently took delight in keeping me at my end of the boat, and in dissuading me from my ardent wish to reach the shore. I said I thought it was time for us to return. She protested. The people would miss us, I assured her, and would be apprehensive that we had met with an accident. She was equally sure that they would not miss us at all. Besides, if they should, a little scare would give piquancy to the night's pleasure, and she would not like to be responsible for such a deprivation. In truth, I think she would have been delighted to keep me on the lake all night.

I finally told her that I held the oars, that if she wished to remain longer she would accommodate me by jumping overboard, and assured her that I would faithfully deliver her last messages. As she made no movement, I dipped my oars and rowed toward the dying lights of the camp-fires, congratulating myself that I should land first, and help her from the boat.

Under the sheltering willows, I received her into my arms, and gave her my first lover's kiss. We walked to her tent hand in hand, like children, and there, while the boys gathered round us to learn where we had been, and to push their good-natured inquiries, I bent and gave her a good-night kiss, which told the whole story to them all.

It seems strange to me now that I could have done so, and that she would have permitted it, but it really was so like a family matter, in which all were interested in the most friendly or brotherly way, that it was quite the natural thing to do. Millie immediately disappeared behind her muslin walls, while I was overwhelmed with congratulations. Nor was this all. One little fellow called for three cheers for Miss Bradford, which were given with a will; and then three cheers were given to Arthur Bonnicastle; and as their lungs were in practice, they cheered Henry and Claire, and Mr. and Mrs. Bird, and wound up that part of their exercise by three cheers for themselves. Then they improvised a serenade for the invisible lady, selecting "Oft in the stilly night," and "The Pirate's Serenade," as particularly appropriate to the occasion, and went to their beds at last only under the peremptory commands of Mr. Bird.

There were two persons among the fifty that lay down upon the ground that night who did not sleep very soundly, though the large remainder slept, I presume, much as usual. I had lain quietly thinking over the events of the evening, and trying to realize the great blessing I had won, when, at about two o'clock in the morning, I heard the word "Arthur" distinctly pronounced. Not having removed all my clothing, I leaped from my blanket, and ran to the door of the tent. There I heard the call again, and recognized the voice of Millie Bradford.

"Well, what is it?" I said.

"There is some one about the camp."

By this time Henry was on his feet and at my side, and both of us went out together. We stumbled among the tent-stakes in different directions, and at last found a man so muddled with liquor that he hardly knew where he was. We collared him, and led him to our tent, where we inquired of him his business. As he seemed unable to tell us, I searched his pockets for the bottle which I presumed he bore about him somewhere, and in the search found a letter, the address of which I read with the expectation of ascertaining his name. Very much to my surprise, the letter was addressed to Henry. Then the whole matter became plain to me. He had been dispatched with this letter from Hillsborough, and on the way had fallen in with dissolute companions, though he had retained sufficient sense to know that the camp was his destination,

Henry broke the seal. The letter was from his mother, informing him that Mrs. Sanderson was very ill, and that she desired his immediate return to Bradford. I entered Mr. Bird's tent and told him of the letter, and then satisfied the curiosity of Millie and Claire. In such clothing as we could snatch readily from our tents we gathered for a consultation, which resulted in the conclusion that any sickness which was sufficiently serious to call Henry home, was sufficient to induce the entire Bradford party to accompany him. He protested against this, but we overruled him. So we simply lay down until daylight, and then rose for a hurried breakfast. Mr. Bird drove us to Hillsborough, and at seven o'clock we took the stage for home.

The ride homeward was overshadowed by a grave apprehension, and the old driver probably never had a quieter fare over his route, than the party which, only a few days before, had astonished him by their hilarity.

On reaching Bradford we found our worst fears realized. The old lady was rapidly declining, and for three days had been vainly calling for her grandson. When he arrived he brought to her a great flood of comfort, and with her hand in his, she descended into the dark valley. What words she spoke I never knew. I was only sure that she went out of her earthly life in an atmosphere of the most devoted filial affection, that words of Christian counsel and prayer were tenderly spoken to her deafening senses, and that hands bathed in tears closed her eyes.

The funeral was the largest and most remarkable I had ever seen in Bradford, and Henry went back to his home, its owner and master.

On the day following the funeral my father was summoned to listen to the reading of Mrs. Sanderson's will. We were all surprised at this, and still more surprised to learn, when he returned, that the house in which he lived had been bequeathed to him, with an annuity which would forever relieve me from supporting him after he should cease to labor. This I knew to be Henry's work. My father was the father of his future wife, and to save him the mortification of being dependent on his children, he had influenced Mrs. Sanderson to do that which he or I should be obliged to do at some time not far in the future.

My father was very grateful and tearful over this unexpected turn in his fortunes. My mother could not realize it at all, and was sure there must be some mistake about it. One of the most touching things in the prayer offered that night at our family altar was the earnest petition by this simple and humble saint, that his pride might not be nourished by this good fortune.

After this the matter came to a natural shape in the good man's mind. It was not Mrs. Sanderson's gift. She had been only the almoner of Providence. The God whom he had trusted, seeing that the time of helplessness was coming, had provided for his necessities, and relieved him of all apprehension of want, and more than all, had relieved me of a burden. Indeed, it had only fulfilled a life-long expectation. His natural hopefulness would have died amid his hard life and circumstances if it had not fed itself upon dreams.

I am sure, however, that he never felt quite easy with his gift, so long as he lived, but carried about with him a sense of guilt. Others—his old companions in labor—were not blessed with him, and he could not resist the feeling that he had wronged them. They congratulated him on his "luck," as they called it, for they were all his friends; but their allusions to the matter always pained him, and he had many an hour of torment over the thought that some of them might think him capable of forgetting them, and of pluming his pride upon his altered circumstances.

It was, perhaps, a fortnight after the death of Mrs. Sanderson, that Henry came to my father's house one morning, and asked me when I intended to begin business. I informed him that I had already been looking for an eligible office, and that I should begin the practice of the law as soon as the opportunity should come. Then he frankly told me that looking after his multiplied affairs was very distasteful to him, and that he wished, as soon as possible, to place everything in my hands. He advised me to take the best and most central chambers I could find, and offered me, at little more than a nominal rent, a suite of rooms in one of his own buildings. I took the rooms at once, and furnished them with such appointments and books as the savings of three industrious years could command, and Henry was my first, as he has remained my constant, client. The affairs of the Sanderson estate, of which I knew more than any man except Mrs. Sanderson's lawyer, were placed in my hands, where they remain at this present writing. The business connected with them was quite enough for my support in those days of moderate expenses and incomes, but it brought me so constantly into contact with the business men of the city that, gradually, the tide of legal practice set towards me, until, in my maturer years, I was almost overwhelmed by it. I was energetic, enthusiastic, persevering, indomitable, and successful; but amid all my triumphs there was nothing that gave me such pure happiness as my father's satisfaction with my efforts.

I never engaged in an important public trial for many years, in which he was not a constant attendant at the court-house. All the lawyers knew him, and my position commanded a seat for him inside the bar. Every morning he came in, leaning on his cane, and took the seat that was left or vacated for him, and there, all day long, he sat and watched me. If for a day he happened to be absent, I missed the inspiration of his interested face and approving eyes, as if he were a lover. My office was his lounging-place, and my public efforts were his meat and drink. A serener, sweeter old age than his I never saw, and when, at last, I missed him—for death came to him as it comes to all—I felt that one of the loveliest lights of my life had gone out. I have never ceased to mourn for him, and I would not cease to mourn for him if I could.

A year after I commenced the practice of my profession, Mr. Grimshaw exhausted his narrow lode and went to mine in other fields. Naturally, Henry was called upon to fill temporarily the vacant pulpit, and quite as naturally, the people learned in a few weeks that they could serve themselves no better than by calling him to a permanent pastorate. This they did, and as he was at home with them, and every circumstance favored his settlement over them, he accepted their invitation. On the day of his ordination—a ceremony which was very largely attended—he treated his new people to a great surprise. Before the benediction was pronounced, he descended from the pulpit, took his way amid the silence of the congregation to my father's pew, and then led my sister Claire up the broad aisle to where an aged minister stood waiting to receive them, and join them in holy wedlock. The words were few which united these two lives that had flowed in closely parallel currents through so long a period, but they were spoken with great feeling, and amid the tears of a crowd of sympathetic friends. So the church had once more a pastor, and The Mansion once more a mistress; and two widely divided currents of the Bonnicastle blood united in the possession and occupation of the family estate.

I do not need to give the details of my own marriage, which occurred a few months later, or of our first experiments at house-keeping in the snug home which my quick prosperity enabled me to procure, or of the children that came to bless us in the after-years. The memory of these events is too sweet and sacred to be unveiled, and I cannot record them, though my tears wet the paper as I write. The freshness of youth has long passed away, the silver is stronger than the jet among the curls of the dear woman who gave herself to me, and bore in loving pain, and reared with loving patience, my priceless flock of children; my own face is deeply furrowed by care and labor and time; but those days of young love and life never come back to me in memory save as a breeze across a weary sea from some far island loaded with odors of balm and whispers of blessing.

Thank God for home and woman! Thank God a thousand times for that woman who makes home her throne! When I remember how bright and strong a nature my young wife possessed—how her gifts and acquirements and her whole personality fitted her to shine in society as a center and a sun—and then recall her efforts to serve and solace me, and train my children into a Christian manhood and womanhood, until my house was a heaven, and its presiding genius was regarded with a love that rose to tender adoration—I turn with pity, not unmingled with disgust, from those I see around me now, who cheapen marriage, the motherly office and home, and choose and advocate courses and careers of life independent of them all.

Neither Henry's marriage nor my own was in the slightest degree romantic—hardly romantic enough to be of interest to the average reader.

It was better so. Our courtships were long and our lives were so shaped to each other that when marriage came it was merely the warrant and seal of a union that had already been established. Each lover knew his love, and no misunderstandings supervened. The hand of love, by an unconscious process, had shaped each man to his mate, each woman to her mate, before they were joined, and thus saved all after-discords and collisions. All this may be very uninteresting to outsiders, but to those concerned it was harmony, satisfaction and peace.

CHAPTER XXVI.

WHICH BRIEFLY RECORDS THE PROFESSIONAL LIFE OF REV. PETER MULLENS.

It must have been three or four years after Henry took charge of his parish, and I had entered upon the duties of my profession, that I met him one morning upon the street, wearing that peculiar smile on his face which said, as plainly as words could have told me, that he was the bearer of news.

"Who do you think spent the night at The Mansion, and is even now reveling in the luxuries of your old apartment?" said he.

"I was never good at conundrums," I replied. "Suppose you tell me."

"The Rev. Peter Mullens."

"Clothed, and in his right mind?"

"Yes, clothed, for he has one of my coats on, which I have told him he may carry away with him; and in his right mind, because he has the coat, and expects to live upon the donor for a few days."

We both laughed over the situation, and then Henry told me that Mullens was in a good deal of perplexity on account of the fact that he had two "calls" on hand, to which answers must be made immediately.

"I have agreed with Mullens," said Henry, "to invite you to dinner, in order that he may have the benefit of your advice."

"Thank you. Is there a fee?"

"Nothing stipulated, but I think you had better bring a pair of trowsers," he replied. "Mullens, you know, wants to see

The Rev. Peter Mullens.

(p. 385.)

the advantages that are likely to come from following your advice, and if he has them in hand he can decide at once."

The prospect of dining with Mullens was not an unpleasant one. I was curious to see what he had made of himself, and to learn what he was going to do. So I congratulated Henry on the new light that had risen upon his domestic life, and promised him that I would meet his guest at his table.

On entering The Mansion that day in my usual informal way, I found the Rev. Peter Mullens lying nearly upon his back, in the most luxurious chair of the large drawing-room, apparently in a state of serene and supreme happiness. He was enjoying the privileges of the cloth, in the house of a professional brother who had been exceptionally "favored." For the time, the house was his own. All petty cares were dismissed. All clouds were lifted from his life, in the consciousness that he had a good coat on which had cost him nothing, and that, for a few days at least, board and lodging were secure at the same price. His hair was brushed back straight over his head in the usual fashion, and evidently fastened there by the contents of a box of pomatum which he had found in my old chamber. He had managed to get some gold-bowed spectacles, and when I met him he presented quite an imposing front. Rising and greeting me with a cordial and somewhat patronizing air, he quickly resumed his seat and his attitude, and subsided into a vein of moralizing. He thought it must be a source of great satisfaction to me that the property which had once been my own, apparently, had been devoted to the ministry, and that henceforth The Mansion would be the home of those who had given themselves to the church.

Mullens evidently regarded himself as one who had a certain pecuniary interest in the estate. The house was to be his tavern—his free, temporary home—whenever it might be convenient for him to pass a portion of his time in the city. Indeed, he conducted himself as if he were my host, and expressed the hope that he should see me always when visiting the town. His assumptions amused me exceedingly, though I was sorry to think that Henry and Claire would feel themselves obliged to tolerate him.

At the dinner-table, Mr. Mullens disclosed the questions in regard to his settlement. "The truth is," said he, "that I am divided on a question of duty. Given equal opportunities of doing good, and unequal compensation, on which side does duty lie? That is the question. I don't wish to be mercenary; but when one Church offers me five hundred dollars a year, payable quarterly in advance, and the other offers me five hundred dollars a year, payable quarterly at the end of the quarter, with an annual donation-party, I feel myself divided. There is an advantage in being paid quarterly in advance, and there is an advantage in a donation-party, provided the people do not eat up what they bring. How great this advantage is I do not know; but there is something very attractive to me in a donation-party. It throws the people together, it nourishes the social element, it develops systematic benevolence, it cements the friendship of pastor and people, it brings a great many things into the house that a man can never afford to buy, and it must be exceedingly interesting to reckon up the results. I've thought about it a great deal, and it does seem to me that a donation-party must be a very valuable test of usefulness. How am I to know whether my services are acceptable, unless every year there is some voluntary testimonial concerning them? It seems to me that I must have such a testimonial. I find myself looking forward to it. Here's an old farmer, we'll say, without any public gifts. Hosannas languish on his tongue, and, so far as I can tell, all devotion dies. He brings me, perhaps, two cords or two cords and a half of good hard wood, and by that act he says, 'The Rev. Mr. Mullens has benefited me, and I wish to tell him so. He has warmed my heart, and I will warm his body. He has ministered to me in his way, and I will minister to him in my way.' Here's a woman with a gift of flannel—a thing that's always useful in a minister's family—and there's another with a gift of socks, and here's another with a gift of crullers, and here's a man with a gift of a spare-rib or a ham, and another with a gift of potatoes, and"—

Mr. Mullens gave an extra smack to his lips, as, in the midst of his dinner, this vision of a possible donation-party passed before the eyes of his imagination.

"It is plain to see which way your inclination points," I said to him.

"Yes, that is what troubles me," he responded. "I wish to do right. There may be no difference between having your pay quarterly in advance and the donation-party; but the donation-party, all things considered, is the most attractive."

"I really think it would suit you best," I said, "and if the opportunity for doing good is the same in each place, I'm sure you ought not to hesitate."

"Well, if I accept your advice," said Mr. Mullens, "you must stand by me. This place is only six miles from Bradford, and if I ever get hard up it will be pleasant to think that I have such friends at hand as you and Brother Sanderson."

This was a new aspect of the affair, and not at all a pleasant one; but I had given my advice and could not retract it.

Mullens remained at The Mansion several days, and showed his white cravat and gold-bowed spectacles all over the city. He was often in my office, and on one occasion accompanied me to the court-room, where I gave him a seat of honor and introduced him to my legal friends. He was so very comfortable in his splendid quarters, so shielded from the homely affairs of the world by his associations, and so inexpensive to himself, that it was a hardship to tear himself away at last, even with the prospect of a donation-party rising before him in the attractive perspective of his future.

He had been several days in the house, and had secured such plunder as would be of use to him, personally, when he surprised us all by the announcement that he was a married man, and was already the father of a helpless infant. He gave us also to understand that Mrs. Mullens was, like himself, poor, that her wardrobe was none of the most comfortable, and that her "helpless infant" would rejoice in garments cast off by children more "favored" than his own. His statement was intended to appeal to Claire and Millie, and was responded to accordingly. When he went away, he bore a trunk full of materials, that, as he said, "would be useful in a minister's family."

Henry and I attended his installation shortly afterwards, and assisted him in beginning his housekeeping. We found Mrs. Mullens to be a woman every way adapted to the companion she had chosen. She was willing to live upon her friends. She delighted in gifts, and took them as if they were hers by right. Everything was grain that came to her mill in this way. Her wants and her inability to supply them were the constant theme of her communications with her friends and neighbors, and for ten long years she was never without a "helpless infant" with which to excite their laggard and weary charities. Whenever she needed to purchase anything, she sent to me or to Millie, or to her friends at The Mansion, her commission,— always without the money. She either did not know how much the desired articles would cost, or there was such danger of losing money when sent by post, or she had not the exact change on hand; but she assured us that Mr. Mullens would call and pay us when visiting Bradford. The burden thus rolled upon Mr. Mullens was never taken up by him; and so, year after year, we consented to be bled by this amiable woman, while the Mullens family went on increasing in numbers and multiplying in wants. It became a matter of wonder that any religious society should be content with the spiritual ministrations of such a man as Mullens; but this society was simple and poor, and their pastor had an ingenious way of warming over his old broth and the old broth of others which secured for him a certain measure of respect. His tongue was glib, his presence imposing, and his self-assurance quite overwhelming.

But at last there came a change. New residents in the parish saw through his shallow disguises, and raised such a storm of discontent about his ears that he was compelled to resign his pulpit and to cast about for other means of living. No other pulpit opened its doors to him. The man's reputation outside of his parish was not a desirable one. Everybody had ceased to regard him as a man capable of teaching; and he had so begged his way and lived upon his acquaintances, and had so meanly incurred and meanly refused to recognize a thousand little debts among his early friends, that it was impossible for him to obtain even a temporary engagement as a preacher.

There was nothing left for him to do, but to become a peddler of some sort, for which office he had rare natural gifts. Leaving his family where they were, he took an agency for the sale of the Cottage Bible. He drove a thrifty business with this publication, going from house to house, wearing always his white cravat, living upon the ministers and deacons, and advertising himself by speeches at evening meetings and Sunday-schools. Sometimes he got an opportunity to preach on Sunday, and having thus made his face familiar to the people, drove a brisk business among them on Monday. His white cravat he used as a sort of pass on railroads and steamboats, or as an instrument by which it was to be secured. Every pecuniary consideration which could be won from a contemptuous business world, by the advertisement of the sacred office which he once held, he took the boldest or the most abject way to win.

It must not be supposed that "old Mullens," as people learned to call him, was really distressed by poverty. Never paying out a cent of money that came into his hands if he could avoid it, he accumulated a handsome property, which he skillfully hid away in investments, maintaining his show of poverty, through all his active life. Henry shook him off at last and helped me to do the same. We heard of him not long ago lecturing to Sunday-schools and buying wool, and it is not ten years since he appeared in Bradford as an agent of a life-insurance company, with specially favorable terms to clergymen who were kind enough to board him during his visit. I shrink from writing here the stories I heard about him, concerning the way in which he advertised his business by mixing it with his public religious teachings, because it associates such base ideas with an office which I revere as the highest and holiest a man can hold; but when I say that in his public addresses he represented the Christian religion as a system of life-insurance of the spiritual kind, I sufficiently illustrate his methods and his motives.

He passed a useless life. He became a nuisance to his professional brethren, a burden to all who were good-natured enough to open their houses to him, and a disgrace to the Christian ministry. Wearing the badge of a clergyman, exacting as a right that which was rendered to others as a courtesy or a testimonial of love and friendship, surrendering his manhood for the privileges of ministerial mendicancy, and indulging his greed for money at the expense of a church to which he fancied he had given his life, he did, unwittingly perhaps, what he could to bring popular contempt upon his profession, and to associate with the Christian religion the meanest type of personal character it is possible to conceive.

Amid the temptations of this poor, earthly life, and the weaknesses of human nature, even the most sacred profession will be disgraced, now and then, by men who repent in dust and ashes over their fall from rectitude, and the dishonor they bring upon a cause which in their hearts they love; but Mullens carried his self-complacency to the end, and demonstrated by his character and influence how important it is that dunces shall not be encouraged to enter upon a high walk of life by benefactions which rarely fail to induce and develop in them the spirit of beggars. I am sure there is no field of Christian benevolence more crowded with untoward results than that in which weak men have found the means for reaching the Christian ministry. The beggarly helplessness of some of these men is pitiful; and a spirit of dependence is fostered in them which emasculates them, and makes them contemptible among those whom they seek to influence.

Though the Rev. Peter Mullens is still living, I have no fear that I shall be called to an account for my plain treatment of him, as he will never buy this book, or find a friend who will be willing to give or lend it to him. Even if he had such a friend, and he should recognize his portrait, his *amour propre* would not be wounded, and he would complacently regard himself as persecuted for righteousness' sake.

CHAPTER XXVII.

IN WHICH I SAY GOOD-NIGHT TO MY FRIENDS AND THE PAST AND GOOD-MORROW TO MY WORK AND THE FUTURE.

THUS I have lived over the old life, or, rather, the young life which lies with all its vicissitudes of pain and pleasure, and all its lessons and inspirations, embalmed in my memory; and here, alas! I must re-write the words with which I began. "They were all here then—father, mother, brothers and sisters; and the family life was at its fullest. Now they are all gone, and I am alone. I have wife and children and troops of friends, yet still I am alone." No later relation can remove the sense of loneliness that comes to him whose first home has forever vanished from the earth.

As I sit in my library, recording this last chapter of my little history, I look back through the ceaseless round of business and care, and, as upon a panorama unrolling before me, I see through tears the events which have blotted out, one after another, the old relations, and transferred the lives I loved to another sphere.

I see a sun-lit room, where my aged father lies propped among his pillows, and tells me feebly, but with a strange light in his eyes, that it is so much better for him to go before my mother! She can do better without him than he can without her! It is sweet to learn that she who had always been regarded by her family and friends as a care and a burden to him, had been his rest and reward; that there had always been something in his love for her which had atoned for his hard lot, and that, without her, his life would be undesirable.

I read to him the psalms of assurance and consolation: "Yea, though I walk through the valley of the shadow of death,

I will fear no evil." I repeat the words of the tried and patient patriarch: "I know that my Redeemer liveth." I join with the family in singing the inspiring lines which he had never undertaken to read aloud without being crushed into sobbing silence:

> "There is a calm for those who weep,
>   A rest for weary pilgrims found;
> They softly lie and sweetly sleep
>   Low in the ground.
>
> "The storm that wrecks the winter sky
>   No more disturbs their deep repose
> Than summer evening's latest sigh
>   That shuts the rose.
>
> "I long to lay this painful head
>   And aching heart beneath the soil,
> To slumber in that dreamless bed
>   From all my toil.
>
> "The sun is but a spark of fire,
>   A transient meteor in the sky;
> The soul, immortal as its sire,
>   Shall never die."

I press his hand, and hear him say: "It is all well. Take care of your mother."

We all bend and kiss him; a few quick breaths, and the dear old heart is still—a heart so true, so tender, so pure, so faithful, so trusting, that no man could know it without recognizing the Christian grace that made it what it was, or finding in it infallible evidence of the divinity of the religion by whose moulding hand it was shaped, and from whose inspirations it had drawn its life. Then we lay him to rest among the June roses, with birds singing around us, and all nature robed in the glowing garb of summer, feeling that there are wings near us which we do not see, that songs are breathed which we do not hear, and that somewhere, beyond the confines of mortal pain and decay, he has found a summer that will be perennial.

The picture moves along, and I am in the same room again; and she who all her life, through fear of death, had been subject to bondage, has come to her final hour. She has reached the door of the sepulchre from a long distance, questioning painfully at every step: "Who shall roll away the stone?" and now that she is arrived, she finds, to her unspeakable joy and peace, that the stone is rolled away. Benignant nature, which has given her so strong a love of life, overcomes in its own tender way the fear of death that had been generated in her melancholic temperament, and by stealing her senses one by one, makes his coming not only dreadless, but desirable. She finds the angels too, one at the head, the other at the foot where death has lain, with white hands pointing upward. I weep, but I am grateful that the life of fear is past, and that she can never live it again,—grateful, too, that she is reunited to him who has been waiting to introduce her to her new being and relations. We lay her by the side of the true husband whose life she has shared, and whose children she has borne and reared, and then go back to a home which death has left without a head—to a home that is a home no longer.

The picture moves on, and this time I witness a scene full of tender interest to me in my own house. A holy spell of waiting is upon us all. Aunt Flick comes in, day after day, with little services which only she can render to her tenderly beloved niece, and with little garments in her hands that wait the coming of a stranger. It is night, and there is hurrying to and fro in the house. I sit in my room, wrapped in pity and feverish with anxiety, with no utterance save that of whispered prayers for the safety of one dearer to me than life. I hear at last the feeble wail of a new being which God has intrusted to her hands and mine. Some one comes and tells me that all is well, and then, after a weary hour, I am summoned to the chamber where the great mystery of birth has been enacted. I kneel at the bedside of my precious wife. I cover her hands and her face with kisses. I call her my darling, my angel, while my first-born nestles upon her arm, wrapped in the atmosphere of mother-love which her overflowing heart breathes out upon it. I watch her day by day, and night by night, through all her weakness and danger, and now she sits in her room with her baby on her breast, looking out upon the sky and the flowers and the busy world.

Still, as the canvas moves, come other memorable nights, with varying fortunes of pain and pleasure, till my home is resonant with little feet, and musical with the voices of children. They climb my knees when I return from the fatigues of the day; I walk in my garden with their little hands clinging to mine; I listen to their prayers at their mother's knee; I watch over them in sickness; I settle their petty disputes; I find in them and in their mother all the solace and satisfaction that I desire and need. Clubs cannot win me from their society; fame, honor, place, have no charms that crowd them from my heart. My home is my rest, my amusement, my consolation, my treasure-house, my earthly heaven.

And here stoops down a shadow. I stand in a darkened room before a little casket that holds the silent form of my first-born. My arm is around the wife and mother who weeps over the lost treasure, and cannot, till tears have had their way, be comforted. I had not thought that my child could die—that *my* child could die. I knew that other children had died, but I felt safe. We lay the little fellow close by his grandfather at last; we strew his grave with flowers, and then return to our saddened home with hearts united in sorrow as they had never been united in joy, and with sympathies forever opened toward all who are called to a kindred grief. I wonder where he is to-day, in what mature angelhood he stands, how he will look when I meet him, how he will make himself known to me, who has been his teacher! He was like me: will his grandfather know him? I never can cease thinking of him as cared for and led by the same hand to which my own youthful fingers clung, and as hearing from the fond lips of my own father, the story of his father's eventful life. I feel how wonderful to me has been the ministry of my children—how much more I have learned from them than they have ever learned from me—how by holding my own strong life in sweet subordination to their helplessness, they have taught me patience, self-sacrifice, self-control, truthfulness, faith, simplicity and purity.

Ah! this taking to one's arms a little group of souls, fresh from the hand of God, and living with them in loving companionship through all their stainless years, is, or ought to be, like living in heaven, for of such is the heavenly Kingdom. To no one of these am I more indebted than to the boy who went away from me before the world had touched him with a stain. The key that shut him in the tomb was the only key that could unlock my heart, and let in among its sympathies the world of sorrowing men and women, who mourn because their little ones are not.

The little graves, alas! how many they are! The mourners above them, how vast the multitude! Brothers, sisters, I am one with you. I press your hands, I weep with you, I trust with you, I belong to you. Those waxen, folded hands, that still breast so often pressed warm to our own, those sleep-bound eyes which have been so full of love and life, that sweet, unmoving, alabaster face—ah! we have all looked upon them, and they have made us one and made us better. There is no fountain which the angel of healing troubles with his restless and life-giving wings so constantly as the fountain of tears, and only those too lame and bruised to bathe miss the blessed influence.

The picture moves along, and now sweeps into view The Mansion on the hill—my old home—the home of my friend and sister. I go in and out as the years hurry by, and little feet have learned to run and greet me at the door, and young lips have been taught to call me "uncle." It is a door from which no beggar is ever turned away unfed, a door to which the feeble, the despairing, the sorrowing, the perplexed have come for years, and been admitted to the counsels, encouragements, and self-denying helpfulness of the strongest and noblest man I know. The ancient mistress of the establishment is quite forgotten by the new generation, and the house which, for so many years, was shut to the great world by the selfish recluse who owned it, is now the warmest social center of the town. Its windows blaze with light through many a long evening, while old age and youth mingle in pleasant converse; and forth from its ample resources go food and clothing for the poor, and help for the needy, and money for those who bear the Good Tidings to the border. Familiar names are multiplied in the house. First there comes a little Claire, then an Arthur Bonnicastle, then a Ruth, and last a Minnie; and Claire, so like her mother in person and temper, grows up to be a helpful woman. I visit my old room, now the chamber of little Arthur Bonnicastle, but no regrets oppress me. I am glad of the change, and glad that the older Arthur has no selfish part or lot in the house.

And now another shadow droops. Ah! why should it come? The good Lord knows, and He loves us all.

In her room, wasting day by day with consumption, my sister sits and sees the world glide away from her, with all its industries and loves, and social and home delights. The strong man at her side, loaded with cares which she so long has lightened, comes to her from his wearying labor, and spends with her every precious flying hour that he can call his own. He almost tires her with tender ministry. He lifts her to her bed; he lifts her to her chair; he reads to her; he talks calmly with her of the great change that approaches; he sustains her sinking courage; he calls around her every help; he tries in every way to stay the hand of the fell destroyer, but it is all in vain. The long-dreaded day comes at last, and The Mansion—nay, all Bradford —is in mourning. A pure woman, a devoted wife, a tender mother, a Christian friend, sleeps; and a pastor, whose life is deepened and broadened and enriched by a grief so great and lasting that no future companionship of woman can even be thought of, goes to his work with a new devotion and the unction of a new power. There is still a Claire to guide the house, and the memory and influence of a saint to hallow all its walls, and chasten all its associations.

The picture sweeps along, and presents to my imagination a resistless river, calm in its beginnings, but torn and turbulent as it proceeds, till it plunges in a cataract and passes from my sight. Along its passage are little barks, each bearing a member of my family—my brothers and sisters—separated from me and from each other by miles of distance, but every one moving toward the abyss that swallows them one by one. The disease that takes my sister Claire takes them all. Each arriving at her age passes away. Each reaching the lip of the cataract, lets go the oars, tosses up helpless hands, makes the fatal plunge, and the sob surge and of the waters, wind-borne to my shrinking ears, is all that is left to me. Not all, for even now a rainbow spans the chasm, to promise me that floods shall never overwhelm them again, and to prove to me that tears may be informed with the same heavenly light that shines in living flowers, and paints the clouds of sunrise.

The noise of the cataract dies away in the distance, the river dissolves, and I sit inside a new and beautiful church. The old one has been torn down to make way for a larger and better one. It is communion-day, and behind the table on which is spread the Christian feast of commemoration sits my boyhood's companion, my college friend, my brother and pastor, Henry Sanderson. The years have strewn silver over his temples and graven furrows upon his face, but earnestness, strength, and benignity are the breath and burden of his presence. An event is about to take place of great interest to him, to the church, and to a large circle of business men. Mr. Bradford, for the first time, publicly takes his stand among the Christian family. He is old now, and the cane which he used to carry for company, and as a habit, has become a necessity. He takes his place in the aisle, and by his side my own dear wife, who from her childhood has stood loyally by him and refused to unite with a church until he could do so. The creed has been revised. The refinements and elaborate definitions and non-essential dogmas have been swept away, and the simple old Apostle's Creed, in which millions of disciples and saints have lived and died in the retiring centuries, is all that is read to him, and all to which he is called upon to respond.

Home at last! Received into the fold where he has always belonged! A patriarch, seated at the table of the Lord from which he has been shut away by children in experience, wisdom, and piety! He is my father now, the grandfather of my children, and the little wife who has trusted him and believed in him all her life has at last the supreme happiness of communing with him and her daughter in the holy festival.

Why do I still watch the unrolling canvas? The scenes that come and pass are not painful to me, because they are all associated with precious memories and precious hopes, but to those who read they must be somber and saddening. Why tell of the news that reached me one day from Hillsborough? Why tell of that which reached me six months afterward from the same place? They sleep well and their graves are shrines. Why tell how Aunt Flick, from nursing one with malignant disease, came home to die, and left undone a world of projected work? Why tell how Mr. Bradford was at last left alone, and came to pass the remnant of his life with me? Why tell of another shadow that descended upon The Mansion, and how, in its dark folds, the lovely mother of my friend disappeared?

It is the story of the world. We are born, we grow to manhood and womanhood, we marry, we work, we die. The generations come and go, and they come without call and go without significance if there be not a confident hope and expectation of something to follow, so grand and sweet and beautiful that we can look upon it all without misgiving or pain. Faith draws the poison from every grief, takes the sting from every loss, and quenches the fire of every pain; and only faith can do it. Wisdom, science, power, learning—all these are as blind and impotent before the great problem of life as ignorance and weakness. The feeblest girl, believing in God and a hereafter, is an archangel by the side of the strongest man who questions her simple faith, and mounts on wings where he stumbles in doubt and distress, or sinks in darkness.

To those of two homes who are living, through six long and ever-memorable evenings, I have read my book, and now they are all with me to-night as I draw the chair to my library-table, to write these closing paragraphs. The center of the group is Mr. Bradford, an old, old man, though he is still strong enough to hold my youngest upon his knee. Henry sits near him, talking with Millie, while the young people are gathered in a distant corner, conversing quietly among themselves about the events I have for the first time fully unveiled to them. Their talk does not disturb me, for my thoughts linger over what I have written, and I feel that the task which has been such a delight to me is soon to pass from my hands. No work can come to me so sweet as this has been. I have lived my life again—a life so full of interest that it seems as if I could never tire of it, even though death should come nearer and nearer to me, waiting for my consent to be pushed from the verge of earthly existence.

I hear the quiet voices around me. I know where and what I am, but I cannot resist the feeling that there are more forms in the room than are visible to my eyes. I do not look up, but to me my library is full. Those who are gone cannot have lost their interest in those who remain, and those who are gone outnumber us two to one. My own, I am sure, are close about me, looking over my shoulder, and tracing with me these closing words. Their arms are intertwined, they exchange their thoughts about me all unheard by my coarse senses, and I am thrilled by an influence which I do not understand. My sister sits by the side of her husband unseen, and listens to the words which he is speaking to my wife, and hears her own name pronounced with grateful tenderness. Mr. Bradford has a companion older than the little one who sits upon his knee and plays with his great gold chain, but sees her not. There are wistful, sympathetic faces among the children, and they cannot know why they are so quiet, or what spell it is that holds them. A severe, restless little woman watches her grandson with greedy eyes, or looks around upon those she once had within her power, but regards us all in impotent silence. Of them, but apart, companions in the new life as they were in the old, are two who come to visit their boys again—boys growing old in labor and preparing to join them in another school, among higher hills and purer atmospheres, or to be led by them to the tented shores of the River of the Water of Life. The two worlds have come so near together that they mingle, and there are shadows around me, and whispers above me, and the rustle of robes that tell me that life is one, and the love of kindred and friends eternal.

To morrow, ah! golden to morrow! Thank God for the hope of its coming, with all its duty and care, and work and ministry, and all its appeals to manliness and manly endeavor! Thank God, too, for the long dissipation of the dreams of selfish ease and luxury! Life has no significance to me, save as the theater in which my powers are developed and disciplined by use, and made fruitful in securing my own independence and the good of those around me, or as the scene in which I am fitted for the work and worship of the world beyond. The little ones and the large ones of my own flock are crowding me along. Soon they will have my place. I do not pity, I almost envy them. Life is so grand, so beautiful, so full of meaning, so splendid in its opportunities for action, so hopeful in its high results, that, despite all its sorrows, I would willingly live it over again.

Good-night!

Holland's Works

TITCOMB'S LETTERS TO YOUNG PEOPLE,
Single and Married. One vol. 12mo, Turkey morocco, $4.00; cloth full gilt, $2.50; cloth, ... $1.50

BITTER-SWEET. A Poem. One vol. 12mo, full gilt, $2.50; cloth, ... $1.50

KATHRINA: Her Life and Mine. In a Poem. One vol. 12mo, about 300 pages. Full gilt, $2.50; cloth, . $1.50

GOLD-FOIL HAMMERED FROM POPULAR Proverbs. By TIMOTHY TITCOMB. One vol. 12mo, cloth, . $1.75

LESSONS IN LIFE: A Series of Familiar Essays. By TIMOTHY TITCOMB. One vol. 12mo, cloth, . $1.75

LETTERS TO THE JONESES. By TIMOTHY TITCOMB. One vol. 12mo, ... $1.75

PLAIN TALKS ON FAMILIAR SUBJECTS. A Series of Popular Lectures. One vol. 12mo, cloth, . . $1.75

THE BAY PATH: A Tale of New England Colonial Life. One vol. 12mo, cloth, ... $2.00

MISS GILBERT'S CAREER: An American Story. One vol. 12mo, cloth, ... $2.00

BRIGHTWOOD EDITION OF DR. J. G. HOLLAND'S (Timothy Titcomb's) SELECT WORKS. In six vols. 16mo, cabinet size, printed from new stereotype plates, upon tinted wove paper, including—

Bitter-Sweet, ... $1.50
Kathrina, ... 1.50
Lessons in Life, ... 1.75
Gold Foil, ... 1.75
Timothy Titcomb's Letters to Young People, . . 1.50
Plain Talks (Dr. Holland's Popular Lectures), . . 1.75

The volumes of this edition may be purchased separately, or they will be furnished in a handsome box for $9.00.

GARNERED SHEAVES.

The Complete Poetical Works of

J. G. HOLLAND (*Timothy Titcomb*).

RED LINE EDITION,

Printed on tinted paper, with sixteen full-page illustrations, and a new portrait of the author on steel. 1 vol., small 4to, 602 pages. Cloth. Price $4.00; morocco, $7.50.

This volume comprises "Bitter Sweet," "Kathrina," and the "Marble Prophecy," with the miscellaneous poems lately issued. The thousands to whom these poems are already as household words, will give them a cordial welcome in this very attractive form.

A New Poem by DR. HOLLAND.

THE MARBLE PROPHECY,

And Other Poems.

By J. G. Holland, Author of "Bitter Sweet," "Kathrina," &c., &c.

One vol. 12mo, with a full-page illustration, cloth, $1.50.

The Marble Prophecy is, next to "Bitter Sweet" and "Kathrina," Dr. Holland's longest and most important poem. But it is very different in subject from its famous predecessors. Taking for his theme the noble group Laocöon, the poet presents, in vigorous and picturesque verse, some of the most vital religious and political questions of the day. The minor pieces of the present collection are many of them already well known to the public. Here may be found such strong and beautiful verse as "Daniel Gray," "The Heart of the War," &c., &c. The Marble Prophecy appears now for the first time, and the other poems have never before been collected. Altogether it is a pure, worthy and notable volume of poetry, and one that cannot fail to win a still wider reputation for this very popular author.

The above works sent, post-paid, on receipt of price.

SCRIBNER, ARMSTRONG & CO.,
654 Broadway, New York.

"The very best, the most sensible, the most practical, the most honest book on this matter of getting up good dinners, and living in a decent Christian way, that has yet found its way in our household."—*Watchman and Reflector*

COMMON SENSE
In the Household.
A MANUAL OF PRACTICAL HOUSEWIFERY,

By MARION HARLAND,

Author of "Alone," "Hidden Path," "Nemesis," &c., &c.

One vol. 12mo, cloth. Price...................... $1 75

SEE WHAT THE CRITICS, AND PRACTICAL HOUSEKEEPERS, say of it:

"And now we have from another popular novelist a cookery book, whereof our housekeeper (this literary recorder is not a bachelor) speaks most enthusiastically. She says that simplicity and clearness of expression, accuracy of detail, a regard to economy of material, and certainty of good results, are requisites in a useful receipt-book for the kitchen, and Marion Harland has comprehended all these. That she has by experience proved the unsatisfactoriness of housekeepers' helps in general is shown by the arrangement of her book. She has appended a star to such recipes as, after having tried them herself, she can recommend as safe and generally simple. Such a directory will be a great help to one who goes to the book for aid in preparing a pleasant and savory meal without much experience in cooking. The language is so simple, and the directions so plain, that a reasonably intelligent cook might avail herself of it to vary her manner of preparing even ordinary dishes. The introduction to the book should be printed as a tract and put in every house. The simple advice for the management of servants, the general directions at the head of each department of cooking, and the excellent pages on the sick-room, make as complete an aid to housekeepers as can well be desired."—*Harper's Monthly.*

"In the hands of the author, whose name is well known in another department of literature, the subject has been treated with thoroughness and skill, showing that a little common sense may be as successful in the concoction of a toothsome viand as in the composition of a romance."—*N. Y. Daily Tribune.*

"It inspires us with a great respect for the housewifery of a literary lady, and we cannot err in predicting for it a wide popularity."—*N. Y. Evening Post.*

"Unites the merits of a trustworthy receipt-book with the freshness of a familiar talk on household affairs."—*Albany Evening Journal.*

"The directions are clear, practical, and so good in their way that the only wonder is, how any one head could hold so many pots, kettles, and pans, and such a world of gastronomic good things."—*Hearth and Home.*

"The recipes are clearly expressed, easy to follow, and not at all expensive. The suggestions about household affairs are *chic*. On a test comparison with three other American cook-books, it comes out ahead upon every count. Beyond this *experto crede* nothing more need be said."—*Christian Union.*

Copies sent, post-paid, on receipt of the price, by

SCRIBNER, ARMSTRONG & CO.,

654 Broadway, New York.

THE WORKS OF GEORGE MACDONALD

PUBLISHED BY

Scribner, Armstrong & Co.,

654 Broadway, New York.

THE HIDDEN LIFE

AND OTHER POEMS.

1 Vol., 12mo, $1.50.

This volume includes "The Hidden Life," MacDonald's well known poem "The Disciple," "The Gospel Women," "A Book of Sonnets," and the "Organ Songs," including the "Ode to Light,"—itself one of the most remarkable of modern poems.

WITHIN AND WITHOUT.

1 Vol., 12mo, $1.50.

This, which is the longest poem and one of the most important works of this popular author, is, in fact, a *Thrilling Story in Verse.*

It deals in a graphic and masterly manner with the deepest human passion, is beautiful with imagination, and intensely interesting in plot. Macdonald is one of the most original and charming of living poets, and the many American readers of his prose works will be delighted at the opportunity of becoming acquainted with his poetry.

"All Mr. MacDonald's usual moral and spiritual subtlety and tendencies are these, and the story is full of the most lovely light."—*Contemporary Review.*

WILFRID CUMBERMEDE.

Author of "Alec. Forbes," "Annals of a Quiet Neighborhood," &c.

1 Vol., 12mo. Price $1.75. Cheap edition, paper, 75c., cloth, $1.25.

CRITICAL NOTICES.

"This book is full of intellectual wealth. It will teach us as many wise thoughts, and nurture as many noble feelings, as either 'Robert Falconer' or 'Alec. Forbes.'"—*British Quarterly Review.*

"It is simple, natural, pathetic, and playful by turns, interesting in plot and development of character, and written in such limpid English as it does one good to meet with."—*N. Y. Journal of Commerce.*

"The best story of him who is the best of living story-writers. It may be enjoyed almost in perfection by one who has not read the beginning, and who will never read the sequel; and it will remain in the memory like a beautiful song."—*N. Y. Independent.*

"Mr. Macdonald's writings are beautiful in style, powerful in description, pathetic and pure in their design."—*Christian Intelligencer.*

☞ *These works sent, post-paid, upon receipt of the price*

The Erckmann-Chatrian Novels

THE CONSCRIPT: A Tale of the French War of
1813. With four full-page Illustrations. One vol. 12mo. Price, in paper, 75 cents; cloth, $1.25.

From the Cincinnati Daily Commercial.
"It is hardly fiction,—it is history in the guise of fiction, and that part of history which historians hardly write, concerning the disaster, the ruin, the sickness, the poverty, and the utter misery and suffering which war brings upon the people."

WATERLOO: A Story of the Hundred Days.
Being a Sequel to "*The Conscript.*" With four full-page Illustrations. One vol. 12mo. Price, in paper, 75 cents; cloth, $1.25.

From the New York Daily Herald.
"*Written in that charming style of simplicity which has made the* ERCKMANN-CHATRIAN *works popular in every language in which they have been published.*"

THE BLOCKADE OF PHALSBURG.
An Episode of the Fall of the First French Empire. With four full-page Illustrations and a Portrait of the authors. One vol. 12mo. Price, in paper, 75 cents; cloth, $1.25.

From the Philadelphia Daily Inquirer.
"Not only are they intrinsically interesting historically, but intrinsically a pleasant, well-constructed plot, serving in each case to connect the great events which they so graphically treat, and the style being as vigorous and charming as it is pure and refreshing."

INVASION OF FRANCE IN 1814.
With the Night March past Phalsburg. With a Memoir of the Authors. With four full-page Illustrations. One vol. 12mo. Price, in paper, 75 cents; cloth, $1.25.

From the New York Evening Mail.
"All their novels are noted for the same admirable qualities,—simple and effective realism of plot, incident, and language, and a disclosure of the horrid individual aspects of war. They are absolutely perfect of their kind."

MADAME THERESE; or, The Volunteers '92.
With four full-page Illustrations. One vol. 12mo. Price, in paper, 75 cents; cloth, $1.25.

From the Boston Commonwealth.
"It is a boy's story—that is, supposed to be written by a boy—and has all the freshness, the unconscious simplicity and *naïveté* which the imagined authorship should imply; while nothing more graphic, more clearly and vividly pictorial, has been brought before the public for many a day."

Any or all of the above volumes sent, post-paid, upon receipt of the price by the publishers,

SCRIBNER, ARMSTRONG & CO.,
(Successors to CHARLES SCRIBNER & CO.),
654 Broadway, New York.

It is the design to present in this Library a series of works by the best authors of the day, the leading characteristics of which shall be elevation and purity of tone, and entire freedom from every thing in the remotest degree demoralizing. A broad page, large and clear type, will make the successive volumes thoroughly readable, and occasionally they will be carefully illustrated.

The following works have been issued during the Spring and Summer of 1873:

MAY.
A NEW NOVEL, FROM ADVANCE SHEETS.
By Mrs. OLIPHANT, author of "At His Gates," "Miss Marjoribanks," "Chronicles of Carlingford," etc.

One vol. 8vo, cloth, $1.50. Paper, $1.00.

The characters are strongly contrasted, while the quaint Scotch humor one or two of them display gives to the story a freshness and heartiness quite unusual.

"Mrs. Oliphant is always original. Her books have a certain stamp of their own. The gem of this novel, "May," is the character of May, or Marjory herself. She is a grand creature, and we congratulate Mrs. Oliphant on the beauty and harmony of her character."—*London Saturday Review.*

GALAMA; or, The Beggars.
By J. B. DE LIEFDE.
One vol. 8vo, cloth, $1.25. Paper, 75 cents.

This is a story of love and adventure, in the times of the Dutch Republic. The characters are drawn with wonderful clearness; they attract the warmest sympathy from the first, and every reader must follow their fortunes to the close with the deepest interest.

"This work gives a striking picture of those famous beggars who founded the 'Dutch Republic,' a nation which has been governed with a thrift not surpassed by the stern economy of Frederick of Prussia and his successors."—*N. Y. World.*

AT HIS GATES.
By Mrs. OLIPHANT, author of "May," "Chronicles of Carlingford," etc.

One vol. 8vo, cloth, $1.50. Paper, $1.00.

Mrs. Oliphant ranks among the first of living novelists, and this is one of the best of her very popular productions.

"It is a better novel, to our mind, than any woman, 'George Eliot' excepted, has given to the world since Charlotte Brontë laid down her pen."—*Louisville Courier-Journal.*

"Revealing a remarkable knowledge of human nature and keen intellectual appreciation of the completeness of detail essential to a really good story."—*Buffalo Commercial Advertiser.*

IN PRESS. WILL BE ISSUED AT AN EARLY DAY:
THE STORY OF WANDERING WILLIE.
By the Author of "Effie's Friends" and "John Hatherton."

☞ *These volumes sent, post-paid, by the publishers on receipt of price.*

SCRIBNER, ARMSTRONG & CO., 654 Broadway, N. Y.

www.ingramcontent.com/pod-product-compliance
Lightning Source LLC
Chambersburg PA
CBHW022104290426
44112CB00008B/539